Storming the City

U.S. Military Performance in Urban Warfare from World War II to Vietnam

Storming the City

U.S. Military Performance in Urban Warfare from World War II to Vietnam

Alec Wahlman

Number 1 in the American Military Studies Series
University of North Texas Press
Denton, Texas

10 9 8 7 6 5 4 3 2 1

Permissions:
University of North Texas Press
1155 Union Circle #311336
Denton, TX 76203-5017

The paper used in this book meets the minimum requirements of the
American National Standard for Permanence of Paper for Printed Library
Materials, z39.48.1984. Binding materials have been chosen for durability.

Library of Congress Cataloging-in-Publication Data

Wahlman, Alec, 1965- author.
Storming the city : U.S. military performance in urban warfare from
World War II to Vietnam / Alec Wahlman. — Edition: first.
pages cm — (Number 1 in the American military studies series)
Includes bibliographical references and index.

ISBN 978-1-57441-610-7 (cloth : alk. paper) — ISBN 978-1-57441-622-0 (ebook)
1. Urban warfare—United States. 2. World War, 1939-1945—Urban warfare. 3. Korean War, 1950-1953—Urban warfare. 4. Vietnam War, 1961-
1975—Urban warfare. I. Title. II. Series: American military studies ; no. 1.
U167.5.S7W45 2015
355.4'26097309045—dc23
2015020381

Number 1 in the American Military Studies Series

The electronic edition of this book was made possible
by the support of the Vick Family Foundation.

Dedication

To mom and dad, who proved an interest in history is contagious.

Contents

List of Maps

List of Photographs

List of Tables

Preface

A key thought in my mind when beginning this study was that urban warfare was a growth industry. Since that time, nearly a decade ago, events in Syria, Iraq, Libya, and Ukraine have reinforced that thinking. Central to military conflict is the seeking of relative advantage, circumstances that play to one's strengths and not those of the opponent. For many combatants that has led them to seek battle in urban terrain, a trend I believe likely to continue.

To facilitate my own learning I researched the four case studies in chronological order, making it easier to see the progression of capabilities, or lack thereof. The case studies are presented in this book the same way so the reader can also better capture that sense of progression. By selecting these particular case studies this book provides a window into how a technologically advanced force fared when the need arose to fight in urban terrain. Understanding those cases in detail will be useful for those pondering future urban operations, despite the changes in the security environment since the last case in 1968.

Acknowledgements

I would like to thank the many archive staff that helped me during my visits, to include those at the Military History Institute (Carlisle, Pennsylvania), the National Archives (College Park, Maryland), the Gray Research Center (Quantico, Virginia), and the Center for Military History (District of Columbia). Their enthusiasm and professionalism was greatly appreciated. Although I never met them personally, I would also like to thank all those whose hard work made many primary and secondary sources available online, notably via the websites of the Combined Arms Research Library (Fort Leavenworth, Kansas), the Donovan Research Library (Fort Benning, Georgia), and the Virtual Vietnam Archive (Texas Tech University).

My many colleagues at the Institute for Defense Analyses (IDA) (Alexandria, Virginia) provided varying forms of important support, as did those who played a role in my education. Professor Williamson Murray introduced me to the discipline of military history, and Professor John Gooch showed me the British twist to it. Two former bosses encouraged me in this study as well, Karl Lowe and Dr. Michael Fischerkeller. Some analytical work on urban warfare early in my career at IDA, with Dr. William Hurley and Joel Resnick, sparked my interest in the subject. Other colleagues and friends were also of great assistance: Jim Kurtz, Kevin Woods, Jim Lacey, Sharon Tosi Lacey, Drew Lewis, and Jeff Jaworski.

As for my parents, neither had an educational background in history, but both had an interest which they passed on to me. Both were proud that I had begun this study, but sadly, neither lived to see its conclusion. My two brothers, Duane and Glen, also played an important role, although they did not know it at the time. All those late nights playing military board games as we grew up, instilled in me a lifelong passion for military history, even though I am sure at times they questioned the wisdom of allowing their little brother to join in.

Acronyms and Abbreviations

1/1	1st Battalion, 1st Marine Regiment
1/5	1st Battalion, 5th Marine Regiment
2/5	2nd Battalion, 5th Marine Regiment
1st ID	1st Infantry Division
1st Marines	1st Marine Infantry Regiment
5th Marines	5th Marine Infantry Regiment
7th Marines	7th Marine Infantry Regiment
17th ROK	17th Republic of Korea Regiment
ARVN	Army of the Republic of Vietnam
BAR	Browning Automatic Rifle
CARL	Combined Arms Research Library, Command and General Staff College, Fort Leavenworth, Kansas
CMH	Center for Military History, Fort McNair, Washington, District of Columbia
CS	Non-lethal riot control gas named for the initials if its inventors
DMZ	Demilitarized Zone
DRL	Donovan Research Library, Fort Benning, Georgia
DUKW	US amphibious truck
FM-31-50	*Field Manual 31-50: Attack on a Fortified Position and Combat in Towns*

GI Government Issue, common term referencing enlisted American personnel

GRC Gray Research Center, Marine Corps University, Quantico, Virginia

LAAW Light Anti-Armor Weapon

LVT US amphibious tractor

MACV Military Assistance Command—Vietnam

MHI Military History Institute, Carlisle, Pennsylvania

NA National Archives, College Park, Maryland. Some footnote citations will use x/x/x/x/x/x/x with each x corresponding to the record group through box numbers, followed by appropriate folder and page notations. See bibliography for additional detail.

NCO Non-commissioned officer

NKPA North Korean People's Army

NVA North Vietnamese Army

Pzkw Panzerkampfwagen—German term for their tanks, but not all armored vehicles

ROK Republic of Korea (South Korea)

RPG Rocket Propelled Grenade

SVN South Vietnamese

US United States

USMC United States Marine Corps

VC Viet Cong

VVA Virtual Vietnam Archive, Texas Tech University, <http://www.vietnam.ttu.edu/virtualarchive/>

Introduction

Cities and Urban Warfare

Table A		
Most Populous World Cities (population in millions)[1]		
1500	1900	1950
Beijing 0.7	London 6.5	New York 12.3
Vijayanagar (India) 0.5	New York 4.2	London 8.7
Cairo 0.4	Paris 3.3	Tokyo 6.9
Hangzhou 0.25	Berlin 2.7	Paris 5.4
Tabriz 0.25	Chicago 1.7	Moscow 5.4

The industrial age changed the relative value of land. Development meant relatively small areas could often be of more value to a nation than vast tracts of undeveloped land. Advances in technology and changing economic patterns both enabled and demanded that populations concentrate. Expanding cities were the manifestation of that trend, particularly their substantial growth in the nineteenth and twentieth centuries. From 1900 to 1950 the aggregate population of the world's five largest cities increased 110 percent, while the overall global population increased only 52 percent (see Table A).[2] The proportion of the urbanized global population increased from 13 to 29 percent between 1900 and 1950. That trend continued, reaching 49 percent by 2005, and is projected to reach 60 percent by 2030.[3]

As the size of cities grew, so did their military importance. Four factors characterize this increasing importance. First, urban areas became more numerous and physically larger, increasing their proportion of the overall terrain mix. Cities also possessed two key commodities needed for waging warfare in the industrial age: population and materiel. In addition, they acted as the hubs for increasingly advanced modes of transportation. Finally, urban terrain muted some of the key advances in military technology, namely lethality and mobility. These factors began to emerge in the nineteenth century, but their impact was not fully felt until the twentieth century.

Prior to the nineteenth century, urban warfare was largely limited to sieges, which were not so much about fighting in a city but about cracking its hard outer shell. The smaller size of pre-industrial cities then facilitated their fortification, and the limits in offensive military technology for breaching those fortifications often meant a prolonged struggle. Once attacking forces were inside the city, the battle was soon over. While armies certainly fought *over* cities, they rarely fought *in* them.

In the late-nineteenth and early-twentieth centuries, that dynamic began to change. Cities were rapidly growing, making it difficult to encase them in any sort of fortification, and even if they had been, advances in artillery were making the hard outer shell less effective. Moreover, by the late-nineteenth century weaponry had made combat in open terrain more dangerous. Man-portable weapons had become far more lethal, through a combination of increased rates of fire and range. Rifles and machine guns could now kill even beyond 1000 meters. Artillery also saw impressive gains in range, lethality, and rate of fire.[4] Armies were slow to react, paying insufficient attention to the warnings from the Boer and Russo-Japanese Wars as to how the firepower-survivability equation had changed.[5] After considerable costs, the combatants in World War I learned to make open terrain less so by digging in. By World War II, more advanced aircraft and armored vehicles further reinforced the trend toward open terrain lethality. Motorization and mechanization added at least the potential for sharply increased mobility.

The characteristics of the new generation of weapons were offset by the modern urban landscape. The new weapons reached out farther and caused effects over larger areas (e.g., exploding artillery shells), but urban areas undermined both those effects, by presenting reduced lines of sight and an abundance of cover. The three-dimensional nature of urban terrain caused most of its surface area to be obscured from even the highest perch, in contrast to the commanding view high ground often provides in rural terrain. This results in shorter detection ranges, and thus shorter engagement ranges. The engagement ranges familiar to Alexander the Great were similar to those frequently seen in twentieth-century urban warfare.[6] Urban structures also provided, depending on the type of construction, excellent cover from small arms fire, mortars, and even artillery. While urban terrain contained dense road networks, rubble could easily block those roads, negating the mobility of even the most off-road-capable tracked vehicle. For armored vehicles, the abundance of cover in urban areas allowed infantry to approach close enough to be lethal, as they too benefited from a new generation of man-portable weapons.

Any combatant feeling disadvantaged in the areas of mobility or long-range lethality could, at least in part, neutralize these factors by retreating into urban terrain, with many sprawling cities to choose from. Urban areas offered instant stealth and cover in an era of increasing demand for both. While an attacker could certainly decline to enter that urban battle space, that in turn would cede control of the operational tempo to the defender. The

German siege of Leningrad tied up substantial German forces over two years in a war where time was not on the Wehrmacht's side. And yet, the world's armies displayed only minimal interest in urban terrain before World War II as a counter to the improvements in mobility and firepower. Most likely, the implications of those improvements were not yet fully understood, and thus the need for a counter was not apparent.

Two mid-nineteenth-century examples of the interplay between urban terrain and advances in weapons technology were evaluated by Jonathan Beall. Beall studied how US troops assaulted Monterey, Mexico (1846) and Fredericksburg (1862), and he found US troops unprepared in both cases. Courses at West Point had addressed siege warfare; however, they taught nothing about fighting in urban terrain. In both battles the assaulting forces were hampered by a lack of urban warfare training, a lack of doctrine, and a citizen army structure that had no formal process for lessons learned. The assault on Monterey was more successful because General Zachary Taylor had the good fortune of possessing more experienced troops, including some with exposure to urban combat from previous fighting in Texas. These more experienced troops improvised and adapted, in part by operating in smaller groups and minimizing their time in the open streets, in a way the Union troops assaulting Fredericksburg did not. [7]

Political unrest in Europe in the nineteenth century and early twentieth century did generate some interest in urban warfare in European armies. For example, the Prussian army had to temporarily withdraw from Berlin in 1848 when it found civilian mobs and barricades too problematic. The six-day battle to clear Dresden of civilian mobs in 1848, the joint operations with the French government to clear Paris in 1871, the wave of strikes in Germany in the late-1880s, and the Russian revolution of 1905 all caused the German military to pay more attention to the "enemy at home" and urban warfare. In 1907 the German General

Staff conducted a study of past urban operations and produced a report entitled *Fighting in Insurgent Towns*, which it distributed to all province commanders. The report described urban terrain as a difficult environment for suppressing civilian unrest, and said the best solution was rapid and decisive action by the army.[8] However, the German focus in urban warfare was on dealing with irregulars, not conventional military forces.

The overall trend through the nineteenth century and up to World War I was a decreasing use of army troops to suppress disorder in urban areas. Two factors were behind this: the establishment of professional police forces in major cities and increasing public outcry about the use of the military against the state's own population.[9] World War I itself presented the world's armies with many questions about the future of warfare, but urban combat was not one of them. Those factors, combined with the intellectual challenges of understanding the many new weapon technologies emerging during this era, appear to have made urban warfare a low priority for most armies.

In the twentieth century no military embraced the advance of technology more than the US military. Although not always the first to field a new technology, improvement and mass fielding were American strong suits. Three factors drove this, the first being the nation's wealth. Be it ships, aircraft, tanks, or electronics, advanced technology came with an advanced cost. A second factor was the American affinity for, and skill with, technology in general. The American economic model encouraged innovation, which often took the form of new technology. General George S. Patton stated, "Americans as a race are the most adept in the use of machinery of any people on earth."[10] A third factor was an American aversion to the human cost of war. In part an aversion to foreign conflicts per se, it was also an eagerness to replace men with machines, human losses with materiel losses. The high American valuation of individual liberty translated into a high valuation on individual life.

The confluence of these trends—the increasing importance of cities, the advances in military technology, and the constraints urban terrain places on military operations—leads to the central three-part question of this study. When the need arose to fight in urban terrain in the mid-twentieth century, how effective were US forces, why, and how did that performance change from World War II to Vietnam? World War II acts as a starting point for US twentieth-century urban warfare, while Vietnam provides a window into how that performance may have changed over several decades.

As will be shown in this study, the short answer is as follows. Across four major urban battles, spread across three wars and over three decades, US forces proved themselves capable of accomplishing their assigned missions to capture each city. Words such as cheap, easy, quick, or clean did not apply to these battles, but in the end, US forces took each city from the enemy. The two central factors behind this performance were transferable competence and battlefield adaptation. Although the American military gave some modest attention to urban warfare in its doctrine before and between these battles, city fighting had almost no impact on force sizing, organization, or major equipment decisions. Urban warfare proved a lesser included case, a problem covered in the preparation for other aspects of warfare. The second factor behind the performance of US forces was battlefield adaptation. The preparation for other types of warfare gave American forces much of what they needed to succeed in urban fighting, but experience was still lacking. Adaptation covered that remaining gap. US troops proved consistently capable of rapidly adapting to the novel demands of urban warfare. The spirit of innovation and flexibility that made this possible can be traced back to the culture of the US military and American culture in general.

From World War II to Vietnam, however, there was a gradual reduction in tactical performance in the four battles. Of the four battles, the most impressive performance was at Aachen, particularly given that the attacking Americans were outnumbered by the defending Germans 3–1. The second best performance was at Manila, against a large and fanatical defending force. Greater problems emerged in Seoul and Hue, as US forces failed to cut off either city before the assault. As a result some North Korean forces escaped Seoul, and communist forces were able to reinforce and re-supply their troops in Hue, prolonging the battle. The overall trend was thus one where US forces were gradually less effective over time. However, this author still considers the performance at Hue to be an overall success, as the city was captured and a very large number of enemy forces were killed in the battle. The trend was not one of a collapse in performance, but rather a gradual degradation.

Study Structure

This study will evaluate four major US urban battles, analyze American capabilities, and explain US performance in each. The four battles are Aachen (1944), Manila (1945), Seoul (1950), and Hue City (1968) (henceforth Hue). These battles provide a useful sampling of major American urban operations across the mid-twentieth century. Each battle will have its own case study chapter, presented in chronological order. Preceding the Aachen case study will be a short chapter examining the presence of urban warfare in American military thought before Aachen. Preceding the Seoul case study will be a second short chapter examining the same for the post-World War II era.

Across this twenty-four-year span from Aachen to Hue, the United States graduated from major power to superpower. The US military became the world leader in many technologies, extending the World War II penchant for technology to new heights. The capabilities fielded in many areas, over these three decades, thoroughly changed the art of the possible. Long-range radar, beyond-visual-range air-to-air missiles, mach-2 jet fighters, aerial refueling, and nuclear weapons all made US military aviation far more capable. Nuclear propulsion, ballistic missiles with nuclear warheads on submarines, surface-to-air missiles, anti-submarine helicopters, and larger carriers with jet air wings similarly enhanced the United States Navy. US ground forces saw advances as well, with radar-guided air defense systems, surface-to-surface ballistic missiles, and the helicopter.

Comparing events separated by time and space allows one to discern patterns and how consistent those patterns are across varying conditions. Although the battles for Aachen and Manila occurred only four months apart, they took place on opposite sides of the globe and against very different opponents. The battles for Manila, Seoul, and Hue were all for large Asian cities, although their respective wars each had its own distinct character. The forces defending Aachen and Manila both contained a substantial proportion of poorly trained non-infantry personnel, with the German force smaller but better equipped. The North Korean defenders in Seoul possessed the largest collection of armor, although the potential for those vehicles was largely unrealized on account of dismal crew training. Somewhat ironically, given the prominent role of communist irregular forces in Vietnam, at Hue US forces met their most conventional and experienced foe. Unlike the battles farther to the south during the Tet Offensive, at Hue the communist forces were mostly veteran North Vietnamese Army regulars. The battles on either end of the timeline, Aachen and Hue, involved the defenders with the best anti-tank capability. While the North Koreans at Seoul had the objective to delay and attrite attacking American forces, in the other three battles the defenders were seeking to hold, in both Manila and Hue to the last man.

Unlike a laboratory scientist who can control for outside factors, historians must accept events as they occurred. Controlling for various factors is replaced with acknowledgement of those factors along with an assessment of their effect. What all these battles have in common is that they involved substantial US forces (at least two battalions), fighting for at least three days to clear a large urban landscape of a sizeable enemy force. That commonality provides a sufficient foundation upon which to compare urban warfare performance.

The objective of the case study chapters is not to provide the definitive account of each battle, as would a book focused on any one of these battles. Rather, this study will explore each battle to a level of detail sufficient for evaluating tactical performance. The operational and political implications for each battle will be discussed, but not given the same emphasis as the tactical. The same will be true of tactical operations that took place outside of urban terrain. While operations proximate to each city were certainly important to events within, they will be discussed only in terms of how they affected operations inside the city, and with less detail. The echelon focus of each battle chapter will vary. While Aachen and Hue were battalion-level fights for American forces, Seoul was regimental and Manila was fought at the division level.

Each case study chapter will follow a similar structure, with the first section addressing the operational context—how the battle fit into its particular strategic and operational surroundings. The second section will discuss the opponent faced by US forces, including their motivations and objectives. The third section will provide a brief synopsis of the battle itself, providing temporal and geographic context for the more detailed analysis to follow. Beginning with the fourth section is the analytical core of each case study. Those sections are:

- Command, control and communications
- Intelligence and reconnaissance
- Firepower and survivability
- Mobility and counter-mobility
- Logistics
- Dealing with the population

These aspects of performance were chosen for their coverage of the landscape of tactical performance in urban operations. They represent a blending of aspects often assessed within the US Department of Defense, and those the author has found useful in previous research.[11] These aspects also provide a similar structure for evaluating each battle, facilitating comparison, and also guiding research efforts. This standardized framework is flexibly applied to each battle, with the length afforded to each section varying in relation to the events in each battle. Certain notable topics not represented in the framework are addressed, although spread across several categories. The orchestration of combined arms will be covered in the sections on "command, control, and communications" and "firepower and survivability." The rules of engagement will be covered in the "firepower and survivability" and "dealing with the population" sections.

The last chapter section on the population deserves special attention. A central principle to good historical analysis is keeping one's judgments within the context of the era in question. In other words, don't overlay today's values on yesterday. The reactions in today's world to civilian casualties during military operations are fundamentally different than they were in the period of this study. After all, that historical scope includes a period when the American public took no real issue with the use of multiple nuclear weapons against enemy cities. Rather than comparing yesterday's civilian casualties to today's values, a more valid comparison is to the enemy treatment of civilians and the context of the broader conflict. Would a slower capture of a city result in more civilian deaths at the hands of the enemy? And what of lives still at the mercy of the enemy regime elsewhere?[12] Context matters. The conclusion chapter will address how American and global values on civilian casualties have changed beyond the scope of this study and the implications of that for future urban operations.

Sources and Other Literature

Unit reports held at various archives formed the foundation for the battle chapters (e.g., National Archives at College Park, Maryland). US Army and Marine Corps doctrinal publications and several professional military journals did the same for the chapters on urban warfare in American military thought. A broad swath of secondary literature played a supporting role throughout, with the sources for Aachen the least useful, the sources for Hue the most robust.

Each of the battle chapters is also supported with non-US sources. For example, the Aachen chapter includes interrogations of a captured German corps commander, the German commander in Aachen, and captured German rank and file.[13] The Manila chapter contains numerous references to Allied Translator and Interpreter Section reports (ATIS in most notes), a mix of prisoner interrogations and captured and translated Japanese documents. In the Seoul chapter Period Intelligence Reports from the X Corp often mentioned information from North Korean prisoners of war, and the Military Intelligence Section of the General Headquarters Far East Command produced an Enemy Documents periodical. The South Korean perspective came from a three-volume history of the war from the Korean Institute of Military History.[14] For the Hue chapter a wealth of captured and translated communist documents were accessed from Texas Tech University's online database the Virtual Vietnam Archive, to include several lengthy North Vietnamese after-action reports on the battle.[15] Sources were also accessed presenting the South Vietnamese perspective and that of Australian advisors to the South Vietnamese.[16]

Several other books mirror this study in looking at urban warfare case studies over a span of time. The three best book compilations are *City Fights* (2003), *Block by Block* (2003), and DiMarco's *Concrete Hell* (2012).[17] Because *City Fights* looks at thirteen case studies, six of which involve American forces, its depth is limited on any one battle. For example, the chapter on Manila is eighteen pages long and draws upon just three sources, all secondary.[18] *Block by Block*, the best of those mentioned above, covers eleven case studies, not all of which were conventional combat operations (e.g., humanitarian relief, counterterrorism). However, coverage of so many battles comes at the cost of depth. For comparison, its chapter on Aachen is but half the length of the Aachen chapter in this study, drawing on only five primary sources on the battle itself, compared to fifty-eight in this study's Aachen chapter. The strength of *Concrete Hell* is its identification of trends and insights across nine urban battles. Its key weaknesses are a lack of footnotes, modest depth on any one battle, and a limited bibliography, particularly a paucity of primary sources.

Kilcullen's excellent *Out of the Mountains* (2013) focuses on more recent historical examples to discuss how four "megatrends" will drive future urban insurgencies. He devotes the bulk of his text to these megatrends, theories of urban functionality, and approaches to dealing with urban insurgencies, with the historical examples in a supporting role. In contrast, a reader of this study will find far more attention to US operations from World War II to Vietnam, the tactical performance of US forces, and operations versus conventional opponents.

The gap this study seeks to fill is between the detailed accounts of single battles and the broad pattern analysis across many battles that lacks tactical detail. By limiting the scope to just four battles, and only those involving American forces in major conventional combat operations, span and tactical detail can coexist. That coexistence then cues up a rigorous assessment of American performance over time that would otherwise not be possible.

Chapter 1

Urban Warfare in American Military Thought before Aachen

Prior to World War II

Prior to World War II no nation's military seriously studied urban warfare against conventional military opponents, including the military establishment in the United States. World War I taught many lessons but urban warfare was not one of them. Open warfare received the bulk of the US Army's attention as it assessed operations during World War I, as opposed to what it perceived as the failure of trench warfare.[1] For the interwar Army, urban warfare had presented itself as a problem so rarely as to be a theoretical issue, dwarfed by larger and more tangible challenges such as airpower, mechanization, and mobilization. The paucity of global attention to this topic during this period meant there was little chance for the Army to take intellectual shortcuts by borrowing from others.

Be it the American apathy toward national defense in the 1920s or the fiscal famine of the 1930s, the Army had few resources to expend on apparently nonessential requirements. Army leaders focused on absorbing the lessons of the Great War, the most important being how to rapidly expand force structure for industrial-age warfare. Austere budgets forced hard choices on the Army's leadership, and the Army prioritized manpower over equipment or concept development for future warfare. Even for an area of mainstream interest such as mechanized warfare, the Army's budget for its armored forces, from 1920 to 1932, annually averaged an amount equal to the cost of just two new medium tanks of the period.[2]

Several other factors served to suppress the serious study of urban warfare. American political culture has always been wary of an expansive internal security role for the military (e.g., 2nd and 3rd amendments to the Constitution), thus reducing civil order as a driver for the development of urban warfare doctrine.[3] Moreover, the isolationist tendencies of American foreign policy during this period precluded any external rationale for prioritizing urban warfare. A factor common to all armies was the rural settings of most bases and training grounds. The need for vast open spaces in which to train, while not disturbing civilian activity, made the military challenge of urban warfare seem even more theoretical and unimportant.[4]

Before World War II the US Army did have some experience with urban operations, but it proved an insufficient catalyst for prompting significant changes in doctrine or force structure. American troops had at least one notable urban operation in both the Mexican-American War and the Civil War.[5] From the end of the Civil War to the end of the century the Army was called out over three hundred times to quell civil unrest, the largest deployments being in 1877 and 1894 when police in several American cities needed assistance. The last urban deployment before World War II was to quell the Bonus Marchers in Washington in 1932.[6]

American military doctrine did give some minimal attention to urban warfare during the interwar period, although only at the close of the era. In the Army's overarching doctrinal publication of 1923, *Field Service Regulations*, a chapter on special operations contained sections on night combat, combat in woods, and combat at river crossings, but no section on urban operations. A one-page section on terrain did mention villages and woods, although only in terms of their use for movement to combat, for shelter, or the placement of reserves.[7] Although the 1938 revision of the Infantry School's *Infantry in Battle*, prepared under the supervision of then-Colonel George C. Marshall, did contain several brief references to urban combat, it made no mention of any special requirements associated with urban terrain.[8] In the 1939 follow-on to the 1923 overarching doctrinal publication, *Field Manual 100-5* (October 1939), the treatment of urban operations was expanded, with a five-page section on "combat in woods and towns," containing (for the first time) specific information on the particular demands of urban warfare.[9]

The tight budgets of the interwar period elevated the importance of professional military journals, as the Army cut back on the issuing of formal publications.[10] In this less formal venue as well, the level of attention to urban warfare was low, even as global tensions increased leading up to World War II, with the Spanish Civil War and Japan's military operations in China.[11] From 1936 through the German invasion of Poland, the US Army's *Military Review*, *Field Artillery Journal*, *Cavalry Journal*, and *Infantry Journal* combined carried only three articles that gave any attention to urban operations. Only one of these three articles gave tactically useful information on urban combat, as it described Japanese operations in Shanghai in the early 1930s.[12] In one article, summarizing the key lessons of the Spanish Civil War, not one of the lessons mentioned related to urban warfare.[13] One possible contributing factor was the censorship exercised at times by the Army's leadership, which suppressed some viewpoints from appearing in *Infantry Journal* that were contrary to official Army policy.[14] United States Marine Corps personnel reading the *U.S. Naval Institute Proceedings* or the *Marine Corps Gazette* would have fared no better, with only three urban warfare-related articles over that same time period. Any reader of these three articles would have been hard pressed to derive any urban warfare lessons.[15]

The modest attention given to urban operations in American military journals and the tardy and minimal presence in doctrine were insufficient to have much effect on training. In an October 1940 catalogue of War Department training materials, not one of the seventy films and filmstrips listed pertained to urban operations, and only one of the 261 printed training publications related to urban operations, if one is willing to count Field Manual 27-15 (abbreviated FM 27-15) *Domestic Disturbances*.[16] The 1941 General Headquarters maneuvers appear to have paid little if any attention to operations in urban areas, and they resulted in no urban warfare lessons learned.[17]

Learning and Experience during World War II

Once World War II began, but well before US ground forces saw significant combat, the American military began learning about urban warfare from others. Once US forces were in action they continued learning from others as extensive American first-hand urban experience was not to be gained until after D-Day. After the fall of France, the British Army gave significant attention to urban warfare, specifically the defense of English towns and cities in case of a German invasion.[18] Allied forces in Italy were involved in several significant urban battles in 1943 and 1944. Soviet experience as well, from the Eastern Front, made its way to the United States, and not just from Stalingrad, but also because the Germans routinely fortified villages and towns. Equally important, the Americans liberally borrowed from German urban warfare lessons and doctrine.[19]

During the war the presence of urban warfare-related articles increased sharply in American professional military journals. From the German invasion of Poland through 1943, the US Army's *Military Review*, *Field Artillery Journal*, *Cavalry Journal*, and *Infantry Journal* together published twenty-nine articles on urban warfare, describing operations in France, Poland, Russia, and Italy. These same journals published an additional twenty-one articles related to urban warfare in 1944 and 1945. *Military Review* in particular presented the foreign perspective with its many reprints from foreign sources. The coverage of urban warfare was notably less for the journals more likely to have been read by USMC personnel, with the *Marine Corps Gazette* publishing only four related articles during the war years and the *U.S. Naval Institute Proceedings* publishing none.[20]

The quality and substance of the articles in these journals varied widely. A few, however, did provide valuable insights that would later prove accurate in Aachen and Manila, well before there was US doctrine specific to urban warfare. A pair of articles from the same author, in the fall of 1942, stood out for their tactical accuracy relative to later battles, and their similarity to the US Army's January 1944 manual on urban warfare (*FM 31-50*). The articles made many prescient points on urban tactics, to include staying out of the streets, moving from building to building through interior wall breeches, sewer movement, and clearing buildings from the top down. And as in the Army's *FM 31-50*, the author had one key point wrong about urban warfare, as he did not see a role for armor. "Enemy tanks can do very little in street fighting."[21] In the fall of 1943 an article by the Soviet commander at Stalingrad, reprinted from a Soviet periodical, also presented an insightful description of urban warfare. For example, the author wrote how offensive operations by large units were not possible. "Here it is the small infantry group that dominates the scene."[22]

Between the informal layer of information distribution represented by journal articles and the release of official doctrine lay another layer during World War II. The War Department regularly issued publications designed to disseminate information across the theaters. *Combat Lessons* was specifically designed to rapidly share lessons, and at least half of the issues released from 1942 to 1945 gave some attention to urban operations. For example, the late-1943 No. 2 issue began with an eight-page section on "Combat in Towns" and the comment, "As major campaigns develop in Western Europe, combat in towns assumes increasing importance."[23] *Intelligence Bulletin* was another regularly released (monthly) information product. The January 1944 issue contained an article examining German urban warfare doctrine along with this statement.

> Now that United Nations forces are fighting energetically on the soil of continental Europe, it must be expected that we shall engage the enemy in towns and cities with ever-increasing frequency.[24]

Two other issues in 1944 contained articles on urban operations, and urban operations received cover story attention twice over 1943 to 1944.[25] Four additional issues in 1945 contained articles on urban warfare, although these were all published after the battles for both Aachen and Manila.[26] Another War Department product, *Tactical and Technical Trends*, carried two articles on urban warfare tactics in 1943, relative to the Eastern Front and the British respectively.[27]

Another information conduit with a more focused dissemination target involved the extensive network of combat observers, deployed across the European and Mediterranean theaters by the Army Ground Forces Headquarters. The reports sent back by these observers were incorporated into lessons learned documents to inform senior commanders.[28] At least ten of these observer reports, for the October 1944 to February 1945 timeframe, addressed urban warfare.[29] In one case the observer's report contains lessons learned from Aachen within one week of the battle's conclusion.[30] While some of the early conceptions that emerged within the US military on urban operations changed over time (e.g., role of armor), the topic of urban operations itself had clearly grown in importance.

The Army reissued its overarching doctrinal publication, *FM 100-5*, in May 1941. The trend towards greater attention to urban operations that began in the 1939 version of this manual continued with "combat in towns" now receiving its own two-page section. Some of the points made in this manual remain valid to this day, such as the significance of decentralized command and control, and the importance of initiative and aggression for small unit leaders. However, this version of *FM 100-5* still retained the 1939 version's pessimistic view on the utility of mechanized forces.

The Army issued *FM 100-5* again in June 1944, with the "combat in towns" section expanding to three pages. Perhaps more importantly, the description of the role of armor in urban operations had changed, to state that the opportunities for tank support would present themselves frequently. Another important addition was references to the need to provide security for civilian infrastructure. Notably, that reference to protecting infrastructure was published some eight months before the XIV Corps commander ordered the 1st Cavalry Division to swing wide outside of Manila to capture key nodes in the city's water supply system.[31]

The American doctrinal magnum opus for urban warfare in World War II was *FM 31-50* —*Attack on a Fortified Position and Combat in Towns*, published in January 1944. Despite being the Army's first urban warfare-specific manual, and the fact that it had to share space with the topic of fortified position assault, this manual managed to get a remarkable number of things right.[32] It is the single strongest piece of evidence that the Army's efforts to learn about urban warfare from others were effective in producing a sound theoretical foundation for the urban battles to follow. Many elements of *FM 31-50* read like lessons learned from the first two major American urban battles, Brest and Aachen, despite its being published over six months before either battle. The most prominent weakness of *FM 31-50* lay in its treatment of armor's potential in urban warfare, echoing the same shortfall in the 1941 version of *FM 100-5* in effect at that time. The manual accurately describes the canalizing effect of urban topography on armor, and its increased vulnerability to infantry with man-portable anti-tank weapons. It then, however, described those conditions as limiting armor's role to tasks such as being held in reserve to react to enemy counterattacks, or to be brought forward to deal with especially strong enemy positions. In a three-page "illustrative problem" describing a rifle squad's attack on a section of houses, there is no mention of supporting armor. Another three-page section on training makes no mention of the need to coordinate infantry with armor. One other limitation of *FM 31-50* was its scope, stated in the manual as for units up to regimental size.[33] As the Army's only urban-specific manual, this left the division and corps commanders at Manila working beyond the scope of urban doctrine. Despite these limitations, one could argue *FM 31-50* had it 80 percent right, an impressive achievement for a manual predating significant first-hand American experience in urban operations. An after-action report from Manila touted the utility of *FM 31-50*.

> Tactics recommended in FM 31-50 for combat in towns were used to great advantage by U.S. Forces in the street fighting in Manila.[34]

To go along with the new doctrine was new training. Driven by a February 1943 directive from Army Ground Forces, the Army's training establishment added combat in cities to the program in mid-1943 for pre-deployment training in the United States. The combat-in-cities fire course included pop-up targets on pulleys that would emerge at random distances of five to fifty yards. The combat-in-cities exercise required small units to clear both the streets and houses of mock villages, include some pulley-controlled dummies that could suddenly emerge on stairways or from closets. This proved so challenging for troops that extra ammunition had to be provided, safety rules relaxed, and an extra week was added to both the basic and unit training cycles. However, the pressures to deploy units did at times cause trainers to cut corners, including in the area of urban warfare training.[35]

For Aachen and Manila, it appears that these changes in urban training had only a modest effect on performance. The divisions involved in those two battles had already deployed overseas before the implementation of changes in training in the United States.[36] Once deployed, there were opportunities for some units to benefit from urban training. While stationed in southern England, all three regiments of the 1st Infantry Division, included the 26th Infantry Regiment whose men would clear Aachen, underwent urban warfare training. The southern coast resort town of Weymouth served as the venue, complete with booby traps and mock enemy defenders. This training took place from December 1943 to February 1944, and while it is difficult to discern from the unit records the total amount of time spent on urban training, at times it involved entire companies spending the day at Weymouth.[37]

Aided by both good doctrine and some training, first-hand experience still played a key role. After the war, despite Aachen having taken place ten months after the publication of *FM 31-50*, and after his regiment had undergone urban warfare training in England, Lt. Col. Derrill Daniel recounted many lessons he and his men learned while in Aachen.[38] Approximately one month before Aachen, elements of three American divisions assaulted the French port of Brest, giving the US Army its first large-scale exposure to urban warfare. A larger battle than Aachen, the extensive German fortifications in and around the city made this a mixed urban and fortified position assault. Although Aachen was the 1st Infantry Division's introduction to urban warfare, lessons learned at Brest, primarily from the 2nd Infantry Division, were collected and distributed to other forces in Europe.[39] However, the unit reports for Aachen, as well as Daniel's later accounts of the battle, do not reference benefiting from the lessons of Brest, so the influence of that battle on the troops in Aachen is unclear.

American military culture, and American culture in general, fundamentally shaped how lessons were learned and shared in the combat zone. Drawing on the American cultural notions of competition, entrepreneurial spirit, ingenuity, initiative, equality, decentralization, and confidence, the US Army's system for learning was decentralized and open to inputs from all levels. Insights often flowed upward, and higher echelon commanders generally avoided comprehensively imposing singular solutions. Both formal and informal information channels flourished. At the battalion level and below word of mouth prevailed, while larger organizations tended to produce written reports. One example of this bottom-up approach can be found in a November 1944 Combat Observer report, intended for the Army's higher echelons of command. This report contained two pages of comments on urban warfare, all of which came from enlisted and non-commissioned officers. Michael Doubler put it well when he described the GI problem-solving approach as doing what came naturally.[40]

The battles of Aachen and Manila, just four months apart but against very different opponents, would test both how well the Americans had learned from others and how well they could learn on the job.

Chapter 2

Aachen–October 1944

The assault on Aachen marked a new phase in the American Army's drive eastward from Normandy into the Reich. The slow, grinding hedgerow fighting of June and July 1944 had given way to frenzied pursuit in August. In September, however, as US forces approached Germany itself, the pursuit phase ended as quickly as it had begun. The slower tempo in turn shaped how American forces encircled and captured Aachen. Aside from the symbolic value as the first German city threatened by Allied ground forces, Aachen was also a useful military objective. The city was the gateway to the Aachen Gap, an avenue into Germany's industrial heart—the Ruhr.

Initial US plans were to bypass Aachen, cut it off, and then mop up the weakened defenders, but those plans were thwarted by unexpectedly dogged German resistance, forcing a more methodical approach. The US effort then shifted to a better resourced pincer movement by two corps, to isolate the city in preparation for the final assault. Strong German counterattacks, and the fortifications of the Siegfried Line, made the encirclement far more demanding and slower than expected. With many forces dedicated to the encirclement and holding off German counterattacks, US commanders strained to find manpower for the assault, and they compensated with extensive armor, artillery, and air support.

While German forces were less short of manpower, their troops were of doubtful quality. Most formations were ad hoc groupings of hastily assembled units of non-infantry personnel, or the shattered remnants of larger formations. German armor was scarce, and air support almost non-existent, although artillery support was relatively abundant.

In the end the 1st Infantry Division cleared Aachen, block by block, with two heavily supported infantry battalions. Methodical thoroughness, and a comprehensive and enthusiastic use of firepower, characterized the operation. Speed was a distinctly secondary priority as US forces advanced across the city over a ten-day period. Perhaps most impressive was the small size of the assaulting US force, roughly one-third the manpower of the defending Germans. Aachen presents a good window into US urban capabilities when confronted by a determined, technically advanced infantry force, well supported by artillery, in the late World War II period. It also serves as an example of the American tendency and skill for substituting machines for men.

Operational Context

In the Normandy hedgerow fighting of June and July 1944, the Allied pace of advance was slow, and the cost high. However, with the breakout from Normandy in late July, a new phase began. The modus operandi became one of pursuit and encirclement rather than clear and hold. Massive numbers of Germans were captured and it appeared to US forces that German resolve was irrevocably broken.[1] US First Army commander Lt. Gen. Courtney Hodges told his staff on 6 September that with ten more days of good weather the war would be over.[2]

Then the pursuit phase ended as suddenly as it began, in part a victim of its own success. While the critical port facilities of Antwerp fell on 4 September to British Field Marshal Bernard

Law Montgomery's 21st Army Group, the essential approaches to the port would not be cleared for two more months, making the port itself unusable. That delay forced the Allies to rely on the already long supply lines back to Normandy. A further drain on First Army supplies was Operation MARKET GARDEN, to the north in Montgomery's sector, which began on 17 September. During the pursuit phase, the First Army had covered 750 miles in six weeks, but it would then need almost six months to advance the sixty miles from Aachen to Cologne.[3]

Three other factors contributed to the slower American advance. The pursuit had worn out US soldiers and equipment. The retreat back into Germany had also shortened the Wehrmacht's supply lines and increased the defender's motivation. And lastly, the Siegfried Line, split into two bands on both sides of Aachen (see Map 2-1), acted both to slow the first US advances around Aachen and shape the later encirclement effort. Lightly equipped German units and fragments of units were able to fall back into these defenses and buy time for the German leadership to reorganize and deploy reinforcements.

In mid-September General Hodges' First Army approached the German border, Aachen, and the Aachen Gap, a historical avenue into Germany. His three corps were (from north to south): XIX, VII, and V. On 11 September the dire logistical situation prompted Hodges to order a two-day halt to all his units. However, even with this modest delay, VII Corps commander Maj. Gen. J. Lawton "Lightning Joe" Collins strained at the leash. Collins requested permission for a "reconnaissance in force" to penetrate the Siegfried Line, where advance was found to be "easy," before pausing for supplies. Hodges granted permission on 12 September to VII Corps in the center of his line, and ordered Maj. Gen. Leonard T. Gerow's V Corps on the southern flank to do likewise.[4]

Collins hoped to punch through both bands of fortifications before the Germans could fully man them. He directed elements of the 3rd Armored Division and 1st Infantry Division (1st ID) to start southwest of the city and drive northeast up to Stolberg, with some infantry units hooking north in a secondary effort to take Aachen. When a combination of German resistance, roadblocks, difficult terrain, and fortifications slowed progress, Collins decided the easy going was not to be had. At that point he jettisoned the goal of capturing Aachen in favor of merely isolating it by taking the dominating hills to its east, which would free up forces for a stronger push toward Stolberg and through both bands of fortifications. XIX Corps, from its position northwest of the city, was to advance east and then south, to link up with VII Corps on the high ground east of the city.[5]

Collins's stronger second push began at dawn on 13 September, led by elements of the 3rd Armored Division and supported by elements of the 1st ID. The 1st ID elements made modest progress

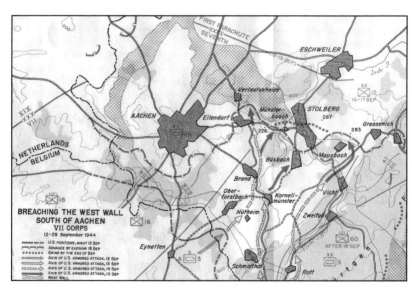

Map 2-1: Breaching the West Wall South of Aachen. *Courtesy Charles B. MacDonald, United States Army in World War II: The European Theater of Operations: The Siegfried Line Campaign* (Washington, DC: Department of the Army, Office of the Chief of Military History, 1963), map section.

pushing through the first band of fortifications west of Aachen. They advanced several miles until they formed a semi-circle on the outskirts of Aachen from its southwest to its east by the evening of 15 September. In the first two days the 3rd Armored Division elements pushed northeast four to five miles to Stolberg itself, four miles east of Aachen, but then progress slowed to a crawl.

The advance into Stolberg had breached the second band of fortifications but VII Corps' units were stretched too thin to exploit the breach. By 18 September Collins realized his momentum was gone and that his forces were stretched to the limit just holding the gains to date, so he ordered his units to consolidate and shorten their lines. By 22 September fighting had died down and VII Corps shifted over to the defensive for the rest of September (see Map 2-1).[6]

XIX Corps' push east and south, to link up with VII Corps units behind Aachen, simultaneously stalled. German resistance was strengthening and any advance meant longer flanks, and more forces needed to protect those flanks. On 22 September all three First Army corps commanders met for two hours with Hodges. At that meeting Hodges authorized the XIX Corps commander, Major General Charles H. Corlett, to postpone his attack indefinitely. There was some concern among the commanders that German forces might be playing dead as they had recently demonstrated some impressive recuperative abilities. With that the bulk of First Army paused.[7]

The Foe

US forces faced a weakened but still dangerous opponent in and around Aachen. While the German standards for organization, leadership, discipline, and equipment were high, this was an army showing the strains of a long war on two fronts. The Wehrmacht was relatively well supported by artillery at Aachen. A 1st ID report called the artillery fire directed at the division while at Aachen the heaviest yet seen by the division.[8] However, the Luftwaffe was largely absent and armor support was almost as scarce. German infantry units had a plethora of tools for dealing with US armor. The towed 88mm dual-purpose flak/anti-tank gun could knock out any tank in the US inventory at long-range, and the more common towed 75mm anti-tank gun was almost as deadly. German infantry itself was a serious threat to Allied armor with the *Panzerfaust* one-shot disposable anti-tank rocket and the bazooka-like *Panzerschreck*. German troops were also equipped with excellent small arms such as the MG42 machine gun and the world's first assault rifle—the *Sturmgewehr* 44.

The German units that had retreated back to the Siegfried Line, and many of those thrown into the fray from Germany, were mostly either fragments or understrength. For example, the 116th Panzer Division had only approximately thirty operationally fit tanks or assault guns in mid-September. One grenadier training regiment, attached to the 89th Infantry Division, provided the division's only artillery—a German 105mm howitzer and an Italian 150mm. Another unit was an *Ost-Batallion* (East Battalion). It had 450 Russian "volunteers" with four 122mm Russian howitzers.[9]

While ragged, the Wehrmacht in September 1944 was far from beaten. In mid-September the Germans had also hastily plugged new units into the Siegfried Line, formed in Germany as a product of the latest mobilization efforts. This effort was guided by Field Marshal Gerd von Rundstedt, reinstated as Commander-in-Chief West by Hitler on 5 September. Both Hitler and Rundstedt recognized the danger in the west and the Aachen sector. On 4 September Hitler assigned the Western Front priority for all new artillery and assault guns. In a 7 September assessment Rundstedt specifically mentioned a desperate need for armor at Aachen. The Germans were able to deploy three full-strength infantry divisions (12th Infantry, 183rd Volksgrenadier, and 246th Volksgrenadier) to the Siegfried Line during the critical period of mid-September. Their transit by train was relatively unhindered, as poor weather precluded most US interdiction efforts. Throughout this period the Germans aggressively used both artillery and counterattacks to hold back US forces.[10]

The American drive to encircle Aachen and breech the Siegfried Line left few American forces to assault the city, but it also drew German forces away from holding it. Both the danger of being cut off inside the city and the threat of a breakthrough to Cologne and the Ruhr beyond caused the German command to limit the forces inside the city. In early October the German corps commander in the Aachen area (LXXXI Corps), General Friedrich Koechling, shifted four infantry battalions from the 246th Volksgrenadier Division from inside the city to north of the city, to stem the advance of the US XIX Corps.[11]

The forces actually inside Aachen in September were an ad hoc mix of the available, and primarily infantry formations. When the assault into the city began, the commander inside Aachen, Colonel Gerhard Wilck, had approximately five thousand troops—most from his own 246th Volksgrenadier Division. That division had travelled by train, at full strength, from Bohemia to the western front in late September.[12] The 246th Division had formed up only two months earlier from various manpower scraps. Forty percent were former naval personnel, while many of the rest were from categories previously excluded from call up: those in marginal physical condition, deferred defense workers, and the previously wounded.[13] Further complicating Wilck's task was his late ascent to command of the forces in the city—on 13 October—two days into the American assault of the city itself.[14] He had approximately five tanks, and these were older PzKw IVs—roughly the equal of the Sherman.[15] Aside from the artillery outside Aachen, Wilck had almost three dozen towed artillery pieces and anti-tank guns inside the city.[16]

The approximate five thousand figure for German strength in the city, at the start of the American assault on 11 October, is not consistently used in all sources. A 7 November 1944 1st ID report is less than clear in that it describes a "more or less constant" figure of 3500, only four pages later to state "not more than 4,000 troops ever made up the garrison of Aachen."[17] However, another 1st ID report dated the same, states that Aachen itself was defended by "approximately 5000 troops."[18] The interview of the captured German commander is of no help as it does not mention German troop strength.[19] The later 1st ID source does mention the number of German prisoners taken, although the 5637 figure is for the entire 1st ID and almost certainly combines those captured in and around the city.[20] The best support for the approximate figure of five thousand comes from an account written by a First Army officer. While undated, this account was probably written within several months of the battle, and it gives a precise tally of the Germans captured within the city, by the 26th Infantry Regiment: 3391. By narrowing the criteria to just inside the city, over the dates of the assault (11–21 October), and just those captured by the 26th Infantry, this source filters out figures for the greater battle around Aachen.[21] MacDonald, who uses the 5000 figure, cites this particular source twice.[22]

In interviews after the battle, Wilck described his available forces.

> The forces at his disposal consisted for the most part of elements of the three regiments of his 246th division: the 404th Regiment in the north, the 689th Regiment in the south and the 352nd in the east. In addition, there were several other make-shift units, like Battlegroup Rink, a machine gun fortress battalion and a replacement battalion.[23]

The replacement battalion was comprised of men 50–60 years old, and the Luftwaffe unit had personnel with little infantry training and poor equipment.[24]

In response to pleas from Wilck, LXXXI Corps commander Koechling sent some reinforcements into the city during the first week of the assault. Eight assault guns made it into Aachen the evening of 14 October, followed the next day by Battlegroup Rink—an ad hoc SS formation which had to disengage from its efforts to stop the VII and XIX Corps linkup.[25] The SS unit derived its name from its commander Obersturmfuhrer Herbert Rink and was composed of roughly one hundred and fifty troops left over from the First SS Panzer Division.[26] Before the city was completely cut off by American forces on 16 October, the Germans also succeeded in pushing into the city some artillery that belonged to the 246th Volksgrenadier Division, and units of the Engineer Assault Regiment 600.[27]

One other trend across the entire Wehrmacht, which started the previous year, affected the defenders of Aachen. Since 1943 the Wehrmacht had reduced manpower in each division, substituting firepower for men (e.g., additional machine guns and more automatic weapons). In early 1944 the standard infantry division was reduced from 16,860 to 13,656 men.[28] The impact at Aachen was a larger number of support weapons per unit in the hands of the defenders.

The Assault

Mid- to Late-September: German commanders misread the build-up of American forces south of Aachen, actually the push on Stolberg, as a precursor to an all-out assault on the city on 16 September. At that time, the Germans expected a direct assault into the city from the south and orientated the bulk of their defenses in that direction. They continued to view the southern threat as the most dangerous until well after the actual American assault from the east in mid-October.[29]

Most of the remaining civilians were driven out by two evacuation orders from the Germans in mid-September. The second order was required because an earlier German commander, who arrived in the city on 12 September, countermanded the first evacuation order. He thought clearing out the civilians, for what looked to him like a hopeless fight, would be unduly harsh on the population.[30]

In late-September Collins had few troops available for the actual assault, since most were encircling the city, holding off the strong German counterattacks from the east. He selected the 18th and 26th Infantry Regiments of the 1st ID, both positioned just south of the city, to complete the encirclement and conduct the assault. The 18th Regiment was to push northward, linking up behind the city with elements of the XIX Corps, as the XIX Corps drove south (see Map 2-2). Once the linkup with XIX Corps was completed, and the city isolated, the 26th Infantry was to advance into the city. Patrols by the two regiments discovered the southern orientation of the German defenses. By waiting until the 18th Regiment had secured ground east of the city, the 26th Infantry was able to enter the city from an unexpected direction, the east.[31] The paucity of available American infantry units required US commanders to replace the 18th Regiment, previously manning the perimeter south of Aachen, with combat engineers.[32]

1 to 9 October: In early October Collins received some much needed help from the Twelfth Army Group commander, Gen. Omar Bradley, who reduced the VII Corps' frontage from thirty-five to twenty miles. However, the problem was Aachen, and the salient it had become in the American line, which created a more pressing requirement to capture the city.[33]

The 18th Infantry Regiment's mission was to capture the high ground several kilometers east of the city, Crucifix Hill and the Ravelsberg (hills 231 and 239, respectively, on Map 2-2), beginning at 0400 on 8 October. The fighting was fierce over 8 to 10 October, with heavy casualties on both sides, although the 18th Regiment succeed in taking and holding both hills.[34] As was common in that resource-constrained environment, even the 26th Infantry

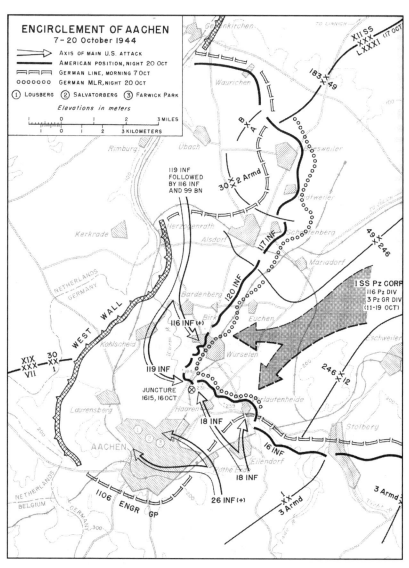

Map 2-2: Encirclement of Aachen. *Courtesy Charles B. MacDonald,* United States Army in World War II: The European Theater of Operations: The Siegfried Line Campaign (Washington, DC: Department of the Army, Office of the Chief of Military History, 1963), p. 283.

Regiment, which drew the assignment of assaulting the city, could not be fully committed. Its 1st Battalion was still resting and refitting from the heavy losses it suffered in the push on Stolberg in September, which left only the 2nd and 3rd Battalions available.[35]

10 to 12 October: While the gap was still not closed behind Aachen, between the 30th Infantry Division (with its 119th Infantry Regiment) and the 18th Infantry Regiment, it was getting smaller and under observed artillery fire by 10 October.[36] That was close enough for the 1st ID's commander, Maj. Gen. Clarence Huebner, to deliver an ultimatum to the Germans in Aachen, demanding surrender within twenty-four hours.[37] While no official reply was received rejecting the ultimatum, German radio reported the ultimatum rejected on 11 October.

That day, at 1100, two days of heavy air and artillery strikes began. While this bombardment was on-going, the 30th Infantry Division was continuing to push slowly southward, with the gap down to 3000 yards late on the eleventh.[38] Northeast of Aachen a German build-up of "considerable proportions" started on the twelfth and continued for several days. The pressure on the 16th and 18th Infantry Regiments outside the city was heavy, but they held.[39]

Both the 2nd and 3rd Battalions of the 26th Infantry Regiment shifted to their assault positions southeast of the city. The 2nd Battalion, commanded by Lt. Col. Derrill Daniel, edged up to the railroad tracks that roughly formed the southern edge of the city.[40] The 3rd Battalion, commanded by Lt. Col. John Corley, pulled off the southern perimeter of the city, leaving one infantry company behind to hold the line, and moved to the edge of the factory district, an industrial section on the eastern edge of the city.[41]

Third Battalion's part of the main assault began the morning of 12 October. The commander of the 26th Infantry Regiment, Col. John Seitz, assigned Corley three objectives to be taken in sequence: the factory district, Farwick Park/Observatory Hill (henceforth called Farwick Park), and the largest hill of the Lousberg (850+

feet).[42] This high ground, at the northeast edge of Aachen, should not be confused with the larger hills several kilometers outside the city to the northeast (Crucifix Hill and the Ravelsberg), captured several days earlier by the 18th Infantry Regiment. All three of Corley's objectives were on the northeast edge of Aachen, the central portion of the city being the responsibility of 2nd Battalion. The Lousberg Heights comprised three hills, forming a rising spine of ground running to the northwest. Corley did not think he could take the latter two objectives without his entire battalion, and Seitz released Corley's third company back to him late that night. The two companies Corley started with pushed off at 1100, and he reported the factory district secured by 1530.[43]

13 to 21 October: While two American battalions were clearing the city, strong German counterattacks on the line east of the city several times came close to breaking through. Over 14 to 15 October the 1st ID commander was sufficiently concerned to order halts in offensive operations for first 2nd Battalion, and then 3rd Battalion, ordering them to prepare for possible threats to their flanks from outside the city. On the nineteenth the Germans unleashed yet another strong counterattack on the line east of the city, supported by armor and what the GIs of the 18th Infantry Regiment called the heaviest artillery fire they had seen to date.[44]

Meanwhile, the progress of the 30th Infantry Division to close the gap behind Aachen continued at a "snail-like" pace. The final push to complete the encirclement of Aachen was successful on 16 October, when patrols from the 30th Infantry made contact with the 18th Infantry Regiment late in the day.[45]

The 3rd Battalion's drive on Farwick Park was slow, in part because of the need to maintain contact with 2nd Battalion to the south, and because of heavy casualties, especially among the officers and NCOs. However, the northwest portion of the park was in American hands by the fourteenth. The ordered pause on the fifteenth gave Corley's men a chance to rest, while consolidating and

The crew of a 57mm anti-tank gun fire upon a German strongpoint in Aachen. *Courtesy of the National Archives and Records Administration.*

improving their positions. On that same day German forces inside the city staged a strong armor-supported counterattack, in an attempt to retake Farwick Park. They managed to cut off one of 3rd Battalion's companies. Corley pushed back, recapturing all the lost ground and regaining contact with his isolated company, but he reported to Colonel Seitz that night he needed 250 replacements (authorized strength was 871). The German attack continued on the sixteenth, with Corley holding only by scraping together infantry replacements from his non-infantry personnel. That evening Seitz reported to General Heubner that 3rd Battalion had had its worst day since landing at Normandy and that it was "nip and tuck." Corley concluded that his battalion was at its limit, and not able to take the Lousberg in its current state.[46]

Third Battalion spent the seventeenth in recovery, an effort not helped by the heavy German mortar fire all day. Corley used this pause in the action to observe the front line and plan the next day's assault. The difficulty and importance of the assault caused Corley to do something he would never do again in the war—issue a written attack order while in combat. After some careful planning by Corley, his battalion renewed its attack to capture the remainder of Farwick Park at 0630 on 18 October. Progress was rapid, aided by the aggressive direct fire use of a self-propelled 155mm gun attached to the battalion. The park was fully captured by 1130. Corley's men discovered that the newly captured Quellenhof Hotel had been a German headquarters. Corley called that day's work by his battalion its best attack of the entire war.

Before dawn on 19 October patrols from the 3rd Battalion had discovered a weakness in the German defenses of the highest hill of the Lousberg Heights—defenses weakened as the Germans pulled out troops for the attacks of 15 and 16 October. That morning, elements of the 3rd Battalion pushed on toward the second hill in the Heights, the Salvatorberg, capturing it by 1500. Late that night the Germans fired an extensive artillery barrage into the city from outside the encirclement.[47]

To aid 3rd Battalion, Task Force Hogan was formed on 18 October from a battalion of tanks (minus one company) and a battalion of armored infantry—both detached from 3rd Armored Division. They worked on the 3rd Battalion's right flank to help complete the capture of the high ground.[48] On 19 October Task Force Hogan made slow but steady progress, sweeping the northern slopes of the Lousberg Heights. Task Force Hogan's objective was to deliver a right hook to that high ground.[49]

The 2nd Battalion's push northwest, and then west through the heart of the city, began on the morning of 13 October. For the first half hour the infantry met little resistance and progress for the day was good, though moving its supporting armor into

A M1919 machine gun team uses the cover available in Aachen as it watches the street. *Courtesy of the National Archives and Records Administration.*

the city took until nightfall on account of the fifteen- to thirty-foot railroad embankment. On the fourteenth Daniel turned his 2nd Battalion westward, for the drive through the city, but then he received orders from the 26th Infantry Regiment to halt, until it was clear the German attacks outside the city would be repulsed. Daniel renewed his advance on the fifteenth, although a strong German counterattack supported by armor managed to temporarily push elements of his battalion back several blocks. October 16 was spent again in an ordered halt, because of strong German attacks to the east of the city. Daniel was advancing westward again on the seventeenth, although his assigned sector was becoming wider (as the city itself was wider to the west) and German resistance was stiffening. Combat engineers of the 1106th Engineer Combat Group, moved into the city to help the 2nd Battalion man the expanding front line. On the eighteenth it became evident to American commanders that even more troops were needed to help 2nd Battalion, so the 2nd Battalion of the 110th Infantry Regiment (28th Infantry Division) was brought into Aachen on the night of 18 to 19 October to help man the line. This additional manpower allowed the 2nd Battalion to continue its advance on the nineteenth into the heart of the city, while maintaining contact with the 3rd Battalion.[50]

By 20 and 21 October, 2nd Battalion was clearing "sporadic" resistance as it pushed out to the western edge of the city, though the Germans defending the Technical High School fought particularly hard.[51] On 20 October, 3rd Battalion continued to press northwest up the Lousberg, against lessening resistance. One company took the summit of the Lousberg, while the other two companies cleared buildings on the hill's southern slope, and Task Force Hogan cleared the northern slopes. On the morning of the twenty-first, as the various companies pressed forward, they encountered what looked to be just another air raid shelter, but unbeknown to the Americans this was the headquarters of the German commander Wilck. Wilck turned himself over to Corley's men and officially surrendered at 1205. At that time he knew the locations of only 500 of his 1600 troops that American forces rounded up after the surrender.[52]

The battle was over and the city itself showed the effects. An observer walking through it immediately afterward described what he saw.

> The city is as dead as a Roman ruin, but unlike a ruin it has none of the grace of gradual decay [...] Burst sewers, broken gas mains and dead animals have raised an almost overpowering smell in many parts of the city. The streets are paved with shattered glass; telephone, electric light and trolley cables are dangling and netted together everywhere, and in many places wrecked cars, trucks, armored vehicles and guns litter the streets.[53]

Command, Control, and Communications

The urban environment of Aachen presented numerous challenges to command and control, including short lines of sight and blocked radio signals. However, US planners recognized the difficulties in urban command and control and constructed an assault plan that mitigated those difficulties. Daniel was specifically concerned about command and control in planning for Aachen.[54] The planned methodical and controlled advance minimized confusion and helped US forces fully exploit their firepower advantages.

The first challenge faced by the Americans was the confusing maze-like topography of Aachen, where the large number of structures and short lines of sight could make one block look like the next. To deal with this, US planners gave each prominent structure and intersection a number and these were marked on the maps given to various echelons of command.[55] This facilitated quick and accurate coordination between ground units for fire support, and assisted with maintaining the integrity of the front line by preventing gaps between US units.

Operations were limited to daylight to further maximize control. Among his seven lessons out of Aachen, Daniel noted, "Daylight operations in street fighting are necessary to take full advantage of maximum fire power and to avoid loss of control."[56] In daylight it was easier to match landmarks with maps, and thus more accurately direct fire support. Darkness facilitated German infiltration attempts, so restricting US movements at that time allowed US troops to consider any night-time movement as hostile.

Another mode of control was the requirement that units positively link up at designated points before moving on. That restriction was in keeping with the overall emphasis on thoroughness over speed. It was important to US commanders that no gaps appear between their units, and they were willing to slow the general advance to do so.[57]

The buildings of Aachen often interfered with radio communications. To compensate, advancing platoons laid large amounts of communications wire, and following units connected these wires laterally to form an effective network.[58] A lessons-learned report from the 1106th Engineer Combat Group, which held the line on the southern edges of the city, cited good communications as key to holding its position. Poor communications meant poor artillery support—an essential element in defeating strong German counterattacks. While at Aachen, the 1106th laid over fifty miles of communications wire, in addition to the wire they took over from other infantry units.[59]

Even when buildings did not block radio communications, there were compatibility issues between the radios used by the infantry and armor.[60] In Normandy there had been communication problems as the radios given to each arm were incompatible. Several solutions emerged, including mounting a field telephone in a box on the back of a Sherman that hooked into the tank's intercom.[61] Another solution was to equip infantry units with "peeps," or jeeps equipped with radios that could communicate with the armored units. The lasting solution began in late-October 1944, with a large-scale program to install infantry radios in tanks. The S-3 log for the 26th Infantry Regiment, from 8 to 21 October, made only a few mentions of communications breakdowns for the regiment.[62]

Commanders recognized these communication issues as they organized the forces and pushed combined arms down to the small unit level.[63] The parceling out of armor and other support weapons to the small unit level improved combined arms coordination. An infantry unit could receive immediate armor support from vehicles directly attached rather than needing to request that support through several layers of command. These attachments reduced reaction times, made the support better suited to each particular situation, and they followed Army doctrine, which called for decentralized command and control in urban environments.[64]

The direct attachment of the M12 self-propelled 155mm guns was rare, although not unprecedented.[65] It is unclear from the sources consulted whose idea it was to attach the two M12s to the two battalions clearing Aachen, but division- and corps-level approval was probably given. An official US Army history states Corley "called for" one of the guns early in the assault on the city, and after it proved effective the 26th Infantry Regiment commander acquired another for the 2nd Battalion. The two guns belonged to the 991st Field Artillery Battalion, which at the time was attached to the 3rd Armor Division, another VII Corps unit holding the line just south of the 1st Infantry Division.[66]

Headquarters elements also moved aggressively forward. Being closer to the front line made it easier for commanders to stay in contact with smaller units and to gather first-hand impressions of the battlefield. Corley operated well forward from a small command post immediately behind his infantry companies. Even the 1st ID commander, General Huebner, had an advanced command post in the suburbs of Aachen.[67]

Another factor aiding both infantry battalions was the tenure of their commanders. Both Daniel and Corley had been in command of their respective battalions since early 1943. Both commanders entered Aachen experienced and they knew their men well. Prior to Aachen, Corley had earned one Purple Heart, two Bronze Stars, two Silver Stars, and a Distinguished Service Cross.[68]

In his master's thesis on unit cohesion and leadership, Michael Runey studied the performance of Corley's 3rd Battalion in the last three months of 1944, including operations in Aachen. Runey praised the quality of the leadership throughout the battalion, which kept it in action despite heavy losses in the city: 292 total battle casualties, sixty-one of which were non-commissioned officers and thirteen officers. Only one of Corley's three infantry company commanders was still in command by battle's end, and another company finished with only two of its authorized six officers. This ability to press on despite the loss of so many leaders was a reflection on the aggression of those leaders and the ability of those remaining to motivate the men. The US doctrinal emphasis on leaders showing initiative and aggression paid off, but it also came at a cost.[69]

Despite the various mitigation efforts, the urban environment of Aachen still made command, control, and communications difficult at times. In the approach to Aachen through its suburbs, on the evening of 10 October, a company of the 3rd Battalion became lost. In the fading light its commander mistakenly entered the industrial complex, which his orders only called for approaching. Upon realizing his error he ordered a withdrawal, which was accomplished without loss.[70] On 14 October a gap developed between the 2nd and 3rd Battalions. A 2nd Battalion 57mm anti-tank gun was lost to German bazooka fire from the flank, from an area that was supposed to be covered by 3rd Battalion. The absent company from 3rd Battalion had missed the linkup point and was "considerably" north of its ordered location. The error was quickly diagnosed and the misplaced company moved to the linkup point early the next day.[71]

Intelligence and Reconnaissance

American intelligence and reconnaissance capabilities in Aachen were rather limited, but US commanders recognized these limitations and adapted. On the positive side they made accurate judgments as to the general orientation of German defenses, and there were good maps of the city's streets, buildings, and surrounding suburbs. Two notable shortfalls were in judging the overall size of the German force and specifically locating German forces. The 1st ID estimates of German manpower in Aachen were low at 3500—relative to the 5000 actually there.[72] The specific locations of most German personnel were not pinpointed until they were encountered by American ground forces. The plan for assaulting Aachen constructed by US commanders recognized the limitations in urban intelligence and worked around them.

In the judgment of the commander of the German LXXXI Corps, US air reconnaissance was generally effective at discovering German positions, although it did not perform well against German positions in wooded or urban areas.[73] For example, officers in the 3rd US Armored Division received detailed 1:10,000 scale maps just a day before a major attack was to commence in February 1945 across the Rhineland. These maps were greatly aided by aerial photo flights over the entire area. On these maps they could identify newly dug minefields, individual German foxholes, and even the difference between foxholes holding riflemen or machine guns (discernible by the firing soot traces left in the snow).[74]

The map situation was notably better:

> Both sides had the same excellent 1/25,000 metric scale maps of the area reproduced from those originally made by the French Army, showing roads, railroads, contour lines, towns, and forests. To offset superior knowledge of the terrain that the Germans enjoyed, the Americans controlling the air, had the advantage of aerial photographs, and they could use their artillery spotter planes while the Germans could not.[75]

There had been a shortage of maps until Allied forces captured a German map factory in Liege, Belgium, in early September. A signal corps cartography group moved in and subsequently produced a wealth of maps. One VII Corps officer reported being well supplied with 1:125,000, 1:62,500, and 1:10,000 scale maps—the first two in color and the last detailed enough to show individual buildings.[76] The battalions of the 26th Infantry Regiment received 500 maps of Aachen in the week prior to the assault, produced by 1st ID support units.[77] The assaulting forces had at least one copy of a brochure for the spa complex at Farwick Park—including a floor plan for the Hotel Quellenhof, which served for a time as the

German headquarters.[78] However, while the GIs had good maps of the city, those maps did not mark everything—such as the German air raid shelters. US forces apparently did not know the location of the first German headquarters, the Quellenhof Hotel in the northern part of the city, nor the new location when the headquarters moved on 14 October, until they captured both positions.[79]

The primary tool for finding German forces was contact. As patrols or larger units moved through the city, they learned where German forces were, and were not, by who engaged them. As the infantry of the 2nd Battalion first entered the city itself on 13 October, after cresting the railroad embankment, they were surprised to find little German resistance for the first half hour. On 16 October what they thought to be a pillbox turned out instead to be a well-camouflaged tank, this being apparent after it was hit with a 155mm round.[80] On several occasions German infantry, and even armor, were able to mount significant counterattacks inside the city. This ability suggests German forces could sometimes move and mass, at least initially, without being detected by US forces.

However, this difficulty in locating German forces was mitigated by a combination of methodical advance and liberal use of firepower. Not knowing if German infantry were in a building before entering was less of a problem if the procedure was to fire heavily into that building anyway. The assumption was that each building was a German position until proven otherwise. Once inside, US infantrymen were thorough in checking every room. On a few occasions they did miss things, as when a steeple was not cleared of German snipers, and when German troops used the sewers to come up behind US infantry.[81]

The Americans solved the problem of sorting German civilians from German soldiers who had changed into civilian clothing by simply evacuating every German found in the city. Each evacuee was interrogated in an attempt to root out any German soldiers. Starting on 13 October the 1st ID's Military Police Platoon was turning over civilians to the Counter-Intelligence Corps for screening.[82] One unit report stated six German soldiers were found on 19 October this way.[83]

One notable source of information was the population of Aachen. The 26th Infantry Regiment's S-3 log for October makes several references to information coming in from civilians, along with the general comment, "Civilians have been very co-operative on information."[84] In many cases the civilians gave information on mines and booby traps. Of the twenty-two reports that came into the headquarters of the 1106th Engineer Combat Group, ten were from civilians, and every one of those reports was later confirmed as accurate. The GIs speculated their motives to be a desire either to protect their own property from damage, to return home safely, or to use the infrastructure safely.[85] Aside from the population, German prisoners provided a modest amount of useful information.[86]

Firepower and Survivability

The American approach for assaulting Aachen was built on a foundation of maximum firepower.[87] While the often cited ratio needed for an attacking force is 3-1, the ratio was 1-3 in favor of the defending Germans at Aachen. The equalizer for American forces was artillery and armor. In planning the assault, the 2nd Battalion commander coined the phrase "Knock'em All Down." Heavy suppressive fire would keep German heads down, artillery and mortars would keep other Germans out, and then the infantry would charge in to clean out buildings with small arms and grenades. Every structure was assumed to be a German strongpoint until proven otherwise.[88]

American commanders preparing for Aachen had the benefit of recent experience. The slow pace and high cost of the Normandy hedgerow fighting of June and July 1944 had caught the Army by surprise. The infantry and tanks found they were ill-prepared to work together. The micro-segmentation of the battle space by an average of fourteen hedgerows per kilometer strained US forces in unexpected ways. They encountered German infantry, anti-tank guns, and armor at short ranges, where US infantry and armor were vulnerable to any breakdowns in coordination between arms. The 3rd Armored division lost eighty-seven Shermans (38 percent of its authorized strength) after penetrating just five miles of German-held territory.[89] The hedgerow country proved an effective but demanding instructor. US infantry and armor units quickly learned much about harnessing the synergistic potential of combined arms:

> On 25 June, the 29th Infantry Division sponsored a conference on coordination of tanks, infantry, and engineers in the assault, and it published a memorandum entitled "Infantry Coordination of Tanks, Infantry & Engineers in Hedgerow Tactics." Two days later, a booklet arrived at the front, courtesy of the XIX Corps, entitled, "The Tank and Infantry Team."[90]

That learning paid significant dividends in the streets of Aachen.

One could argue the experience from Normandy was more useful preparation for urban warfare than the Army's urban warfare doctrine of the time, at least in one key area. *FM 31-50*, published in January 1944, had most things right about city fighting with one notable exception: the role of armor. Unlike the operations in Aachen, *FM 31-50* described a rather narrow role for armor in urban warfare. This narrow view of armor's role was also described in a March 1942 Army manual for armored forces. However, the June 1944 version of *FM 100-5*, the Army's overarching manual on operations, took a different view—likely influenced by Allied operations in Italy and Stalingrad. While it still described urban areas as hampering armor's mobility, it stated "Opportunities will present themselves frequently where the support of tanks in such situations becomes desirable."[91]

One factor aiding the coordination between the tanks of the 745th Tank Battalion and the foot soldiers of the 26th Infantry Regiment was familiarity. Of all the independent tank battalions serving in the European Theater of Operations, no other was attached longer to the same unit as the 745th was attached to the 1st ID, the two having worked together since 6 June. This was a significant bonus for both. Several tank battalion commanders wrote in their after-action reports for Normandy that long-term attachment was essential to maximize cooperation, one even suggesting attachment should occur when the infantry unit was formed.[92]

An Army rifle battalion in 1944 included a headquarters company, three infantry companies and a heavy weapons company. The commanders of both battalions entering Aachen parceled out much of the equipment from their heavy weapons companies to the infantry companies. This equipment included water-cooled heavy machine guns, extra bazooka teams, flame throwers, and towed 57mm anti-tank guns. Small groups of engineers were also added at the company level, parceled out by the 1st ID from its 1st Engineer Combat Battalion.[93] The 2nd Battalion commander described these units as small company task forces.[94] This push of support weapons down to smaller units reflected a recognition by US commanders that Aachen would be a small unit fight of close range engagements and difficult command and control. Attaching these weapons at that level gave the companies better support and reduced reaction times.

A similar augmentation to smaller units occurred with armor. Infantry companies were assigned a few Sherman medium tanks or M10 tank destroyers to exploit the American advantage in armor where it most mattered—at the front line with the infantry. From the 634th Tank Destroyer Battalion came Company A (authorized strength of twelve M10 tank destroyers), from the 745th Tank Battalion came Company C (authorized strength of eighteen Shermans), and the 745th's Assault Gun Platoon of Shermans with

M10s from the 634th Tank Destroyer Battalion on the hunt in Aachen. *Courtesy of the National Archives and Records Administration.*

105mm guns (authorized strength of five tanks).[95] The actual number of armored vehicles available to the infantry companies varied from day to day due to combat losses, breakdowns, and replacements and was difficult to identify precisely, but the number available varied between half and full strength.[96]

US troops were aggressive in their application of firepower. They would sweep the streets with fire before moving on them, as prescribed in doctrine.[97] In storming buildings the infantry used extensive suppressive fire and grenades: both rifle grenades and hand-thrown. Generally GIs explored interior spaces first with firepower, only then visually checking for the presence of Germans. The grenade of choice was the "offensive" MkIIIA2, designed to emphasize blast over fragmentation, with a bursting charge nine times larger than the standard fragmentation grenade (more commonly recognized by its pineapple shape). That greater blast was further amplified when confined to interior spaces.[98]

The US small arms available at Aachen were effective, and in the view of the German LXXXI Corps commander, "completely equivalent" to those carried by the Germans for urban combat. The standard issue US rifle, the M1 Garand, allowed eight rapid shots before reloading was necessary. Captured German soldiers described American infantrymen with their M1s as "formidable opponents."[99] The short engagement ranges in urban combat put a premium on speed, and the semi-automatic Garand was superior to the bolt-action rifles such as the K98 carried by some German troops. However, by October 1944 many Germans were carrying fully-automatic submachine guns or the world's first assault rifle—the *Sturmgewehr* 44.[100] The Browning Automatic Rifle also fit the operations of Aachen well. Unlike the otherwise excellent MG42 German light machine gun, the Browning with its twenty-round box magazine was well suited for use by a single man on the move. The US M1917 water-cooled heavy machine gun was perfect for the sustained fire role to sweep the streets. This pinned Germans inside buildings being assaulted and kept away reinforcements.

Other tools for the infantry were towed 57mm anti-tank guns and flame throwers. Towed anti-tank guns appear to have been of little utility, probably because they were too large and heavy to readily move inside buildings, and the infantry wanted to avoid spending much time in the streets. Man-portable flame throwers were of more value. Flame throwers had proven useful in complex terrain in most theaters of World War II. Aside from their psychological impact, they had the ability to turn good cover from direct-fire weapons into a death trap. Entering through small openings, such as a firing aperture or window, the flames could expand and splatter, filling the room. Though their range was limited to thirty meters, they were useful for dealing with especially stubborn defenders. No tank-mounted flame throwers were available at Aachen.[101]

A Sherman tank and M10 tank destroyer work together in the confines of Aachen's urban landscape. *Courtesy of the National Archives and Records Administration.*

In spite of the surplus of firepower—and aggressive use thereof—clearing Aachen remained a dangerous business. Considering the small number of forces that assaulted the city, the infantry losses were significant. In less than two weeks the 2nd Battalion suffered 206 battle casualties and the 3rd Battalion 292. As a percentage of authorized strength (871 per battalion), this represented losses of 24 and 34 percent respectively. In the case of the 3rd Battalion the actual loss was worse as it began the battle understrength with 752 personnel (making the loss 39 percent).[102] The 3rd Battalion's losses in officers (thirteen of thirty-six authorized: 36 percent) and NCOs (sixty-one of 155 authorized: 39 percent) were also heavy.[103] These figures did not denote reductions in strength for these units, as both received a considerable number of replacements during the battle, but rather the overall cost of capturing Aachen.[104]

Despite the inflow of replacements, at the battle's heaviest point for 3rd Battalion, Corley told his regimental commander on the night of 15 October that he needed 250 replacements to be "up to par." On that day alone he had lost thirteen NCOs. Two days of heavy fighting on 15 and 16 October cost Corley's lead company its commander and reduced its available manpower from 155 to 115. Two-thirds of the battalion's "combat fatigue" losses were suffered over these two days. Corley had held off strong German counterattacks, although only by scraping together non-infantry personnel as infantry replacements. Corley concluded that his battalion was at its limit, not able to take the Lousberg in its current state.[105]

While these losses were substantial, they were not more severe than those suffered by other units in the area. Closing the ring around Aachen to the north had cost the 30th Infantry Division nearly 2000 casualties.[106] On the day the 18th Infantry Regiment took Crucifix Hill to the east of the city, it suffered sixty killed.[107] In mid-September, the 1st Battalion of the 26th Infantry Regiment had been aiding the 3rd Armored Division in breaching the Siegfried Line in the Stolberg area. In one eight-day period it suffered 229 casualties.[108]

In the urban environment of Aachen, US armor performed well. The paucity of German armor in the city meant there were few tank-on-tank engagements. The main work of US armor was to engage German infantry and towed artillery pieces, and to provide suppressive fire support to US infantry. The two principal US armored vehicles in Aachen were the M4 Sherman medium tank and the M10 tank destroyer. Most of the Shermans had 75mm main guns and the M10s had higher velocity three-inch guns (76.2mm). There were a few "assault gun" Shermans in Aachen, equipped with a short 105mm howitzer. Relative to the need in Aachen for firepower, the 75mm-equipped Sherman was moderately superior to the M10, while the 105mm-equipped Sherman was excellent—arguably the best American tank of the war for urban operations.[109] The M10 had only one turret-mounted machine gun (a .50 caliber) that required a crewman be exposed to use, while the Sherman had two .30 machine guns that could be fired from inside the tank. The 75mm-equipped Sherman had two more advantages well-suited for urban operations: a faster power traversing turret and room for more stowed main gun ammunition (up to ninety-seven rounds as opposed to only fifty-four for an M10).[110] In a close-range urban engagement, quickly slewing the turret for a quick shot was a key advantage.

The primary threats to US armor were indirect artillery fire, mines, anti-tank guns, and German infantry with man-portable anti-tank weapons. In the area of survivability the Sherman (both versions) was superior to the M10 in the urban environment. The M10 had noticeably thinner armor, but its real Achilles heel was its open turret, which made the crew vulnerable to grenades and small arms fire. That vulnerability was an outgrowth of American tank destroyer doctrine that downplayed the need for combined arms and emphasized speed, use of cover, and firepower over armor protection. The 1942 US Army *Field Manual 18-5* (*FM 18-5*) described tank destroyers as "ill-suited to close combat against strong forces of hostile foot troops." In July 1944 the Army released a revised *FM 18-5*, which placed increased emphasis on combined arms, although this was too late to impact the design of the M10.[111] The M10s in the Huertgen Forest suffered from their open turrets. Because a large percentage of the incoming artillery and mortar rounds were airbursts as they struck trees, M10 crews fashioned log roofs such as the infantry did for their foxholes. In August 1944 the Army developed a standardized roof armor kit, although there is no evidence these kits were employed at Aachen.[112]

The Sherman, however, was far from invulnerable. The key at Aachen was not surviving the blow but rather preventing it—usually accomplished with heavy suppressive fire and careful coordination with the infantry. Even some of the heaviest tanks then in

GIs work closely with an M10 tank destroyer as it moves down a street in Aachen. *Courtesy of the National Archives and Records Administration.*

service in any Army did not have enough armor to protect them from German anti-tank guns engaging at the typical close ranges seen in Aachen, or the highly effective man-portable *Panzerfausts* or *Panzerschrecks*.[113]

The 634th Tank Destroyer Battalion's A Company lost three M10s to the Germans, one to a grenade thrown inside the turret and the other two from unspecified causes. Total casualties by Company A were four killed and nine wounded.[114] The 745th Tank Battalion's Company C lost five 75mm Shermans and two 105mm Shermans, four to German "bazookas" (either the *Panzerfaust* or *Panzerschreck*), two more to 120mm mortar fire, and one to an unspecified cause. Total casualties were two killed and ten wounded.[115] It is unclear whether these units entered Aachen at full strength, and both received replacement vehicles during the action, so these losses do not describe the strength of these units at battle's end.

In contrast to the modern vision of urban terrain being the most dangerous for armor, some armored units outside Aachen fared as badly or worse than those inside the city. Over the same dates as the assault on the city, Company B from the 634th Tank Destroyer Battalion lost four M10s holding the line east of the city.[116] The 743rd Tank Battalion, helping the 30th Infantry Division finish the encirclement of the city, lost twenty-two tanks in the month of October—a loss rate roughly proportional to that of Company C inside the city. From July 1944 to April 1945, the 3rd Armored Division lost on average 135 of its authorized strength of 232 Shermans; a 58 percent monthly loss rate. In support of an advance in the Huertgen Forest of only 3000 yards, less than the advance across Aachen, the 746th Tank Battalion lost twelve tanks from 6 to 25 October.[117]

The air and artillery support provided to the 2nd and 3rd Battalions was extensive. The VII Corps commander, Collins, had something to do with this. He had a strong background in artillery, being one of only two US Corps commanders in WWII to have completed the Army's advanced artillery course (unusual for an infantryman), and having been a strong proponent of heavy artillery support to infantry operations while a divisional commander in the Pacific theater.[118] The heavy use of artillery was also supported by US doctrine.[119] Daniel provided a description of the air and artillery support:

> The air was to bomb anywhere in the city except within 500 yards of the railroad tracks in our zone; the artillery was to start on a line 100 yards from the tracks with the light guns and the mediums and heavies were to cover from 300 yards to 500 yards from the tracks. Our own mortars would work over the area from the tracks to the artillery line 100 yards beyond. Jump-off time was set for 0930, at which time all the artillery was to lift 200 yards and the air was to stop except for targets marked by colored smoke.[120]

The artillery support was effective, although not primarily for killing Germans in their fortified positions. Despite the heavy preparation bombardment, delivering over 500 tons of munitions in the first two days, when the 2nd and 3rd Battalions crossed into Aachen itself they found German resistance still strong.[121] The stout construction of Aachen's buildings, the air raid shelters, and the fortification German troops had built provided good cover.

As the two battalions and their attached units pushed westward through the city, the supporting artillery units to the south were well positioned to fire parallel to the front line. Because artillery rounds tend to fall in a long, thin oval with lateral aiming errors being less than distance errors, this allowed American artillery to fire closer to the advancing GIs with less chance of friendly fire losses—in some cases into the same city block. Daniel deemed this one of his major lessons from Aachen. US artillery units also used delayed fuses to allow the shells to penetrate a few floors into a building before exploding. This sometimes drove German defenders out into the streets where US infantry and armor could more easily engage them.[122]

A standout fire support tool used by US forces in Aachen was the self-propelled M12 155mm gun (not a howitzer) used in the direct fire role. The M12 was a dramatically more powerful direct fire weapon than anything else the assaulting forces possessed. The 155mm high explosive round was almost three times larger than the 105mm round from the assault gun Shermans (thirty-three pounds vs. ninety-five pounds).[123] This was not a new use of the 155mm self-propelled guns, as US forces had used them in direct fire mode against hard targets such as bunkers over the previous month of Siegfried Line-breaching operations.[124] The first use in Aachen was on 13 October by the 3rd Battalion, when it encountered some stoutly constructed apartment buildings in the factory district that had shrugged off the fire of tanks and tank destroyers. The single 155mm gun attached to the 3rd Battalion dropped one building with its first round. This so impressed the 26th Infantry Regiment commander that he soon acquired a second 155mm gun from VII Corps for his 2nd Battalion.[125]

The 155s proved useful against several difficult targets. On 18 October US infantry started taking sniper fire from behind, which was coming from a church steeple. This steeple withstood all return fire, including main gun rounds from tanks and tank destroyers, so the 155 was brought up. Again, one round was enough, taking down the tower—which was later found to be reinforced with concrete. On another occasion, two German tanks were destroyed by 155 fire, one that American troops thought a bunker, and the other that had the bad luck to drive underneath a high explosive round in flight. The 155s also played a role in securing the final surrender of the German commander by shelling his command bunker.[126]

The most unusual fire support tool used by US forces, over several days starting 8 October, was the "V-13," a series of three streetcars loaded up with munitions and rolled downhill into the city by US engineers. While the first did not make it into the city before exploding, the second two did, but with no real damage inflicted.[127] Aside from garnering some press attention for the engineers, the V-13 did have some value in boosting US troop morale.[128] Both the V-13 and the 155mm guns are good examples of the American affinity for firepower and the creativity and improvisation in its application.

Mobility and Counter-Mobility

The slow pace of the advance across Aachen's battered landscape mitigated the need for mechanized mobility for the infantry. While wet weather had some impact on the delivery of supplies into the city, inside the city it had no real effect on mobility.[129] Even with debris-filled streets, distance was not an issue for dismounted infantry given the average advance of 300-400 meters per day and Aachen's modest size of four to five kilometers across at its widest point.[130] The infantry spent most of their time either inside buildings or outside on foot. Riding in a halftrack or on a tank was too dangerous, given the German anti-tank weapons, and would have prevented them from properly supporting the armor and clearing buildings.[131] Where mobility mattered more for the infantry was indoors. US troops spent as little time as possible in the street, going from building to building through holes in walls, some of which they created themselves (e.g., with bazookas). Daniel described it this way, "We quickly relearned that in street fighting, strange to relate, one should stay out of the street."[132] They did not always have to create their own holes as on some blocks they discovered the cellars already connected.[133] The 26th Infantry Regiment parceled out the engineer squads across the assault force to help with wall breaching, road clearing, and booby traps.[134] When a street had to be crossed, it was often first covered with smoke (e.g., 75mm smoke rounds from Shermans). The troops preferred to clear a house from the top down when possible, sometimes knocking a hole in the roof, as Germans in the cellar were less of a problem than those on the top floor. When dealing with snipers they moved slowly and stayed together. Against a heavy defense the infantry moved fast, dispersed, and kept moving.[135] The infantrymen also stripped themselves down to only those items they needed for the day's fighting, the assumption being they would be resupplied each night. This worked well in that it left the infantrymen unencumbered for climbing around and over urban clutter.[136]

Wheeled vehicles had their own set of problems. While most armored vehicles were tracked, the support vehicles ran on wheels that were susceptible to puncture on the rubble-strewn streets.[137] Medical evacuation became enough of a problem that wheeled ambulances were augmented by drafting the Weasel, a small tracked supply vehicle, to assist in transporting wounded.[138] In spite of this augmentation, vehicle limitations put the litter bearers under considerable strain.[139]

Tracked vehicles fared the best in Aachen. They could handle many of the rubble-clogged streets—but the environment of Aachen still presented problems.[140] As the assault kicked off on the morning of 13 October in the 2nd Battalion's sector, the armor had trouble following the infantry across a steep fifteen- to thirty-foot railroad embankment.[141] There was only one pre-existing underpass, which the Germans had destroyed and US engineers needed twenty-four hours to clear. With the initial assault, two tanks did cross over the embankment successfully, although the tank crews were worried others might roll or have their thinly armored undersides exposed to German anti-tank fire. In another example of battlefield adaptation, a solution was found by US personnel. With portions of the train station walls blown out, tanks could then drive through the station to the other side of the tracks. By nightfall on the thirteenth all the attached armored vehicles were across.[142]

Even after the German surrender, the engineers needed three days to clear two designated main supply routes through Aachen. As late as 31 October, engineering unit records noted continued clearing operations and mines still being found "everywhere." Some filled craters had to be dug back up when it was discovered there were mines buried deep within them.[143]

The primary counter-mobility tool for US forces was firepower. This fitted well with two aspects of the American approach to the assault. First, the assault was coming in from a direction US planners thought the Germans would not expect (the east), and they were right.[144] Second, the paucity of US manpower meant that firepower had to be substituted wherever possible. Eventually the Germans were going to realize the attack from the east was the main effort and attempt to shift their forces accordingly. The fire support plan was designed to slow just such a shift, and raise the German losses suffered with that movement.

The key contribution of US artillery was in restricting German movement and dealing with counterattacks.[145] To benefit from the cover available, German infantry had to stay inside. This presented a quandary to German forces—stay undercover and then get assaulted in place by advancing US forces, often from unexpected directions, or attempt to redeploy and suffer casualties from the nearly constant artillery fire. American artillery units directed harassing fire at intersections and roadways most nights, where German forces were likely to be moving. It is notable that in the less built-up areas around Aachen, where the battle raged to encircle the city, artillery played a more lethal role. A captured senior German commander estimated that 60 to 70 percent of German losses around Aachen were from US artillery.[146]

The role of air support was similar to that of artillery in that its primary contribution ended up being in the area of counter-mobility. The early bombardment was heavy, about 300 fighter-bombers dropping 172 tons of ordnance in the first three days, to include napalm, although it failed to break the back of German resistance.[147] When weather permitted, patrols over Aachen could spot German movement and attack on their own initiative, or pass on the information to the artillery from spotter aircraft.[148] The other major contribution of airpower was to keep the skies over Aachen relatively free of German aircraft.[149] This left US forces free to mass and limited German awareness of the location of US units. German soldiers were impressed with the Allied air support in general, stating: "American and British planes are the best in the world."[150]

On the front line a key source of US firepower was the main gunfire of M10s and Shermans (3 inch, 75mm, and 105mm). Used on buildings until just before US infantry assaulted, this fire kept fresh German troops from entering while driving those already in the building out or down to the cellar. The streets were also swept by M1917 heavy machine guns, and the machine guns on the armored vehicles. While using the same round (.30 caliber) as its lighter, air-cooled M1919 cousin, the M1917 was water-cooled. This allowed more sustained fire, but with roughly twice the weight (M1919 forty-four pounds, M1917 eighty-nine pounds). A heavy rate of 250 rounds/minute could be sustained for several minutes.[151]

One urban-unique counter-mobility problem for US forces was the city's sewer system. While US forces methodically cleared buildings and evacuated all German prisoners and civilians, on a few occasions they still took small arms fire from behind. They soon discovered that the Germans were using the sewer system to pass underneath the front line, emerging behind US forces into previously cleared buildings. US forces then backtracked, cleared out the infiltrators, and located each manhole. They threw grenades down every manhole, and then thoroughly blocked them before moving on.[152]

Engineer units manning the southern perimeter around Aachen employed rather conventional counter-mobility solutions. While it was illustrative of the US manpower shortfalls to have engineers manning the line, these units were well suited to holding the perimeter. What they lacked in firepower they made up for in counter-mobility tools. Elements of the 1106th Engineer Combat Group extensively emplaced anti-personnel and anti-tank mines, booby traps, and wire entanglements to hinder German movement.[153]

Logistics

The single largest logistical challenge for US forces in Aachen was the sharp increase in munitions required for the aggressive application of firepower. In storming buildings, the infantry used a great deal of suppressive fire and grenades. This preventative fire method was effective at both killing Germans and reducing US casualties, but it increased demand for many types of infantry munitions. Even the infantry's tactic of creating holes in walls inside structures to facilitate movement increased the demand for munitions. "We used great quantities of dynamite, beehives, and bazooka ammunition in blowing these holes."[154] However, this did not come as a surprise to US forces, and their planning efforts addressed this increased demand. Daniel had the battalion ammunition dump moved forward to be closer to the troops.[155]

The US armor in Aachen was also a heavy consumer of ammunition. In one thirty-two-hour period during the assault, the company of M10 tank destroyers (authorized strength of twelve vehicles) sent into the city expended 393 rounds from their 3-inch (76.2mm) main guns.[156] On average, each tank or tank destroyer expended approximately fifty rounds of main gun high explosive ammunition per day.[157] Besides their main guns, the armor also expended large quantities of machine-gun ammunition.

There were problems moving wheeled vehicles into the city during the assault, due to debris in the streets. As most of the logistical vehicles were wheeled, this complicated the forward delivery of supplies. This problem was in part mitigated by the modest size of the city, four to five kilometers across at its widest part. As the problems with wheeled transport became evident, US personnel adapted by substituting tracked vehicles to press supplies forward.[158]

Ammunition shortages did affect the fire support given to infantry in the city. During the assault on Aachen, 81mm mortar ammunition, normally a staple of infantry battalions, was scarce.[159] Conversely, there was a surplus of 4.2-inch mortar ammunition. A 26th Infantry Regiment report for October makes a number of references to shortages of both 60mm and 81mm mortar, but also refers to 4.2-inch ammunition as "unlimited."[160] This required adaptation coincidently made fire support more effective, as the much larger 4.2-inch mortar rounds (24.5 pounds vs. 10.6 pounds for the heaviest 81mm round) were better for attacking targets with overhead cover.[161] On several occasions, US infantry augmented their fire support with captured German mortars.[162] While there were some limitations imposed on larger caliber artillery ammunition use leading up to the assault, by the time the 2nd and 3rd Battalions actually pushed into the city, the big guns were well supplied.[163]

Dealing with the Population

While the pre-war population of Aachen was approximately 165,000, the actual number in the city when the assault began was far less. Several German evacuations in September, and the air strikes and artillery fire leading up the assault, had reduced the population to 7000–15,000 by 12 October.[164] This was to the benefit of US forces for several reasons. First, it simplified the task of sorting civilians from combatants during operations. Second, it reduced the burden on US forces of evacuating and caring for those civilians as they fled or were moved outside of the city.

The issue of civilian casualties was not a significant shaping factor in the planning for Aachen. The 2nd Battalion's commander later explained the mindset of American planners: "At that time we would have been willing to plow up Aachen and sow it to salt as was done to Carthage."[165] That mindset was also evident in the extensive use of air and artillery bombardment, and the presumptive use of firepower inside structures.[166] It could be that the sharply reduced size of the population influenced planners into considering it less of an issue. Another influencing factor on planning could have been that US forces were now dealing with the citizens of the Reich themselves, and thus less concerned with their safety. At times, the Wehrmacht showed a disregard for civilian safety, as when on the evening of 19 October German artillery outside the city fired an extensive barrage into Aachen.[167]

While US tactics and plans did not afford the population much protection, the system of air raid shelters in the city did. Of those civilians still in the city during the assault, many packed themselves into the large air raid shelters. Daniel's men captured three large air raid shelters, one with three stories, walls fifteen feet thick, and 200 soldiers and over 1000 civilians inside.[168] However, these shelters were ill-designed for extended stays by massive numbers of people. Multi-story structures, solidly built of concrete, they had no windows and only limited ventilation through three-inch pipes.[169]

The rules of engagement given to US forces in Aachen were liberal. The 1st ID commander had ordered a 4.2-inch mortar battalion to use white phosphorous rounds with the goal of burning the city down. Although an uncooperative wind thwarted his effort, the mindset was clear.[170] The S-3 report for the 26th Infantry Regiment for 11 October mentions a new white phosphorous rifle grenade that had "A fine incendiary effect for burning down buildings." [171] An interesting contrast can be found with one example of more restrictive rules of engagement in a non-urban setting. A

An aerial view of the ruins of Aachen after the battle; in the foreground are the remains of the cathedral where Charlemagne was crowned emperor. *Courtesy of the National Archives and Records Administration.*

tank destroyer platoon commander, fighting just south of Aachen in the Huertgen Forest, stated:

> In hindsight, we could have plastered that patch with phosphorous and smoked them out, but we didn't. We had been told not to use it, as Germans claimed it was gaseous and hence in violation of the Geneva Convention.[172]

The only evident concerns for collateral damage related to architecture. Firing proximate to some cultural and historical buildings was restricted.[173] In this regard they met with limited success. On 19 October soldiers in the 2nd Battalion were asked to investigate a church for damage to which they reported back, "On the church they wanted us to investigate if they want to repair they will have to start at the foundation."[174] A junior US officer who toured the city after its capture described seeing only one out of six churches not heavily damaged.[175]

As to the civilian death toll in Aachen, there is little information. US forces gave no official account and no other estimates exist in the available sources. Considering the damage done to the city itself, the number of civilians in the city at the time, and the number evacuated, the number killed could be anywhere from the low hundreds to a few thousand.

US forces enforced a strict policy of evacuation of all Germans, military or civilian, as they pushed across the city.[176] The primary purpose of this was to protect US troops by preventing German troops in civilian clothes from sniping from the rear.[177] It also served to unclutter the battlefield and reduce the need for US troops to discriminate civilian from combatant. The utility of the evacuation was strongly espoused in a lessons-learned document from one of the units involved:

> Civilians must be promptly and vigorously expelled from any area occupied by our troops. Failure to do so costs lives.[178]

Evacuated German civilians were cared for at a captured Wehrmacht barracks in Brand, five kilometers southeast of Aachen. At the barracks they were screened, fed, and housed by American forces, with 3300 civilians living there by the end of October.[179]

> The Counter Intelligence Corps screened the evacuees, looking for any spies, would-be saboteurs, and high-ranking officials. Suspected spies were turned over to the First Army Military Commission for trial.[180]

Conclusions

Despite only modest preparation specific to urban warfare, and little if any direct experience fighting in cities, US forces at Aachen were successful in clearing the city. What carried them through was their overall competence in warfare, which proved transferable to urban terrain, and an ability to quickly adapt to the particulars of urban warfare.

The quality of American small unit leaders was a key factor. US doctrine placed a great deal of emphasis on leaders showing initiative and aggression. Although urban warfare was not a driver behind this, it nevertheless paid dividends on the streets of Aachen. Even after suffering heavy losses in officers and non-commissioned officers, Corley's men still proved capable of advancing and absorbing German counterattacks. The greater independence afforded small unit leaders, when visually cut off from their commanders by the short lines of sight, does not appear to have substantially hindered the effectiveness of those small units.

Another key set of factors was the American emphasis on firepower, the logistical support to make it consistently available, and the skill at orchestrating combined arms. US commanders made up for the paucity of infantry by augmenting with armor, heavy weapons, artillery, mortars, and air support. Again, this was not something emphasized within the Army because of urban warfare, but rather warfare in general. Not only were those other elements pushed forward with the infantry, but they were employed aggressively and with considerable skill. Commanders put few restrictions on the employment of firepower, the logistical system kept most munitions plentifully available, and the small unit commanders maximized the utility of this additional firepower. As one historian put it, "There was no attempt to avoid collateral damage; in fact, the troops displayed a degree of enthusiasm in wrecking a German city." [181] The employment of the M12 self-propelled 155mm guns, and the coordination between infantry and armor, are two of the best examples of this. A German captured at Aachen, who had served on both the Eastern and Western Fronts, compared his experiences:

> You Americans are the master of your equipment—
> and your equipment is plenty good. You are better as
> individual fighters than the Russian but you lack his
> tenacity. Your strongest point is, I believe, a minute
> coordination between all your weapons.[182]

Even the much maligned Sherman tank proved a good fit in Aachen. While clearly at a disadvantage against much of the German armor in more open terrain, in the close-range combat role supporting the infantry, it proved well-suited. The experiences of the hedgerow fighting in Normandy were a significant factor in this coordination between various combat arms. Having paid a price for poor coordination in June and July of 1944, American units learned better how to tie the various arms together in an environment of short lines of sight.

In addition to the competencies that proved transferable to urban warfare, American troops also proved able to readily adapt to the particular demands of Aachen. The substitution of wire for radio communications, the mandated linkups between units to maintain the integrity of the front line, and the sealing of sewer entrances are good examples of this. Battlefield adaptation had long been a theme in the Army's doctrine. Even the first revision of the Army's overarching manual after World War I, *Field Service Regulations* (1923), stated the expectation that men of all ranks "show initiative in meeting the different situations as they arise." This emphasis on initiative continued as a central theme in the subsequent 1939, 1941, and 1944 versions of *FM 100-5*.[183]

Success at Aachen was also the product of the strong emphasis senior American commanders put on isolating the city. This required substantially more resources than clearing the city itself, and involved heavy losses, but senior commanders were nevertheless aggressive in cutting off Aachen. In taking the high ground northeast of the city, the 18th Infantry Regiment suffered sixty killed in one day, and one of its companies dropped in manpower from 160 to sixty in just four days.[184] Those efforts weakened the defenders in the city, prevented reinforcements in the last half of the battle, and protected the flanks of both battalions in the city.

Today urban operations are often viewed as the worst-case scenario, although that was not so for US forces entering Germany in 1944. Losses among US infantry and armor were significant but not as high as those suffered by some US units fighting in some non-urban environments, especially considering the size of the defending force. Just south of Aachen was the Huertgen Forest, a large and densely packed tree farm. Operations in the Huertgen began at the same time as Aachen. In terms of both US losses, and the time taken to advance, the capture of the Huertgen Forest was far more difficult. First Army's operations in the Huertgen cost it 24,000 battle casualties plus 9000 more from the harsh winter conditions. It was one of the few campaigns where German losses were less than those of the western allies.[185] Collins, whose VII Corps forces cleared both Aachen and the Huertgen, said of the Huertgen Forest: "That was the deadliest fighting of the war."[186]

In the end, US forces completed their mission of capturing the city. American commanders recognized the limitations of their forces, and the problems presented by the urban environment, and worked around them. They also recognized their strengths and aggressively employed those to maximum effect. At Aachen, US forces demonstrated that a numerically smaller force could win in the urban landscape.

Chapter 3

Manila—February 1945

To make full use of the Philippines in their drive on the Japanese home islands, US forces needed to capture the northernmost island of Luzon; to make full use of Luzon, US forces needed to capture Manila. However, the attention given to Manila itself was minimal during US planning for the Luzon campaign. A mixture of hope, denial, and faulty intelligence reports led General Douglas MacArthur to believe the Japanese would not fight for the Philippine capital city, but rather would declare it an open city, as he had done three years earlier. That was not to be, contrary to even the wishes of the top Japanese commander on Luzon, General Tomoyuki Yamashita.

After US forces landed in Lingayen Gulf on northern Luzon on 9 January, it took them almost a month to move south across the Central Plain to Manila. Waiting there was a mixed Japanese army-navy force, thrown together by local Japanese commanders from the manpower scraps available. It took another month of hard fighting for two reinforced US divisions to clear the city. The end result was significant losses for the US forces, the elimination of the Japanese force, large-scale civilian casualties, and heavy damage to the city.

Although the defending Japanese force was composed mostly of support troops, they were well equipped with crew-served weapons, demonstrated typical Japanese fighting spirit, and made effective use of the urban landscape. While not part of the overall Japanese commander's master plan, the battle for Manila did slow the conquest of Luzon and substantially weakened participating US forces.

Occurring just four months after Aachen, the battle for Manila was against a different foe, in a larger city, with a large friendly civilian population present, and it involved much larger forces for both sides. These factors made Manila a much larger urban battle that presented its own set of challenges to US forces.

Operational Context

The US Joint Chiefs of Staff, after vigorous internal debate, selected the Philippines over Formosa as the next major target in the fall of 1944.[1] MacArthur decided to begin his assault of the Philippines by striking at the archipelago's center—at Leyte.[2] This allowed US forces to isolate the southernmost large island of Mindanao, while providing a springboard for the assault on Luzon, the largest and northernmost island. Luzon was the key, as it contained the best port (Manila), the best airfield facilities (Clark Field), and it was the closest to the Japanese home islands and other Japanese-held territory. US landings were made on Mindoro in December to capture airfields closer to Luzon.[3]

Lt. Gen. Walter Krueger's Sixth Army landed four divisions on 9 January 1945 at Lingayen Gulf, on Luzon's northern coast (see Map 3-1). The two divisions of I Corps were on the left, while the two divisions of XIV Corps were on the right, and by nightfall 68,000 men were ashore and had pushed inland an average of four miles.[4] While the early going was easy for the Sixth Army, and beyond the expectations of planners, the pace of advance was cautious.

> The opposition encountered on the advance to the Agno River was so light that the high command looked for some deep-laid plot conceived by the enemy.[5]

The units of the XIV Corps, on the right flank, progressed without difficulty southward down the Central Plain, while I Corps encountered significant Japanese forces on the hilly left flank. This asymmetrical resistance quickly exposed the left flank of Maj. Gen. Oscar Griswold's XIV Corps. Krueger favored a slow advance southward but his boss felt otherwise. MacArthur, Southwest Pacific Area Commander, thought the danger of counterattack from the left was minimal and that the Japanese would not fight for Manila—two points on which Krueger disagreed.[6]

The success of XIV Corps' advance southward was a reflection of the Japanese commander's defensive plan. General Yamashita, the 14th Area Army commander, did not plan on defending the Central Plain, nor Manila itself. Yamashita had only two primary goals for Luzon: maximum attrition of US forces and maximum delay. Everything else was secondary—including the survival of his forces. His plan centered on holding three mountainous redoubts, one east of Manila, one west of Clark Field, and the main redoubt in northeast Luzon (see Map 3-1).[7] The weak link in his plan was transportation. Getting his forces to the various redoubts was easy; moving the quantities of supplies he would need for his large force to hold out for extended periods was not.

Manila was a vast storehouse of supplies for Yamashita's forces, although with American air dominance little could move by day without inviting attack, and the lightly equipped Japanese forces had few trucks. In the last month before the Lingayen Gulf landings, Yamashita had moved only about 6 percent of the supplies out of the city to his redoubts.[8] He wanted to hold the city only long enough to extract the maximum amount of these supplies, and had no intention of committing large forces to its defense.

Aside from Krueger's caution over the exposed left flank of XIV Corps, the drive down the Central Plain also slowed when the corps encountered its first substantial Japanese forces at Clark Field, approximately half way to Manila, in the last week in January

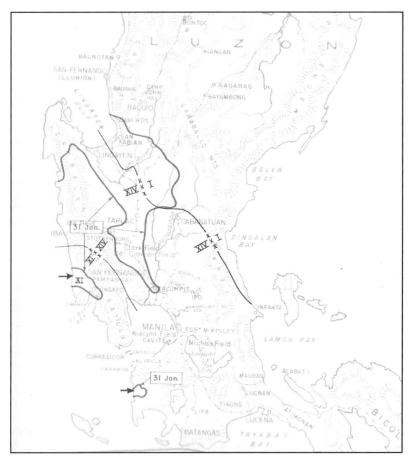

Map 3-1: The War with Japan—Philippine Campaign. *Courtesy The Department of History, United States Military Academy at West Point.*

(see Map 3-1).[9] The further south I Corps advanced, the stronger Japanese resistance became as the Japanese tried to preserve the last transport routes to the northeast redoubt. A counterweight to these factors was MacArthur's constant demand for greater speed—to capture the prize of Manila that he saw as ready for the taking—and to liberate a population he felt personally responsible for.

In the closing days of January, several events set the stage for a final dash into Manila. The resistance around Clark Field was crumbling and Japanese forces in the area retreated farther west up into the mountains, reducing their ability to threaten XIV Corps' supply lines back to the beachhead.[10] On 27 January a new division landed at Lingayen Gulf, the 1st Cavalry Division, and it immediately began moving south, soon to be attached to XIV Corps.[11] On 29 and 31 January the Americans conducted two supplementary division-size landings (see Map 3-1) north and south of Manila Bay. The northern landing at Subic Bay aimed to free up XIV Corps units around Clark Field, and cut off the Bataan Peninsula as a possible redoubt for Japanese forces. The southern landing at Nasugbu (11th Airborne Division) had two aims: to present a threat to Manila from the south, and to prevent Japanese reinforcement of the city from southern Luzon.[12]

On 30 January MacArthur went to the front line to personally observe the pace of the advance of XIV Corps elements and he decided it was time for a rapid drive on Manila.[13] Adding to MacArthur's sense of urgency were intelligence reports of several large groups of Allied internees and prisoners of war (POWs) whom the Japanese might kill before they could be liberated.[14]

Later on 30 January Krueger ordered the drive on Manila with the 37th Infantry Division assigned a lane on the right, and the 1st Cavalry Division on its left; both divisions were by then a part of XIV Corps. Map 3-1 shows the extent of the American advance southward as of 31 January. As elements of the 37th Infantry were still involved in securing Clark Field, the 1st Cavalry was first off the mark, sending two "flying columns" southward, starting at 0001 local time on 1 February.[15] The flying columns lived up to their name, covering more than one hundred miles in sixty-six hours, and the first American forces into Manila entered the northern suburb of Grace Park at 1830 on 3 February.[16]

While the 11th Airborne Division's drive toward Manila from the south had progressed well since its 31 January landing, aided by a brigade-size airborne assault on 3 February, its progress ground to a halt over 4 to 5 February at the southern outskirts of the city.[17] The Japanese had expected the primary threat to the city to come from that direction and had laid the Genko Line across this avenue of approach. The Japanese anchored this wide and thick belt of minefields, mutually supporting concrete pillboxes (many two or three stories tall), and many large artillery pieces, to the shore of Manila Bay and extended it well inland.[18]

The Foe

After the surrender of US forces on Corregidor in May 1942, the Philippines became a strategic backwater for the Japanese, with Manila important only as a logistical and transportation center. By the summer of 1943, only 25,000 Japanese troops were on Luzon. That changed in May 1944, when the Japanese Imperial Headquarters developed their Sho Plan (Victory Plan), which envisioned a decisive air, land, and sea battle around the Philippines. Troops and aircraft then began arriving and a new commander was brought in, the hero from Malaysia and Singapore, General Tomoyuki Yamashita. He had been serving in quasi-exile in Manchuria, in part due to a rivalry with Prime Minister Tojo, but the fall of the Tojo government in July 1944 cleared the path for his return to an active theater.[19]

Yamashita arrived in Manila on 14 September 1944. Just one week later, US aircraft staged a major raid on the harbor facilities of Manila and nearby airfields. This served as a wakeup call to the Japanese and defensive preparations were accelerated. On 15 November Yamashita ordered the Kempeitai (secret police) to begin conducting punitive sweeps for armed guerrillas in the city while sealing off large areas. With the already weakened economy, foodstuffs began to disappear and the first civilian deaths from malnutrition were recorded in December.[20]

A severe Japanese inter-service rivalry, and a lack of unity of command, hampered the Japanese defense of Manila. While the overall commander of Japanese forces on Luzon was the army's Yamashita, a semi-autonomous Japanese naval chain of command controlled navy units. Yamashita assigned the mountain redoubt east of Manila, Manila itself, and the remainder of southern Luzon to Lt. Gen. Shizuo Yokoyama and his 80,000-man Shimbu Group. Yamashita's orders for Manila were not to defend it but rather to extract as many supplies as possible—blowing bridges as needed to slow the American advance—and then to withdraw eastward into the mountains.[21]

However, in a variation on the phrase "no plan survives contact with the enemy" Yamashita's plan did not survive contact with the Japanese Navy. Approximately one-quarter of Yokoyama's Shimbu Group were naval troops under the command of Rear Admiral Sanji Iwabuchi. However, Iwabuchi had a second boss in the overall Japanese naval commander in the Philippines, Vice Admiral Denshichi Okochi. Okochi ordered that control of his naval forces in and around Manila would pass over to Yokoyama only when those forces had completed the tasks assigned them by Okochi, and only in those areas Okochi deemed of "primary army interest." Essentially, Iwabuchi's naval orders trumped those of Yokoyama's and Yamashita's. Worse still, Yokoyama did not learn of this redefinition of his command until 6 January, just three days before the first American landings on Luzon. Several subsequent conferences failed to resolve the matter and Yokoyama finally relented, granting Iwabuchi command of all 18,000 troops in Manila, one-quarter which were army troops.[22]

The primary task Okochi assigned Iwabuchi's newly named Manila Naval Defense Force was to fortify Manila, a decision Okochi apparently arrived at on his own. While Yamashita viewed Manila as too hard to defend, the Imperial Japanese Navy felt otherwise.[23] Similar to Yamashita's overall objectives in defending Luzon, Iwabuchi wanted to inflict the maximum casualties on US forces while delaying their advance as long as possible. While the navy's orders for the defense of Manila included the large-scale destruction of civilian infrastructure, most notably the city's water system, it is not clear that was a part of Yamashita's plan to withdraw from the city.[24]

Iwabuchi's defensive scheme for Manila was essentially static and focused on threats from the south and Manila Bay (the west).[25] The Genko Line of bunkers, minefields, and artillery protected the city from the south. While the northern quarter of the city was relatively open, the Pasig River formed a formidable natural barrier to the rest of the city southward. Emptying into Manila Bay, the river initially cuts due east into the city and then changes to a south-east direction, with the bulk of the city south of the river. The core of the Japanese defense lay south of the Pasig, in the sixteenth-century Spanish fort, the *Intramuros*, and the many large buildings, some of which were American-built earthquake-proof government structures. That core was thus protected by the Genko line to the south, the mountains to the east, and the Pasig to the north, with all its bridges blown by Japanese forces.[26]

Inside the city Japanese preparations were extensive. The defenders fortified most large buildings by bricking up windows and doors, cutting firing ports into walls, sandbagging roofs and windows, installing internal pillboxes, and digging tunnels below.[27] However, the firing positions in many of these fortified buildings were narrow, and the various strongpoints were not well designed for mutual support.[28] The Japanese also constructed extensive barriers on most roadways with a mix of obstacles and mines.[29] What the minefields lacked in camouflage, they made up for in number, variety, and explosive power, sometimes including aircraft bombs and even depth charges.

The greatest strength of the Japanese defenders was their fighting spirit. A captured Japanese order dated 15 February reflects this:

> In the all-out suicide attack every man will attack un-
> til he achieves a glorious death. Not even one man
> must become a prisoner. During the attack friends of
> the wounded will make them commit suicide.[30]

The Americans would take few Japanese prisoners in Manila; most Japanese died at their positions as ordered or in suicidal charges.

In the few months before the landings at Lingayen Gulf, American attacks destroyed most Japanese airpower in the Philippines, and Yamashita kept what Japanese armor there was on Luzon well outside the city, trying to preserve the links between the main northeastern Luzon redoubt and Manila. That left the artillery to aid the infantry defending Manila. Artillery was not a strong suit of the Japanese ground forces, due to Japan's less industrialized economy and a military culture that emphasized face-to-face combat. In Manila the Japanese substituted resourcefulness for mass, often placing their limited artillery on the upper floors of buildings or on trucks for shoot-and-scoot missions. Japanese artillery units also suffered from weak coordination. These units were rarely able to fire in mass, and when firing indirectly, poor spotting support resulted in poor accuracy. Compared to most major militaries of the time, the Japanese were weak in anti-tank capabilities. US forces recovered only five of the moderately effective 47mm towed anti-tank guns after the battle.[31]

While Japanese infantrymen were normally not well equipped with heavy weapons by World War II standards, resourcefulness helped here as well. There were many partially sunk hulks in Manila Bay and destroyed aircraft at local airfields. The Japanese stripped a large number of cannon from those ships and aircraft and improvised weapon mounts for ground use. After the city was captured, US forces recovered more 20mm cannons (990) than light and heavy machine guns combined (600). These cannon were so common they even supplanted the rifle as the primary Japanese weapon.[32]

The overall supply level for the Japanese defenders was good. Aside from a glut of food and ammunition in the city that Yamashita so desperately wanted to move, there was also some Japanese military production of smaller weapons in the city, such as grenades and mines. Several large buildings held "months" worth of food when US troops entered the city.[33]

One factor the Japanese did not allow to hamper their defensive scheme was the presence of the large civilian population. Aside from giving no consideration for their safety or provision, the Japanese actively used the population as a shield from American firepower.

The Japanese command and control capabilities were weak, inflexible, and poorly supported by communications, in part due to a paucity of radios. However, the static nature of the Japanese defense lessened the stress on the Japanese command and control system.[34]

In Manila, the Japanese demonstrated some flair for urban camouflage, partially making up for their static defense and limited heavy equipment. Most of their positions were inside buildings, in some cases even pillboxes so far inside they were not detected until GIs were inside. The Japanese disguised some positions to look like common urban features, such as burial mounds, rubble, or partially destroyed structures. Japanese attempts to camouflage their personnel with civilian clothes, longer hair, and in one case American uniforms and equipment, were less effective.[35]

The single greatest weakness of the Japanese defenders was the quality of their manpower. Units were provisional in the extreme, with many of the men only recently grouped together and few with an infantry background, with most coming from the support services.[36]

The Assault

The Japanese were caught unprepared in two ways by the American assault into the city. First, they did not expect an attack from the north. Two weeks after US forces landed at Lingayen Gulf, Iwabuchi did finally realize the primary threat to the city was from the north, and he ordered a major realignment of defenses on 23 January. However, this left only two weeks before the arrival of US forces, which was insufficient to fully shift defenses northward.[37]

The arrival of the 1st Cavalry Division's flying columns late on 3 February also surprised the Japanese. The initial slow rate of advance down from Lingayen, while not the intention of US commanders, had generated a Japanese expectation they would have more time to prepare the city's defenses.

As the cavalrymen swept into the city north of the Pasig, with the aid of local guerrillas, they liberated 3500 civilian internees at Santo Tomas University after a short fight. The speed of their advance was so fast that bypassed pockets of Japanese were able to temporarily isolate the freed internees and cavalrymen by blowing a bridge behind them the next morning (4 February).[38] The euphoria of the rapid advance moved up the chain of command and MacArthur attempted to enter the city on 4 February, but he was thwarted by the same blown bridge that cut off the leading cavalry units.[39] The leading elements of the 37th Infantry Division were close behind, entering the city the day after the 1st Cavalry. On the evening of 4 February, the infantrymen freed 465 more civilian internees and 810 US prisoners of war at Bilibid Prison, not far from the university.[40]

As the 1st Cavalry Division reached the city, the stout nature of the Japanese defenses north of the Pasig became more apparent. The XIV Corps' Griswold ordered the 37th Infantry Division to clear the densely populated section of the city north of the river, while sending the 1st Cavalry wide left. The 1st Cavalry's sweep through the eastern suburbs was intended to capture key nodes of the city's water system, and then the division was to sweep back westward toward the bay, cutting off Japanese defenders from outside support.[41]

Japanese resistance was strong, but the 37th Infantry Division made steady progress southward, toward the river. On 5 February leading elements of the 37th Infantry were minutes away from crossing the last intact bridge in their sector when the Japanese demolished it. The Japanese succeeded in destroying all six bridges across the Pasig before American forces could cross. Meanwhile a large number of fires broke out in the 37th Infantry's sector, most set by Japanese forces, requiring a partial retreat as the flames swept through densely packed wooden buildings. The infantrymen spent most of 5 and 6 February fighting these fires, evacuating liberated internees and prisoners, and continuing to reduce Japanese resistance. Trailing elements of the 1st Cavalry Division showed up to reinforce this effort, and then they moved on eastward to follow their fellow cavalrymen.[42]

On 7 February Griswold ordered the 37th Infantry Division to force a crossing of the Pasig, which it did in amphibious tractors and assault boats, pushing two full infantry battalions across in five hours. Japanese resistance was stiff but uncoordinated, and by nightfall the bridgehead was 500 yards deep. By the next morning a pontoon bridge was in place to speed the crossing of troops, with one full infantry regiment plus two infantry battalions across by late afternoon on the 8 February.[43]

The 1st Cavalry's sweep eastward progressed quickly until heavy resistance was encountered in the eastern suburbs on 7 February. The Americans had bypassed many pockets of Japanese, which caused problems with logistics, and some artillery fire came from the hills east of the city. The water system nodes tasked by Krueger to the division were taken relatively intact by 9 February, many wired for demolition or with Japanese intercepted en route to destroy them.[44]

From 6 to 10 February the 11th Airborne Division slowly ground its way north, through the heavy defenses of the Genko Line, toward Nichols Field and Fort McKinley. The 11th Airborne

A bazooka team from the 1st Cavalry Division prepares to fire through a hole in a wall around the baseball stadium in Manila, where Japanese forces were heavily dug in. *Courtesy of the National Archives and Records Administration.*

was too lightly equipped for rapid progress through the heavy defenses and had to await assistance from other units cutting back into the city from the east. So many Japanese naval guns (many six inch in caliber removed from ships) were encountered in the Genko Line that one company commander quipped, "Tell Halsey to stop looking for the Jap Fleet. It's dug in on Nichols Field." [45]

By nightfall on 10 February the 37th Infantry Division had finished clearing the city north of the Pasig and about half of the division had moved south of the river. The 1st Cavalry Division had made its own crossing of the Pasig at two points starting late on 9 February, both about five miles southeast from where the 37th Infantry crossed. Aided by surprise, the 1st Cavalry bridgeheads were expanding rapidly toward the city center. One quarter of the city below the Pasig was in American hands by this point, although the XIV Corps' intelligence section concluded that the hardest fighting was still ahead.[46]

In that first week as US forces pushed hard into the city, Iwabuchi apparently had second thoughts about holding in place. On 9 February he moved his headquarters to Fort McKinley, less than ten miles southeast of the city. At this time the first intelligence of the battle reached Yokoyama in the mountain redoubt to the east, in spite of Iwabuchi being less than forthcoming. Yokoyama grossly underestimated US forces in the city at this point at one regiment. He planned a counterattack for the following week, hoping to cut the Americans off and open an escape route for Iwabuchi.[47]

After crossing the Pasig, the 37th Infantry Division had pivoted westward and began a slow and costly advance across a seemingly neverending series of building strongpoints. Losses mounted sharply and the 37th Infantry's commander, Maj. Gen. Robert Beightler, asked for and received permission from XIV Corps to loosen the artillery rules of engagement. Previously, artillery fire had been limited to observed Japanese positions and air support was essentially prohibited.[48] Armor support arrived south of the river several days after the 37th Infantry crossed, once US engineers laid heavy bridges across the river.[49] Some large structures took days to reduce and capture, even with extremely heavy use of indirect and direct fire artillery. For example, the fortified New Police Station took eight days of hard fighting and only fell after the fourth time US infantry gained entry.[50] The 129th Infantry Regiment (37th Infantry Division) called it the most formidable defense its soldiers encountered in the war. The 1st Cavalry Division would encounter similar strongpoints as it drove into the heart of the city.

On 11 February Iwabuchi moved his headquarters back into the city as he felt his new location at Fort McKinley might fall before the rest of the city. At this point, Iwabuchi had no knowledge of Yokoyama's planned counterattack. On 13 February Yokoyama received more information on the battle and ordered Iwabuchi to pull out with his force. Yamashita wondered why Iwabuchi was going back into the city and on 15 February Yamashita ordered all Japanese forces out of the city. However, neither of these orders reached Iwabuchi until 17 February, when he was cut off, and he made no real effort to follow them. On 23 February all communications between Iwabuchi and Yokoyama were lost. Yokoyama's seven infantry battalion counterattack of 15 to 19 February from outside the city failed miserably, costing the Japanese 950 killed while causing only ninety-nine 1st Cavalry Division casualties—most of whom were wounded.[51]

While previously part of the Eighth Army, the 11th Airborne Division was transferred to XIV Corps on 10 February, as the

Aerial view of Manila during the battle, with the Pasig River on the left and the bulk of the fires burning south of the river. *Courtesy of the National Archives and Records Administration.*

paratroopers continued to slowly push northward. They made contact with the 1st Cavalry Division the next day, completing the encirclement of the city. On 13 February Nichols Field fell to the 11th Airborne.[52]

Minutes after making contact with the 11th Airborne Division, elements of the 1st Cavalry Division reached the shore of Manila Bay. Those units then turned north to clear the docks up to the Pasig, which separated the Intramuros from the bay. Along the way the cavalrymen had to clear the Rizal Stadium, which required Shermans to batter their way onto the baseball diamond and engage Japanese bunkers around the field. On 14 February, the 37th Infantry Division and 1st Cavalry coordinated on a big push westward, through parts of the city center still held by the Japanese. Progress was modest against the many Japanese strongpoints, and by 16 February room for maneuver became an issue. Griswold pulled out elements of the 1st Cavalry from the city and directed them eastward toward the Japanese positions in the hills, or southeast toward Fort McKinley, which fell on the nineteenth to the 11th Airborne.[53]

XIV Corps had known since 12 February that the sixteenth-century Intramuros would be one of the final strongpoints for the Japanese. This roughly one-kilometer-square Spanish fort, in the center of the city, had stone walls up to twenty-five feet high and forty feet thick at their base. Requests for use of heavy air support were made and approved up the chain by the commanders of the 37th Infantry, XIV Corps, and Sixth Army, only to be denied by MacArthur. US commanders believed there to be several thousand Japanese defenders inside, along with many civilian hostages. The Americans directed increasing amounts of artillery fire over several days at the Walled City, as they called it, culminating in a massive one-hour bombardment on the morning of 23 February. The artillery fire created several breeches in the thick walls with direct fire from large XIV Corps artillery assets (e.g., 8-inch howitzer,

240mm howitzer). The artillery barrage was immediately followed by artillery smoke screens and a two-battalion infantry assault of the stunned defenders. Initial progress was good, although it still took several days to clear all the basements, dungeons, and tunnels of the Intramuros.[54]

With the fall of the Intramuros, the only organized Japanese defenses left in the city were three large earthquake-proof government buildings a few hundred yards south of the Walled City. The defenses of the Finance, Agricultural, and Legislative Buildings were strong and each took days to reduce with the heavy use of artillery, flame throwers, and demolition charges, but on 3 March Griswold was able to report to Krueger that all organized resistance in Manila had been eliminated. Iwabuchi did not live to see this, as he and his staff had committed suicide at his headquarters in the Agricultural Building at dawn on 26 February.[55]

Command, Control and Communications

The American plan for Manila was ad hoc. In an eleven-page section on planning for Luzon, Krueger's memoirs include only a few mentions of Manila as an objective, and never discuss how it was to be captured.[56] The division of labor between the 37th Infantry and 1st Cavalry divisions was driven by the initial defenses encountered north of the river. Krueger's decision to send the 1st Cavalry wide left, in large part to capture key nodes of Manila's water system, was both timely and wise, sparing many civilian lives dependent on that water, and presenting an effective second front to the Japanese defenders.[57] The priority given to protecting the water infrastructure, while not directly ordered by MacArthur, was inspired by the tone of concern he set for the Filipino population.

The fact that the Japanese expected the primary thrust to come from the south was fortunate happenstance and does not appear to have guided the American decision to land the main force at

Lingayen. Predicting Japanese preparations was of limited use anyway, as Japanese actions differed sharply from Yamashita's plans. Presenting a southern threat to Manila with the 11th Airborne Division did limit the shift of those southern defenses northward and stop reinforcement from Japanese forces on southern Luzon.

South of the Pasig, and in some of the eastern suburbs, the advancing Americans discovered a strongpoint-based defense that quickly increased the cost of advance. Rapid adaptation came in the form of a slower methodical advance, with a more liberal use of artillery and armor support. Absent those quick changes, US casualties would have been higher, the city would have taken weeks longer to capture, the civilian population would have suffered even more from Japanese violence and the collapse of city services, and other US efforts would have suffered with the delay in access to the port facilities of Manila.

Some elements of this adaptation had to be pried loose from the top of the American chain of command. Griswold made several references in his diary during the battle for the city to MacArthur's underestimation of Japanese defenses and unrealistic "visions of saving this beautiful city intact." While Griswold did not get the air support he asked for from MacArthur, he received enough changes in the other fire support rules to preserve his units and maintain momentum. That penchant for flexibility was still evident late in the battle with the assault on the Intramuros, as half the area inside the walls was left unassigned as an objective, awaiting progress in the initial assault.[58]

XIV Corps benefited from experienced leadership and continuity at several levels. The corps commander and commander of the 37th Infantry Division had been in command since mid-1943 and late-1940 respectively. The 37th Infantry, a federalized National Guard division, had not seen the bulk of its officers drawn away to form other divisions, as had happened to many of the divisions formed at that time.[59]

The short-range nature of the combat in Manila took its toll on American command elements, but control was maintained. The 145th Infantry Regiment (37th Infantry) lost two battalion commanders in its first two weeks in Manila.[60] The commander of the 1st Cavalry Division, Maj. Gen. Verne Mudge, was seriously wounded by a grenade on 28 February. In his diary, over February 7 and 8, Griswold noted six Japanese infiltrators killed inside his command post in the city.[61]

With the different vectors of the three divisions early in the battle, the need for coordination between divisions was minimal. However, with the subsequent 1st Cavalry Division sweep back into the city, and the 11th Airborne's drive northward, the convergence of all three divisions demanded greater management from XIV Corps. This was well executed by Griswold and on 14 February the 37th Infantry Division and 1st Cavalry launched a coordinated push into the city center. On 10 February the 11th Airborne Division was transferred from Eighth Army to the Sixth Army's XIV Corps. XIV Corps artillery units subsequently supported the lighter airborne division in its assault on Nichols Field, and Griswold ordered the 11th Airborne not to advance north beyond the airfield.[62]

The attachment of units across and below echelons was routine, even across corps and divisional boundaries.[63] The 37th Infantry's after-action report described its 145th Infantry Regiment as operating below the Pasig with a platoon of Sherman tanks, amphibious tractors, three platoons of 4.2-inch mortars, and its "usual" artillery battalion.[64] That willingness of US commanders to distribute assets to the infantry units on the line, and the ability of those infantry units to use those assets effectively reduced casualties and aided the advance.

A key element supporting rapid adaptation and the attachment of heavy weapons at lower echelons was the quality of American small unit leaders. Small unit leaders had been trained to show initiative and to be aggressive, in keeping with long-standing tenets of US doctrine. [65] These traits were well suited to the urban environment where short lines of sight and difficulties in communications made many engagements small unit fights. These small unit leaders made the most of the additional firepower, applying it effectively in the urban terrain that was new to them.[66]

With the converging of the various units in the city there were some difficulties in tracking unit locations, maintaining contact between units, and friendly fire incidents, but these difficulties did not seriously undermine the overall effort. On 16 February the 11th Airborne Division was ordered to halt its attack on Fort McKinley by XIV Corps, because the Corps headquarters erroneously believed some elements of the 1st Cavalry Division were already there.[67] The 148th Infantry Regiment needed several days of patrolling to make contact with elements of the 1st Cavalry on its flank as the cavalrymen cut back into the city.[68] On 11 February artillery fire from the 1st Cavalry killed twelve men in the 37th Infantry, including a company commander, and it took ten to fifteen minutes to get the firing stopped.[69] From 9 to 25 February the journal of the 37th Infantry Division's Artillery headquarters notes four more cases of US artillery fire that landed on or near soldiers of the 37th Infantry, in one case wounding five GIs.[70] On Provisor Island, in the Pasig River, tank destroyers from the 640th Tank Destroyer Battalion either mistook infantry of the 129th Infantry Regiment for Japanese, or simply lost track of their location, killing two and wounding five.[71]

To minimize command and control difficulties on the front line, units were halted at night. Restricting night movement made locating Japanese minefields easier, reduced the chance of missing hidden groups of Japanese, and allowed any night movement to be equated with the enemy, countering the Japanese tendency to counterattack and infiltrate at night.[72] To maintain the integrity of the line, units advancing faster often halted to allow others to catch up at designated intersections or city blocks. US commanders were willing to trade speed of advance for a more leak-proof front.[73]

Communications in Manila worked reasonably well. At the company and platoon level, field phones and runners were the most effective. For larger units the backpack SCR-300 radio worked best, though it usually needed to be operated from the upper floors of a building.[74] Communications security was "only fair," but there is little evidence the Japanese exploited this.[75] As the large American units squeezed into a smaller area later in the battle, distance became less of an issue than frequency overlap. Units with the same assigned frequencies were close enough to interfere with each other's communications. The extensive cross-attachment of units also caused some communications problems, as sub-elements sometimes lacked the capability to contact a distant parent unit.[76] There was even frequency overlap with some Japanese units, and on a few occasions the Japanese ineffectively tried to jam US communications by simply talking continuously over their radios.[77] American signalmen found communications wire vulnerable to damage from the large number of tracked vehicles present, so it was essential to keep it mounted off the ground. Japanese sniper fire did impede communications between the infantry and tanks, as it made using the phones on the rear of vehicles hazardous.[78]

Intelligence and Reconnaissance

There were significant shortfalls in the overall quality of US intelligence on Manila and its Japanese defenders. US commanders had basic information on the ad hoc composition of the defending Japanese units, the size of the defending force, the static nature of the defense, and its southern orientation.[79] However, intelligence personnel were slow to understand the intent of some elements within the Japanese force to seriously defend the city. MacArthur began operations on Luzon believing the Japanese would not fight for Manila, and those views survived longer than they should have, until US troops had been in the city a week. Griswold's assessment was more accurate: he wrote in his diary on 7 February, "My private opinion is that the Japs will hold that part of Manila south of the Pasig River until all are killed."[80]

The Japanese command structure experienced its own confusion and dissonance, as Yamashita's intent to abandon the city was disregarded by a naval chain of command with its own agenda. US intelligence analysts had a difficult time reading intent and predicting action because of the conflicting Japanese plans and actions. It was not until the Americans overcame the significant Japanese resistance north of the Pasig that the true nature of the Japanese defense became apparent to US commanders.[81] After the battle, the American understanding of Japanese intentions was still being clarified. The 37th Infantry's after-action report, written several months after the capture of Manila, stated "There were some indications that the enemy did not intend to defend the City of Manila."[82]

Once inside the city US forces usually found Japanese units and strongpoints by contact. Specific intelligence prior to contact remained limited, although that available was well integrated and distributed. Maps produced within the 37th Infantry Division blended the latest aerial and ground photos, observation post reports, and information from former residents, recent escapees, and prisoners of war. US intelligence personnel provided frequent updates to maps every few days to account for the changes in the urban landscape wrought by the heavy use of artillery. They also gathered a wealth of intelligence from captured Japanese documents, many taken from dead Japanese. Artillery spotter planes were of considerable value in tracking Japanese positions and movement. Observation posts set up in tall buildings proved a rich source of information, combining good lines of sight and persistence. Intercepts of Japanese radio transmissions played only a small role as an American intelligence input, largely because the Japanese had so few radios.[83]

Intelligence on the city itself was somewhat better, due in no small part to the long-term American presence prior to the war. US intelligence units produced and distributed terrain hand-books for Manila, and the after-action report for the 37th Infantry Division noted that the overall Luzon operation was better supported with maps than any of its previous operations. When US intelligence received indications on 5 February that the Japanese were planning on destroying key nodes in Manila's water system, US commanders knew where to send the 1st Cavalry Division to protect those nodes. However, there were still limits to how well the troops knew the city. When trying to locate and secure one of two key electrical substations, US troops mistakenly captured a bill collection office for the Manila Electric Company.[84]

Making the job of US intelligence personnel more difficult was the Japanese resourcefulness in urban camouflage. They kept many of their positions hidden inside buildings; often using rubble and destroyed structures. In one case, the Japanese put several pill-boxes with 25mm cannons in a cemetery and disguised them as burial mounds, complete with sod, flowers, statues and crosses.[85] Locating Japanese artillery was complicated for US spotters because the Japanese mounted it on trucks, emplaced it on the upper floors of buildings, and occasionally shielded it behind smoke.[86] The Japanese also exploited the difficulty US troops had in telling them apart from the civilian population by employing some of their troops with longer hair and civilian clothes as spies, or simply having their troops change into civilian clothes for infiltration attempts.[87] Japanese infiltrators often hid during the day under the plethora of tin roofing scattered around the city, and then attempted to cross the American lines at night.[88]

Three key sources of intelligence came from humans: the Filipino population and guerrillas, captured Japanese, and escaped or rescued Allied internees and prisoners of war. A flood of information from the population and guerrillas came into US units when they entered the city. Experience demonstrated that this information had value, but required considerable vetting.[89] The 37th Infantry's language detachment of three officers and seven language specialists was found to be "totally inadequate," as was the overall number of personnel capable of processing such intelligence inputs.[90]

While US troops took prisoner fewer than 1000 Japanese, those prisoners were usually very forthcoming with information.[91] "Excellent artillery targets were provided by almost all prisoners."[92] The Japanese military had so denigrated the concept of surrender that most of those who did so felt little or no obligation to conceal militarily useful information.

One cost to the Japanese for their extensive use of human shields in the city was maintaining control of all those hostages in the chaos of the American assault. Escaped civilians or prisoners of war often informed US assaults on Japanese positions. For example, when escapees brought out information on the large stockpiles of food and ammunition in three government buildings south of the Intramuros, the XIV Corps changed its initial plan to starve out the Japanese held up in those buildings.[93]

Firepower and Survivability

While US troops had no major urban combat experience as they entered Manila, they did have experience assaulting Japanese jungle bunker complexes over the previous several years. The largely static strongpoint-based Japanese defense of Manila made that jungle experience relevant. US commanders and troops adapted quickly to the presence of a large civilian population (to the degree possible), the need to account for the city's infrastructure, and the tactics of moving and fighting in buildings. The clearing of northern Manila also served as on-the-job training.[94]

The Army's urban warfare field manual, *FM 31-50*, which combined the topics of combat in towns and the attack of fortified positions, matched well with the tactics chosen by the Japanese in Manila. The after-action report from the Sixth Army praised *FM 31-50*, "Tactics recommended in FM 31-50 for combat in towns were used to great advantage by U.S. Forces in the street fighting in Manila."[95] While the field manual had most of it right, there were a few departures from doctrine that emerged as the troops fought and adapted their way across Manila. Armor was found to be more useful overall and artillery larger than 155mm was found to be useful in the direct fire role.[96] Another limitation of US Army doctrine was the scale at which it addressed urban warfare. As the field manual title suggests (*Attack on a Fortified Position and Combat in Towns*), its focus was on smaller urban areas, not large cities such as Manila, so it did not address issues that arose when operating division-size units in a large city.[97]

Not surprisingly, given the past experience in fighting Japanese defenses, the training for units designated to land on Luzon focused on bunker assaults and small unit infantry-armor-engineer cooperation, which paid big dividends in Manila. The artillery appears to have been less a part of this training and more focused on the open terrain aspects of Luzon.[98] In a lessons-learned report prepared after the battle, the headquarters of the 754th Tank Battalion credited the rigorous and comprehensive training it conducted with the 37th Infantry Division before the Luzon landings as making it more effective when working with the infantry of the 37th Infantry, as compared to the infantry of other divisions.[99]

US commanders attached heavy weapons, engineers, armor, and artillery across units and generally pushed them down to the small-unit level.

> Squads were organized into small assault teams with bazookas and demolitions. Heavier assault weapons

such as flame throwers were kept with the platoon Hq. group available on call.[100]

The heavy water-cooled M1917 machine guns, normally in the infantry battalion heavy weapons companies, were distributed out to the infantry companies. Infantry regimental cannon companies, which by this point in the war had upgraded from short-barrel towed 105mm howitzers to self-propelled M7 105mm howitzers, were attached directly to the infantry battalions. Commanders assigned 105mm- and 155mm-equipped field artillery battalions to support infantry battalions.[101] They also distributed armor to various infantry units by attaching Sherman medium tanks, assault gun Shermans with 105mm guns, M10 tank destroyers, and even a small number of light Stuart tanks.[102] Small unit leaders proved adept at employing this additional firepower and maximizing the synergy of combined arms.

As there appears to have been no detailed American planning for the assault on Manila, there was no clear idea across all US commanders how they would conduct the battle before American troops arrived in the city. Prior to that, the only operational principle was a minimum use of fire support, as dictated by MacArthur, to protect the population. Once the nature of the Japanese defense became clear, and American losses mounted, the mindset quickly changed.

> To occupy and secure any one of these virtual fortresses without prohibitive and decimating casualties, required the constant employment of direct fire weapons such as Cannon Company M-7s, tank destroyers, medium tanks, 155mm howitzers, to blast openings in walls and sufficiently neutralize buildings and eliminate the enemy forces remaining therein.[103]

While MacArthur lifted the restrictions on artillery in the first week, he stuck by his prohibition on air support. The known presence of civilians did affect US artillery support but did not stop it, as when the Philippine General Hospital was subjected to artillery

The heavily damaged Manila Post Office, the scene of heavy room-to-room fighting as it had been a Japanese strongpoint, including pillboxes inside the building. *Courtesy of the National Archives and Records Administration.*

fire only on its first floor and foundation level after US troops learned of a large number of civilian hostages within.[104]

The overall American emphasis on firepower resulted in a substantial advantage over the Japanese. American infantry enjoyed a marked advantage in the quality of their small arms over the Japanese. The semiautomatic eight-shot M1 Garand was a generation more advanced than the standard issue bolt-action rifles of the Japanese military. Moreover, US infantry companies and battalions were better equipped with machine guns and mortars than comparable Japanese infantry formations.[105] Japanese units also exhibited a marksmanship disadvantage, a cost of using so many non-infantry personnel.[106]

Japanese units partially made up that gap in firepower with the large number of crew-served 20mm and 25mm cannons taken from ships and aircraft. However, these weapons were heavy, requiring the Japanese to construct improvised mounts, and the Japanese usually set them up with narrow fields of fire. Thus, the Japanese employment of these weapons made them poorly suited for dealing with any rapid US infantry attack from an unexpected direction.[107]

Demolition charges, grenades, bazookas, and flame throwers played a major role in clearing the Japanese strongpoints. Demolition charges allowed US troops to breach walls and clear rooms so infantrymen did not have to clear them, as did grenades. GIs used bazookas to support assaults and for nightly preparation fires to soften up Japanese strongpoints for the following day's assault, aiming in many cases to burn out buildings with white phosphorous rounds.[108] Flame throwers proved most useful in attacking bunkers and buildings with bricked up windows and doorways.[109] The jet of flaming fuel could enter a small firing slit and spread across the interior, breaking down an otherwise strong defensive position. Man-portable flame throwers were plentiful in the 37th Infantry Division but less so within the 1st Cavalry.[110] When some Japanese positions resisted even flame throwers, such as basements and caves dug under buildings, US troops would pour gasoline or oil down into these positions and ignite it.[111]

US infantry endeavored to enter buildings from the top and work their way down, as doctrine prescribed.[112] When that was not possible GIs would try to create their own entry points from unexpected directions with demolition charges. Working up through a building tended to be more costly in casualties as the Japanese defenses were usually built for that, and they could roll grenades down on US troops. Once inside, stairways were the primary avenue of advance, supply, and evacuation.[113]

Increasing the effectiveness of these various man-portable weapons was their aggressive use by US troops. GIs would enter a building with all guns firing.[114] In many instances individual or pairs of GIs accounted for large numbers of Japanese with their hand-carried weapons. A single two-man M1919 light machine-gun crew, who dashed forward and set up their gun in the path of the attack, stopped one Japanese night counterattack. At sunrise thirty-two Japanese bodies were piled around their position.[115] One two-man Browning Automatic Rifle team dashed forward to within sixty yards of the Japanese strongpoint in the Paco Railroad Station and its 300 defenders. Over the next 2.5 hours they accounted for at least eighty-two Japanese, one heavy machine gun, and one 20mm cannon before exhausting their 1600 rounds of ammunition.[116] One daring bazooka operator, in two days' work, knocked out five Japanese machine guns, blew up one ammunition dump, and killed twenty-seven Japanese. A bold flame thrower operator, despite wounds in both his legs, charged a strongly held Japanese building to use his weapon on the firing slits. GIs then cleared the building and found twenty-eight charred Japanese bodies inside.[117] The aggression, skill, and weapons of the infantry made it as important in capturing Manila as armor and artillery.

The large amount of American artillery present in Manila was a mix of towed and self-propelled and ranged from small 75mm pack howitzers to the huge twenty-nine-ton 240mm howitzer.[118] Of the three divisions in and around Manila, the 11th Airborne Division had the least organic artillery, with just one battalion of towed short-barrel 105mm howitzers and two battalions of 75mm pack howitzers.[119] The 1st Cavalry Division and 37th Infantry Division between them had seven towed 105mm howitzer battalions, one towed 155mm howitzer battalion, and several companies of self-propelled M7 105mm howitzers attached at the regimental level.[120] XIV Corps also had substantial artillery assets of its own: one 4.2-inch chemical mortar battalion, five 155mm howitzer battalions, one 155mm gun battalion, one 8-inch howitzer battalion, and one 240mm howitzer battalion. Once the 11th Airborne transferred to the XIV Corps, it began receiving artillery support from XIV Corps, a rare instance of a unit receiving artillery support from a unit to its front.[121]

Despite the strong American naval forces in the Pacific, there was no naval gunfire support in the battle for Manila. The Japanese held islands in Manila Bay, had mined its waters, and had devoted a considerable numbers of suicide boats to counter any American naval presence in the bay. To gain entry to the bay, the US Navy first needed to take back the largest of these islands at the mouth of the bay, Corregidor. As Corregidor was some thirty miles from Manila, US ships remained out of gun range of the city. The combined amphibious and paratrooper assault on the island started on 16 February, and took two weeks to clear its 5000 defenders, costing US forces over two hundred killed. Even after US forces secured Corregidor, it took until 16 April to secure all of the islands in the bay. [122]

While the primary use of artillery was indirect fire support, there were many cases of direct fire, some at close range. The M7 self-propelled 105mm howitzer excelled in the direct fire role with its mobility and partial small arms protection for its crew (no roof). US commanders attached towed howitzers, up to 155mm, to infantry units for direct fire support, sometimes firing at ranges down to 150 yards.[123] The use of artillery in the direct fire mode made the fire more accurate and coordination with the infantry easier, but this did place the artillerymen at greater risk. Japanese indirect counterbattery fire was rarely effective, although if an American artillery piece could see its target, then those at the target could see them.[124] In a two-day close-range artillery preparation on the three government buildings south of the Intramuros, Japanese small arms fire damaged two howitzers, killed five artillerymen, and wounded fifty-four.[125]

To protect the population the initial rules of engagement for artillery were restrictive, requiring US troops to first precisely locate Japanese positions. A 6 February journal entry for the 37th Infantry Division's artillery headquarters stated a requirement that artillery support of the 37th Infantry's infantry units from divisional artillery assets receive its approval. That same journal entry stated the XIV Corps commander did not want any area shelling, had expressed a preference for direct fire, and cautioned that artillery fire should avoid hitting buildings.[126] MacArthur soon lifted those restrictions as casualties climbed south of the Pasig and US intelligence indicated that the Japanese had turned many buildings into strongpoints in the southern part of the city. The three infantry regiments of the 37th Infantry were rapidly weakening. The 148th Infantry Regiment had suffered over five hundred casualties in just three days (7–10 Feb) from an authorized strength of just over three thousand, and it had entered Manila already understrength. By 10 February the 129th Infantry was 700 men understrength.[127] As the engagement rules loosened, artillery use soared, and some locations were hit with area fires.[128] Night time "protective fires" became the norm, both to soften up the next day's objectives and to hamper Japanese night movement.[129]

US troops quickly learned lessons about the effects of their artillery on Japanese strongpoints. High-angle indirect fire was minimally effective against the heaviest buildings; 155mm direct fire the most effective. Unfuzed projectiles proved useful for opening holes in heavy walls. The fissures produced by such rounds were bigger than those of high explosive shells with delayed fusing. Subsequently, US troops fired delay fuse rounds into those fissures with good effect.[130] If the objective was simply to demolish the building, then it was best to first fire at the lower floors, to minimize the number of surviving Japanese in pockets left after the building collapsed. If the intention was to storm the building, then it was best to start the artillery fire at the top and work down, forcing the defenders into the basement before US infantry entered.[131] Though the 4.2-inch mortar was not effective against the heaviest buildings, it was still popular with the infantry units for its short response time and accuracy—an important consideration for targets close to US infantry. The large mortars were also a key delivery vehicle for smoke screens.[132]

Sherman medium tanks and M10 tank destroyers composed the bulk of the US armor in Manila. There were a few Stuart light tanks in the city, although they played a minor role. A platoon of assault gun Shermans, with their very effective 105mm guns, was also present.[133] Most of the Shermans and M10s came from the 754th Tank Battalion and the 640th Tank Destroyer Battalion, both subordinate to the XIV Corps.[134] Griswold did not fully commit either battalion to the battle for Manila, but rather employed one to two companies from each in the city at any one time.[135] While the new heavy M26 Pershing tank was entering frontline service in Europe in February 1945, the first Pershings did not arrive in the Pacific until July on Okinawa.[136] The machine guns on the Shermans and M10s proved most useful, often catching Japanese driven out of bunkers or buildings by main gun fire, or when the Japanese rushed a vehicle with hand-carried anti-tank weapons.

Aside from the usual bunker and building targets, the vehicle crews found other uses for the Sherman and M10 main guns. They used these main guns to destroy Japanese barges, other watercraft in the bay and on the Pasig, and partially sunken ship hulks holding Japanese with crew-served weapons.[137] In the artillery preparation for the assault on the Intramuros, M10s were used to blast footholds in the seawall (adjacent to the Pasig) for the infantry.[138] The tankers of the 754th Tank Battalion used improvised canister rounds elsewhere on Luzon but it does not appear that they were used in Manila.[139] Canister ammunition may have been used by the light Stuart tank platoon in the 37th Infantry.[140] When firing at heavy buildings the higher-velocity 3-inch main gun of the M10 was more effective than the shorter 75mm on the Sherman.[141]

A small number of flame thrower-equipped Shermans were present in Manila. While their use was rare, they were effective, in one case shooting flame up a staircase.[142] The flame thrower unit took the place of the bow machine gun in the Sherman's hull. After the battle, the headquarters of the 754th Tank Battalion called for more tanks equipped with larger flame throwers.[143]

Air support played a modest role in Manila. The most significant contribution came from the small artillery spotter aircraft, which located targets for the artillery and provided overall information on Japanese forces. The restrictions imposed by MacArthur limited airstrikes in the city to fewer than two dozen sorties after US forces arrived.[144] With one notable exception, when a single Japanese aircraft bombed a tank company bivouac, killing its commander and three enlisted men, US aircraft kept the skies free of Japanese airpower.[145]

Despite all the firepower tools available to US forces, and their effective combined arms coordination, the reduction of Japanese strongpoints was a costly and time-consuming affair. One example was the joint effort of the 37th Infantry Division and 1st Cavalry Division to capture the Philippine University and hospital complex. It took over 2000 rounds of 105mm high explosive, 1100 rounds of 4.2-inch mortar high explosive, and another 264 rounds of 4.2-inch white phosphorous over five days before US infantry could gain a toehold. When one of the participating infantry regiments from the 37th Infantry left the front line and handed over its positions to the 1st Cavalry, its infantry companies were on average 40 percent below authorized strength. It took ten days to clear the complex, and total US losses were sixty killed, 445 wounded, and another 105 non-battle casualties from heat exhaustion, sickness, and combat fatigue.[146]

An interesting contrast in US infantry loss rates can be seen in the first week of fighting relative to the later weeks. In that first week, with the strict artillery rules of engagement and the absence of most armor, the burden of advance rested on the infantry—and the casualty rates reflect this. From 6 to 12 February the 37th Infantry Division lost 105 killed and 787 wounded. The following week (13 to 19 February) those totals dropped to seventy-nine killed and 762 wounded. By the third week (20 to 26 February), when the use of artillery was heavy and the combined arms coordination fine-tuned, those numbers dropped further to fifty-two killed and 555 wounded.[147] Despite encountering heavier Japanese defenses as the 37th Infantry pushed farther into the city, the combination of learning and firepower reduced losses.

The culmination of that trend came in the storming of the Intramuros. Over several days, extensive artillery fire was directed inside and against its outer walls. Artillery as large as 8-inch and 240mm battered several gaps into the walls that were forty feet thick at their base.[148] The intense bombardment of 23 February, preceding the final assault, was the most prominent example of US firepower against Japanese determination. In just one hour almost 8000 artillery, mortar, tank and tank destroyer main gun rounds were fired into a roughly one kilometer square area—a total of 185 tons of ordnance.[149] Griswold called it the most intense artillery fire he had seen in the Southwest Pacific theater.[150] That prodigious use of fire support proved effective, minimizing US losses to twenty-five killed, a low cost relative to the taking of other Japanese strongpoints in the city and the roughly two thousand Japanese defending the Intramuros.[151]

There were non-combat threats as well to the GIs: poor sanitation, bad local food, venereal disease, and rotting bodies. Waste disposal proved a serious health issue in Manila by late February. With the breakdown in the garbage removal and sewage systems, civilian garbage and human waste began piling up around the city. Compounding the problem was the massive number of dead bodies rotting in the heat. The fly population exploded, with "clouds" of flies blanketing the streets, so that even eating without ingesting some was difficult.[152] This led to a rapid rise in the dysentery rate for US troops, sufficient to "seriously affect the efficiency" of some units.[153] Civilians tended to cluster around US field kitchens, further contaminating the military food system and exposing military personnel to a range of tropical illnesses unfamiliar to American immune systems. Access to local food establishments and local women also generated non-battle casualties. Stomach ailments were a serious problem, and the venereal disease rate "went on a rampage."[154] The weekly disease rate for the 37th Infantry Division increased roughly five-fold from late January to late February (356 to 1614 cases).[155]

The total casualties suffered by US forces primarily came from the 37th Infantry and the 1st Cavalry, and most were infantrymen.[156]

> Most casualties suffered fragmentation wounds caused by artillery, mortars, and automatic cannon. Those killed outright were killed by rifle bullets at close range.[157]

The often cited total casualty figures of 1010 killed and 5565 wounded overstate the actual losses in Manila as those figures include the losses of the 11th Airborne, which did not fight in the city. A more accurate total is 780 killed and 4700 wounded.[158]

Even with the lower US casualty figure estimate, the cost of capturing Manila was greater than for other locations on Luzon. At the capture of Manila, all units of the Sixth Army on Luzon had counted 65,204 Japanese dead, while suffering 3480 killed and 13,164 wounded. Thus, the general exchange ratio for the Sixth Army on Luzon from the Lingayen landings until early March was one American casualty for every 3.92 dead Japanese. However, inside Manila that ratio was only one American casualty for every 3.04 dead Japanese (5480 US casualties and 16,665 dead Japanese).[159]

Armor losses at Manila were light considering the number of vehicles employed. Only one M10 was destroyed, by a mine, though the open-topped vehicles exposed the crews. Five M10 crewmen were killed and thirteen wounded—most by small arms fire.[160] Attempts by Japanese infantry to rush tank destroyers with hand-held anti-tank weapons were decidedly unsuccessful, as were their frequently fired, but poorly directed artillery and mortar rounds.[161]

Despite their heavy use in Manila, only one Alligator amphibious tractor was lost, in the 7 February crossing of the Pasig.[162] Sherman tank losses were even lower with no total losses. Seven Shermans were damaged, mostly by mines.[163] In Manila five Sherman crewmen were killed and eleven wounded, but four of the killed and seven of the wounded were from one rare Japanese air attack.[164]

The armor losses in Manila were generally lighter than those suffered outside the city. Sherman losses were higher elsewhere on Luzon for the 754th Tank Battalion, which lost five Shermans—with ten more damaged outside of Manila.[165] The 640th Tank Destroyer Battalion lost only one seriously damaged M10 outside Manila, although it suffered thirty-one casualties (all but two wounded).[166] In comparison, the 4th Tank Battalion on Iwo Jima, a comparable amount of armor to that sent into Manila, lost eleven destroyed Shermans and eight more damaged in its first four days in action.[167]

Mobility and Counter-Mobility

Simply getting into Manila was a challenge for some elements of the US forces pushing southward down the Central Plain. The many destroyed bridges north of Manila often produced gaps between the infantry and its supporting armor and artillery. The infantry could more easily be shuttled across rivers and streams in amphibious tractors, or cross on quickly emplaced light pontoon foot bridges. The heavier equipment had to await the construction of vehicular bridges, which took longer to build and were in shorter supply. The 37th Infantry's armor support was approximately two days behind the division's leading infantry getting into Manila.[168]

The single greatest obstacle to US mobility was the Pasig River. Running due east from Manila Bay for five miles, and then southeast across the eastern portions of the city, it separated the northern Japanese defensive positions, and those in the eastern suburbs, from the main strongpoints at the city center. As American forces were clearing northern Manila, the Japanese demolished all six of the vehicular and railroad bridges across the Pasig—in some cases minutes before US infantry would have seized them. As these bridges were 100–400 feet long, US engineers could not easily replace or repair them.[169]

US commanders quickly marshaled Alligator amphibious tractors and assault boats for a forced crossing of the river on 7 February several miles inland from Manila Bay. That afternoon approximately twenty Alligator amphibious tractors, thirty man-paddled assault boats and two assault barges began repeated trips across the river until they had ferried two infantry battalions from the 37th Infantry's 148th Infantry Regiment across five hours later. Heavy Japanese fire was directed at all except the first wave, but losses were modest as a low jetty provided cover for the first half of the crossing, the Japanese had poor visibility of the loading site, and the later waves were covered with US artillery-delivered smoke and suppressive high-explosive fire missions.[170] One Alligator, one assault barge, and four or five assault boats were destroyed, and many of the Alligators took some damage. The crossing owed a large part of its success to US reconnaissance elements finding a weak point in the defense of the southern bank.[171]

More battalions and supplies followed in the next two days until the bulk of the 148th and 129th Infantry regiments were across. Under heavy Japanese mortar and artillery fire, US engineers began constructing a 1.5-ton capacity pontoon bridge on the afternoon of 8 February, completing it at 0300 the morning of 9 February.[172] Poor Japanese observation again limited the effectiveness of their mortars and artillery, one hundred rounds landing within one hundred yards of the bridge but with no direct hits. A northward refugee flow across the river did present a traffic control problem, which the Americans addressed by using barges and Alligators to carry civilians. By the night of 12 to 13 February, a heavy forty-six-ton capacity vehicle bridge was across the Pasig on the site of the

7 February crossing, again constructed under heavy fire. US engineers constructed several smaller pontoon footbridges, on either side of the heavy bridge, to handle civilian traffic.[173]

With its left sweep through Manila's eastern suburbs, the 1st Cavalry Division was ready to cross the Pasig two days after the 37th Infantry. Just an hour after reaching the river late on 9 February, elements of the 1st Cavalry started crossing in assault boats. The next morning other elements of the division began crossing at a second site using a combination of Alligators and small native canoes. The speed of these crossings surprised the Japanese, and US troops made rapid progress on the far shore. The Japanese were able to react later that day with heavy artillery fire on the crossing points, damaging several pontoon bridges under construction. By the morning of the 13 February a heavy vehicle bridge was over the Pasig. Over the next several days the Japanese succeeded several times in floating explosives down the river and destroying some of these American bridges. However, Alligators maintained the flow of forces and supplies across the river while the bridges were repaired.[174]

The last major river crossing was in support of the storming of the Intramuros on 23 February, when a battalion of infantry crossed the Pasig as the artillery preparation inside the Walled City ended. This crossing was closer to the shore of Manila Bay than the first crossing of the river on 7 February. The infantry climbed up the bank and moved through a gap blasted in the seawall by artillery, tank, and tank destroyer fire. In just 2.5 hours, engineers constructed a 400-foot light walkway across the river, during the assault, to speed movement. They added a heavier vehicle bridge on 26 February, and a second on 28 February, to allow two-way traffic.[175]

Aside from the river, the other major obstacle to US movement was the extensive Japanese minefields and obstacles—usually mixed together. The Japanese blocked most roads and intersections with a wide range of obstacles and a menagerie of conventional and improvised mines. Obstacles included large factory machines, I-beams and railroad rails buried vertically in the pavement, barrels filled with sand, water, or cement, cars, trucks, trolley cars, and barbed wire.[176] Interestingly, the Japanese use of obstacles matched closely that prescribed in US doctrine for defending urban terrain.[177]

Japanese minefields were an odd mix of whatever munitions were available, including conventional anti-tank and anti-personnel mines, aircraft bombs, naval mines, and even depth charges. However, those mines were usually poorly camouflaged and thus easy to spot. Obstacles and mine belts were often poorly linked to nearby belts, sometimes leaving gaps US forces could pass through, or sometimes not covered with observation so that fire could not be called down on US engineers trying to clear them. Sometimes the Japanese rigged entire buildings with explosives, to be detonated by the defenders as US troops entered.[178]

US engineers quickly developed tactics for clearing these easy-to-find mines. A tank would roll forward close to the minefield with engineers crouched close behind while the infantry laid down suppressive fire. The tank would stop and engineers would dash out, disable the mine (often in ten to fifteen seconds), attach a cable back to the tank, and then dash back behind the tank. The tank would then reverse, pulling the mine out and away. This was done repeatedly until they had cleared the field. After the battle, engineers created a fifty-ton pile of these munitions. Throughout the battle at least two companies of engineers were attached to each infantry regiment. The clearing capability they brought was essential for combined arms, as it allowed armor to stay close to the infantry.[179]

Apart from the river and obstacle/mine belts, the only other major impediment to vehicle movement was rubble. In a few parts of the city where the buildings were of heavy construction, densely packed, and often multi-story, rubble often blocked the streets after heavy artillery use. Fortunately those conditions were rare, as the densely packed structures north of the Pasig tended to be of light construction, and the large structures in most of the city south of the river were widely spaced. Inside the Intramuros, rubble was a problem after the heavy artillery preparation and bulldozers were needed to clear lanes for the tanks and other vehicles.[180]

US infantry perfected dismounted movement tactics in the operations north of the Pasig, and they followed US Army doctrine by keeping time in the street to a minimum. The preference was to enter one building from another, either by starting from the roof down or by blowing a hole in the wall in an upper floor. The infantry then worked its way down via the stairwells, or, if those were blocked, by blowing holes in the floor. All attacks were heavily supported by small arms fire, armor, and artillery. The GIs marveled at how the Japanese usually held their ground even though the progression of explosions had to let them know the Americans were coming.[181]

The key US counter-mobility tool was artillery/mortar fire, not surprising given the overall American emphasis on firepower. Aside from the heavy fires directed nightly on known Japanese positions, harassing fires were also directed at intersections and other open areas Japanese forces might move across under the cover of darkness. One 14 February journal entry for the Artillery Headquarters of the 37th Infantry Division notes 1500 rounds for "fires for PM." The one-kilometer-square Intramuros and its surrounding area received over nine hundred and fifty rounds of harassment fires during the night of 21 to 22 February, with even heavier fires the next night.[182]

Not all of the counter-mobility fires were indirect. A large number of Japanese infiltrators were killed by small arms fire while probing for gaps in the American line. In one night two battalions of the 145th Infantry killed ninety-four Japanese infiltrators.[183] Sherman tanks sank a number of Japanese barges trying to move up and down the Pasig.[184] On 7 February the Japanese attempted to turn the flank of the 145th Infantry north of the Pasig with a barge assault up the coast of the bay. Heavy mortar, cannon, and anti-tank gun fire killed most of the Japanese on the water, and the twenty who made it to shore shortly thereafter. Long-range heavy machine-gun fire from American positions north of the river hampered movement on the streets visible south of the river.[185]

However, the resourceful Japanese still found some effective modes of transportation. A number of sailboats, fishing boats, and even rafts were used in Manila Bay. US forces attacked these occasionally, with artillery or aircraft, but often US commanders were too unsure of the occupants of those boats to approve requests to engage. Many civilians had ignored the American prohibition against civilian boat traffic.[186] A limited number of Japanese probably escaped the city in this manner. The Japanese also had tunnels dug between many positions in the city, including some that may have been under the Pasig.[187]

Logistics

A major logistical challenge in Manila was the heavy consumption of artillery ammunition. Once MacArthur eased the restrictive rules for artillery use, ammunition consumption soared, with nightly harassing fires, nightly preparatory fires on specific targets, and increased supporting fires during the day. The XIV Corps' average daily expenditure of 105mm howitzer ammunition from 22 February to 3 March was four times that for operations after the capture of Manila.[188] In a single night, one infantry battalion's 81mm mortar platoon set a unit record by firing over four thousand rounds of high explosive and white phosphorous into buildings scheduled for attack the next day.[189] The intense one-hour artillery preparation of the Intramuros on 23 February involved almost eight thousand rounds of artillery, mortar, tank, and tank destroyer fire.[190] Moving that vast amount of ammunition was difficult as most of it had to come from the Lingayen beachhead, a round trip of over 350 miles.[191] The average daily quantity of 75mm howitzer, 105mm, and 155mm ammunition alone used by XIV Corps from 22 February to 3 March filled seventy-two trucks.[192] Despite these difficulties, the robust American logistical system came through. The abundance of American weapons proved effective only because they were supported by the capability to keep them supplied.

Aside from ammunition the other major logistical issue was supplies for the civilian population.

> One of the most difficult problems of the entire campaign was the provision of minimum essential supplies for the civilian population, particularly in the Greater Manila area.[193]

The medical capabilities of the Philippine Civil Affairs Units proved inadequate and other US units had to make up the shortfalls

Emergency relief supplies of rice and other food stocks are loaded from landing craft that came up the Pasig, to trucks that will distribute them within Manila. *Courtesy of the National Archives and Records Administration.*

by providing medical care to civilians. The scale of support needed to supply the large population strained the already extended US logistical system. Large stocks of captured Japanese supplies did provide some relief.[194]

Inside the city several other logistical issues emerged. Some units, such as tank destroyers, did not have allotments of ammunition that reflected their heavy infantry support roles. The extensive cross attachment of units complicated logistics, as separation from the normal parent unit sometimes meant separation from needed maintenance support.[195] The heavy use of the Alligators, both in the approach to the city and for several major river crossings, pushed those vehicles and their crews to the limit.[196] After several years of jungle fighting, the GIs' sudden contact with a large civilian population exposed a serious shortfall in prophylactic supplies.[197]

Dealing with the Population

US commanders allocated significant resources and forces to providing for the civilian population. The 1st Cavalry's sweep wide left around the city was in part motivated by Krueger's desire to secure key nodes in the city's water system. US troops shared food and medical supplies with the population, and river crossing operations often accounted for the needs of civilian traffic.[198] While close contact with the population at times proved unhealthy for the GIs, US commanders did not allow this to prevent support to the civilians. Processing the heavy flow of information coming in from the population was a challenge, although that information did prove valuable in understanding Japanese defenses.

The tone of how the Philippine population would be treated was set from the top of the US military chain of command—by MacArthur. His ban on air support in the city, the initial strict limitations on artillery support, the designation of infrastructure as objectives, and the logistical support to civilians were all influenced by MacArthur's tenure in the Philippines prior to the war. MacArthur embraced the role of liberator on a personal level.

Although US planners underestimated the scale of support needed for the population in Manila, that effort did receive significant resources. Thirteen forty-nine-man Philippine Civil Affairs Units were assigned to Luzon by the Sixth Army—many staffed by Filipino expatriates from the United States.[199] These units were trained in relief and civil government operations.[200] The planning estimate of 200,000 needy in the city was almost doubled when the pool of supported reached 350,000 in Manila. A XIV Corps after-action report called for double the number of civil affairs units, and greater internal medical capabilities in those units, for any future operation comparable in size to Manila.[201]

Unlike US forces, the Japanese in Manila did not allow the presence of the civilian population to interfere with their operations.

Some of the few Japanese to surrender in Manila, being led by an officer in the 1st Cavalry Division. *Courtesy of the National Archives and Records Administration.*

In fact, they actively used the population as both shields and targets.[202] This was not out of character for the Japanese military, as they had killed an estimated 260,000 non-combatants in Nanking over a few months in late-1938 and early-1939.[203] On one occasion, an American forward observer spotted some Japanese moving supplies, while twenty Filipinos were held at gunpoint nearby, including a Filipino girl tied naked to a tree, to avoid drawing American artillery fire.[204] On another occasion, Japanese troops told hospital workers to fashion large red cross symbols for the roof, and on completion of the symbols the Japanese troops ejected all workers and patients; troops and weapons moved in to replace them. Several times the Japanese suddenly released large numbers of Filipino civilians toward US lines to slow the American advance, when their utility as hostages waned.

Differentiating between friend and foe was no easy task for US troops. Both US unit logs and captured Japanese documents refer to Japanese infiltrators in civilian garb.[205] While most of the population in Manila was hostile to the Japanese, there were some pro-Japanese collaborators. These collaborators aided the Japanese by acting as spies, conducting sabotage behind US lines, and holding pro-American Filipinos hostage.[206]

The violent struggle for Manila cost an estimated 100,000 civilian lives.[207] No accurate count exists of how many of those died from US versus Japanese actions, but it is probable Japanese intent played a greater role than American accident.[208] A criticism sometimes leveled at US forces operating in Manila is that the heavy use of artillery killed many civilians.[209] While true in isolation, that critique's validity evaporates in the context of Manila. American forces could control the amount of artillery fire they directed on targets, which often had the potential of housing civilians, and in some cases were clearly known to. What US commanders could not control, however, was the ongoing and continual assault on the population by the Japanese, which US commanders were well

A visual example why a prolonged siege of Manila was not a viable option. This emaciated Filipino girl was typical of many civilians who would crowd around US Army field kitchens during and after the battle, looking for any food available. *Courtesy of the National Archives and Records Administration.*

aware of.[210] Above and beyond the civilian deaths from the collapse of the city's infrastructure, Japanese forces were systematically denying civilians medical care, food and water—and in many cases murdering them outright.[211] The interrogation of captured Japanese and many captured Japanese documents illuminated the extensive nature of the killing—including one diary that stated,

> 7 Feb 45—150 guerrillas were disposed of tonight. I personally stabbed and killed 10. 9 Feb 45—Burned 1,000 guerrillas to death tonight.[212]

Absent offensive action by US forces, Japanese actions in the city would have steadily increased the civilian death toll. Japanese actions forced some difficult choices on American commanders. The single most important thing the Americans could deliver, both for the larger war effort and the residents of Manila, was the rapid liquidation of the Japanese defenders, and that was delivered with vigor and skill.[213]

The American conduct of operations in Manila should also be judged in the context of World War II. The complete destruction of the Japanese empire, rather than simply reducing its geographic footprint, was as just a cause for war as any in the twentieth century. Every day that empire existed meant death and misery for hundreds of millions of people. Every day the Japanese controlled Manila and the Philippines meant more Filipino civilians, Allied internees, and POWs would perish.[214] Both the military and moral imperatives called for maximum speed, and the heavy use of firepower was the only tool that could provide that speed. Manila needed to be captured to facilitate its use in subsequent operations, and the participating units could not be sacrificed in the process.

Conclusions

American forces in Manila faced a stark challenge. The enemy force was large, well-entrenched in a large urban battle space crowded with civilians, and determined to hold at all costs. And yet, with a relatively modest advantage in manpower of approximately 1.5–1, US forces managed to capture the city. It was not quick or cheap, but they completed their mission.

One reason for this was that a number of American general war-fighting competencies proved applicable in the urban environment. The emphasis on small unit leader aggression and initiative paid dividends as squads and platoons cleared buildings, bunkers, tunnels, and basements. The distribution of heavy weapons out to the infantry units on the front line, and the large supply of these weapons, gave the infantry the firepower they needed to kill Japanese defenders who had spent months preparing their positions, often in heavy structures. Further augmenting the firepower at the tip of the spear was the armor and artillery, often attached to the infantry units and firing at close range. Absent a credible Japanese armor threat, or serious anti-tank capability, American armor was at its best supporting the infantry. Perhaps most importantly, US commanders and their troops proved capable of blending these various combat arms into an effective whole that was greater than the sum of its parts—the essence of combined arms. Underlying all this firepower was a logistical system that could supply vast quantities of munitions, making it possible to substitute firepower for manpower. That sort of logistical support was far from ad hoc, but rather built into the organization of US forces years earlier. The emphasis on mobility in the US Army proved useful inside the city, as amphibious tractors and extensive engineering capabilities made opposed crossings of the Pasig seem almost easy. The past battlefield experiences of the XIV Corps also proved transferable to Manila. Previous operations against Japanese jungle bunker complexes prepared US units well, and the Sixth Army's after-action report cited the similarity in Japanese tactics in Manila to those earlier operations.[215]

Where some pre-existing capability did not apply, US commanders and the troops were quick to improvise. With MacArthur's ban on air support, commanders substituted additional artillery support. The engineers and tankers developed a system for cooperatively clearing Japanese minefields and barriers. When attacking the heavy structures in the city's center, artillerymen quickly learned what combination of artillery calibers and ammunition worked best. Commanders quickly learned that the Japanese preferred to attack and infiltrate at night, so they halted the advance of their units at dusk to better thwart these actions.[216] The tendency for rapid adaptation was not only a part of US Army doctrine, it was indicative of the overall American military culture and even American culture itself. Michael Doubler's study of American battlefield adaptation in World War II found this to be true in Europe, and the same can be said for the Americans in Manila.[217]

In a sense, the first few days of fighting north of the Pasig acted as a sort of laboratory for urban warfare, testing the effectiveness of an infantry-centric approach against a determined foe in urban terrain. The armor support was several days behind the infantry, air support was prohibited, and the rules of engagement greatly restricted the use of artillery. The high losses suffered by the lead US infantry units quickly brought about a relaxation of the artillery use rules, and put to rest any notions of urban warfare being an infantry-only operation.

Although it is unclear whether Japanese commanders would have either evacuated the city if given the chance, or how seriously Japanese commanders outside the city wanted to reinforce those forces in Manila, US commanders took those options away from them by isolating it. The left hook of the 1st Cavalry Division seized the initiative in the city by limiting how long the Japanese could drag out the battle.

Manila was a much larger urban battle than Aachen, and the defending enemy was substantially different as well. However, the methods used by US forces were very similar: combined arms, maximum firepower, isolation of the city, and methodical advance—all tempered with a spirit of adaptation. Neither battle was low cost or quickly concluded, but in both cases US forces were victorious.

Chapter 4

Urban Warfare in American Military Thought after World War II

After World War II

In the post-World War II era, the US military for the most part went back to its pre-war apathy toward urban warfare. Shortly after V-E Day (Victory in Europe), the US Army's European Theater Headquarters commissioned a sweeping lessons collection effort that resulted in 131 General Board reports on a wide range of subjects, with distribution throughout Europe and the Army's school system.[1] In these reports urban warfare was rarely mentioned and never presented as a serious challenge needing future attention. In *Study No. 1*, on the strategy employed by the United States and allied militaries in Western Europe, a section on the terrain obstacles facing the allied forces in August 1944 did not mention cities. In a later section, assessing the same issue of terrain obstacles for November 1944, terrain features around Aachen were mentioned but not urban terrain as such. Brest was mentioned, although in terms of siege operations, and Aachen only in terms of being the location where the Siegfried Line was first penetrated. The study listed Lt. Col. John Corley, a battalion commander at Aachen, as one of those interviewed, so it is not that those with first-hand experience were not consulted.[2] The report on tank battalions never mentioned urban warfare and the report on infantry divisions stated that overall US doctrine was proven sound without any mention of problems with urban terrain.[3] The report on tank destroyer units stated, "Fundamentally, there was no such thing as different employment of tank destroyers in various types of operations."[4]

This minimalist coverage of urban warfare was not the product of some collective amnesia, but rather a reflection of the US Army's belief that urban warfare was a rarely occurring problem that was already solved. Brest and Aachen had been difficult fights, with significant casualties and a slow tempo, but so had many other types of operations. American forces clearing German troops from the Huertgen Forest just south of Aachen at around the same time suffered forty-eight times as many casualties (wounded, killed, captured, and missing) than in Aachen. Armor losses in Manila were far lower than those on Iwo Jima.[5] General George S. Patton's view of urban warfare reflected this attitude: it was "simply a variation of pillbox fighting."[6]

Immediately after the war, the US military establishment had far more pressing problems to address. The rush to demobilize, combined with the sharp reduction in funding levels, meant there was little attention and no resources to spare for peripheral problems. Far more important were the implications of nuclear weapons and the revolution in electronics, both factors that made massing ground forces for a methodical urban battle seem not just old fashioned but self-defeating. In an address to the Infantry School in 1954, US Army Vice Chief of Staff General Charles L. Bolte described the new nuclear battlefield: "Mass, in the old sense of concentrating units and material to achieve a breakthrough or to mount an assault, becomes suicidal."[7]

When the Korean War broke out, and United States Marine

Corps (USMC) units barely out of their peacetime modes of operation proved capable of quickly clearing Seoul, the perception of a solved problem was reinforced. While the dream of a nuclear panacea to all military problems died on the ridgelines of the Korean Peninsula, the revival of attention to conventional ground combat within the US military did not include urban warfare. By fiscal year 1958, the United States Air Force's share of total American defense spending had ballooned to more than 48 percent, leaving just 29 percent for the US Navy and Marine Corps, and 21 percent for the US Army. With that historically small slice of funding the Army focused on high technology. In fiscal year 1957, it devoted 43 percent of its research and development funds to nuclear weapons and missiles, with less than 5 percent going to artillery, new vehicles, or aircraft.[8] The 1950s also witnessed both Army and Marine Corps attempts (later aborted) to change the organizational structure of their ground units, either to better survive the nuclear battlefield or to enhance air transportability. In neither case were these changes directed at improving performance in urban operations.[9] A study published by the US Army Command and General Staff College on the evolution of US Army tactical doctrine from the end of World War II to the mid-1970s mentions urban warfare only twice, and in passing. Another study from the Staff College, of Army organizational changes from the end of World War II to the 1990s, mentions urban warfare only once as a rationale behind reorganization, and this in reference to the 1980s.[10]

Any Marine officer reading the *U.S. Naval Institute Proceedings* after the end of World War II and up until the battle for Hue looking for urban warfare articles, would have been sorely disappointed. While numerous articles were critical of the notion that technology had diminished the need for ground combat, only two articles in that entire period gave attention to urban warfare, and neither of those provided any useful tactical detail.[11]

The *Marine Corps Gazette* was a different story. From V-J Day until Hue, the *Gazette* published a dozen urban warfare-related articles. Although some of these articles would have been of minimal value for someone fighting in Seoul or Hue (e.g., articles covering urban riot control), others offered substantial learning value.[12] Two of the more useful articles, published in 1945 and 1948, presented many of the tactical principles then contained in the Army's *FM 31-50*, although neither mentioned that manual by name.[13] This crossover of Army urban warfare doctrine to affect USMC thinking would not be the only example of such influence. From 1951 to 1952 the *Gazette* published five articles that gave detailed accounts of the battles for Seoul and Stalingrad. These articles gave attention to the operational context of these battles along with sufficiently rich tactical detail to be instructive. For example, one article devoted two pages to Marine air support operations over Seoul.[14] In short, there were examples of insightful journal articles on urban combat between 1945 and 1968, just not very many of them.

Despite this general sense of apathy toward urban warfare, the solid US Army doctrinal foundation from World War II continued to evolve through the 1950s and 1960s. The Army released revised versions of *FM 31-50* in 1952 and 1964. The same two-subject division of the 1944 version was retained, with "attack on a fortified position" preceding the section on urban combat, although by 1964 the total length of the manual decreased by half. The most significant change in the 1952 version was a greater role ascribed to armor, as well as to other supporting heavy weapons. In a section on attacking towns, about 1.5 pages describe the role of tanks in detail, more space than was given to any other supporting arm. Although the section on training did not explicitly mention tanks, it did call out the need for combined arms training, something not done in the 1944 version.[15] The 1964 version continued the strong emphasis on combined arms, now including helicopters. The 1964 manual also explicitly and succinctly addressed the conundrum of urban warfare in the nuclear age.

Such an attack might expose the attacker to the risk of having a large part of his force destroyed by nuclear, chemical, or biological weapons. If, however, the built-up area is critical to the attacker, the commander may be required to accept this risk.[16]

As a testament to the quality of the original 1944 manual, many of the illustrations in the 1964 version were only slightly changed versions of those used in the 1944 version.[17]

Another notable change in *FM 31-50* during the post-World War II years was its treatment of gas. The 1944 and 1952 versions both mention the use of "chemical" mortars (i.e., the 4.2-inch mortar in both the US Army and USMC inventories), but only as a means to employ high explosive or smoke ammunition.[18] These versions make no other mention of the employment of chemical weapons for urban operations, including any necessary precautions for defending against the chemical threat. The 1964 version changed this with references to the employment of chemical weapons, including two that specifically mention non-lethal agents. Because of the potential for civilian casualties, "especially in friendly territory ... incapacitating chemical and biological agents are ideally suited for the integration with conventional fire support."[19]

Post-World War II Marine Corps doctrine also gave significant attention to urban warfare. The August 1945 manual for rifle squads contained a section on urban warfare along with many of the same tactical suggestions made in the Army's *FM 31-50*, such as clearing buildings from the top down and preceding room entry with a grenade. Interestingly, this manual was signed by the then-commandant of Marine Corps Schools, Brigadier General Oliver P. Smith, who would command the 1st Marine Division five years later as it cleared Seoul.[20] The 1966 rifle squad manual expanded its treatment of "Combat in Built-up Areas." The 1965 *Marine Rifle Company/Platoon* manual dedicated ten pages to urban warfare.[21]

In 1949 the Marine Corps released its own dedicated urban

warfare manual, *Combat in Towns*. This thirty-eight-page manual contained many of the tactical principles of the 1944 version of *FM 31-50*, but also the more limited role for armor that would change in the Army's 1952 revision of its manual. About one-third of this short Marine manual was given over to a detailed historical example of the 1943 Canadian assault on Ortona, Italy. While the battle description cited several flaws in execution, it did point out that the attacking Canadian forces were outnumbered 1500 to 500 by the defending German paratroopers. Much like Aachen, this was a reminder that the defensive advantages of urban terrain could be surmounted, even if outnumbered.[22]

However, in manuals for larger or more specialized USMC units the coverage of urban warfare dropped off sharply. The 1964 *Marine Infantry Battalion* manual did not have a dedicated section for urban warfare. In a section describing a major component of the battalion's firepower, the 106mm recoilless rifle, which would play a key role at Hue, no reference was made to its possible utility in city fighting.[23] The 1964 580-page manual *Field Artillery Support* contained only one page on urban warfare, and the 1966 manual titled *Air Support* contained special sections for deserts, mountains, jungles, and cold weather, but no section for urban terrain.[24] The 1965 300-page manual on *Tank Employment* did a little better with a four-page section on urban operations, which it described as a fight better suited to infantry.[25] The manual for engineering operations contained a brief one-page section on urban operations, instructing the reader to see the Army's *FM 31-50* for "additional information," another example of the influence of Army urban warfare doctrine on the Marine Corps.[26] When Lt. Col. Ernie Cheatham realized that he and his battalion were shortly to deploy to Hue, he conducted a crash review of field manuals at his command post on urban warfare, and the Army's *FM 31-50* appears to have been on his reading list.[27]

Hammel, in his two books on Hue, states that the USMC had

not analyzed the urban warfare lessons from World War II, and by the time of the Vietnam War had "virtually cut" urban warfare training from its Vietnam-era training, while having "no plan, no doctrine, not even a concept" when it came to urban warfare. While he appears to be correct with regard to training, his comments on doctrine are incorrect.[28] Raymond Murray, one of the Marine regimental commanders at Seoul, stated after the battle that he had undergone some urban warfare training, but characterized it as an exposure to the theory rather than "any real practice."[29]

Significant real world experience was not available, outside of the battles for Seoul and Hue, to make up for the shortfalls in Marine urban training. No major urban battles involved the Marines from after Seoul up until Hue, and there was just one urban deployment of note. A peak strength of over eight thousand Marines served over 1965–1966 in Santo Domingo, the capital city of the Dominican Republic. Their mission was to quell fighting between various sub-national groups. A study commissioned by the Department of Defense described many lessons from that deployment that would echo those from Hue, although the fighting in Santo Domingo was far less intense. One example is the study's reference to civilian road maps, gathered from gas stations, as a key source of information. The Marines in Hue would avail themselves of the same source. Although the study was completed after Hue, it is possible the Marines who were in Santo Domingo passed on their insights to others in the Marine Corps.[30]

For both services, there does not appear to have been any strong desire to redeploy those with urban warfare experience to major urban battles after World War II. This may be another indicator of Marine Corps and US Army apathy toward urban warfare, or at least a sense that it did not require significant special expertise or preparation. John Corley, a battalion commander at Aachen, was in Korea when Army and Marine units landed at Inchon and drove on Seoul. However, he was acting as a regimental commander in the Pusan Perimeter at the time, having flown in as an emergency replacement for another commander, who had been wounded.[31] Robert H. Barrow, a captain at Seoul who drove his company deep into Yongdungpo, unhinging the enemy defense of that key suburb, was in Vietnam at the time of Hue. Then-Colonel Barrow was commander of the 9th Marine Regiment, which did not take part in Hue.[32] Lieutenant Colonel Murray, a Marine regimental commander at Seoul, was also in Vietnam at the time of Hue, as the Deputy Commander of III Marine Amphibious Force, a parent unit to the Marine battalions in Hue. However, then-Major General Murray returned to the United States the same month (February 1968) as the battle for Hue.[33]

It was in this setting of doctrinal evolution but little else that the battles for Seoul and Hue took place. Both of these Asian cities acted as transportation hubs and held special political or cultural significance in their respective countries. While driven by similar ideological motives, the opponents of American forces at Seoul and Hue would differ in force size, type of force, objective, and tactics employed to defend each city. This mix of variables would test the US Marine Corps' assumptions and preparations for urban warfare.

Chapter 5

Seoul-September 1950

eneral Douglas MacArthur's bold Inchon landings on 15 September 1950 were but a means to an end. The true objective of Operation CHROMITE was Seoul, as its capture would simultaneously cut off the bulk of the North Korean People's Army (NKPA) in the south from its primary supply hub and its principal escape route back north. An added incentive, especially for someone with MacArthur's flair for publicity, was the notoriety of recapturing an allied capital city.

Most of the defenders of Seoul were North Korean units that had been recently assembled, with little experience or training for the rank and file. Some of these units were leavened with experienced officers, and a few other units rushed up from the south. However, the caliber of most of these defending forces was not the same as those NKPA units that had crossed the 38th parallel four months earlier.

Unlike Aachen and Manila, which involved forces seasoned by several years of war, US forces at Seoul were a hastily assembled collection of units that included some personnel with World War II combat experience, but many without. Another difference from the two World War II battles was the reduced level of effort by US commanders to seal off the city. Unlike the combination of skill and luck that allowed American forces to avoid the primary enemy defensive positions guarding Aachen and Manila, the primary American thrust into Seoul would run headlong into the primary NKPA defensive position holding it.

However, the essence of the military problem was the same: a major urban area that needed to be captured from enemy forces. The particulars stressed the American military's urban combat capabilities in some new ways, although the core objectives were the same: capture of the city in a timely manner and at a reasonable cost. The battle for Seoul would give insights into how the US Marine Corps could perform in a major urban battle and the degree to which lessons were learned from World War II.

Operational Context

As Commander-in-Chief Far East Command, MacArthur saw August 1950 as time for a bold and decisive counterblow in Korea, one he thought should happen at Inchon.[1] In its attempt to push the United Nations forces off the peninsula, the NKPA had driven most of its forces deep into the south, leaving only scattered rear area units to guard the lines of communication needed to support those southern forces. Inchon was the second largest port in Korea, second only to Pusan, and more importantly, it was only twenty miles from Seoul. Seoul was the key because it was the rail and road hub for central Korea, and MacArthur called its capture "the primary purpose" of the Inchon landings.[2] Most of the north-south and east-west railroads and highways went through the city. MacArthur planned to follow up the surprise landing at Inchon with a rapid advance on Seoul. Its recapture would make the North Korean deployments in the south unsustainable, and better yet, offer the possibility of cutting them off and destroying them completely.[3] Furthermore, Kimpo airfield, between Inchon and Seoul, was the best in all of Korea.[4]

Gathering the needed troops for the landings was challenging for a US military that just a few months earlier had been on a peace-time footing. MacArthur set up a new organization for the landings that was independent from the other forces in Korea: X Corps. He assigned his own chief of staff, Maj. Gen. Edward Almond, as commander. X Corps' headquarters became operational on 31 August, just fifteen days before the landings.[5] The United States Marine Corps (USMC) was the primary supplier of ground forces for this amphibious assault. The 1st Marine Division was composed of the 5th Marine Regiment (already in Korea), the 1st Marine Regiment (assembled in the United States) under the command of the legendary Col. Lewis "Chesty" Puller, and the 7th Marine Regiment (assembled from Marine units in and out of the United States). In addition to this core of three infantry regiments, the 1st Marine Division had an artillery regiment (11th Marine Artillery Regiment), a tank battalion (1st Marine Tank Battalion) and assorted other units. MacArthur augmented these Marine forces with the Army's 7th Infantry Division, to cover the southern flank of the drive on Seoul, and two South Korean regiments.[6]

The Inchon landings began on the morning of 15 September, with elements of the 1st and 5th Marines, and the largest naval force assembled since World War II: four aircraft carriers, two escort carriers, six cruisers, and thirty-three destroyers. While there were some modest difficulties with locating landing beaches and friendly fire, the landings were a success, perhaps exceeding even MacArthur's expectations. Despite considerable risk, MacArthur's plan to assault directly into a city paid off, as on day one US forces held a major port facility.[7]

The drive inland was rapid for the first several days, beginning to cross the approximately twenty miles separating Inchon from Seoul. NKPA resistance was scattered and disorganized. The North Koreans mounted a few significant counterattacks, but these were either broken up by US air attacks, or impaled on the defensive positions Marine units set up nightly as they halted. The 5th Marines advanced eastward in parallel with the 1st Marines, with the latter to the south, advancing along the Inchon–Seoul highway. In these first few days both carrier-based aircraft (Marine and Navy) and naval gunfire support greatly aided the advance. Halfway to Seoul, before crossing the Han River, the 5th Marines angled to the northeast, securing Kimpo airfield by the morning of 18 September (see Map 5-1).[8] Kimpo would prove key to subsequent operations, as a forward base for close support aircraft and for flying in supplies directly from Japan. After capturing Kimpo, the 5th Marines pushed on to a crossing point on the Han, approximately eight miles northwest of Seoul. They crossed on the morning of 20 September, in amphibious tractors (LVTs), amphibious trucks (DUKWs), and motorized barges, and then turned southeast toward Seoul.[9]

The first major hurdle for the 1st Marines was an industrial suburb of Seoul called Yongdungpo, located to the southwest of Seoul itself, with the Han River in between. The Marines dealt with it separately from the rest of the city, taking the suburb in heavy fighting over 21 and 22 September that required all three battalions of the regiment. Between Yongdungpo and Seoul were the remains of three bridges across the Han, but each was heavily damaged so they were not a viable entrance into the city.[10] On 24 September the 1st Marines crossed the Han just north of Yongdungpo, and then pivoted right to form up on the right flank of the 5th Marines for the drive into Seoul.[11]

The 5th Marines had encountered even stronger resistance northwest of Seoul, in a string of hills shielding the northwestern edge of the city, where the NKPA had chosen to place its main line of resistance. Marine after-action reports praised the quality of the NKPA field fortifications on these hills, and the tenacity with which the North Korean forces held their ground. Even with heavy air and artillery support (naval gunfire support now being out of range[12]), and several battalions of Korean marines, the 5th Marines needed four days to clear the hill mass. Losses for the

5th Marines were heavy, and the hills would not be fully cleared until 25 September.[13] The ferocity of the fighting was evident in the experience of one Marine infantry company, which suffered 178 casualties out of 206 men in one day. The few men remaining

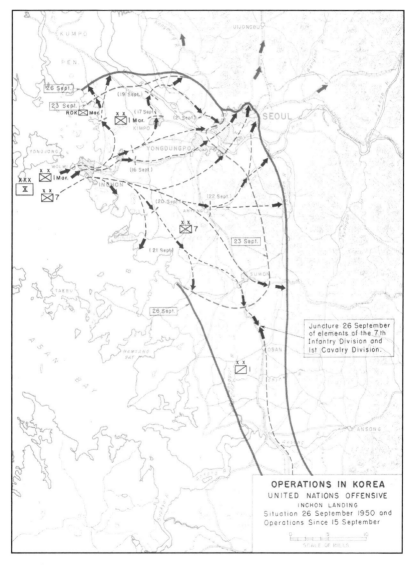

Map 5-1: Operations in Korea—United Nations Offensive. *Courtesy The Department of History, United States Military Academy at West Point.*

succeeded in taking a ridge covered with dead North Koreans. They stopped counting bodies when the number reached 1500.[14] The commander of the 5th Marines, Lieutenant Colonel Raymond Murray, described the battle for that high ground as more difficult than the fighting in Seoul. "Once we got past those two hills, we didn't have all that much difficulty in the city itself."[15]

Around this time the two supporting drives of the operation came into play. The 7th Infantry Division's (US Army) 32nd Infantry Regiment and the 1st Marine Division's 7th Marine Regiment both arrived in Inchon several days after the initial landings, simply because they were not available earlier. While roughly equal in size to the two USMC regiments driving on the city itself, planners decided their later arrival better suited them for supporting roles. The mission of the 32nd Infantry Regiment was to relieve the 1st Marines south of the Inchon–Seoul highway and guard against any NKPA thrusts northward from the Pusan perimeter, sealing off Seoul from the south. Planners recognized that once the threat to Seoul became clear, the NKPA might drive northward toward Seoul with significant forces. By 24 September the 32nd Infantry had cleared the south bank of the Han immediately below Seoul. The 7th Marines crossed the Han on 23 September at the same point as the 5th Marines. The 7th Marines then drove due east, across the hills north of Seoul, to deny that terrain as either an escape route or reinforcement avenue for the NKPA.[16]

By 25 September all three infantry regiments of the 1st Marine Division were in a line, north of the Han, near the western edge of the city. The south bank of the Han was clear, allowing X Corps to place several artillery battalions there, ready to support operations in the city.[17] Lastly, the 32nd Infantry Regiment was ready south of the city. It had taken ten days, but the final assault was set. Map 5-1 gives an overview of the two Marine thrusts toward the city as of 23 and 26 September, the 5th Marines crossing the Han northwest of the city then driving southeast toward the city, while the

1st Marines drove toward Seoul through Yongdungpo. The map also shows the advance of elements of the U.S. Army's 7th Infantry Division south of the city and southeast to link up with other US forces breaking out from the Pusan Perimeter.

As the battle for Seoul was an early battle in the Korean War, the previous experience and training of the participants were important issues. It is unclear what proportion of the US personnel had World War II combat experience, although experience level was less at the lower enlisted ranks and the first few ranks of officers. One officer in the Army's 31st Field Artillery Battalion described "at least half" of the enlisted men below the rank of sergeant as without World War II experience.[18] The Marines began the war with thirty fighter reserve squadrons with 95 percent of their officers with combat experience, although that was not necessarily the ratio for the pilots over Seoul.[19] In some cases the lack of experience related to equipment. The men of the 1st Tank Battalion had only the briefest introduction to their M26 Pershing tanks, as the unit simultaneously received its orders to deploy to Korea and notice that most of its Sherman tanks were to be replaced with Pershings.[20] Fortunately for the Marines, their air and ground units had undergone a considerable amount of training in the previous year that partially made up for the short deployment notice.[21] The units of the Army's 7th Infantry Division were hampered by a massive influx of untrained Korean replacements, as directed by MacArthur, with approximately half the division's manpower being these men. While that infusion allowed the 7th Infantry Division to quickly expand, the Koreans were of dubious value with so little time for US forces to train them (in addition to the language barrier).[22]

The Foe

The Inchon landings apparently caught the North Koreans by surprise.[23] The NKPA units encountered by US forces in the first three days were mostly reserve and rear security forces. However, starting on 20 September, Seoul's defenders began erecting barricades in the streets, and by the time the 5th Marines crossed the Han and the 1st Marines attacked the high ground just west of Yongdungpo, the units they encountered were ready for them.[24]

In their scramble to find units to reinforce Seoul and its vicinity, the North Koreans drew upon uncommitted reserve units pulled up from the south, units on their way to the south but held in Seoul, recently formed units sent down from the north, and hastily assembled local units of whatever manpower they could find.[25] Some of the NKPA units actually consisted of recently drafted South Koreans, being held in the rear until they were needed at the southern front as replacements.[26] At the time of the landings there were 8000–10,000 NKPA in the Seoul area, which later climbed to over 20,000.[27] As almost all of the larger combat formations were in the south surrounding the Pusan perimeter, those available for the defense of Seoul were mostly regimental-size or smaller and composed of inexperienced men. The sole division-size NKPA unit present in the Inchon-Seoul campaign was the 18th Rifle Division, which the NKPA called back on its way south. Prior to the Inchon landings, the NKPA had engineer and anti-aircraft units in Seoul. These two unit types would prove useful in the coming defense, especially the 1200-man 19th Antiaircraft Artillery Regiment.[28]

More capable NKPA units arrived just in time to delay US forces at Yongdungpo and the hill mass northwest of Seoul (north of the Han). According to a NKPA POW the 78th Independent Regiment, one of the units that was to give the 5th Marines considerable trouble in the hills, only arrived at that main line of resistance on 19 September, just one day before the 5th Marines crossed the Han.[29] The primary defenders of Yongdungpo, the 87th Regiment, arrived on 20 September, just as the 1st Marines were ready to attack.[30]

The NKPA at Seoul was largely a foot-mobile infantry force, with modest armor and artillery support, but no air support. Even the more capable combat formations were short of experienced manpower, such as the 78th Independent Regiment, composed primarily of newly recruited students.[31] These raw recruits exhibited poor marksmanship, but the plethora of Russian sub-machine guns, light machine guns, and heavy machine guns at the rifle company level allowed them to dispense heavy volumes of small arms fire.

Inexperience, however, was not the case with the officers, many of whom were veterans of China's civil war.[32] The Marines attributed the stout defense exhibited by many NKPA units to the triumph of fear of the officers over low morale.[33] In one notable case, the Marines even suspected a Russian was among the NKPA officers. "Fireproof Phil" was taller and of lighter complexion than his men, and he continually exposed himself to Marine fire while rallying his troops in the hills northwest of Seoul.[34]

The NKPA's artillery and mortar support was the opposite of its small arms: low volume but high accuracy. The NKPA had a large number of 82mm and 120mm mortars, 76mm field guns, and a smaller number of 122mm howitzers.[35]

> The outstanding aspect of the enemy use of mortars is the accuracy with which they are employed, indicating in most cases that they kept at least one expert for each weapon and that much of their fire is observed, as is the case with their artillery.[36]

And yet, fortunately for American forces, the North Koreans did not mass their artillery and mortar fires. One battalion of the 5th Marines noted it saw no barrage of greater than six rounds in the Inchon-Seoul campaign. The Marines surmised this was because the NKPA parceled out its artillery and mortars in small detachments to infantry units.[37]

The anti-tank capability of the NKPA was significant on paper, but it proved grossly inadequate on the battlefield, primarily due to poor gunnery.[38] The artillery component was mostly towed 45mm guns, towed 76mm guns, and self-propelled SU-76s (76mm gun). The 76mm guns had adequate performance against the lighter armor of the Shermans, but were insufficient against the Pershing.[39] The infantry had satchel charges and a large number of Soviet 14.5mm anti-tank rifles.[40] The satchel charges usually required a risky dash to within throwing distance of the target, while the anti-tank rifles had ceased being useful against anything except light armored vehicles since the early years of World War II. Mines proved the most effective NKPA anti-tank tool, although they were less effective once the Americans realized their prevalence.[41] The weapon with the most potential was the NKPA's own tanks. Armed with a powerful 85mm gun, roughly the equal of the Pershing's 90mm, the T-34/85 (the only NKPA tank type encountered) had the penetration potential to deal with even the Pershing's heaviest armor out to approximately 500 meters.[42] The armor on this variant of the T-34 was insufficient to survive hits from the Pershing's 90mm, however. Several NKPA tank units arrived in Seoul after the Inchon landings, although many of their vehicles were lost in counterattacks outside of the city. The last to arrive, on 23 September, had ten to fifteen tanks, making the total number in the city probably fewer than twenty.[43]

The North Koreans were most adept at camouflage. "Outstanding in the enemy's conduct of his defense was his ability to camouflage."[44] Gun emplacements and field fortifications would make good use of the terrain and natural materials. Their soldiers were also camouflaged in that most carried a set of civilian clothes with them at all times. They would don these clothes to allow for safe movement between positions, for dispersion and escape, and for the infiltration of agents and spotters behind US lines. In some cases, entire platoons put on civilian clothes and then continuing to operate as tactical units.[45] This tactic was effective with the large number of civilians present in Seoul. There were also at least two reported instances where NKPA personnel used American clothing and equipment.[46]

Some of the NKPA tradecraft was learned from the Chinese and Soviets. Red Army advisors had trained the NKPA in mine warfare, and US prisoners of war (POWs) reported seeing Soviet officials in Seoul the day after the Inchon landings (16 September). Prior to the landings, US military intelligence had received many reports of Soviet advisors working with NKPA units.[47] The 1st Marines reported, "The city was undoubtedly organized under the supervision of Russian Officers."[48] A Chinese field fortification manual, captured by US forces from the North Koreans, had sections on urban fortification and how specifically to deal with a mechanized attacker.[49] Also captured was a 1948 Soviet manual (translated into Chinese) titled "Tanks in Battle," which described the defensive use of tanks in urban areas.[50] However, the adoption of Chinese and Soviet tactics by the NKPA was limited. While they had many of the smaller details correct (such as individual camouflage), the NKPA fell short on the larger and more important issues, such as combined arms and flanking maneuvers.[51]

On the defensive, the North Koreans did prove themselves capable of "conducting a most skillful delaying action," both outside and inside Seoul.[52] Their urban barricades reduced the mobility of the Marines, but they could not completely halt the advance of the Americans. NKPA fortifications were certainly extensive inside Seoul, although the degree of integration of their defensive positions is less clear. The 1st Marines reported:

> Defensive positions on the outskirts of Seoul and especially in the city were extensive, well planned and mutually supporting and displaced in depth.[53]

The reference to "mutually supporting" may be describing fortifications outside the city, but only on a local level in the city, as the same after-action report describes independent and usually isolated pockets of resistance inside Seoul.[54]

In sum, while hardly the cream of the NKPA, the North Koreans defending Seoul exhibited selected although important areas of expertise. Their performance in fortification, counter-mobility, small unit leadership, and indirect fire support all supported their operational goal of holding Seoul as long as possible. To this point in the war, the NKPA had shown considerable skill in offensive operations, leaving their prowess in defensive warfare an unknown. The Inchon-Seoul campaign would show the NKPA to have significant defensive capabilities as well.

The Assault

September 25 was the first day of fighting in Seoul itself, mostly by the 1st Marines. On this first day in Seoul, however, Puller's men had to fight without their armor support. The crossing site used by the 1st Marines on the previous day lacked the heavy pontoon barges needed to move the tanks, so the tanks had to drive further north, to the location where the 5th Marines had first crossed. Those tanks made it across the Han on the morning of the twenty-fifth, but poor terrain, enemy contact, and mines all combined to keep them out of the city for the day. Even without that support, elements of the 1st Marines pushed 2000–2700 yards into the city, against heavy enemy resistance, before setting up their night-time defensive positions.[55] Map 5-1 shows the drive of Puller's Marines through the city center.

Delays in the 5th Marines' efforts to clear the northwest hill mass prompted Almond to order the 32nd Infantry Regiment and 17th ROK Regiment (paired with the 32nd) to attack into the city from the south. On the morning of the twenty-fifth, the 32nd Infantry did just that, crossing the Han in amphibious tractors, advancing toward their objective of South Mountain, or Namsan to the Koreans. After driving 3500 yards north, aided by fog and surprise, they captured their objective by 1900, a 260-meter hill overlooking the city. While South Mountain itself was not urban terrain, it was important for the visibility it gave of the entire city. The 32nd Infantry was quickly followed across the Han by the 17th ROK Regiment, which then turned right to capture a series of hills to the east.[56]

The 5th Marines spent the twenty-fifth with split duty, with some of its troops clearing the rest of the hills at the edge of the city, and others pressing into Seoul.[57] The 7th Marines were north of the city, where they remained throughout the battle. X Corps had assigned them a series of high-ground objectives lying just north of the city.

The North Korean reaction to these initial penetrations into Seoul was twofold. First, they started moving forces out of the city to the northeast, apparently thinking this was an option soon to be precluded by the American advance north and south of Seoul. Second, they launched several strong counterattacks against US units in or at the edge of the built-up area. Unfortunately for X Corps, Almond recognized only the first reaction.

Earlier, on 25 September, US aerial reconnaissance had reported a large number of enemy leaving the city to the northeast. This led Almond to conclude the North Koreans were in full retreat, and he then ordered the 1st Marine Division, late that night, to conduct an immediate attack. The 1st Marine Division commander, Maj. Gen. Oliver P. Smith, objected strenuously, but he was overruled by the X Corps chief of staff, and Smith set 0200 (26 September) for both the 1st and 5th Marines to attack.

Just minutes before the attack was to commence, a forward reconnaissance patrol for the 1st Marines reported that a major enemy counterattack was about to begin in their sector. Puller reacted by calling in all the artillery support he could get, and his men spent the rest of the night in what was arguably the largest urban

Marine Corps legend Colonel Lewis "Chesty" Puller, commander of the lead Marine regiment (1st) recapturing Seoul, consults with Marine Brigadier General E. A Craig at a command post overlooking city. *Courtesy of the Library of the Marine Corps.*

fire fight in US military history. The Marines estimated the attacking force as at least a full battalion of infantry, supported by heavy mortars and fourteen tanks and self-propelled guns.[58] Puller's men held, supported by seven tanks, decimating the attackers. It was an indication that the fight for Seoul would be more like that for Yongdungpo than Inchon. Also hit that night were the 5th Marines and the 32nd Infantry Regiment. The attack on the 5th Marines was smaller, but approximately one thousand NKPA troops struck the 32nd Infantry in their positions. One company of the 32nd was overrun before US reserves threw the attackers back by morning.[59]

X Corps had assigned the majority of Seoul to the 1st Marine Division. The 1st Marine Division tasked the 5th Marines with a smaller zone, in the northwest of the city, probably in recognition of the heavy losses they had suffered clearing the hills outside the city. The 1st Marines were assigned the largest sector, a wide strip through the center of the city, starting from the southwest corner and continuing to the northeast edge. X Corps assigned the remainder of the city to the 32nd Infantry Regiment and the 17th ROK Regiment. X Corps attached several battalions of Korean marines to various US units to aid with mopping up and flank protection.[60]

On the morning of 26 September the assault recommenced, and US forces soon learned the rest of the NKPA defensive plan. At most intersections, North Korean forces had set up barricades made mostly of rice bags filled with dirt. These barricades were covered by infantry in nearby buildings, mines in front of the barricades, and often artillery and/or tanks.[61] US troops quickly developed a process for breaking through each barricade, but it was time consuming. The 1st Marines were able to advance 1000–1500 yards to the northeast against heavy resistance that day, while the 5th Marines made "limited gains" against similar resistance in their sector.[62] The 32nd Infantry Regiment, along with the 17th ROK, continued to push eastward, taking more of the high ground between the city and the Han, and inflicting heavy losses on enemy columns moving east of the city.[63]

On 27 September the 32nd Infantry Regiment pushed north and west of South Mountain, to clear parts of the city not in the zone of the 1st Marines, making contact with the Marines before noon.[64] The 5th Marines pressed on in their sector, initially against heavy resistance, but by late afternoon they were mopping up.[65] The 1st Marines continued to advance against a "most skillful delaying action," while South Korean marines mopped up behind them.[66]

By the afternoon of 28 September, organized resistance in the city was broken, with the remaining NKPA forces having retreated out of the city to high ground to the north and east.[67] The 17th ROK Regiment and the 7th Marines had both advanced eastward, although at no time during the battle was the city cut off. "By late afternoon, both Division Commanders reported Seoul had been cleaned up except for very minor sniper fire."[68] Mines were still a significant impediment to movement through the last remaining portions of the city, but the battle was over.[69]

Command, Control, and Communications

Several operational factors made command and control in Seoul difficult. The first was the short time available for planning. The plan for the Inchon-Seoul operation, Operation Plan 100B, was not published until 12 August, and the X Corps headquarters was not operational until 31 August.[70] The short planning cycle led to many ad hoc command arrangements and disorganization in units and personnel. The planning rush kept the focus on the big picture, and left many details to be worked out later. A dearth of intelligence on crossing sites for the Han was a key factor.

> Since exact river crossing sites could not be predetermined, detailed plans for the seizure of Seoul could not be prepared by division until the lower downstream crossing of the Han had been secured.[71]

After the 5th Marines had crossed the Han, Almond met with the 1st Marine Division and 7th Infantry Division commanders, to plan the assault on Seoul. Smith wanted a frontal assault from the northwest to punch through the increasing resistance facing his 5th Marines, with all three of his infantry regiments, while Almond favored attacking the city from several directions. Almond gave Smith his frontal assault, although with a deadline of 24 September to enter Seoul. When that did not happen, Almond ordered the 32nd Infantry Regiment and the 17th ROK Regiment to cross the Han northward into Seoul on the twenty-fifth.[72]

The other crucial operational factor was Almond himself. Having spent the preceding eighteen months before the landings as MacArthur's chief of staff, Almond shared some of MacArthur's over optimism and taste for publicity.[73] When the 5th Marines crossed the Han on 20 September, MacArthur told the commander of the 5th Marines that the NKPA forces would "evaporate very shortly."[74] On several occasions Almond told Smith that he wanted Seoul captured by the twenty-fifth, so he could issue an announcement on the three-month anniversary of the North Korean attack.[75] When the rate of advance was substantially behind this timeline, Almond declared the city captured anyway, just before midnight on 25 September.[76] Almond was strongly influenced by intelligence reports from X Corps reconnaissance aircraft that large numbers of NKPA troops were leaving the city, just prior to dusk on 25 September.

Based on that information, at 2040 on 25 September, Almond ordered the 1st Marine Division to attack into Seoul immediately. "You will push attack now to the limit of your objective in order to insure maximum destruction of enemy forces."[77] Smith was aghast, and he called back to X Corps to explain,

> The inadvisability of attacking at night in an unfamiliar oriental city the size and complexity of Seoul, and in which there was no indication of the enemy fleeing the Division front.[78]

The X Corps chief of staff told him the order stood. The two large counterattacks that hit just minutes before the Marines were to launch their own attack demonstrated the considerable gap between conditions in Seoul and Almond's perception. Almond's diary makes no mention of this episode, with no entries from 1700 on the twenty-fifth until 0900 the next morning. Smith's reaction may have been a reflection of USMC doctrine at the time.[79] A 1949 USMC manual on urban combat states,

> The larger the town and the longer it has been occupied by the enemy, the more thorough must be the preparations for the attack.[80]

The critical difference between Almond and Smith was that the 1st Marine Division commander saw Seoul as a fundamentally more difficult objective. Mirroring his superior's error at Manila, Almond did not think the enemy could or would fight seriously for the city. Chesty Puller's vision for Seoul was more accurate, when he predicted to a news correspondent that the North Koreans would defend Seoul in a manner that would require the Marines to destroy it.[81] Fleet Marine Force Pacific commander Lt. Gen. Lemuel C. Shepherd Jr. shared Puller's outlook, telling MacArthur shortly after the 5th Marines crossed the Han, that the NKPA would fight to the last in Seoul.[82]

Two other significant command errors occurred. Failure to foresee the NKPA main line of resistance resulted in the primary American thrust into the city being delayed for several critical days, during which substantial NKPA forces continued their escape northward. The 5th Marines' drive into the city, from the northwest, ran headlong into the primary NKPA defensive position. From a topographical standpoint, the hill mass northwest of Seoul should have been viewed as a likely major defensive position, even more so given its history as a training ground for both Japanese and South Korean troops. A 1st Marine Division photo interpretation report, dated the day before the 5th Marines crossed the Han (19 September), referenced the "entire area" north of the Han and Kimpo as having been used by the Japanese and Koreans for training, and also mentioned numerous empty defensive positions.[83] Had this hill mass been bypassed to the north, it is difficult to imagine the NKPA defense being as effective as it was. The NKPA forces in those hills might have moved out and counterattacked the 5th Marines, but the Marines proved themselves most capable at handling such counterattacks throughout the Inchon-Seoul campaign. Almond and Smith share the blame for this error, Almond for being fixated on a particular date of liberation, and Smith for insisting on the most direct, but also the most predictable, route into Seoul from the 5th Marines' crossing point on the Han.[84]

The other error was the low priority Almond gave to isolating the city. Almond put too much emphasis on capturing the city itself, rather than denying its utility as a transit point to retreating NKPA forces. He focused on the tactical while losing sight of the operational. Almond assigned the task of cutting off the city to the later-arriving 7th Marines and 32nd Infantry Regiment. This resulted in an escape route out of the city to the northeast remaining open during the battle, when resistance slowed the advance of the first two Marine regiments. Given the resources available to Almond, cutting off the city would not have been an easy task, but the low priority he gave that effort increased the likelihood his forces would fail to trap any NKPA in the city.

The two key regimental commanders, Murray of the 5th Marines and Puller of the 1st Marines, were both highly experienced and decorated. In eighteen months of combat operations in the Pacific in World War II Murray had won two Silver Stars and a Navy Cross.[85] Puller, already a legend in the Marine Corps, had won four Navy Crosses by this point in his career.[86] Prior to Seoul, they had never met, although once it became clear the two regiments would be clearing Seoul side-by-side, Murray flew over to Puller's command post in a helicopter. Helicopters were sometimes used by high ranking officers (e.g., Almond) to visit units forward, but this does not appear to have been the case for units inside the city.[87]

Once inside the city the styles of Murray and Puller differed. Murray used as little artillery as possible, doing minimal artillery preparation and relying on his forward commanders and artillery observers to call in artillery on identified enemy positions. After the battle he was particularly proud, and the South Koreans thankful, that the Korean president's house (the Blue House) in his sector was not destroyed.[88] While Puller had sometimes been criticized during World War II for not using enough supporting arms, in Seoul he used artillery heavily.[89]

Establishing and maintaining contact between units in the city proved difficult at times for US forces. On the night of the heavy counterattacks (25 to 26 September), the 5th Marines were unable to make contact with the 1st Marines to their south, and the 7th Marines just north of the city could not make contact with the 5th Marines to their south.[90] Over the course of 26 September, the 1st Marines made contact with the 5th Marines on their left and the 32nd Infantry Regiment on South Mountain on their right.[91] The likely cause was the shorter lines of sight in the urban terrain, as compared to the usual open Korean countryside. As the Marines moved into the city, the requirement for troops per unit of distance to maintain visual contact would have changed considerably. Apparently they adapted, although with some modest delay.

Marines advance down a burning street in Seoul, accompanied by a M26 Pershing tank. *Courtesy of the Library of the Marine Corps.*

The control and integration of Marine aircraft into the combined arms team was outstanding. On-station Marine aircraft could deliver close air support as quickly as artillery, and were "always immediately available" during the day.[92] X Corps attached Marine air controllers to Army units, and this offered such a radically improved level of support over what the Army units were used to from the Air Force that the Marines had to "conduct a running seminar on how to use air support."[93] In January 1951, the then-commander of the 7th Infantry Division wrote a letter to the commandant of the Marine Corps praising the quality of the close air support given his division by the 1st Marine Air Wing over the previous four months. He cited over one thousand sorties without a single friendly casualty.[94] Marine units were also pleased with the "excellent" quality of their air support, with some targets engaged within one hundred yards of friendly units.[95]

There were no significant command and control problems across service and national boundaries in Seoul. During the heavy NKPA counterattack early on 26 September against the 1st Marines, fire support duties were skillfully handed off from Marine artillery to Army artillery, by lower ranking officers, even though the Army artillery had been previously tasked by X Corps to support another unit.[96] An Army staff sergeant from an Army tank unit attached to a Marine regiment found working with Marine infantry effective.[97] Several battalions of Korean marines were attached to the 5th and 1st Marines, along with some Korean National Police, and they worked well clearing out bypassed pockets of NKPA and stragglers disguised as civilians. Almond attached the 17th ROK Regiment to the 32nd Infantry Regiment, and those two units worked well in clearing out the high ground to the city's southeast.[98] Almond had given extra attention in the planning of CHROMITE to coordination between the 1st Marine Division and the 7th Infantry Division.[99]

Almond's rules of engagement for artillery and aircraft were liberal. Unit reports and personal recollections from the battle make few references to restrictions on the use of firepower. The restrictions that are mentioned relate to unit boundaries, suspected prisoner of war holding facilities, and certain historic structures.[100] The mindset was apparent on 20 September, when the 1st Marines reported, in a rather business-like fashion, they were "leveling the southern part of Yongdungpo."[101] The controls in place were apparently sufficient in terms of limiting losses due to friendly fire as only a few instances occurred.[102]

While there were significant communications problems inside Seoul, they were less so than during the rapid movement phase toward the city. The pace of advance from Inchon was too fast for US communications specialists to lay wire, which then placed a heavy burden on radio equipment.[103] The Marines found their radios too heavy, insufficient in range, disrupted by hilly terrain, fragile, and powered by weak batteries.[104] One exception was the SCR-300 backpack radio, which the 1st Marines called "the best, and most valuable, piece of equipment rated by the infantry regiment."[105] Once inside the city both the 1st and 5th Marines reported better communications, probably because the slower pace of advance allowed wire-laying activities to catch up.[106] Communications with aircraft were functional but still in need of improvement, both for aircraft and ground units.[107] The age of Marine radios was an issue, many having been in storage since World War II.[108] The Marines did encounter two urban-specific communications problems: signal blockage from steel-reinforced buildings, and frequencies that were close enough to commercial radio frequencies that interference resulted.[109] In one case, a company from the 1st Marines spent a night isolated in the heart of Yongdungpo out of radio contact. The company had found a gap in the NKPA line and its battalion headquarters ordered it to press forward. By sunset, when the company had set up on a key hill inside Yongdungpo, its radio's batteries had run out, and it is unclear how much was known about this company's situation by other units. The regimental commander, Puller, stated in an interview years later, that he was unaware of the company's location until the next day.[110]

That same company's night alone provides insight into the quality of American small unit leaders. Its commander, Captain Robert H. Barrow, recognized the value of the terrain his company occupied, and he held that hill all night, despite being out of contact, under repeated heavy attack, and low on ammunition.[111] Barrow was not the only example of high quality small unit leadership in the difficult urban environment. While only minutes from executing orders to attack into Seoul itself, more of Puller's small unit leaders were able to quickly shift into a defensive posture and hold back the powerful NKPA night-time attack of 25–26 September. Marine small unit commanders also proved adept at orchestrating combined arms, with the support and weapons pushed out to smaller units, particularly as was needed for dismantling the NKPA barricades. This level of performance was particularly notable as Puller's regiment conducted the bulk of the clearing operations inside Seoul. Unlike Murray's 5th Marines, which had experience inside the Pusan Perimeter, the 1st Marines had been hastily assembled in the United States just prior to the Inchon landings. They had less time to come together as a regiment, placing greater demands on those small unit leaders. The Marine Corps urban manual emphasized this when it stated urban combat "Will resolve itself into small independent actions; and will place a premium upon initiative and aggressiveness of the small unit commander."[112]

In sum, there were considerable problems with higher level command and control, particularly the decisions made on how to enter and isolate the city. And yet, once fighting in the urban landscape, command and control at the regimental level and below was effective in clearing the city.[113]

Intelligence and Reconnaissance

US intelligence reports prior to the landings included detailed maps of the city down to the individual building level, but the estimates of NKPA troop strength (5000) were almost half of the actual strength (8000–10,000).[114] The reports did describe accurately the rear area quality of most of the units, the presence of anti-aircraft and engineer units, and the limited ability of the NKPA to reinforce the Seoul area.[115] Interestingly, American intelligence personnel gave significant attention in their pre-landing intelligence estimates to the possibility of Chinese intervention in the battle for Seoul, as distinct from an approach to the Yalu. "Although the international implications of such a move are considerable, the possibility cannot be overlooked."[116]

American tracking of the locations and strength of NKPA units during the battle proved challenging, with the arrival of many units into the area, the NKPA's re-designation of some units, and the NKPA's creation of some entirely new units. Many of the captured North Koreans could not describe to their American captors how their unit fit into the overall NKPA order of battle.[117] Despite these difficulties, US intelligence reports during the battle presented a fairly accurate picture of the aggregate NKPA units involved. "No groups of enemy were met that were not previously known and their general positions established."[118] It appears that US estimates on the evolving strength of NKPA forces in the general area of the city were fairly accurate as well. A X Corps intelligence report of 21 September, which estimated 15,000 NKPA in the Seoul area, roughly matched the "more than 20,000" peak NKPA strength given in the 1st Marine Division's after-action report, the difference from NKPA reinforcements arriving after the twenty-first.[119]

Far less accurate were the intelligence estimates on how well those enemy forces would fight. It was true that many of the North Korean units in the Seoul area largely consisted of recently drafted students and farmers, but NKPA efforts to fortify them with experienced officers proved successful. Even after the battle, the X Corps war diary summary did not give these units proper credit, stating these "Hastily mobilized recruits did little to increase the enemy potential in the objective area."[120] Another X Corps G-2 section report, issued during the battle on 24 September, disagrees with this assessment by describing the resistance of these units with raw recruits as "determined."[121] Perhaps the X Corps war diary was reflecting the views of its commander, who underestimated the NKPA before the battle. That sort of misjudgment occurred again a few months later, as United Nations forces approached the Yalu, although with far more serious consequences.[122]

The hasty planning cycle for the Inchon-Seoul operation put considerable strain on the intelligence organizations responsible for providing maps and other information on Seoul. While the X Corps planning staff did have 6400 highly detailed 1:12,500-scale maps of the city for distribution, not all of their maps used the same grid system, and there was no time to reprint them with the standard Universal Transverse Mercator grid.[123] Some American engineers made their own up-to-date maps of the Inchon urban area at a 1:5,000 scale, using recent aerial reconnaissance photos.[124] The Far East Command Intelligence Section produced a detailed terrain handbook for Seoul in mid-August, with information on the city's road network, infrastructure, and structural patterns.[125] Given the rapid pace of advance from Inchon to Seoul, intelligence units had difficulty delivering the relevant maps to some units, and there were reported shortages for pilots and at the regimental level.[126] There were a few instances of units being misled by errors on maps outside the city, and one tank company became temporarily lost in the city, but such events were rare.[127] The overall availability of maps and information on Seoul appears to have been sufficient for the needs of American forces in the city.

The belated recognition of the northwest hill mass as the NKPA main line of resistance was not solely a shortfall in intelligence or reconnaissance, but one shared with generals Almond and Smith. As early as 19 September, before the 5th Marines crossed the Han, a 1st Marine Division intelligence report mentioned the area as a Japanese and Korean training ground.[128] On 21 September, as the 5th Marines approached the hill mass, a 1st Marine Division intelligence report characterized NKPA positions there as "apparently thin and hastily organized" and called the stronger defense of Yongdungpo evidence of it being the most critical front to the NKPA. However a photo interpretation section to that same intelligence report mentioned a "system" of trenches fortifying the hill mass.[129] Just one day later, on 22 September, an X Corps intelligence report would call the defenses there "well-organized," and held by at least two reinforced regiments with the intention of holding their positions.[130] Two days later, on 24 September, the 1st Marine Division called the hill mass the enemy's main line of resistance.[131] Smith and Almond, given the location of the hill mass and its previous use for training, should have deduced an alternative to a frontal assault in case the need presented itself. US intelligence personnel did not predict the "just in time" arrival of the NKPA forces to the hill mass, although such a reaction was sufficiently obvious that both Almond and Smith should have accounted for it in their plans.

Almond also erred when he concluded prematurely, late on 25 September, that the NKPA was fleeing the city. Just before dusk on 25 September, US aircraft reported columns of NKPA streaming northward out of the city, and Almond's G-2 section stated in its report for that day, "Remnants of the defeated enemy appeared to be withdrawing to the north and east of the city."[132] Previously, on 24 September, the 1st Marine Division issued a report stating that, according to an informant, the NKPA was pulling out its regular forces and replacing them with "student volunteers."[133] The next day another 1st Marine Division report cited civilian accounts of

NKPA movement out of the city, and prisoner of war reports that few NKPA remained in Seoul.[134] However, missing were any corresponding reports from the Marine regiments in the city of a similar retreat. Any underestimation of the NKPA's ability to mount effective delaying actions should have been purged from Almond's mind after the 5th Marine's four-day fight for the northwest hill mass. The next day, 26 September, the X Corps G-2 section reports changed their tone to use words such as "determined" and "stubborn" in reference to the NKPA units still in the city.[135]

Air reconnaissance was an important element in the US collection apparatus. US intelligence units did not complete the first "photo mosaic" of the Inchon to Seoul area, in 1:25,000 scale, until two days after the Inchon landings.[136] The tasking of photo reconnaissance missions fell behind the initial advance of the forces moving out from Inchon, but Seoul's status as the main objective meant it was the target of many sorties. Photo analysts reported approximately 250 targets in the city to the Fire Support Coordination Center.[137] The principal shortfall in photo reconnaissance was the time required from request to delivery, a minimum of seventy-two hours.[138] In addition to photo reconnaissance, 720 visual reconnaissance flights were flown in the Inchon-Seoul operation.[139] However, the light aircraft primarily used for this mission were in short supply, vulnerable to ground fire, and needed for liaison duties. The vulnerability of the light aircraft was exacerbated by the need to fly low (often under 2500 feet) so that well-camouflaged NKPA targets could be acquired. Making the task for US aerial observers easier were the obvious general locations of NKPA positions, as given away by the street barricades.[140]

Other significant sources of intelligence on the NKPA were North Korean prisoners and civilians. Captured NKPA soldiers were a major source, with both X Corps and 1st Marine Division intelligence reports heavily seeded with references to information generated from interrogations. Civilians, sometimes walking for miles, passed on the locations of enemy forces, weapons and ammunition caches, and NKPA movements. While generally accurate, their reports did tend to exaggerate enemy numbers. Captured documents were sometimes a source of information, but it was apparent to US intelligence personnel that the NKPA had been careful to leave little documentation behind as they retreated.[141]

> Without the help of R.O.K Officers on battalion level tactically information from prisoners, natives and documents would have been non-existent.[142]

One important shortfall was noted in the 1st Marine Division's after-action report: "The art of reconnaissance patrolling was a largely lost art."[143] While the first 5th Marine patrol sent across the Han failed to discover the NKPA on the far bank, a patrol from the 1st Marines did give critical warning of the impending attack in Seoul on the night of 25 to 26 September.[144]

The skill with which the North Koreans employed camouflage made reconnaissance and surveillance more difficult for US forces. US military police set up checkpoints to screen out North Korean soldiers in civilian clothes moving with the refugees, while attached ROK police proved invaluable at these checkpoints as they could spot hiding North Koreans and "Without doubt saved the lives of considerable American soldiers."[145]

Firepower and Survivability

The effective use of combined arms by US units was central to their success in Seoul, as was the overall emphasis on firepower. The toll on the NKPA was heavy, as the 1st Marines estimated they alone were killing 500 NKPA per day in their push through Seoul.[146] "Tank Infantry coordination was found to be sound except for the limited number of tanks available, this was especially true in the city of Seoul."[147] Engineers were integral to the team, especially in the advance through the NKPA barricades, but they too were in short supply at times.[148] An Army tanker, whose unit was often attached to Marine units, praised how the Marines integrated tanks and infantry. "The Marines used tanks very well."[149]

The intermixing of different combat arms, from both the standard tables of organization and temporary attachments, was extensive. Each Marine infantry regiment had five M26 tanks, twelve 4.2-inch mortars, and twelve 75mm recoilless rifles organic to it, in addition to 81mm mortars and heavy water-cooled machine guns at the battalion level.[150] The 1st Marine Division headquarters also distributed additional tanks, from the 1st Tank Battalion, and engineers to the infantry regiments.[151] US commanders designated the regiments Regimental Combat Teams because of the extensive attachment of divisional support units. As an outgrowth of lessons learned in World War II, US Army units had reorganized to facilitate combined arms. Infantry regiments lost their towed 57mm anti-tank guns and towed 105mm howitzers, but gained a heavy mortar company and tank company (twenty-two tanks).[152]

The effective employment of combined arms by US forces proved sufficient to make up for rather limited specific training for urban operations. The commander of the 5th Marines described the training his men had received for house-to-house fighting as "some training, but not much" and more an exposure to the theory rather than a real chance to practice. Some of this training had occurred back in the United States, in a village mock-up, plus "lectures and blackboard illustrations," and classes held aboard ships of the assault fleet. A lieutenant in the 1st Marines recalled:

> The street fighting that we encountered in Seoul was the first that I had seen and I am sure the first that 99% of the company had seen.[153]

However, the general lack of integration across the various NKPA defensive positions limited the problems caused by the paucity of training.[154]

The small arms and machine guns used by US forces in Seoul were little changed from those of World War II. The M1 Garand was still the primary infantryman's weapon, and the Marines praised its performance.[155] The Browning Automatic Rifle (BAR) was still the squad automatic weapon, with three per thirteen-man Marine squad, and one or two per nine-man Army squad.[156] The BAR's box magazine and light bipod configuration were a good fit for rapid room clearing. The light M1919A4 machine gun was adequate, although the Marines wished for something lighter than a tripod for fast-paced street fighting.[157] The heavier water-cooled M1917 was not brought along by some units, but those that did found it most useful for its heavy sustained fire capability. The 3rd Battalion 1st Marines, which took the brunt of the 25 to 26 September counterattack, expended 30,000 rounds from its ten M1917s in four hours that night.[158] That suite of small arms was effective, although the NKPA could claim to have one advantage in the excellent PPSh sub-machine gun, that was issued widely to its troops—an ideal weapon for urban operations with its fully automatic capability, low recoil pistol-type cartridge, and seventy-round drum magazine (compared to eight rounds in the M1). The Marines repeatedly commented on the high volume of fire NKPA infantry could produce.[159] "Always in great numbers among the troops themselves as individual arms is the very effective Soviet 7.62-mm PPSh 1941 Sub-Machine Gun." [160] US marksmanship was certainly superior to that of the NKPA, but the PPSh at least partially offset that advantage.

The extensive firepower capability at the company level was evident from the example of Captain Barrow's Able Company from the 1st Marines, which spent the night of 21 to 22 September isolated in Yongdungpo, holding a key piece of ground. With a few extra M1917s attached, they managed to hold off an attack by five T-34s and five separate infantry attacks. In the morning they found 275 dead NKPA surrounding their position.[161]

US mortars also differed little from those used in World War II. Marine and Army infantry companies each had a section of three 60mm mortars, infantry battalions had four 81mm mortars, and each regiment had an organic mortar company of twelve heavy 4.2-inch mortars.[162] Target marking with white phosphorous rounds from the 81mm proved useful, but there was a shortage of illumination rounds for the 60mm and 81mm—a high demand item during night attacks.[163] The weakness of the 4.2-inch was its limited traverse. Once dug in, the weapon could respond to fire requests only within a narrow arc, and firing outside of that arc required that the weapon be re-emplaced, which happened during the large counterattack early on 26 September. This delayed the response of the mortar company of the 1st Marines, though once reset the mortar company was still able to fire 700 rounds in support.[164]

Marines advance through a residential section of Seoul. *Courtesy of the Library of the Marine Corps.*

Two new support weapons were the 3.5-inch bazooka and the recoilless rifle. The 3.5-inch bazooka corrected its 2.36-inch World War II predecessor's principal shortcoming, the inability to penetrate the frontal armor on many tanks, giving US infantrymen an effective tool for dealing with the T-34 on their own. Some units found the 3.5-inch most useful in hitting NKPA positions in buildings, as man-portable artillery.[165] Army platoons had one bazooka while Marine platoons usually operated with two. In the southern city of Taejon, in July, US infantry had found the new larger bazooka most effective against NKPA T-34s, destroying eight inside the city.[166] Able Company survived its long night of isolation in Yongdungpo in part because its 3.5-inch bazookas allowed it to fend off attacks by five T-34s, destroying one and damaging two others.[167]

The other new weapon was the recoilless rifle, present in both 57mm and 75mm versions. While the recoilless rifle first appeared in US units late in World War II, for Korea they were a well-established part of the equipment set. Army rifle companies had a section of three 57mm variants, which the Marines did not use. At the Army battalion level, four 75mm variants were present, while the Marines held twelve 75mm variants in the regimental Anti-Tank Company.[168] Despite the Marine organizational structure, the Marines used their 75mm recoilless rifles more as forward deployed direct fire artillery than in an anti-tank role. This was probably because of the many other anti-tank weapons available to the Marines (bazookas, air support, tanks), and the marginal lethality of the 75mm shaped charge-projectile against the T-34.[169]

Armor was essential to the successful advance across Seoul, due to both its survivability and its firepower. On paper at least, the North Koreans had considerable anti-tank capability, although their performance in Seoul was well short of that potential. "The anti-tank weapons employed by the enemy were chiefly ineffective by lack of training, poor coordination, and inaccurate gunnery."[170]

Apparently not a single Marine tank was lost in the Inchon-Seoul operation to an NKPA tank. Over the three peak days of fighting in Seoul, the entire 1st Tank Battalion, only portions of which were inside the city, suffered just fourteen casualties, none of whom were killed.[171] NKPA tanks, artillery and infantry *combined* managed to knock out only one Marine tank inside Seoul—a Sherman lost to a daring NKPA infantryman who tossed a satchel charge on its engine deck. That loss made the infantry covering the tanks more vigilant, and subsequent NKPA attempts to repeat that success failed.[172] The North Koreans were more successful with mines, putting "a few" tanks of the 1st Tank Battalion out of action temporarily. The large amount of rubble in the streets made the mines more difficult to detect.[173] While not lethal, the massive volume of NKPA small arms fire, and fire from 14.5mm anti-tank rifles, did on several occasions cause extensive damage to the outside of US tanks, including vision blocks, antennas, external phones, and anything else stored on the outside.[174]

The survivability of US armor allowed it to be employed extensively by US commanders. Marine infantry regiments had their own organic tanks (five Pershings) plus additional tanks attached from the 1st Tank Battalion (usually one company of fifteen tanks per regiment), on orders of the 1st Marine Division headquarters. Compared to the armor used at Aachen and Manila, US tank crews enjoyed significant increases in firepower. The primary Pershing tank had a larger 90mm gun that dealt easily with the tanks of the NKPA, and its power-traverse turret allowed it to react faster to surprise targets than the hand-cranked turret on the T-34/85. One round of regular armor-piercing ammunition from the Pershing was usually sufficient to destroy a T-34 and kill its crew—Hyper Velocity Armor Piercing ammunition being unnecessary.[175] The Pershing's high-explosive round was also an improvement over that of the World War II 75mm Sherman, weighing over 50 percent more (23.4 pounds versus 14.7 pounds), though ammunition storage space on the Pershing was less, dropping from ninety-seven main gun rounds to seventy.[176] The other tanks brought into Seoul by the Marines were two Sherman variants, one equipped with a dozer blade and the other with a large flame thrower. Both Sherman variants also mounted 105mm howitzers. The dozer variant was used to bury NKPA infantry in their trenches or caves outside the city, and inside it was useful for clearing road debris and barricades. The flame thrower variant was not the same as that used in Manila, but rather a much larger flame throwing mechanism mounted next to the main gun. The flame thrower was not used extensively, although when it was it had great effect—especially psychologically. When there was a temporary shortage of 90mm high-explosive ammunition, the tank units relied more on the Sherman's 105mm. The Sherman had thinner armor than the Pershing, and so was often kept further back from enemy positions, but its large thirty-three-pound high-explosive round was very effective. The overall mix of tanks in the 1st Tank Battalion heavily favored the Pershing, with B Company, for example, having only two Shermans out of fifteen tanks.[177] The 1st Marine's after-action report called tanks "invaluable" and said more should be organic to the regiment.[178]

Artillery support was another area where US forces enjoyed a distinct firepower advantage. The initial advance from Inchon was covered by excellent naval gunfire support, but by 24 September the 1st Marines, 5th Marines, and 32nd Infantry Regiment were all too far inland for further naval gunfire. Even the 16-inch guns of the battleship *Missouri* could not reach Seoul.[179] Marine regiments and the Army's 32nd Infantry had no organic artillery larger than their 4.2-inch mortars, so their artillery support came from the division and corps levels. Within the 1st Marine division was the 11th Marine Artillery Regiment, with fifty-four towed 105mm howitzers and eighteen towed 155mm howitzers. X Corps had five additional artillery battalions totaling thirty-six towed 105mm howitzers and fifty-four 155mm howitzers (mix of towed and self-propelled). Almond allocated these X Corps assets across the Marine and Army regiments under his command. These assignments were fluid throughout the Inchon-Seoul operation, including Army artillery units supporting Marine regiments.[180]

The Marines used their artillery mostly at night, their preference being to use close air support during the day. Night missions included softening up targets for the next day, harassment fires to prevent movement, and reactions to the frequent NKPA counterattacks.[181] The best display of artillery fire support was during the major NKPA counterattack on the night of 25 to 26 September. The 1st Marine Division had three battalions of 105mm howitzers (54 howitzers in total) in range to support the 1st Marines when the counterattack began at 0200. The Marine artillerymen fired so fast that first ammunition shortfalls, and then overheated gun tubes, required them to cease fire. Just one of these 105mm battalions (eighteen howitzers) fired over 3700 rounds that night.[182]

Then, with a mix of skill and luck, another source of fire support emerged. A liaison officer, 1st Lt. James H. Dill, from an Army artillery unit, whose attachment to the 1st Marines had officially ended the day before, decided on his own to remain at Puller's command post overlooking the city. Dill had been following the battle, both visually and over the radio, and when the Marine 105s stopped firing he radioed his home unit, the 31st Field Artillery Battalion, to request they fire in support of the 1st Marines. X Corps had reassigned the 31st to support another unit inside the city for that night, the 32nd Infantry Regiment, so Dill's request constituted a major reassignment, especially since the battalion's towed 155mm howitzers would need to be re-emplaced to deal with the different firing arc. His request was passed all the way to the artillery battalion commander, who asked on whose authority the request was being made. Lieutenant Dill, in an exaggeration of historic proportions, replied that it was the Corps commander's request. Almond was spending the night at Puller's command post, and Dill had earlier heard Almond mention the importance of artillery support for Puller's men in the city. The artillery battalion commander took the young lieutenant at his word and ordered the fire mission accepted. Dill could not locate the first few spotting rounds, in the city aflame at night, until he had the innovative idea to ask for white phosphorous spotting rounds. The white smoke produced by these rounds stood out enough from the background that he was able to correct the fire onto the center of the NKPA attack, and 360 rounds of 155mm high-explosive soon arrived. That fire broke the back of the attack. Puller came up on the radio net and said, "I don't know who in the hell you are, but THANK GOD. Out." The next morning Almond told Dill, "That was some of the finest artillery shooting I have ever seen in my service, and I've seen a lot of artillery." Dill and the two enlisted men working with him received Bronze Stars.[183]

Marine reports cite several other positive aspects of artillery support during the Inchon-Seoul operation. The Korean War was the first opportunity for the Marines to combat test their new Target Grid System of fire direction. While not all Marine artillerymen had been trained on this system, introduced in 1949,

> The system proved to be far superior to the old system in that it eliminated much of the long technical training required of observers and fire direction personnel.[184]

During the night attack of 25 to 26 September, Marine artillerymen were able to use their maps to fire, without forward observation, onto some of the more obvious avenues of attack for NKPA forces. The Marines also found their white phosphorous ammunition most effective, especially for marking targets and creating extensive damage via the fires they sparked in the city. The after-action report from the 5th Marines had this overall comment,

"The infantry was never without artillery support in quantities required."[185] Aside from some relatively minor problems, the artillery support of US forces at Seoul was a key source of their firepower advantage over the NKPA.[186]

Air support was another major advantage enjoyed by US forces in Seoul. The excellent coordination between Marine ground units and Marine aircraft that facilitated the approach toward Seoul also aided the advance across the city. The capture of Kimpo, the best airfield in Korea, gave the Marines an excellent base of operations less than five minutes' flight time from the city center. The primary Marine aircraft was the F4U-4B Corsair, a proven veteran of World War II, which carried a mix of napalm, rockets, one-hundred- to one-thousand-pound bombs, and 20mm cannons. The Marines found napalm to be the most effective overall, even against tanks, in part because of its psychological effect on NKPA troops. The heavy use of the 20mm cannon is evident in after-action reports that describe the aircraft as carrying "only" 800 rounds. Two twelve-aircraft squadrons of Corsairs operated out of Kimpo focused on supporting operations inside Seoul.[187] Several other squadrons participated from either bases in Japan or carriers off Inchon.

The Marines found that six aircraft were the most they could effectively control over a target at any one time, with other aircraft best left orbiting outside the city until needed. Aircraft received their targets from either forward observers on the ground or forward air controllers in light observation aircraft over the city. The weather was good for air operations but the extensive smoke from burning buildings did make some targets difficult to engage.[188] During the fight for Seoul, the number of close air support missions (a target engaged by one or more aircraft) managed by the Air Support Section of the 1st Marine Division surged to the highest level since the Inchon landings—55 percent of the missions that were conducted inside the city.[189] Throughout the Inchon-Seoul operation, the skill of Marine forward air controllers regularly allowed aircraft to engage targets within 150 yards of friendly forces, and sometimes within one hundred yards.[190] US Army units, which were not used to being supported by Marine aircraft, lavished praise on the support they received.[191]

However, unlike American armor, American aircraft did not operate with impunity. US aircraft usually delivered their ordnance at low altitudes, and excellent enemy camouflage required low altitudes for visual identification of targets. These low altitudes, combined with an abundance of NKPA anti-aircraft weapons and the experience the North Koreans garnered from dealing with US aircraft in the battle for the northwest hill mass, enabled the NKPA to successfully down aircraft over the city.[192] Light and slow observation aircraft proved especially vulnerable, prompting US commanders to try substituting F7F Tigercat fighters on

Marine walks past a breached North Korean barricade, typical of the barricades placed every few blocks. *Courtesy of the Library of the Marine Corps.*

several occasions for reconnaissance over Seoul. While more sur-vivable, those aircraft performed poorly in the observation role.[193] The new helicopters were also vulnerable, and after several were lost, Marine commanders instituted more stringent rules on where they could fly.[194] Corsairs had their own limitations, as a peacetime cost reduction effort, ordered by the Bureau of Aeronautics, had removed the armor plating around the aircraft's oil cooler and that order had never been rescinded, making them vulnerable to even small-arms fire.[195] NKPA anti-aircraft fire in the Inchon-Seoul campaign claimed eleven Marine aircraft, resulting in seven dead aircrew. The worst day for Marine aircraft was 25 September, the first day US forces entered Seoul. The commanders of three dif-ferent squadrons, one in a Corsair and two in Tigercats, were all shot down within a few hours.[196] Aside from the vulnerability of aircraft, other problems cited by the Marines were an excessively high dud rate on napalm canisters (30 percent), a shortage of na-palm, too many 20mm cannon jams on the Corsairs, and the need for an additional forward air controller per infantry battalion.[197]

As with any close combat, the infantry paid the highest price. It is difficult to deduce from unit records the casualties specific to Seoul in the Inchon-Seoul operation, as they usually provide breakdowns by units that were only partially involved in the city, or cover dates beyond those related to the fight for the city itself. For both the 7th Infantry Division and 1st Marine Division, their daily casualty figures did spike to their highest levels of the cam-paign over 25 to 28 September, the dates operations in Seoul were at their peak.[198]

For the 1st Marine Regiment it is possible to be slightly more precise, by narrowing the losses they suffered to those from 24 to 30 September, after they were finished clearing Yongdungpo and focused on clearing Seoul. Over those seven days, the 1st Marines suffered 400 casualties as opposed to 453 for 15 to 23 September. While certainly substantial, the 1st Marine losses suffered clearing Seoul were actually slightly less than those suffered getting there. The fight for Yongdungpo, though itself a notable urban landscape, mainly occurred outside the built-up area.[199]

The other major Marine unit to enter the city was the 5th Marine Regiment, a unit that had suffered its heaviest losses breaking through the northwest hill mass. The regiment's 2nd Battalion suffered 281 casualties, its heaviest losses of the war, in the last three days of the hill mass clearing operation.[200] Probably on account of the heavy losses outside the city, the 1st Marine Division assigned the 5th Marines a smaller sector in the city, which lowered the casualties it took in the city.[201] However, this did not spare the lead battalion (3rd Battalion) which Murray sent into the city on 26 September. It was that unit's worst day of the campaign, with one hundred casualties. The only other losses specified in the 5th Marines' after-action report were eleven casualties suffered by the 1st Battalion on 27 September.[202]

If the losses for the 1st Marines (400) are combined with the loss figures available for the 5th Marines (111), one ends up with 511. A Marine Corps history of the battle for Seoul lists total Marine casualties at "more than 700" although that figure appears to be significantly overstated for operations inside the city itself. With no specific reference as to where this figure of 700 comes from, it appears to be based on a chart, several pages later in that history, with daily casualty figures for the entire 1st Marine Division.[203] Two problems arise from using those figures as a source. First, one of the Marine regiments listed (7th Marines) never fought in the city. Second, by including casualties suffered on the twenty-fifth, the heavy losses of the 5th Marines in their last day clearing the hills outside of the city become included in the total for Seoul. A better rough estimate for Marine casualties suffered in the city, given the incomplete figures for the 5th Marines, is 550. The official Marine Corps history of the Inchon-Seoul campaign cites 163 casualties for the Army's 32nd Infantry Regiment over 26 and 27 September, when it was involved in heavy action north of the Han.[204] However, strictly speaking, even north of the river the 32nd Infantry spent much of its time outside of built-up areas (South Mountain not being an urban landscape). That same Marine history credits the 32nd Infantry with clearing 15 percent of the city. Assuming some additional casualties for the 32nd Infantry over 25 and 28 September, and pro-rating those losses down to estimate the number actually lost in urban fighting, the 32nd Infantry suffered approximately fifty casualties in the city. Thus, an approximate figure for total US losses in the city is 600. This compares to the overall X Corps casualties of just under 3500 for 15 to 30 September.[205]

Medical care for American wounded was excellent, with two notable advances.[206] The first was helicopter evacuation. While a crude early rendition of the technology, capable of carrying only one stretcher patient at a time with the patient's feet hanging out the window, the Sikorsky HO3S-1 ferried 139 wounded Marines back to medical facilities during the Inchon-Seoul campaign.[207] The second medical advance had to do with the personnel at these facilities.

> Medical officers regarded the operation as a landmark because of the four Navy surgical teams, each composed of three doctors and ten corpsmen, which went in behind the assault troops on the LSTs.[208]

One US military hospital in Seoul reported treating over five hundred military patients with only one death. Another military hospital near Kimpo lost only four patients out of 1702 admissions.[209] The one notable problem with medical care was a shortage of litter bearers, which required units to divert valuable manpower from other tasks.[210]

Mobility and Counter-Mobility

Although counter-mobility was central to the NKPA's strategy in Seoul, and the 1st Marine Division described "a most skillful delaying action," the Marines proved capable of pressing the advance.[211] Even before US forces entered the city, the North Koreans had recovered from their initial surprise at the Inchon landings, relying on mines to slow the American advance. The 1st Marines and their supporting armor encountered large minefields along the Inchon-Seoul highway, which damaged or destroyed several vehicles. However, these minefields were sometimes not well camouflaged or covered by fire.[212]

That changed inside the city, where the NKPA combined mines with barricades, and kept both nearby and under the observation of infantry, crew-served weapons, artillery, and tanks. The barricades were mainly composed of earth-filled rice bags, spanned the full width of the street, were approximately ten feet high and five feet thick, and emplaced at every major intersection (200–400 yards). Covering forces were usually waiting in adjacent buildings or on nearby rooftops. Any approach by US forces sparked heavy fire from small arms and crew-served weapons.[213] While the main roads in Seoul were wide, paved, and straight, the secondary roads were not. The North Korean focus on the major roads was prudent as many of the secondary roads were also dead ends.[214] Some of the US troops tried exploring the secondary roads and found them too narrow for their vehicles.[215] Even on the main roads, debris and downed power and telephone lines made travel difficult, causing many flat tires.[216]

These mutually reinforcing elements at each defensive position required US forces to carefully combine many elements of their own capabilities to continue the advance. The infantry-armor-engineer team had to work well together to keep US losses low and maintain the pace of advance. Tanks would move forward and suppress the NKPA fire in the area, so that the engineers could advance and clear the mines. Aircraft contributed by strafing and rocketing.[217] Mines were especially difficult to deal with inside the city because they were harder to find in the rubble and debris in the streets.[218] The infantry would cover the armor, so NKPA infantry could not exploit the limited visibility of the buttoned-up tank crews and charge forward with satchel charges. Once the mines were cleared, the armor would blast holes in the barricades and charge through (some with dozer blades), while continuing to engage enemy forces behind the barricade. Some of the infantry would continue to cover the tanks; others would then clear the nearby buildings and rooftops. US troops repeated this process over and over, the average barricade taking forty-five minutes to clear.[219] Sometimes it took longer, and sometimes tanks were knocked out by mines, but progress was steady.[220] Despite the advantages afforded a defender in urban terrain, and the NKPA focus on counter-mobility, the Marine advance across the city still sometimes exceeded 2000 yards in a day.

While Marine Corps doctrine on urban warfare did not specifically prescribe these methods to clear barricades, they were in line with the spirit of the doctrine. The Marine Corps' manual on urban warfare mentioned the utility of "obstacles" for defensive urban warfare and the section on street fighting in the Marine Corps' manual for rifle squads was immediately followed by a section on attacking fortified areas, which it defined as any area where military construction had enhanced the defensive characteristics of the terrain.[221]

The weak link in this choreography of arms was de-mining. While the 1st Marine Division had distributed extra engineer units across the assaulting forces, they were still in short supply. Occasionally the advance stalled while the infantry waited for engineers to arrive. The division's after-action report called for more training of the infantry in de-mining. When armor was not present, as during the day on 25 September for the 1st Marines, the pace of advance was slower and the cost higher. Several times, when dozer blade-equipped Shermans tried pushing through the barricades without the engineers, they were knocked out by mines.[222]

The Korean War was the debut for one radical improvement in US mobility, the helicopter, but this was not a mode of transportation ready for the urban environment. The first generation HO3S-1 helicopters did facilitate the rescue of downed pilots, medical evacuation, and the movement of commanders around the battlefield, but they were vulnerable to small arms fire. The Marines had only eight helicopters (the only helicopters then in Korea), and several were lost to ground fire, resulting in a command policy to minimize their exposure to fire.[223]

The primary counter-mobility tool for US forces was aircraft. Even several days prior to the Inchon landings, US carrier-borne aircraft were roaming thirty miles inland to attack NKPA forces and restrict any early North Korean reaction.[224] Both US Navy and Marine Corps aircraft maintained a continuous cap of twelve aircraft during daylight hours.[225] On 16 September alone US air units reported destroying 200 trucks just south of the 38th parallel, in addition to seven tanks across the patrol zone.[226] The NKPA response to the danger of daylight movement was to reserve most of its movements for the hours of darkness. To counter this, there were a number of night fighters in use (F7F Tigercats and a night fighter version of the Corsair), some flying from Japan, and then later out of Kimpo.[227] C-47 "flare ships," each carrying hundreds of one-million-candlepower flares, sometimes supported night interdiction missions.[228]

At night, the two best US counter-mobility tools were mines and harassing artillery fire. Each night US forces dug in, often laying out mines to protect against the frequent NKPA night-time counterattacks. In the large NKPA attack on the night of 25 to 26 September, the lead T-34 was knocked out by a Marine mine.[229] At times harassing fires were directed into Seoul, as the 4.2-inch Mortar Company of the 1st Marines did "throughout the night" of 23 to 24 September.[230]

Logistics

The firepower-intensive operations in Seoul required large quantities of ammunition, and while strained at times, the American logistical system proved capable of supplying that need. Only two general shortages of artillery ammunition occurred. As the demand for white phosphorous ammunition sometimes exceeded the supply, artillerymen had to substitute high explosive rounds. The Marine 4.5-inch rocket battery was rendered useless because the wrong type of fuses had been brought from Japan, a problem that was not corrected until after Seoul had fallen. This was discovered when a full salvo of 144 rockets was fired into Yongdungpo, supporting the 1st Marines, and not a single rocket detonated.[231] During the NKPA night attack of 25 to 26 September, Marine 105mm howitzer battalions ran low on ammunition, which interrupted their fire missions, before overheated howitzer tubes did the same. Despite those problems, as previously discussed, another US Army artillery unit was in range and was able to shift its support to the Marines in Seoul.

Heavy ammunition consumption by the units in Seoul did draw down the 1st Marine Division's overall stockpile, but the supply flow was "never seriously interrupted."[232] This was in part because Marine logisticians aggressively pushed supply dumps forward. By 22 September several were in Yongdungpo, and the first dumps were set up across the Han on 24 September. While American logisticians established no dumps in Seoul until after its capture, one was on the city's outskirts on the first day of the assault, 25 September.[233]

When local supplies ran low, US personnel usually found a rapid remedy. During that same heavy attack of 25 to 26 September, an emergency request came from the 3rd Infantry Battalion (1st Marines) for more ammunition. The regimental supply dump was moving and could not respond. However, the supply dump for another battalion in the regiment was in place nearby, so several officers using a jeep conducted an emergency resupply from its stocks. They navigated the debris-filled streets at night, directly resupplying the companies in need while under fire. When the regimental dump arrived at 0330 that night, it sent several amphibious trucks full of ammunition to those same companies. Captain Barrow's Able Company ran low on supplies, as it spent a night isolated in Yongdungpo. His men managed by scavenging some NKPA supplies they captured, and then a resupply run of five American tanks arrived in the morning.[234]

Supplying the tanks in Seoul did present some difficulties, but not sufficiently to detract from their supporting role. Even before the 1st Tank Battalion shipped out from the United States, its personnel discovered a nation-wide spare parts shortage for the M26 Pershing, which logisticians could never solve during the Inchon-Seoul operation. The supply of 90mm high explosive and white phosphorous ammunition for the M26 was low at times (although not "critical"), and tank units shifted to using the Shermans with their 105mm guns.[235] The 1st Marines complained that their supporting armor spent too much time away from the front line refueling and rearming at distant resupply points.[236] At times the advance of the infantry halted until the armor returned.[237] The armor supporting the Marine infantry was a mix of organic and attached from the 1st Tank Battalion, and the Marines found the infantry regiments lacked the maintenance capabilities to support these large contingents of tanks.[238] This was exacerbated by delays in movement of support elements of the 1st Tank Battalion across the Han.[239]

Several operational logistical factors were present during CHROMITE, but the tempo of operations in the city was not affected. Some units experienced resupply difficulties because they had not brought their full complement of trucks, driven by shipping limitations and the rushed planning for the Inchon landings.[240] Another constraining operational factor was the Han. The lack of bridging material, at least before Seoul was cleared, required all units and supplies to move across via motorized pontoon barges, amphibious tractors, or amphibious trucks, creating long lines at the three crossing points.[241] Helping matters was the success of US engineers in rapidly restoring at least partial rail service in the

Inchon-Seoul area, and the early capture of Kimpo, into which US transport aircraft flew over 1700 tons of supplies from Japan during the fighting in Seoul (25 to 27 September). US forces also captured significant amounts of NKPA supplies in the advance on Seoul.[242]

Dealing with the Population

During the abbreviated planning phase for Operation CHROMITE, US planners addressed support for the civilian population and stipulated an aggressive schedule for handing over responsibility to the South Korean government. X Corps estimated that 15 percent of Seoul's population, which had been 1.5 million in 1949, would be destitute and require direct assistance.[243] To that end, the invasion fleet carried with it 2500 tons of rice for distribution to civilians. US intelligence reports on the city included the location of hospitals, water system components, power plants, and lists of those civilians known to be hostile or friendly to the United Nations forces.[244]

Medical care emerged as the salient service provided by US forces to the population. In the first few days after the Inchon landings, only the medical facilities of the 1st Marine Division were ashore, and those facilities were overtaxed supporting the injured from the Marines, Army, Navy, ROK, POWs and "hordes of civilian casualties."[245] Also in those early days, the 1st Marine Division set up a hospital in Inchon for treating civilian casualties, staffed with US personnel and some "rounded up" local Korean nurses. US forces had some initial difficulty supporting this facility, but this was soon corrected with supplies carried by the assault fleet, flown in from Japan, and captured from the NKPA.[246]

As US forces approached Seoul, it became apparent to the 1st Marine Division Surgeon that the fight for Seoul would generate greater than expected civilian casualties. He took this matter up with headquarters X Corps on 25 September, stating his estimate of five thousand casualties would overwhelm US military medical capabilities ashore at that time, and that there could be political repercussions should this need not be met. Two days later, a letter from the 1st Marine Division commander to Almond estimated a minimum of five thousand civilian casualties and suggested "urgent attention." Over the next two days, the Marines began establishing two more civilian hospitals, in Yongdungpo and Seoul. Given the overall transport shortfalls for X Corps, few trucks were available to transport civilian wounded, but those most seriously injured were moved in US military vehicles. Out of concern for the spread of insect-borne diseases, resulting from the disruptions to civil services and the number of unburied dead, US forces conducted insecticide "fogging" operations in Seoul and Inchon. Several days before US forces entered Seoul, former city officials were flown up from Pusan on US aircraft, including public health and welfare personnel. Once US forces were inside the city, they established collection points for civilian casualties in the city, and US troops passed captured medical supplies on to the local South Korean officials. In the Inchon-Seoul operation, civilians represented 35 percent of the patients treated by the 1st Marine Division's 1st Medical Battalion, and the medical company sent by that unit into Seoul actually treated more civilians than it did Marines (615 vs. 518). Additional civilians were cared for at the regimental level, although the 1st Marines' after-action report identified the need for expanded preparation for this.[247]

Key to the success in the X Corps support of the population was the rapid transition back to South Korean civilian control, something MacArthur had personally emphasized.[248] The Americans flew Seoul's mayor, police chief, and other city officials up from the south into Kimpo. The mayor of Seoul officially resumed his duties in Seoul's City Hall on 28 September.

> Under direction of the mayor of Seoul a program was initiated to establish the civil police, public health and sanitation, reconstruction of public utilities in-

cluding water and electricity, and to clear, in general, the destroyed portions of the city.[249]

Civilian police units were slow to reorganize, but US MPs augmented with ROK personnel and self-organized groups of civilians were reasonably effective in restoring order in the city.[250] Marine after-action reports, however, noted that many units needed more civil affairs personnel.[251]

The rules of engagement under which US forces operated in the city allowed for the extensive use of firepower, understandably given the operational military considerations and the nature of the foe. As Puller's 1st Marines encountered stiff resistance outside of Yongdungpo, he asked for a free hand in applying artillery and air strikes inside the suburb, and Almond "authorized the burning of Yongdungpo." The 11th Marine Artillery Regiment lamented the lack of proper 4.5-inch rocket fuses as they "Would have been very effective in destroying the town of Yong-Dong-Po."[252] They also directed extensive harassment, interdiction, and supporting artillery fire into Seoul itself. One Marine 4.2-inch mortar company fired 700 rounds of high-explosive and white phosphorous and reported "the burning out of several blocks within the city."[253] Restraint in the use of firepower was occasionally evident, but this was most often out of concerns for the safety of friendly military personnel.[254]

An aggressive use of firepower made sense from an operational perspective. The speed at which US forces captured Seoul had a direct connection to the duration of the war in the minds of the American commanders. To that end, US commanders needed an abundance of firepower to overcome the delaying tactics of a determined defender. A shorter war would mean fewer overall civilian casualties. Puller's mix of regret and determination were evident in his comments to the press.

I am sorry I had to use that stuff [155mm artillery] last night. The Koreans won't forget this in 500 years.

> I'm convinced the Reds are holing-up deliberately to
> force us to use artillery and flame throwers.[255]

Speed was also important for the welfare of the civilians and
American POWs. The Marines received reports from informants
in the city of NKPA atrocities there, including that approximately
50 percent of the damaged buildings were due to NKPA arson, in
a planned scorched earth policy.[256] US units also received reports of
American POWs being killed by the NKPA in the city.[257] A captured
NKPA memorandum "Directive Re Slaughtering of Captives," dated
16 August 1950, complained that too many NKPA units were still
slaughtering captured Americans, and urged that they should stop as
it was no longer useful since the war effort was going so well.[258]

The human cost to the civilian population of Seoul is a moot
subject in US after-action reports. The chaos of the battle and the

A pair of North Korean vehicles (T-34/85, SU-76) in Seoul, probably knocked
out during the initial North Korean nighttime counterattack on the 1st Marines
when the Marines first entered the city. *Courtesy of the Library of the Marine Corps.*

preceding three-month North Korean occupation explain the absence of an accurate count as to the number of civilians actually present in the city, but the number was likely a large proportion of the 1.5 million pre-war figure.[259] Even the official South Korean history of the war avoids the topic. In its eleven-page section describing the battle and handover to South Korean government control, not only is there no estimate of civilian casualties, there is not even a mention of civilian dead.[260] While the duration of the fight inside the city was short, the liberal use of firepower by both sides probably cost considerable civilian life. A gross estimate could be in the low thousands.[261]

Conclusions

The capture of Seoul presented a range of problems, including minimal planning for the fight in the city itself, a hasty operational planning cycle, and some units that were recently created, but US forces overcame these and proved capable of accomplishing their mission. Despite the paucity of attention in the US military to city fighting in the period after World War II, the Marines managed to break through determined resistance at several points outside the city and clear Seoul in just three days. As was the case in Aachen and Manila, the two key drivers behind that success were transferable competence and adaptation.

Carried over from World War II, the USMC's emphasis on firepower and combined arms—in training, organization, and equipment—paid handsomely on the streets of Seoul. The skillful blending of armor, infantry, artillery, engineers, and air support allowed steady progress against the NKPA barricades—which were themselves a blending of capabilities (mines, infantry, artillery, and armor). When the NKPA chose to attack, Marine firepower was even more effective, as when the NKPA's offensive capability in the city was largely destroyed on the night of 25 to 26 September.

Equally as important, the American logistical system was able to provide the large amounts of ammunition needed for such a fire-power-intensive approach. The NKPA did possess some significant armor and anti-armor capabilities, at least on paper, but poor crew quality and training resulted in a decided armor advantage for the Marines.

Unlike the previously examined battles in Aachen and Manila, the Marines at Seoul had no recent experience that carried over into urban warfare. The 5th Marines had just come from the Pusan Perimeter, but none of the American units involved had fought extensively in urban terrain or dealt with the NKPA on the defensive. The quality of Marine personnel, including its small unit leaders, helped make up for that lack of experience. The Marine doctrinal emphasis on aggression and initiative fit perfectly with the needs of the urban landscape. Small unit leaders also contributed greatly to the NKPA's effectiveness, particularly in the hill mass northwest of the city.

Adaptation by US forces inside the city was minimized by the short duration of the battle, but there were still some examples of adaptation. The 1st Marines' combined arms solution to the NKPA barricades was not fully applied until their second day in the city, although only because problems with crossing the Han delayed the arrival of its armor into the city. When the US Army first lieutenant could not see the spotting rounds for the badly needed artillery support during the NKPA night attack of 25 to 26 September, he requested a switch to white phosphorous, which proved much more visible amid the many burning buildings.

The greatest difficulties in Operation CHROMITE were induced by higher-level decision making—the relatively low priority given to the isolation of the city, and the direct approach taken by the 5th Marines into the city. Unlike the commanders at Aachen and Manila, Almond gave low priority to cutting off the city before beginning the assault. Perhaps this came from a belief that the city would fall quickly, but his assigning of that task to his two later arriving regiments resulted in the NKPA escape routes remaining open during the battle. A 1st Marine Division intelligence report, produced at the end of the battle, stated,

> His [the NKPA] determined delay through the city has afforded him ample time to regroup and reorganize his remaining forces for a determined stand along a line of his choosing.[262]

The route into Seoul from where the 5th Marines crossed the Han took them directly into the NKPA's main line of resistance. This both delayed the capture of the city and weakened the 5th Marines sufficiently to relegate them to a secondary role in the fighting inside Seoul. Once by plan, and once by accident, US troops entering both Aachen and Manila had managed to bypass the enemy's main line of resistance.

The battle for Seoul was a decisive point in the Korean War, and probably the most operationally important urban battle in US military history. Of the 70,000 NKPA troops around the Pusan Perimeter, only an estimated 25,000 made it back to North Korea.[263] US forces, mostly Marines, conducted the battle in an aggressive and largely competent manner, ending the first phase of that war. Perhaps most impressively, it was conducted only three months into a war that had shaken the United States out of its demobilized daze. The battle also proved a strong rebuttal to the notion that nuclear weapons had marginalized conventional ground combat operations.

Chapter 6

Hue—February 1968

The battle for Hue began with US and South Vietnamese (SVN) forces in possession of the city. The initial communist assault rapidly captured most of the city, but this chapter focuses on the subsequent four-week US/SVN counteroffensive that followed. During the initial assault there were so few American forces present in the city that an examination of that phase would shed no useful light on American capabilities. The communist forces at Hue comprised both North Vietnamese Army (NVA) regulars and Viet Cong (VC) guerrillas. Hue would also be unlike the other urban battles as US forces could leverage their control of the sea to lend extensive naval gunfire and logistical support. The American forces in Vietnam had benefited from advances in air strike, air mobility, and aerial resupply capabilities since Korea, although those advances created a greater dependency on fixed- and rotary-wing aircraft by the ground forces. That dependency would cause difficulties when the weather at Hue seriously hampered US air operations.

The similarities of Hue with the earlier urban battles begin with the almost purely infantry enemy force, as at Manila. Much like Aachen, Hue was a city of considerable historical importance. It had been a center of political power in Vietnam for centuries, even well before it served as the capital from the early-1800s until 1945. As such, the city was of great psychological importance to the people of South Vietnam, no small matter in a long drawn-out war over hearts and minds.[1] As at Seoul, the enemy forces in Hue were not isolated during the battle.[2] Hue was conducted years into a war, as Aachen and Manila had been, so that US forces were fully on a war footing for this fight. Combat operations in Hue were protracted, as they were in Manila, while the compact size of the city was close to that of Aachen. Hue's peacetime population was similar to that of Aachen; however, while the German city's population at the time of the battle was down sharply due to evacuation orders, the population had swelled in Hue at the time of the battle (approximately two hundred thousand).[3]

Operational Context

The US military had divided South Vietnam into four Corps zones, with the farthest north I Corps including the five northernmost provinces. Thua Thien, and its provincial capital of Hue, was separated from the Demilitarized Zone by one other province. Map 6-1 is a modern map of Vietnam, showing Hue's location close to the coast and far north of Saigon (Ho Chi Minh City on this map). Not shown is the location of border with North Vietnam from 1968, just south of the top edge of this map. The I Corps zone was home to the bulk of USMC operations and by the end of 1967, five of the seven USMC regiments in Vietnam were operating there.[4] January 1968 was a period of confusion in the I Corps zone, as many new US units were moving into the area, straining the existing infrastructure. This influx of new units was driven by General William Westmoreland's concern that the communists were getting ready to launch a major offensive along the Demilitarized Zone in Quang Tri Province. The attack on the large American base at Khe Sanh in Quang Tri that began on 20 January reinforced these concerns.[5]

Hue was an important battleground for both sides. The only

major north-south road in the I Corps zone, Highway One, went through Hue. The city also sat astride the Perfume River (Song Huong to the Vietnamese), another major transportation artery. Although a railroad line went through Hue, the South Vietnamese railway system had not run that far north for years, likely since the days of the French Indochinese War.[6] To the South Vietnamese Government Hue was important, as were all cities, as the source of power for the governing elites.[7] It was of special importance for the prominent role it had played in Vietnam's history. Long a seat of

Map 6-1: Vietnam. *Courtesy Central Intelligence Agency, accessed 16 January 2015*, https://www.cia.gov/library/publications/cia-maps-publications/map-downloads/vietnam-physiog.jpg/image.jpg

imperial power, it was home to the French-designed Citadel, and within it the Imperial Palace. The loss of such a venerated symbol could severely damage the legitimacy of the Saigon regime, or so Hanoi thought.[8]

In attacking Hue, Hanoi sought to attack the status quo and unbalance a war that was looking increasing like a stalemate. The war in the countryside was driving 500,000 rural South Vietnamese per year into the cities and away from communist strongholds, denying the communists access to a key source of manpower. A communist drive into the urban areas would prove to the population that the South Vietnamese government could not protect them even there, spark uprisings in support of the communists in the cities across the country, and would strike at US political will when it was most sensitive, in the election year of 1968. The communist leadership ordered the offensive in July 1967. The plan was to attack Saigon, thirty-nine of the forty-four provincial capitals, and many other urban areas.[9]

The communist offensive itself was expected by some US and South Vietnamese commanders, though many other commanders still looked at incoming intelligence on a communist build-up though a lens of skepticism. The urban focus of Tet surprised US and South Vietnamese forces. US forces had identified two NVA regiments within a day's march from Hue, but the aggregate NVA/VC strength and intentions were less clear.[10] Those American and South Vietnamese perceptions, combined with a desire in both Washington and Saigon to put a Vietnamese face on the war, resulted in a minimal US troop presence in South Vietnamese cities.[11] In Hue there was only a small US presence, at the Military Assistance Command—Vietnam (MACV) compound, which housed Army officers and trainers, a few US Marines, and some Australian trainers.

On the eve of the Tet holiday, and the concurrent ceasefire agreed to by both sides, a key breakdown occurred in the communists' command and control that had major implications for Hue. Some communist units, particularly those furthest south, mistakenly used an obsolete calendar that Hanoi had recently replaced for timing their attacks. The result was a rash of attacks in the far south one day early, on the night of 29 to 30 January 1968. This gave South Vietnamese and US forces critical early warning for the main assault the next night. The ceasefire agreement went into effect at 1800 on the twenty-ninth, but with the widespread violations later that night, the South Vietnamese government cancelled the agreement on the morning of the thirtieth.[12]

Hue's geography played a key role. For NVA and VC forces, dispersed infiltration was a common modus operandi for movement to a battle. Hue's location, just eighty kilometers south of the Demilitarized Zone, made it easier for Hanoi to mass its troops near the city. Hue was split into northern and southern sections by the Perfume River, complicating movement within the city but offering an alternative avenue for movement into it. The city was also near the coast, some twelve kilometers to the east, which allowed for US naval gunfire support. Within the city the dominant feature was the Citadel, completed in 1820 by the French, a 2500 x 2500-meter fort making up most of the city north of the river. The Citadel was modeled after Beijing's Forbidden City, and was encircled by a thick five-meter-high outer wall, a moat, and a smaller inner wall.

The Foe

Unlike the previous three battles in this study, this foe was a mix of regular and irregular troops, North Vietnamese Army (NVA) and Viet Cong (VC). Moreover, those forces had less time to fortify their positions in the city before the American offensive took place. Largely light infantry, the communist assault force was seven to ten battalions strong, mainly under the command of three NVA regiments, with perhaps five more battalions arriving later.[13]

Augmenting the light infantry were sapper and light mortar units. An exact number of communist troops in the city is difficult to gage, as the strength of the NVA/VC units varied considerably over the course of the battle, and the steady flow of reinforcements into and casualties out of the city meant that this was a number in constant flux. Further confusing the picture were the many communist units near but not in the city, tasked with isolating it and acting as reserves for units inside.[14] A South Vietnamese source estimated some 7500 communist troops fought inside the city, the bulk of this manpower being NVA.[15] A US Fleet Marine Force—Pacific report for February 1968 stated the VC losses at just over 1000 killed in Hue, with at least 200 more communist "local infrastructure" personnel captured, while regular troop losses were "nearly 4,000."[16] This force mix during Tet was unusual, as in most parts of South Vietnam VC units composed the bulk of the assaulting forces. This bias toward more NVA troops may have been the result of proximity to the Demilitarized Zone and/or the importance the communist leadership placed on the capture of Hue.[17]

Communist efforts to hold Hue were aided by the prolonged and guerrilla nature of the war to this point. The VC had decades of practice infiltrating personnel, weapons, and supplies into enemy-controlled areas, and they did this to great effect in Hue.

> As judged by the appearance and excellent condition of the enemy troops and their weapons, and the already in-place stocks of ammunition and supplies, it was immediately evident that large elements of the enemy force appearing in Hue on 31 January had been there for some time.[18]

Despite that apparent success a communist after-action report called the infiltration efforts "not complete."[19] Overall logistical preparations included nearby villages, south and west of the city, where the communists had "developed regular and well-organized rear areas" to support their forces in the city.[20] The infiltration of large formations of regular troops into the area around Hue was not without its own difficulties. According to a captured North Vietnamese report, the journey down from the north had sapped personnel strength, due to sickness, and the volume of support weapon ammunition that could be transported by such a stealthy manpower-intensive system was low.[21]

Communist pre-assault intelligence efforts collected extensive details on Hue's infrastructure, government, military deployments, and even items such as the monthly doctor schedule for Hue Hospital. This intelligence included details on individuals, their suspected political loyalties, relationships, behavior patterns, family, and even those who had lost family to communist activities in the past. This intelligence helped the creation of "wanted lists" used by communist forces combing Hue's streets for individuals, in some cases even aided by copies of ID cards.[22] Communist planners used a detailed eight-square-foot model of the city, and laid out 314 immediate objectives.[23] Preparations included the study of previous urban operations, what little there was, by communist forces.[24] However, there were some indications that communist agents in the cities were over-reporting the degree of support for the communist cause, in part because these agents wanted to retain their relatively comfortable assignments in the urban areas.[25] A communist after-action report for Hue complained of shortfalls in intelligence on the enemy situation and terrain reconnaissance, highlighting other communist intelligence shortfalls.[26]

Communist plans were to both use and abuse the population:

> The general plan was to combine attacks with uprising. The people must be strongly urged to stand up, because our armed forces alone would fail to win.[27]

While the grand visions of uprising harbored in Hanoi were never to come to fruition, the darker aspects of political purge would. At Hue, US forces faced a foe that planned, months in advance, to cull thousands of the population, and aggressively use the population to further their political and military aims in the city.

For a primarily light infantry force, the communists at Hue were well equipped. US and South Vietnamese forces captured a wide assortment of small arms in Hue, including AK-47s, SKSs, US M-1 rifles and carbines, US M-3 sub-machine guns, US M-14s and M-16s, assorted Soviet and Chinese light machine guns, and even a few Soviet World War II-era PPSh sub-machine guns. The AK-47 was the single most prevalent weapon, but probably not more than 40 percent of the communist troops were so equipped. The AK was a superb weapon for urban combat, arguably no less effective in that realm than any weapon created since the Vietnam War, and it possessed the advantage over USMC M-16s of a larger magazine (thirty rounds vs. twenty rounds for USMC magazines used at that time).[28]

What the AK did for NVA/VC small arms firepower, the shoulder-fired Soviet RPG (rocket propelled grenade) did for their anti-tank capability. At the time of Hue there were two main variants in Vietnam, the RPG-2 and RPG-7. The latter was newer, penetrated more armor, and was first fielded by communist units in South Vietnam one year earlier.[29] Communist troops in Hue possessed both weapons, although in most cases the weapons carried were probably North Vietnamese produced copies. Accounts of the battle mention communist forces equipped with B-40, B-41, B-50, RPG-2, and RPG-7 rocket launchers. The B-40 was a copy of the RPG-2, the B-50 an up-sized version of the RPG-2, and the B-41 a copy of the RPG-7. The B-50 was rare and not as effective as the other two B variants.[30] While difficult to precisely define, it appears there were far more B-40s at Hue than other variants. Whatever the variant, these man-portable anti-tank weapons were employed by the hundreds, in some cases a third of VC infantrymen were so armed.[31]

Other supporting weapons included recoilless rifles (57mm,

75mm, and possibly 82mm), mortars, and heavy Soviet 12.7mm machine guns. The recoilless rifles were heavier, and thus harder to move, but they were more lethal than RPGs against both vehicles and infantry.[32] The heavy 12.7mm machine gun rounds were very dangerous as they could produce extensive secondary masonry fragments and could easily kill even after ricocheting.[33] The NVA made limited use of 122mm rockets, firing them from outside the city. The communists may have also employed a 20mm six-barrel cannon, removed from a downed US aircraft, against South Vietnamese forces in the Citadel.[34] Communist plans for the battle specifically called for the employment of such captured weapons. Communist forces employed even heavier weapons, using several captured SVN M113 armored personnel carriers, and possibly a few M41 light tanks.[35] These vehicles were used only against South Vietnamese forces, as American units reported no combat actions against them.

An NVA/VC capability employed to only a limited degree was tear gas. US unit reports make references to capturing enemy gas masks and recapturing US tear gas grenades in enemy possession.[36] American battalion reports make no mention of the enemy using tear gas, but Australian advisors to the ARVN reported mortar-delivered gas coming from the communists.[37] NVA/VC personnel had limited access to gas masks, field-expedient masks, and basic treatment options, but there were specific sub-units assigned to mitigating the effects of tear gas.[38]

The Assault

South Hue, below the Perfume River, had a more open topography, with wide streets and more space between the buildings, a reflection of its later construction and French design influences. Most of northern Hue was inside the Citadel's walls and moat. There the buildings were closely spaced with narrow streets. The

Citadel was square, with a corner aligned roughly with each point of the compass. Inside the Citadel was the much smaller Imperial Palace, a fortress within a fortress, along the southeast wall. The only significant built-up area in northern Hue outside the Citadel was Gia Hoi, a wedge-shaped island to the north separated from the Citadel by a narrow canal.

The primary South Vietnamese military presence in Hue was Brigadier General Ngo Quang Truong's 1st ARVN Division headquarters. Most of Truong's units were based outside the city, spread across two provinces, leaving him with several companies of infantry and about two hundred personnel from his headquarters staff, inside the city. The 1st ARVN headquarters compound covered the northern corner of the Citadel.[39] The American enclave was the lightly-manned but walled MACV (Military Assistance Command—Vietnam) compound in south Hue, which sat next to Highway One, just before that roadway crossed over the Perfume on the large Nguyen Hoang Bridge. On 30 January, after hearing of the previous night's attacks, Truong cancelled leave for all of his troops, putting his division on full alert. He remained at his divisional headquarters throughout the following night, until the NVA/VC attack commenced in the early hours of 31 January. His actions, as commander of the most significant defending forces in the city, proved key in limiting the success of the initial NVA/VC assault.[40]

The initial NVA/VC assault into the city achieved considerable success but it was not decisive. The combination of VC units already inside the city and NVA battalions sweeping in from the south and southwest succeeded in taking most of both southern and northern Hue by the afternoon of 31 January.[41] However, communist coordination shortfalls gave the defenders of both the 1st ARVN Division headquarters and MACV compounds time to organize their defenses. The two compounds held out against several attacks in a communist offensive phase that was mostly over in twenty-four hours. These two remaining bastions proved critical to undermining the communist plan for holding the city. The threat to NVA/VC units now came from both inside and outside the city.[42]

The initial US/SVN reaction was swift but unguided by an accurate understanding of the situation. Truong ordered several of his units outside the city to immediately press inward. Some of them made it while others were destroyed in the attempt—impaled upon large NVA/VC units with the mission of preventing just such a reinforcement. On 31 January USMC helicopters did lift SVN airborne personnel into Truong's compound and US Marines into south Hue. Marine truck convoys from Phu Bai (the nearest large American base, ten kilometers to the southeast) brought in more Marines, so that several infantry companies were in south Hue by day's end. The initial agreement between US and SVN commanders, clearly influenced by the ground held by their respective forces, was that the US Marines would clear south Hue, while SVN forces would clear the north (see Map 6-2).[43]

Several days were to pass before US commanders, at Phu Bai and elsewhere, realized how different Hue was from the usual communist tactics of hit and run. Both the size of the enemy force then in Hue, and their willingness to stand and fight, far exceeded initial US assumptions. In those first few days, US commanders outside the city ordered several ill-advised attacks by the small USMC forces in the city, over the objections of onsite commanders, with resulting heavy losses.[44] Aside from those attacks, the US/SVN forces in the city in the early days were largely focused on consolidation, reinforcement, resupply, and assessing the true nature of the fight ahead.

In the next week, with the arrival of several more 1st ARVN Division elements, the SVN forces in the Citadel gradually expanded their perimeter to cover half of the Citadel (See Map 6-3).[45] USMC units in south Hue, now reinforced to two under-strength infantry battalions and a tank platoon, slowly cleared their side of the Perfume.[46] Those NVA/VC south of the river fought

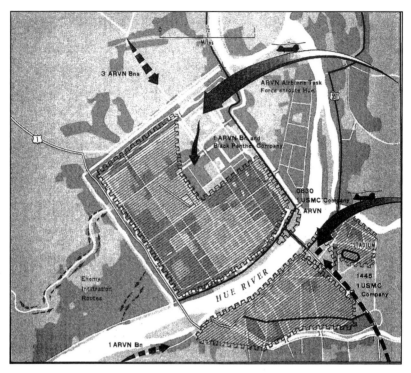

Map 6-2: Early US/SVN Reaction (31 January 1968). *Courtesy Fleet Marine Force, Pacific, Operations of U.S. Marine Forces Vietnam, February 1968*, undated, GRC, p. 11.

aggressively, but their defensive scheme had assumed complete success in the initial communist assault. The Marines attacking out from the MACV compound unhinged that defense. In the Citadel, against less well-equipped SVN forces, the defending NVA/VC made better use of the terrain, eventually halting the progress of the SVN forces.[47] Communist forces coordinated these urban defenses with rural interdiction efforts, which caused serious logistical difficulties for US and South Vietnamese forces.[48] Conversely, the NVA/VC units enjoyed an open supply route southwest of the city, which allowed reinforcements and resupply until the final days of the battle.[49] Nevertheless, as described in captured communist documents, the communist forces struggled with the novelty of urban operations, especially in the areas of command and control and fighting in concentrated formations.[50]

By 12 February the southern portion of the city was clear, and an additional USMC infantry battalion joined SVN forces in the Citadel to aid their stalled advance.[51] The 1st Battalion, 5th Marines (1/5) moved into the Citadel on a mix of USMC helicopters and US Navy landing craft, the latter by way of the Perfume River. The Marines filled in behind exhausted ARVN units, taking over the eastern third of the front (see Map 6-4).[52] It took 1/5 almost two weeks of hard fighting and heavy losses to advance the approximately 800 meters to the southeast Citadel wall. The NVA/VC had set up defenses in depth with well-camouflaged locations, covered most streets with fire, and often held a position

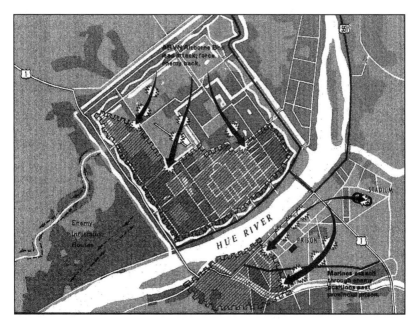

Map 6-3: First Week of US/SVN Counteroffensive (1-6 February 1968).
Courtesy Fleet Marine Force, Pacific, *Operations of U.S. Marine Forces Vietnam, February 1968*, undated, GRC, p. 14.

to the last man.[53] The 1st Battalion, 5th Marines, would not take a single prisoner in its two weeks in the Citadel.[54] With the added weight of the USMC battalion, the SVN mix of ARVN and South Vietnamese Marine units regained some momentum, and they slowly pressed on toward the last pockets of enemy resistance, in and around the Imperial Palace, on 25 February.[55] After the recapture of the Imperial Palace, SVN troops cleared out the last of the communist forces, from Gia Hoi just north of the Citadel's northeast wall, in a brief and rather anticlimactic effort.[56]

Throughout the battle inside the city, US Army units fought their own war with NVA/VC blocking forces outside it. Beginning just a few days after the communist assault, two battalions from the 1st Cavalry Division operated north and west of Hue, with the mission of isolating the city and clearing away any proximate enemy forces. However, the enemy forces they encountered were much larger than expected, and proved too much for these two cavalry battalions. The cavalrymen had to settle for blocking some of the enemy-held corridors, and harassing others by calling in air and artillery strikes on observed movement. Not until 19 and 20 February did two additional battalions join this effort, another from the 1st Cavalry Division and one from the 101st Airborne Division. This larger force was then able to advance to within five kilometers of the southwest portion of the Citadel by nightfall on 21 February, and 2.5 kilometers by 22 February. Thus the NVA/VC resupply and reinforcement corridors into the Citadel remained viable until the battle's final few days.[57]

Command, Control and Communications

With the major influx of new American units into the I Corps sector on-going when the Tet Offensive began, Tet caught the US military command structure off balance. The 1st Marine Division was one of the new units to the I Corps area, and it did not expect

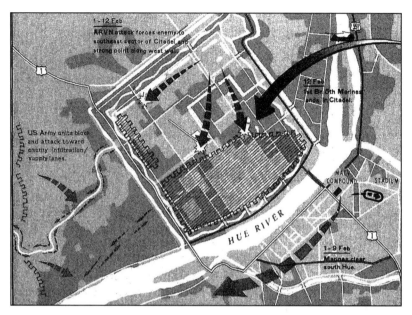

Map 6-4: Second Week of US/SVN Counteroffensive (12 February 1968). *Courtesy Fleet Marine Force, Pacific, Operations of U.S. Marine Forces Vietnam, February 1968*, undated, GRC, p. 16.

to be fully functional until mid-March.[58] The division had a forward headquarters (Task Force X-Ray), commanded by Brigadier General Foster C. LaHue, at Phu Bai (ten kilometers to the southeast), with Hue in its area of operations. While Task Force X-Ray was under the administrative control of the 1st Marine Division, it was under the operational control of III Marine Amphibious Force (Lieutenant General Robert E. Cushman). Lieutenant General Hoang Xuan Lam was the senior SVN commander in the I Corps zone.[59] General Westmoreland realized, about halfway through the battle for Hue, that the command structure in I Corps was overwhelmed and he established a MACV Forward headquarters in the Hue-Phu Bai area on 9 February.[60]

The overtaxed command structure in I Corps did not perform well in responding to the initial communist assault on the city. LaHue and other senior American commanders erred in three ways: they assumed away enemy capabilities, they acted too aggressively in an intelligence void, and they placed too low a value on unit integrity. The assumption that the enemy would neither mass in a city, nor seriously attempt to hold it, led the III Marine Amphibious Force headquarters in Danang, via LaHue in Phu Bai, to order an ill-advised attack into the Citadel on the battle's first day, 31 January.[61] Lieutenant Colonel Marcus Gravel, the senior Marine to have arrived at that point and commander of the 1/1 Marines, was also in charge of those Marine forces in Hue not from his battalion. LaHue's orders to Gravel were to send the bulk of his then small force at the compound across the main bridge to link up with the 1st ARVN Division. Gravel was lucky to extract his men from the Citadel after G/2/5 lost one-third of its manpower killed or wounded. There is evidence that Gravel met with "the senior ARVN advisor" US Army Colonel George O. Adkisson, when Gravel first arrived in Hue, and was told that the Citadel "was in fine shape" but that help was needed evacuating US citizens. Gravel appears to have argued strongly against the attack into the Citadel, although he was overruled by LaHue.[62] Despite the heavy losses of that first day, Task Force X-Ray ordered Gravel to launch another attack that night, this time southward from the MACV compound, to recapture the prison and provincial headquarters. This too struck the Marines in the city as a gross overreach, but their objections to Phu Bai only succeeded in delaying the attack until the next morning. That attack too fared poorly.[63]

The allocation of units to Hue by senior American commanders was piecemeal, with little attention to unit integrity. The first two companies deployed were not even from the same regiment (A Company, 1st Battalion, 1st Marines and G Company, 2nd Battalion, 5th Marines). The 2nd Battalion, 5th Marines was ordered to the city by Task Force X-Ray one company at a time, much to the chagrin of the battalion commander. Two infantry companies from 1/1, and one infantry company from 2/5, never were ordered to Hue.[64] Apparently the fight in south Hue was worth five infantry companies, but not one whole battalion. This practice continued late into the battle, when 1/5 had to begin its assault in the Citadel minus one of its infantry companies.[65] An American advisor with SVN forces in Hue commended SVN commanders for waiting to deploy SVN marines to the Citadel until two battalions were ready.[66]

Compared to senior American leaders outside the city, the Marine commanders inside Hue were more effective. On the battle's first day Gravel arrived in the city (commander 1/1), followed two days later by Lieutenant Colonel Ernest "Ernie" Cheatham (commander 2/5) and Colonel Stanley Smith Hughes, commander of the 1st Marines Regiment and the newly named Hue City Task Force which included all Marine forces in Hue. Hughes was a veteran of both World War II, when he won a Navy Cross and Silver Star, and Korea. He gave very simple mission-type orders to his subordinates: he told them go dig out the enemy and let him know what the regiment could do to help.[67]

Both Gravel and Cheatham rapidly adapted to their new urban battle space, despite their own lack of experience in urban combat.[68] On Gravel's first day in Hue, he realized he needed a safer pathway to the helicopter landing zone, so he had the tanks plough one through some buildings.[69] When Cheatham was at Phu Bai and learned he was going into Hue the next day, he tracked down several footlockers with field manuals, looking for materials addressing urban combat for a hasty study session. It is likely he read both US Army and Marine Corps manuals.

From these manuals he derived that urban operations were about gassing the enemy, maximum firepower, and swift assaults on one building after another. He then ordered his men to stock up on extra weapons and ammunition.[70] Once sufficient Marine infantry had arrived to allow prolonged offensive operations out from the MACV compound, Cheatham and Gravel worked well together. Cheatham in particular was aggressive in being up front with his men. Both Cheatham and Colonel Hughes earned the Navy Cross for their efforts in Hue.[71]

Major Robert Thompson, commander of 1/5 for just ten days prior to coming to Hue, had a more difficult fight on his hands in the Citadel. The enemy there had more time to dig in, and the terrain was more suitable for the defense—with densely packed buildings, foliage, and the wall of the Citadel itself. Perhaps most importantly, Thompson had no room to maneuver such as there was in south Hue. His one option was a frontal attack.[72] Like Cheatham, Thompson had his battalion gather extra weapons and ammunition, on the advice of veterans of Hue he met in Phu Bai.[73] He was aggressive in his use of fire support, and when his battalion was fatigued and weakened by heavy losses after nine days of combat, he successfully changed tactics to include some night attacks.[74] Late in the battle for the Citadel, tensions between Thompson and III Marine Amphibious Group commander Cushman resulted in Thompson's announced replacement, but this was not carried out when 1st Marines commander Hughes strongly backed Thompson.[75]

Rapid adaptation became common for lower ranking officers and the enlisted personnel. This is a credit to the overall command and control environment in those units, that innovation was both encouraged and rapidly disseminated. The young officers and enlisted men quickly learned more effective ways to employ their weapons in urban terrain, and their commanders encouraged experimentation and reinforced success (see later Firepower section for details).[76] The Marine manual for rifle squads stated, in a section on urban warfare, "The outcome of the fighting depends largely upon initiative and aggressive leadership of unit leaders."[77] Several company commanders used tourist maps to guide their advance and coordination with other commanders.[78] A tank platoon commander came up with the idea of pairing one tank with one

Ontos recoilless rifle vehicle, which allowed each vehicle to cover for the other's weaknesses.[79]

Most importantly, both the battalion commanders and the more junior officers kept the men going, despite the heavy losses and a steadfast foe. After nine days in the Citadel, 1/5 had lieutenants still in charge of only three of its ten platoons then on the line, and D/1/5 had but a single officer left. [80] Gravel lost the commander of A/1/1 on the run into Hue and his B/1/1 commander on 7 February.[81] Later to be a major general, Captain Ron Christmas, commander of H/2/5, was severely wounded on 13 February by a mortar barrage, along with several of his officers.[82] Despite these losses, Marine Corps training was shown to produce men and units that could hold together under severe strain.[83] Company commanders at Hue earned three Navy Crosses and four Silver Stars.[84]

American commanders' coordination with their South Vietnamese allies was largely about assigning sectors on a map. The initial agreement between US and SVN commanders was that the US Marines would clear south Hue, while SVN forces would clear the north.[85] However, by 9 February General Truong realized his stalled forces in the Citadel needed help. He requested and received, from LaHue in Phu Bai, Thompson's 1/5 from outside the city. When Thompson's battalion approached on 13 February, to take over the easternmost third of the line inside the Citadel, the handoff from the ARVN airborne was sloppy. The ARVN troops left the line too early and did not inform the Marines, and Thompson's men took significant casualties retaking ARVN positions in surprise contact with the enemy. Going into Hue, Thompson was given strict orders by LaHue that despite working alongside SVN troops inside the Citadel, he was not to take his orders from General Truong, but only from Colonel Hughes, and only SVN troops were to take the Imperial Palace.[86] American forces aided their SVN allies with extensive transportation, logistical, fire support, and air support, though the lack of a single commander directing the battle meant units had to compete for support assets and there was no unified plan for retaking the city.[87] In the "last stages" of the battle, General Abrams of MACV-Forward established a central coordinating agency with enforcement authority at the 1st ARVN division's headquarters.[88] Although the command arrangements at Hue violated the general principle of unity of command, this was more a by-product of the political context of the war than any shortfall on the part of senior American commanders.

When not restricted by weather or the rules of engagement, the Marines on the ground in Hue were supported by a wide range of artillery, naval gunfire, and air strikes (mostly fixed-wing). Airborne forward air controllers guided the majority of aircraft and most strike aircraft pilots did not know their targets until over Hue.[89] Artillery forward observers moved with the infantry companies and Marine spotters directed naval gunfire support on point targets. The two largest problems for directing artillery support were the lack of a single coordinating agency for most of the battle, and the proximity of the combatants. Competition for fire support meant artillery missions were often cut short, before those calling in the fires wanted them to end. There was also some confusion as a result of there being eleven different fire support agencies present in Hue. In the Citadel, the small 800 x 800-meter target area across from 1/5 was a challenge to hit without endangering friendly forces, especially for navy ships that were sometimes over 20,000 yards distant and firing low trajectory rounds. With practice, the artillery spotters became comfortable enough to bring in fire missions to within one hundred yards of friendly forces.[90] Practice also helped overcome the initial slow response for artillery and naval gunfire support.[91]

To simplify command and control, commanders in Hue reassigned the Ontos vehicles, normally a part of the tank battalion organizational table, to be under the command of the tank platoons. In

1/5 in the Citadel, infantry company commanders sent requests for armor support back to the battalion command post. At the battalion command post the tank platoon commander worked out the details, with the infantry, of the target location and ingress/egress routes. Then the tank platoon commander dispatched vehicles to support the attack (often one M-48 and one Ontos). At least in 1/5, the tank platoon commander also had control of the 106mm recoilless rifles mounted atop the small M274 Mechanical Mule vehicles.[92]

For American tankers, operating in a "parceled out" fashion away from their parent tank units was common in the Vietnam War.[93] Other less mobile or indirect fire support weapons were sometimes parceled out to the infantry companies.[94] Engineers were also provided by the 1st Marine Engineer Battalion, working forward with the infantry to destroy enemy fighting positions.[95]

There were instances of friendly fire in Hue, unsurprising considering the proximity of combatants, the non-unified command structure, and the short lines of sight. The three infantry battalion command chronologies mention about half a dozen artillery or mortar incidents, at least suspected as friendly fire, many described as "short," that resulted in one killed and eight wounded Marines.[96] An errant Marine Corps air strike on 26 February killed four and wounded two Marines in 2/5, but this was south of the city.[97] On 4 February CS gas employed by Cheatham's 2/5 drifted into the sector of 1/1, temporarily stalling their advance.[98] On 23 February a Marine tank in the Citadel mistook movement at the battalion command post (in a building) as enemy, and fired both its .50 caliber and 90mm gun at the command post—though without casualties.[99] There were also a few instances of SVN or US forces firing on the other that generated a small number of casualties, but the clearly defined geographic division of labor kept these to a minimum.[100]

At the battalion level none of the three infantry battalions reported any serious communications problems.

The primary means of communication within the Battalion was radio and proved to be very reliable. The Battalion Command Post was constantly very close to the attacking companies hence utilization of messengers to augment the radio, particularly for administrative traffic, was utilized and found to be expedient. Internal wire was utilized to a limited degree as the tactical situation allowed.[101]

Thompson's 1/5 also reported communications with higher headquarters as good at all times, though a "crowded" fire support net "presented difficulties."[102] While the Command Group for 2/5 displaced nine times in February, its Radio Section and Wire section became adept at quickly setting of communications in a new location. Radio whip antennas proved critical in the urban environment, often making the difference between effective communications, and no communications, with the interference sometimes encountered from buildings.[103] The tall whip antennae were not without their drawbacks, as they made the radiomen easy to spot, giving them a casualty rate similar to point men and platoon commanders.[104]

At the smaller unit level communications were more difficult. The standard issue Marine infantry PRC-25 platoon radio, which weighed about twenty-five pounds, worked well for contact with the company level and support radio nets. Some tank crews in Vietnam carried PRC-25s as well, to communicate with the infantry, and apparently at least some of the tanks at Hue were so equipped. While the M-48 tanks had rear fender-mounted telephones, some infantry officers preferred to call them via radio, even though it was less reliable, as the tanks were sometimes too swept by fire for the phones to be safely used. The infantry squads usually had one PRC-6 radio, but this overgrown walkie-talkie was "completely useless" indoors, unable to penetrate structure walls, according to one platoon leader in the Citadel. The Marines adapted to this problem by switching to runners for cross-squad communication.[105]

A Marine CH-46 helicopter offloads South Vietnamese troops into Hue to reinforce other South Vietnamese counteroffensive north of the Perfume River. *Courtesy of the Library of the Marine Corps.*

Intelligence and Reconnaissance

The first shortfall of US intelligence was allowing communist forces to achieve "complete tactical surprise."[106] While US military intelligence knew of two NVA regiments close to the city, the enemy's capability to attack and hold the city was underestimated by American commanders, and his intentions were misread. Moreover, the extensive communist infiltration of personnel, weapons, and supplies into the city itself was completely missed.[107]

> Most estimates of the enemy's capabilities were sadly astray; for apart from indicating the enemy's lack of intent to attack Hue few believed he had the capacity.[108]

One author attributes at least some of this underestimation to a feedback loop from the strategic message of success, coming from Washington and senior US military officers. Despite the existence of some intelligence that an attack was coming, it seemed too fantastic, and at odds with the apparent successful progress of the war. The mistimed early attacks in the southern part of the country did give a late warning to senior US commanders in South Vietnam, but that awareness never translated to any preparation by US personnel in Hue, in part due to communications problems and the all-too-common "maximum alert" messages from US commanders in Saigon.[109]

The US intelligence picture of the enemy force in the city during the battle was also distorted. Bad information, or no information, appeared to be guiding the orders of senior US commanders outside the city in the early days of the battle.[110] This persisted in a MACV monthly summary report, issued almost two months after the battle's end, which stated that by the end of 2 February "only northern portion Citadel complex occupied by en [enemy] forces" when actually the reverse was true, as that was the only part of the Citadel held by friendly forces.[111] The initial US reinforcements sent into the city were small company-size packets, for a fight that eventually engaged the better part of three infantry USMC battalions. Both the overland reinforcement efforts from Phu Bai and the US Army advance down from the north ran into resistance that far exceeded the expectations of US commanders. In a memorandum to President Johnson on 11 February, the Chairman of the Joint Chiefs, General Earle Wheeler, made no mention of difficulties in reinforcing Hue. But in another memorandum five days later he described a "considerable enemy" force outside of the city.[112] The orders in the first few days from Phu Bai, for the Marines in south Hue to go on the offensive, both in south Hue and across the river into the Citadel, baffled the Marines in the city. It was clear to them that commanders back in Phu Bai had no idea how large the enemy force was.[113] The Marines in the city had to feel their way forward, discovering for themselves the enemy strength.[114] Depending on the source, the estimates ranged greatly. On 8 February, when most of south Hue was secured, the 1st Marine Regiment estimated six enemy battalions in the city, plus five more companies.[115] For 11 February, estimates on enemy strength in the Citadel ranged from two to three companies to two to three battalions.[116] A two-page memorandum on 11 February to President Johnson from General Wheeler spent only two sentences on Hue stating, "Sniper fire continued at Hue."[117] The flow of enemy units in and out of the city via the communist-held southwest corridor made it even harder for US forces to gauge enemy strength.[118] A 1st Marine Division after-action report, written in May, complained that accurately tracking enemy strength had been impossible, in part because of the presence of enemy units "not carried in the order of battle."[119]

The communist intent to hold the city was something that only slowly dawned on US commanders outside the city. For the Marines inside the city, it only took a few days of hard fighting to realize the communist jungle shoot-and-scoot modus operandi no longer applied.[120] At least to SVN forces in the Citadel, it was apparent by 4 February that communist forces were planning on holding the city "as long as possible."[121] In case any further proof was needed, on 16 February the 1st Marine Regiment intercepted enemy radio traffic in which the commander of forces inside the Citadel was denied permission to withdraw, despite heavy losses, by his superiors outside the city.[122]

US intelligence was even less aware of the robust resupply/reinforcement corridor to the city's southwest. A MACV monthly summary for February, written in April, made no mention of such a corridor.[123] On day two of the battle (1 February) the Marine commander of Task Force X-Ray, General LaHue, stated, "I don't think they have any resupply capabilities, and once they use up what they have brought in, they're finished."[124] By the time 1/5 had spent several days operating in the Citadel, the communist support effort outside the city was more grimly apparent. A battalion of the US

Army's 1st Cavalry Division, 12th Cavalry Regiment moving southward toward the city, was fortunate to extricate itself from contact with much larger communist blocking forces it encountered, north of the city during the battle's first week. Over 19 and 20 February, US and SVN units in the Citadel found dead enemy troops affiliated with fresh units that had recently infiltrated the city.[125]

The precise location of enemy positions inside Hue was largely discovered through contact. The plethora of cover available gave communist forces many options for their defensive positions, and the only sure way to know was when US Marines took fire. The dense building pattern and narrow streets in the Citadel made for short lines of sight, usually less than twenty-five meters, so enemy movements behind the front line were difficult to observe. Even in south Hue's more open layout, convoys coming north from Phu Bai generally saw only those enemy forces that fired upon them. When H/2/5 secured the provincial capital building in south Hue, they discovered it to be an enemy command post, and only after capturing several enemy positions inside the Citadel did US Marines realize that the dense old-growth vegetation in between the closely spaced buildings often harbored enemy positions.[126]

Detecting enemy personnel was not made any easier by the efforts of the enemy to blend into the population. On several occasions Marines encountered VC posing as civilians, or individuals dressed as civilians carrying weapons and ammunition.[127] One Marine clearing Hue Hospital was only saved because the VC posing as a nun he encountered suffered a pistol misfire.[128] Some VC personnel carried both civilian clothes and SVN uniforms. Screening the mass of refugees was beyond both the skill and capacity of the US Marines, so SVN troops took over the bulk of those duties.[129]

Two important sources of information were the South Vietnamese military/police and the population. While the US Marines received little intelligence from SVN military units, they fared better with individual SVN personnel and the SVN police.[130]

The rapid communist capture of the city had trapped many SVN military personnel away from their units, many on leave in the city. Some of these individuals managed to elude capture, observe enemy patterns for days, and then escape across to US units.[131] The Marines praised the SVN police, citing their apprehension of almost 500 enemy and enemy supporters.[132] The flood of refugees flowing through Marine units was a modest source of information, in part because of the language barrier. The Kit Carson Scouts (former VC) working with Marine units helped in surmounting that language barrier, assisting with prisoner interrogations and processing captured enemy documents. One particularly useful enemy document, captured by 2/5 on 6 February, showed enemy positions in the city.[133]

Other contributing sources of intelligence were radio intercepts, sniper teams, aircraft, and wounded Marines evacuated from the city.[134] On 16 February, ARVN troops in the Citadel intercepted an enemy radio transmission ordering a large attack into the ARVN section of the Citadel, by a battalion-size force outside the city. An American advisor with the ARVN called in massed artillery fires on the route of advance, stopping the attack and inflicting many enemy casualties.[135] Sniper teams, who usually placed themselves in locations with good visibility, could report back to nearby units what they saw. The typically poor flying weather curtailed aerial reconnaissance, and the bulk of fixed-wing sorties were attack missions, but helicopters and light aircraft did modestly contribute to the reconnaissance picture.[136] After the first few days of combat in the city, subsequently deploying Marine units in Phu Bai found wounded Marines there another window into the nature of the fight.[137]

There was a serious map shortage for the first Marine units into the city. Initially, Cheatham had just three detailed city maps to share across his entire battalion, which he had scrounged from US Army personnel at the MACV compound, the local police headquarters, and a gas station. Some of these maps, along with some later received, would number key buildings and landmarks.[138] In some cases, the lack of information on internal building layouts caused the Marines some problems. Better 1:10,000 maps were issued by the time 1/5 deployed to the Citadel.[139]

Firepower and Survivability

Because Hue had a large population, a prominent place in Vietnam's history, and to this point had been largely untouched by the war, Saigon began the battle very concerned about the use of heavy firepower in the city. On 1 February the top SVN commander in the I Corps zone, Lieutenant General Hoang Xuan Lam, requested US forces not use any heavy artillery, naval gunfire, bombs, or napalm from aircraft in Hue—which US forces agreed to, though the Marines were cleared to "level buildings" if needed (with their direct fire weapons). On 3 February the South Vietnamese agreed to lift these restrictions on supporting arms for the Marines in south Hue.[140] In cautioning his 2/5 Marines against excess damage to the city, Cheatham told his company commanders, "Use good judgment, but protect our Marines."[141]

In the Citadel more restrictive rules applied. When Task Force X-Ray ordered G/2/5 across the Nguyen Hoang Bridge into the Citadel, on the battle's first day, the company was told by Task Force X-Ray it could not even have mortar support once across the river.[142] While these restrictions seemed hypocritical to some Marines, who saw SVN A-1 Skyraiders dropping bombs over the Citadel, a careful review of a sortie database by this author for the battle's first week shows the South Vietnamese delivered these bombs (one hundred to one thousand pounds each) either outside of the Citadel, or at its edge—possibly the wall.[143] The South Vietnamese may have not objected so much to the use of firepower in the Citadel, but to the American penchant for applying it on

A Marine fires a M79 40mm grenade launcher at a Communist sniper position. *Courtesy of the Library of the Marine Corps.*

suspected enemy positions (e.g., harassment and interdiction artillery fires frequently fired at night onto jungle pathways).

When 1/5 entered the Citadel the rules of engagement were the same as those that applied to south Hue in the later stages of that fight, except that the Imperial Place was still off-limits to heavy US firepower. The problems encountered by 1/5 on its first day, 13 February, were primarily the result of a poor handoff from ARVN units. On that first day, all available direct fire weapons were used, followed the next day by heavy artillery and airstrikes. One personal account of the battle asserts that very strict rules of engagement were in effect for the first several days that did not even allow tank main gun fire, 3.5-inch bazookas, or 60mm mortars, but other sources present a more credible account that contradicts this description.[144] In Thompson's "commander's analysis" section of the 1/5 Command Chronology he makes no mention of rules of engagement hindering his attack, and that same document contains copies of orders from the 1st Marines to 1/5 on the first day of the assault to "attack utilizing maximum fire support."[145] Other sources that disagree with the "strict rules of engagement" account are the well-researched histories by Hammel and Nolan, and the official South Vietnamese history of Tet.[146] On 22 February, General Lam relaxed the rules of engagement for the Imperial Palace, within which communist forces were stubbornly holding on. The subsequent airstrikes there caused significant damage.[147]

The awful (but not unusual) weather in February, along with initially restrictive rules of engagement, relegated air strikes to a minor role in the battle, something out of character in the Vietnam War.[148] In Hue in February 1968 twenty-four days had cloud ceilings below 1000 feet, and half of those days the ceiling was below 500 feet.[149] That month 1/1 was supported by only five close air support missions (sometimes multiple aircraft) against 185 artillery fire missions.[150] The commander of 1/5 described the shortage of close air support as "sorely felt" by his battalion and said it resulted in increased casualties.[151] Cheatham's 2/5 saw but twelve supporting airstrike missions in the month.[152] SVN aircraft contributed just over half of the total sorties during the battle. US aircraft employed a range of munitions, including CS gas dispensers, though the 1/5 commander called napalm by far the most effective. Although some of the American aircraft did have radar bombing systems, they were not accurate enough given the proximity of enemy and friendly forces in the city.[153]

Artillery, naval gunfire, and mortars played a more extensive supporting role. The early rules of engagement restricted heavy fire support, while the proximity of combatants sometimes made artillery too dangerous to employ, especially in the last days inside the Citadel.[154] Beginning on 5 February, flat trajectory naval gunfire support from the US Navy's Seventh Fleet began hitting targets in the city, from as far away as 26,000 yards. The armor piercing shells of the naval guns proved effective in breaching enemy fortifications virtually impervious to other weapons. The US Navy fired 4780 rounds of naval gunfire into the city, while approximately twice that number of artillery shells was fired by assorted artillery units. The Marine 8-inch howitzers were a popular fire support option because of their accuracy and destructive effect on heavy structures such as the Citadel wall.[155] From within the city, USMC infantry garnered fire support from 81mm mortars organic to the battalions (but sometimes attached to companies), 60mm mortars organic to the companies, and two 4.2-inch (107mm) heavy mortars from the 11th Marine Regiment operating near the MACV compound.[156] The more vertical trajectory of the mortar rounds, short minimum range, reduced blast, and quick reaction time made them useful tools for attacking the enemy closest to US forces.[157]

The most important direct fire heavy support weapons were the M48A3 tanks and Ontos 106mm recoilless rifle vehicles. The first tanks into Hue arrived by a rather fortunate accident, when four tanks from the 3rd Marine Tank Battalion, on a pre-planned transit through the city, joined the initial in route infantry reinforcements. The two M48A3 (90mm guns) and two M67A2 flame tanks would spend the next several weeks as the only heavy armor support in south Hue.[158] Over the next few days, the tanks were joined by several Ontos recoilless rifle vehicles, at least two Army M42 Dusters with twin rapid-fire 40mm guns, and two Army M55 trucks with quad-.50 caliber machine gun mounts. There were also at least two ARVN M41 light tanks in south Hue, but these played little offensive role. [159] Supporting 1/5 in the Citadel, another platoon of five M48A3s from the 1st Marine Tank Battalion arrived there (via landing craft from Danang) around the same time as 1/5, with a few more tanks possibly arriving in the Citadel over the next week (for a total in Hue of seven to nine M48s). More Ontos vehicles arrived in the Citadel as well, bringing the total in the city to ten.[160]

The Marines employed these armored vehicles aggressively. The limitations on air and artillery support left the armor as the most reliable form of fire support for the infantry. The M48A3s carried a 90mm main gun with two machine guns, while the Ontos carried six 106mm recoilless rifle tubes, externally mounted on a light tracked chassis. The Ontos was faster and packed more firepower, but was more vulnerable given its thin armor. Sometimes with a mixed M48A3/Ontos pair, the armor would dash forward and fire on an enemy position, followed by a quick retreat and an infantry assault. Lines of sight in the Citadel were very short, due to the narrow streets and crowded buildings, often requiring that targets be approached to within thirty meters. Some streets were too narrow for the tanks to traverse their guns, and occasionally the tanks could not elevate their guns sufficiently to engage a target. The M48A3's 90mm gun was most effective when concrete piercing fuses were used, allowing for reliable penetration of walls in two to four rounds while reducing ricochets. The tremendous firepower of the Ontos proved "significantly more effective" than other supporting arms, especially against heavy buildings or enemy positions in the Citadel wall. Three rounds were often sufficient to open a four-meter-square hole in a wall, or completely collapse it.[161] Also present at Hue were two M67A2 flame tanks, based on the M48 but with the main gun replaced with a large flame projecting system, although they played a minor role. Their unplanned arrival in south Hue meant many of the specialized support vehicles they needed for continuous operations were not present, and the South Vietnamese were concerned about the danger of spreading fires, so their flame projectors were used only about half a dozen times.[162] The use of man-portable flame throwers was minimal as well.[163]

A key firepower component owned by the infantry battalions themselves were the 106mm recoilless rifles, with eight normally in each battalion's heavy weapons company.[164] Some were mounted on M274 Mechanical Mules, making them better at quickly relocating after firing, while others were tripod-mounted and could go some places the Mules could not, such as the upper floors of buildings.[165] The 106mm rounds were useful at breaking down walls and their backblast could act as a pseudo smoke screen.[166] The 2/5 called the 106mm one of its "invaluable" weapons for urban combat.[167] Over 10,000 rounds of 90mm and 106mm ammunition were transported into Hue during the battle.[168]

Some added understanding of the value of these various heavy supporting arms can be gained from the Vietnamese perspective. The various SVN units in Hue lacked the same complement of direct fire weapons and armor. Australian advisors noted "Small, well-positioned enemy detachments were able to repeatedly hold up company attacks."[169] The few ARVN M41 light tanks available had smaller 76mm guns that had considerably more difficulty penetrating the heavy buildings in the Citadel.[170] A captured communist document assessing their operations in Hue stated, "We suffered heavy casualties caused by enemy firepower and armored vehicles."[171] The 1st Marine Division concluded the NVA/VC "underestimated the effectiveness of supporting arms in a built-up area."[172]

The smaller man-portable weapons used by the Marines at Hue were a curious mix of the old and the new. The infantry battalions that went to Hue had recently traded in their 3.5-inch bazookas, the weapon that was new at Seoul, for the newer LAAW (Light Anti-Armor Weapon). From Cheatham's late night doctrinal cram session in Phu Bai, and information coming back with the wounded of Hue, word passed around that the larger 3.5-inch bazooka was the better tool for this fight (89mm versus 66mm diameter round). All three Marine battalions pulled their 3.5-inch bazookas out of storage and even scrounged some additional launchers from other battalions.[173] In the quest for maximum firepower, the Marines also kept their LAAWs, some Marines carrying three or four. Training was somewhat of a problem with the older 3.5-inch, but the officers and NCOs managed to find enough experienced infantrymen.[174] One Marine fired approximately one hundred rounds through his 3.5-inch in a single day, and there was at least one case of a launcher wearing out to where newly loaded rounds simply fell out.[175] The LAAW and M79 40mm grenade launcher were both used extensively by the Marines, although the heavier punch of the 3.5-inch made it a standout support weapon. Hand grenades, of course, were used extensively, with the Marines frequently throwing them into any space about to be entered.[176]

The small arms carried by the Marines were a key element of their arsenal because so much of the fighting was at close range. The commander of H/2/5 described city fighting as, "It's all fighting that's done within thirty five meters."[177] The 5.56mm M-16A1 rifle (henceforth M-16) carried by the Marines was a substantial advance over the 7.62mm M1 Garand used at Seoul. The M-16's magazine was larger (twenty rounds versus eight), it had lower recoil that enabled more rapid and sustained fire, and it was 20 percent lighter and four inches shorter. Those last two character-

Marines from A Company, 1st Battalion, 1st Marine Regiment leave a church in Hue after capturing it from Communist forces. *Courtesy of the Library of the Marine Corps.*

istics were important for infantrymen scrambling over rubble or maneuvering through tight interior spaces.[178] Unfortunately for the Marines, some of the communist forces carried the AK-47, a weapon at least as good as the M-16.

Replacing the three layered set of automatic weapons from World War II and Korea—the Browning Automatic Rifle (BAR), the M1919 light machine gun, and the M1917 heavy machine gun—was the M-60 machine gun. At a full ten pounds lighter than the M1919 (twenty-three versus thirty-three pounds), the M-60 with its bipod was better suited for rapid assaults and even firing while on the move.[179] Both the M-16 and M-60 used cartridges that were smaller and lighter than those used in the previous generation of weapons, allowing for large amounts of ammunition to be carried by each infantryman. For example, the lighter 5.56mm M-16 ammunition allowed 420 rounds to be carried with the same weight as 184 rounds of the larger 7.62mm for the M1 Garand.[180]

In H/2/5, there was an interesting reversal of the tendency to push support weapons down to the lowest levels. Captain Ron Christmas, H/2/5's commander, decided most of his M-60s should be pulled up from the infantry platoons and kept together to form a company base of fire, often emplacing them on rooftops or at second-story windows.[181] It does not appear this was done across the Perfume in the Citadel in 1/5.[182] This change in the commonly seen patterns in urban fighting may have been the result of Christmas seeing more need for massed fires in the more open street plan of south Hue, as his men dashed across open areas to assault buildings. Each infantry company was authorized six M-60s, residing in the company's Weapons Platoon.[183]

Scout-sniper teams played an important role in Hue. The term sniper is often misapplied, in both primary and secondary sources, to any infantryman (especially enemy) taking singular carefully aimed shots. However, at Hue there were fully trained and equipped Marine scout-sniper teams working with the Marine infantry. They were equipped with 7.62mm bolt-action rifles with scopes, though some sources refer to "sharpshooters" armed with the 7.62mm M14 rifle.[184] The accuracy of the snipers both reduced the risk to civilians and proved highly lethal against enemy troops hiding in the urban cover.[185] Night vision scopes had been employed by US forces in Vietnam by 1968, often by snipers, but it does not appear the Marines in Hue had any. Only one source mentions the use of night vision equipment in the vicinity of Hue during Tet, and this a US Army unit outside of the city.[186]

The greatest difference in firepower for US forces in Hue, relative to earlier battles, was the extensive use of nonlethal gas, which had not been used at all in Aachen, Manila, or Seoul. CS gas was approximately ten times more effective than the earlier generation CN tear gas. The first US use in Vietnam in early 1965 was accompanied with a stated policy that it was only to be used in riot control situations. However, the utility of CS when dealing with enemy mixed in with civilians proved too powerful, and its use expanded well beyond that initial limited role. At the time of Hue, the most important international convention related to chemical weapons was the 1925 Geneva Protocol. However, the US government had not ratified that treaty and maintained that it did not prohibit the use of riot control agents in warfare.[187] Moreover, MACV had issued general rules of engagement for urban areas that encouraged the use of CS "to the maximum extent possible."[188]

All three USMC battalions at Hue deployed CS, as was strongly encouraged by Colonel Hughes, via a mix of hand grenades, man-portable multi-round grenade launchers, 4.2-inch mortar rounds, and aircraft (bombs and spray tanks).[189] The hand-thrown grenades worked well for room clearing, while the 4.2-inch rounds could punch through roofs and fill a structure with CS. The thirty-five-pound disposable E-8 launcher was carried by the infantry as a backpack, and then set on the ground for firing. Its sixteen launch tubes each enclosed a stack of four 35mm CS gas grenades, and all sixty-four grenades could be fired quickly at a target up to 150 meters away, creating a gas cloud within thirty seconds that could cover an area at least forty by eighty meters. An effective area weapon, the E-8 worked less well against buildings with few openings. CS was generally effective at disorganizing enemy defenses but was not decisive on its own.[190] Communist troops in Hue had either standard issue or field-expedient gas masks, along with personnel specifically assigned to aid in the treatment of gas exposure.[191]

On the survivability side of the equation, US aircraft had their access to Hue restricted by the weather: when they could fly into or over the city the low cloud ceilings forced them to fly low, where the principally small caliber communist anti-aircraft weapons were most effective.[192] While no fixed-wing strike aircraft were shot down over the city, a significant number were damaged.[193] Helicopters fared worse, as their slower speed, lower altitude, and vulnerability during take-off and landings all made them more at risk from enemy fire. The precise number of helicopters shot down or damaged is unclear, but the USMC parent organization for many of the helicopter squadrons supporting operations in Hue experienced its highest number of hostile fire incidents since 1965 in the month that operations were on-going in Hue, with 140 aircraft hit.[194] At least two CH-46s and two UH-1 Hueys were downed by fire from communist forces in Hue.[195] More commonly, helicopters turned back due to heavy fire, damage, or wounds to the aircrew.

Despite the intention of their design, inside an armored vehicle was a very dangerous place to be in Hue. While the M48A3's armor was moderately thicker in places than that of the earlier generation M26 that was employed in Seoul, that level of protection was no match for the RPGs employed extensively by the communist troops.[196] RPG rounds could penetrate the tank's armor from any angle out to several hundred meters. These penetrations were small, and the damage done to the tank itself was modest, but the crews suffered heavily from fragmentation sprayed about the interior. The tanks themselves were usually back in operation after an overnight trip to the rearmament and repair facility just blocks behind the front line. The five tanks supporting 1/5 in the Citadel received a total of thirty-four RPG hits, although nightly repairs, and replacement crews, ensured four or five tanks were operational at all times. Of the original fifty-five tank crewmen who went into the Citadel, only eleven were still with the tank unit six weeks later, and on several occasions tanks were side-lined for lack of crew.[197] The RPG threat was not new, as it had been used by communist forces since 1965 to knock out American tanks, and M48s assigned to base defense were often protected by sandbags and wire mesh, but this could not be done for the more mobile fight in Hue.[198] Two Marine tanks were apparently destroyed in south Hue, one when an RPG round detonated the tank's ammunition load, and another that took seven 57mm recoilless rifle hits.[199] The design of the M48A3 included a 12.7mm machine gun (.50 caliber), mounted in an enclosed armored cupola, to allow the tank commander to engage targets while remaining protected. Unfortunately the side-mounting of the machine gun resulted in frequent jamming, forcing the crew to either not use the machine gun or remount it externally, and exposing them to enemy fire.[200]

The city was dangerous for lighter vehicles as well. While the Ontos vehicles in the Citadel survived without loss, likely due to their shoot-and-scoot employment, at least three were knocked out by enemy fire in south Hue.[201] Other lighter vehicles were knocked out, either temporarily or permanently, including several M42 Dusters, M55 quad-50 trucks, and other trucks. The Mechanical Mule did surprisingly well, with its small size and speed making it more survivable.[202]

Of course, the infantry were the most exposed to enemy fire. Discerning the number of USMC casualties inside the city is challenging because of the many partial units involved and the difference in official records between Operation HUE CITY (city plus surrounding countryside) and operations in the city itself. Further complicating matters, some sources report all wounded and others only those evacuated from the city. The best single source for USMC casualty totals inside the city is from a Fleet Marine Force—Pacific report: 142 killed and 857 wounded and evacuated.[203] These figures are widely repeated in many of the secondary sources.[204] However, a tally of casualty figures from the three USMC infantry battalions (1/1, 2/5, 1/5) produces notably lower figures. Between them these three battalions reported ninety killed and 700 wounded—substantially lower than the 142/857 figures given by the Fleet Marine Force—Pacific report. [205] The actual losses inside the city are probably somewhere in between these two sources: perhaps 100–120 killed and between 700–800 wounded. Offsetting the modest inclusion of non-Hue casualties by the infantry battalions were casualties suffered in the city by the attached tank platoons and personnel from other units.[206] The elevated casualty figures from Fleet Marine Force, which do stop at 25 February (when the battle in the city ended), likely include losses suffered by 1/1 and 2/5 as they pushed out south and east from south Hue after 12 February.

A US Navy study of Hue's casualty rates (per employed personnel) found them much higher than those suffered by USMC units elsewhere in Vietnam at the peak of USMC involvement (mid-1968). In Hue Marines were seven times more likely to be killed or wounded. The same study found the USMC casualty rates in the Citadel approximately 20 percent higher, per employed personnel, than in south Hue.[207] In terms of total casualties, SVN forces suffered four times the killed, and three times the wounded, of US forces in the city.[208]

In the case of 2/5, a heavy influx of replacements kept the manning level above 90 percent for almost the entire month of February, though by the end of the month the battalion had seen a 47 percent turnover in personnel.[209] 1/5 fared worse, suffering heavy casualties over a longer timeframe and receiving fewer replacements. By 18 February each of 1/5's four infantry companies was below one hundred effective personnel, out of an authorized 216. When Thompson pulled B/1/5 off the line and sent it back to Phu Bai for rest and refit, on 23 February, it was down to sixty-one men.[210]

The principal causes of these American infantry casualties were enemy mortars and small arms fire. The frequency of enemy mortar fire caused the Marines to often avoid the upper stories of buildings.[211] Engagement ranges were brutally short, often within thirty-five meters, and flying debris and shrapnel caused many wounds.[212] The early generation of body armor available to the Marines (M55 vest) saved some lives, as it could often stop fragments and flying debris, but usually not rifle bullets. Tank crewmen found the vests too bulky for use inside of their tanks, so they generally did not wear them unless dismounted or riding outside of the hatch.[213]

The medical care system for the injured generally functioned well. Marine units emplaced medical facilities forward, close to the front lines in the city itself, and extensively employed medical evacuation via helicopter to more robust and distant medical facilities. These forward facilities displaced as the front line changed, but they were often overflowing with wounded, which in part motivated the extensive use of helicopter evacuation. Eight US Navy Corpsmen were attached to each Marine rifle company, and they provided the initial treatment, directing wounded further back as needed to a forward aid station. The more seriously wounded were then further evacuated back to the Battalion Aid Station by medical personnel driving either trucks or Mechanical Mules.[214]

The substantial casualties suffered by the US Marines in Hue can be linked back to the decision of the communists that Hue would be a climactic battle. The enemy force was large, and it fought with determination, so Marine losses need to be judged in that context, along with the huge number of enemy killed within the city.

Mobility and Counter-Mobility

The first mobility problem encountered by US forces was getting forces into Hue. An extensive NVA/VC interdiction effort around Hue severely disrupted travel on the road network. The principal overland route for US ground convoys to Hue came from Phu Bai, a major US base (with airfield) approximately ten kilometers to the southeast, connected by the primary Vietnamese north-south roadway, Highway One.[215] Communist attacks cut Highway One for approximately one week, starting on 4 February, at a key bridge between the city and Phu Bai, which delayed the arrival of 1/5 into the Citadel by a day.[216] US ground mobility assets were further strained by the occasional need to transport allied Vietnamese forces.[217]

Given the plethora of helicopters possessed by US forces, and the proximity of the large airbase at Phu Bai, "helilift" was a logical substitute for truck transport. However, the weather for the entire month of February made for poor flying conditions (not unusual for Vietnam in February), as did heavy enemy fire over the city.[218] Despite those difficulties helicopters moved significant numbers of troops into the city. USMC CH-46 helicopters brought two USMC infantry companies into the MACV compound over 1 and 2 February, and two companies of the 1/5 into the Citadel over 11 to 13 February.[219] Over two harrowing days at the beginning of the battle, a squadron of USMC CH-46s flew 468 ARVN soldiers into northern Hue, though four of the nine CH-46s involved had to divert on the second day due to damage suffered in and around Hue.[220] Aside from troops, helicopters also carried equipment as heavy as 650-pound 4.2-inch mortars and 400-pound 106mm recoilless rifles.[221]

An alternative route into Hue was via the Perfume River, which was both deep and wide (250–400 meters across) at Hue, allowing large vessel access.[222] However, the NVA/VC interdicted this avenue of approach as well. Vietnamese Marines arrived in Hue on a mixture of US and Vietnamese landing craft.[223] Tanks from the 1st Marine Tank Battalion arrived in northern Hue on US landing craft. Despite the capabilities of the helicopters and landing craft, they could not fully replace the interdicted road network. On 8 February there were in excess of two hundred replacements awaiting transport into the city.[224]

Helicopters played an important role for medical evacuation but additional modes of transport were required. Both poor weather and the danger of take-offs and landings close to enemy forces made ground transport essential. The 1st Battalion, 5th Marines, complained about frequent problems with getting helicopter medevac support in the last ten days of the battle. During this period, "Army helicopters were utilized for the bulk of evacuees."[225] Despite the problems with helicopter evacuations, a large number of casualties were flown out of Hue and Marine

Marine infantry work with a Marine M48 tank to clear Communist forces from Hue University early in the battle. *Courtesy of the Library of the Marine Corps.*

Aircraft Group 36 alone averaged forty-one medevacs per day in February (over 1200 total), in and around Hue.[226] Trucks or the M274 Mechanical Mule often provided the first leg of evacuation to nearby medical facilities or to where helicopters could safely transport the injured to more distant facilities. The 870-pound M274 was essentially a cargo pallet with four-wheel drive and a motor. Given its 1000-pound cargo capacity, the Mule was one of the few cargo vehicles capable of hauling more than it weighed. Its small size (four by ten feet) made it an "invaluable" medevac tool, able to negotiate rubble-strewn streets and narrow alleys.[227] The Mule was an example of a piece of equipment not necessarily designed for urban operations that proved very useful in that environment. The combination of ground transport and helicopter medevac gave American medical personnel a flexible set of options for both dangerous frontline evacuations and fast transport to rear area medical facilities.

A major shaping factor on ground movement within the city was the NVA/VC destruction on 7 February of the large 400m Nguyen Hoang Bridge that connected north and south Hue, and was the path for Highway One over the Perfume River.[228] With the Nguyen Hoang destroyed, and south Hue secure, US forces used helicopters and various water craft to move forces to the northern portion of the city.[229] On several occasions heavy enemy fire cut short helicopter flights into north Hue. Most of 1/5 transited from south Hue to the Citadel on US landing craft or motorized patrol junks of the South Vietnamese Navy.[230] These water craft sometimes carried South Vietnamese troops as well, and the craft at times encountered significant enemy fire or CS gas drifting out from the Citadel.[231] US engineers also operated floating bridge components to ferry troops between northern and southern Hue.[232]

Inside the city the slow rate of advance, and the short distances involved, minimized the need for vehicles to move personnel (unwounded). The vehicles that were needed were those lending direct fire support, such as M48 tanks, Ontos, and those 106mm recoilless rifles mounted on Mules. In the Citadel some of these vehicles had difficulty with narrow streets, closely spaced buildings, dense foliage in between buildings, and rubble.[233] Tanks sometimes encountered streets so narrow the tracks rubbed on buildings on both sides.[234] On the battle's first day, the retreat from the ill-advised Marine probe into the Citadel was aided by civilian vehicles hotwired by Marines.[235]

For dismounted US Marine infantry Hue presented a range of urban mobility problems. Hue's buildings were sometimes closely grouped together, with pockets of foliage between them that could be ten to fifteen feet high (coconut and palm trees), and many of the houses had hedgerows laced with barbed wire. Even if no NVA/VC were holding a particular area, moving through it was slow going for Marines on foot.[236] NVA/VC troops dug into the Citadel wall (five meters high) had excellent fields of fire, which required Marine units to set up buffer zones next to some wall sections, where Marine infantry would not go until the later stages of the battle.[237] On a number of occasions, the Marines used direct fire weapons and satchel charges to blow holes in the walls surrounding some of the larger buildings, or to breach the buildings themselves.[238] The Marines also found the NVA/VC units not very security conscious at night, allowing Marine infantry on occasion to move small units into key positions around well defended larger buildings, easing subsequent daylight assaults.[239] For those 106mm recoilless rifles not mounted on Mules, the Marines had to man-handle them—no mean feat for a 400-pound weapon.[240]

The central counter-mobility shortfall for US forces at Hue was the failure to seal off the city itself.

> Prisoner interrogation indicated no shortages of ammunition during the battle, and indicated that resupply was constant and virtually automatic to the front lines.[241]

The NVA/VC had established well-organized rear areas and conduits for resupply and reinforcement to the south and west of Hue.[242] US Marines within the city, and US Army units outside, did not completely cut off these avenues of resupply/reinforcement until the city fell. The substantial communist forces dedicated to preserving the conduits into the city proved stronger than the American forces assigned to close them by US commanders. Over the course of the battle the NVA managed to reinforce the seven to ten battalions it had in the city with perhaps five more, some of which had redeployed from Khe Sanh. By one estimate, it would have taken sixteen battalions to totally isolate Hue, battalions the Americans and South Vietnamese would have been hard pressed to find during the nationwide communist offensive.[243] Late in the battle some high ranking NVA/VC officers and political officials were able to escape from the city using these same routes.[244]

US engineers attached to 2/5, along with American artillery

fire, destroyed several smaller bridges over the Phu Cam Canal into southern Hue. This demolition took place over 8 to 10 February, as 2/5 finished clearing south Hue, and was fiercely resisted by communist forces in the area. Marine commanders were concerned about an NVA/VC counterattack into south Hue from below the Phu Cam Canal, and they judged it easier to drop the bridges than fully secure each with infantry.[245] Another Marine counter-mobility tactic in south Hue, with its more open street layout, was to park a tank at an intersection, with the coaxial machine gun pointed down one street, and the cupola-mounted machine gun pointed down another, to cover any enemy movement between blocks.[246]

While nightly harassment and interdiction artillery fire was a common US tactic in Vietnam, not to mention earlier US urban battles, this was not the case in south Hue. The two factors that drove this were the initially restrictive rules of engagement, and the slow realization by American commanders as to the seriousness of the enemy commitment. North Hue was a different story. US artillery and mortar units fired nightly harassment and interdiction missions until 20 February, when the enemy-held portion of the city became too confined for this to be safely done given the proximity of US and South Vietnamese forces.[247]

Countering communist units moving into and throughout the city was made even more difficult by their movement methods. During the initial assault some NVA/VC entered the city floating on blocks of plastic and makeshift rafts.[248] Once inside the city, these units were instructed to minimize movement along larger streets, and when possible to use underground pathways or wall breaching (via explosives and crowbars).[249]

Logistics

The logistical difficulties experienced by US forces in Hue were considerable, and they began with the effective NVA/VC interdiction effort on the road network around Hue. With the interruption of ground transport, the logical alternative was aerial resupply, but the persistently bad flying weather hampered that as well. The helicopter types involved were a mix that included UH-1 Hueys, CH-46s (medium lift), and CH-53s (heavy lift). When windows opened up in the weather, helicopters could deliver substantial amounts of supplies into the city. On 15 February, two large CH-53s flew thirty-three sorties into Hue's Citadel, bringing in 60.5 tons of cargo from nearby Phu Bai, but those supplies represented over one-third of the total delivered by that helicopter squadron during all of the battle.[250] There was one attempt to parachute supplies to an isolated group of US personnel early in the battle, but this was not successful and was not tried again.[251]

A third option was naval resupply by landing craft launched from Da Nang, travelling north along the coast to the mouth of the Perfume River, and then up the river to the landing craft ramp at Hue. However, in many places the NVA/VC controlled one or both banks of the river, allowing them to fire on landing craft and mine the river. Armed American patrol boats acted as escorts, but the resupply convoys needed the assistance of helicopter escorts as well, something often precluded by the weather. Under heavy fire from NVA/VC forces near Hue, US forces shut down the landing craft ramp at Hue from 31 January to 4 February. The first landing craft of supplies arrived there on 5 February, though the landing ramp was only used during daylight hours. The enemy interdiction efforts reached such a level of severity that US forces ceased running convoys up the Perfume over 18 to 20 February.[252] Despite the use of convoys, patrol boat escorts, and occasionally helicopter escorts, over two dozen US vessels were damaged in February travelling to and from Hue (including one sunk at the Hue ramp), resulting in five killed and twenty-nine wounded US personnel. The February monthly total for supplies delivered to Hue, via the Perfume, was 5600 tons—only 24 percent of that delivered the previous month.[253]

An added burden on the American logistical system was the need to support South Vietnamese units in and around the city. The initial wave of communist attacks destroyed many Vietnamese Air Force helicopters, and the ARVN logistical system broke down. Until 8 February most resupply for South Vietnamese units came from American helicopters. According to Australian advisors working with the South Vietnamese, "Neither the 1 ARVN Division in Hue nor the many scattered units could have survived without US assistance."[254]

Once supplies entered the city, US forces were hampered by a shortage of trucks, an extension of the overland difficulties.[255] The Marines, however, found two smaller vehicles effective as substitutes in moving supplies over Hue's narrow and often rubble-covered streets. The M-422 Mighty Mite was a light-weight (1700 pounds empty) mini-jeep that could haul 850 pounds, plus another 1000 pounds in a trailer.[256] Marines used them at the company level to move supplies. The Mule also proved excellent for resupply duties.[257]

Ammunition use in the city was heavy. While the first arriving units underestimated the requirement for ammunition, word quickly spread as to the true need. The Marines of F/2/5 arrived in Hue on 1 February without even their packs, but as H/2/5 prepared to enter the city the next day, the company commander ordered them to gather all the ammunition they could carry.[258] Ammunition had top priority on all modes of transport into the city, in some cases bumping infantry off helicopters. The total haul of ammunition into the city during the battle was massive, including: 1,000,000 rounds 5.56mm, 550,000 rounds 7.62mm, 30,000 rounds 81mm, 6000 rounds 106mm, 4000 LAAW rockets, 350 E-8 CS launchers, 12,300 fragmentation grenades, and 4700 CS grenades.[259]

The heavy ammunition use and transportation difficulties combined to curtail some operations within the city. For example, the 1st Battalion, 5th Marines used forward supply points to push supplies the final distance to their forward combat elements; however, the insufficient flow of supplies into the battalion itself on two separate occasions caused the battalion commander to call off attacks.[260] These supply shortfalls for 1/5 were at their worst at the midpoint of the battalion's fight for the Citadel: 18 to 20 February.[261] Improved logistical support to 1/5 would likely have aided their advance and possibly reduced their casualties. This could be judged as one result of the strong communist effort to isolate the city that paid benefits for the fight within.

US forces adapted to the breakdown in the usual logistical system. Rear area maintenance units sent small teams of maintainers forward into the city, who provided "invaluable" support, most notably keeping the armored vehicles operational.[262] Despite the repeated damage to tanks from RPGs, 1/5 reported four or five tanks always available for duty out of the seven in the Citadel.[263] Inside the city, senior Marine commanders shifted the Ontos vehicles, normally assigned to infantry units, to the tank units present. This simplified logistical support by having all of the armored vehicles under one command.[264]

Dealing with the Population

The existence of a long-standing host nation government allowed US forces in the city to share the task of caring for the population. The initial shock of Tet did disrupt the coherence of the South Vietnamese Government, across all of the I Corps area, but it gradually recovered and undertook relief efforts for refugees both inside the city and those who had fled. The communist occupation and targeting of SVN government officials left the city government itself largely paralyzed, though Hue's police did recover enough to provide some semblance of law and order in cleared portions of the city.[265] Civilians streamed into US- and SVN-controlled territory at every opportunity. By 3 February nearly 2000 refugees had made their way to the USMC-controlled portion of south Hue, totaling 5000 by 7 February.[266]

The earliest efforts, in south Hue, fell to American forces, who used loud speakers to direct civilians to various collection points and temporary shelters. Operation RECOVERY, begun on 25 February, was a ninety-day joint US-SVN effort of relief and reconstruction designed to aid the civilians from Hue who were homeless, some twenty thousand who were still inside the city. By 2 March, at least in south Hue, the electrical and water systems were partially restored. In the last two weeks of February, US personnel inoculated over twenty-eight thousand civilians against diseases that might spread because of the breakdown in city services.[267] Figures on the total displaced population range from 32,000 to 116,000.[268] By 29 February displaced civilians were returning to their homes at a rate of 2500/day, and by 5 March 20,000 had done so.[269]

Marines help evacuate civilians from Hue to the safety of a South Vietnamese collection point. *Courtesy of the Library of the Marine Corps.*

At the beginning of the battle, civilians were "conspicuously absent" from the battlefield, creating little hindrance on American operations. This changed as 1/1 and 2/5 began liberating an expanded perimeter around the MACV compound. The roads became crowded as increasing numbers of civilians tried to return to their homes and businesses. The task of handling these growing crowds was primarily dealt with by US personnel not on the front line, and Vietnamese security personnel, though US company commanders did divert some manpower for this. In the Citadel, Thompson was concerned about NVA/VC infiltrators amongst the civilian throngs, so he cordoned off the battlefield and assigned an ARVN battalion attached to him (by General Thuong) to handle the civilians.[270]

The strong desire on the part of many civilians to return to their homes and businesses was likely influenced by the ARVN penchant for looting. There were numerous instances of such, which at times exhibited a disturbing degree of organization.[271] Looting was enough of a problem that the 1st Marines headquarters ordered all its subordinate units to report any observed instances, and the American ambassador mentioned it as a key complaint from the population in Hue to President Johnson.[272] The official South Vietnamese history of Tet stated "thievery and looting were widespread" but referred only to communist culprits.[273]

The South Vietnamese quickly relaxed their initially strict rules of engagement, which US forces had agreed to follow. While driven by military necessity, the change in rules of engagement would be a double-edged sword for the population. The use of heavier direct fire weapons, artillery, naval gunfire, and air support accelerated the advance of US forces, while simultaneously reducing US casualties and reducing the duration of the communist occupation. Gia Hoi for example, the triangle-shaped portion of the city northeast of the Citadel, was liberated last by the ARVN. While this part of the city did not experience the extensive destruction that others did, its population suffered longer under the communists.[274] The Marine use of tear gas helped clear buildings while saving civilians inside. The Treasury Building and hospital complex in south Hue were each cleared with the aid of gas, by 2/5, and almost five hundred civilians were rescued from within.[275] The extensive Marine use of snipers was driven, at least in part, out of a desire to limit civilian casualties.[276] On occasion the Marines halted their fire if they discovered proximate civilians, but overall the presence of civilians did not dissuade them from using heavy firepower. The extensive communist use of the population for carrying wounded and supplies and digging field fortifications increased the likelihood civilians would be caught in the crossfire.[277] Overall, the city suffered badly from the heavy use of firepower, with some 80 percent of the structures damaged or destroyed.[278]

The duration of the occupation mattered because the communists were not there just to hold the city, but also to reshape it politically. Hanoi had been disappointed to that point by their limited political success in Hue, and Tet was their chance to accelerate matters. The communists undertook a detailed mapping of the human political landscape in the city, starting many months before Tet, and they used that intelligence to conduct a rapid and bloody purge of Hue. Captured communist documents boasted of the dual military and political victory in Hue.

> Hue was the place where reactionary spirit had existed for over ten years. However, it only took us a short time to drain it to its root.
>
> We eliminated 1,892 administrative personnel, 38 policemen, 790 tyrants, six captains, two 1st lieutenants, 20 second lieutenants and many N.C.O.[279]

While the remains of some of the killed were discovered by US and SVN military units as they took back portions of the city, most were not discovered until later (in some cases several years) in mass graves outside the city—called by one author the "most extensive political slaughter of the war."[280]

The total loss of civilian life is difficult to determine. Oberdorfer says the total count of bodies found in and around Hue was 2800 while Nolan says 3000 plus another 2000 missing. A US Fleet Marine Force report, written a few months after the battle, lists an oddly exact figure of 4094 dead civilians in Hue, or 80 percent of all civilians killed in the I Corps zone for February. An SVN history of Tet, written sometime in 1968 or 1969, lists only 944 civilians "known" killed; however, the same history gives a rough number of 1000 being buried in mass graves by the VC, suggesting the 944 was but an interim number.[281] If the highest figure from Fleet Marine Force is used (4094), along with communist documents that cite 1892 killed administrative personnel and 790 "tyrants" (a common term in communist documents referencing politically undesirable types), that equated to the communists crediting themselves with 66 percent of the civilian fatalities. Based on these sources, it could be argued that the heavy US and SVN use of firepower killed only half as many civilians as did the communist purge.

A slower rate of US advance, from a reduced use of firepower, would have probably caused fewer direct civilian fatalities.[282] Two other factors, however, would have increased civilian casualties if progress had been delayed. According to at least one captured communist document, they wished they had more time to more thoroughly purge the city.[283] Moreover, the breakdown in city services posed a danger to those still in the city. Most problematic was the lack of water, with the supply faltering in some parts of the city as early as 3 February.[284] A desperate population would drink from unsafe water sources, exposing them to water-borne disease at a time the local healthcare system was severely disrupted. In a more protracted battle this could have killed a great many more civilians. Irrespective of the rationale behind the SVN/US decision, quickly retaking the city was the best thing that could have been done to save Hue's citizens.

Conclusion

Hue presented the Marines with a very different challenge from most other engagements they had fought in Vietnam. And yet, the Marines adapted to the constraints and surmounted the obstacles to accomplish their mission. The two major components of that success were their overall excellence in warfare and adaptation.

The Marines trained their leaders to be aggressive and show initiative, precisely the traits needed to root out several regiments of NVA determined to fight to the last man. When solutions were needed to problems specific to the fighting in Hue, they were not long in coming. Lieutenant Colonel Gravel needed a safer route for his wounded to the helicopter evacuation zone, so he had the tanks plough a path through the buildings.[285] When an early Marine probe of the Citadel came at the cost of heavy casualties, the Marines augmented their ground evacuation capability by ho-twiring civilian vehicles.[286] When the nature of the RPG threat in urban terrain became evident, a young Marine lieutenant came up with the idea of pairing one M48A3 with one Ontos, to maximize potential of each. Initiative and aggressiveness made up for the lack in urban-specific training and experience.

An essential enabler for that aggression was the heavy firepower available to the Marine units, both organically to the infantry battalions and in the form of external support. Although because of weather the Marines received only a modest amount of air support, other means including artillery, naval gunfire support, tanks, Ontos, and the weapons of the infantry filled in where needed. The skill at which these various arms were combined was key. The Marines were adroit in finding the right firepower solution for various problems, be it CS gas for NVA heavy buildings, pairing the M48A3 with the Ontos, or quickly augmenting the infantry's firepower by pulling 3.5-inch bazookas out of storage. Moreover, the Marines had the logistical capabilities to make all those firepower systems employable on a continual basis. While the 1/5 Marines did have to curtail operations on occasion to await more supplies, the fact that infantry were sometimes bumped from helicopters to make room for ammunition demonstrated the priority on firepower. For an enemy determined to hold in good defensive terrain, all that firepower was essential. By one estimate over 5000 communist troops were killed in Hue.[287]

The most notable shortfall at Hue for American forces was the failure to isolate it. The strength of the communist forces in the city, and the duration for which they held certain locations, were both increased by the enduring resupply and reinforcement corridor to the southwest of the Citadel. The problems presented by the broader Tet Offensive, and the substantial forces the communists committed to preserving its corridor into Hue, certainly made isolating it a difficult task for American and SVN commanders. Those circumstances are cause to moderate criticism of the failure to close off the communist resupply corridor. However, the modest priority American commanders gave to this effort is more open to question. At the battle's midpoint, when more forces were available, commanders deployed them into the Citadel rather than assigning them to isolate Hue.

The overall spirit of adaptation applied to logistics as well. Every mode of resupply was hampered in some way at various times, be it by destroyed bridges for the truck convoys, weather for the helicopters, or enemy held sections of shoreline on the Perfume. Despite these ever-changing difficulties, American forces adapted and managed to push both supplies and men into the city throughout the battle.

The communist thrust into Hue, and even more their attempt to hold the city, surprised senior American commanders. Into that blind spot Hanoi aggressively inserted a powerful force. The core strengths of NVA/VC forces in Hue were their large number, fighting spirit, and excellent man-portable weapons. As 2/5 reported, they faced a "tenacious and professionally competent enemy."[288] A USMC sergeant put it more bluntly, "The NVA in Hue were mean, motivated bastards."[289] The communist command structure was gambling that a decisive offensive—centered around the battles for Saigon and Hue—could repeat 1954. Although the strategic course of the war slowly trended in Hanoi's favor after 1968, the quest for tactical success at Hue would fail.

Conclusion

The central three-part question this study sought to answer was: *When the need arose to fight in urban terrain in the mid-twentieth century, how effective were US forces, why, and how did that performance change from World War II to Vietnam?* The four battles analyzed were chosen because they each tested the US military's capabilities in a major urban battle while together presenting a range of conditions across three wars and over three decades. And yet, despite the variations in conditions, resources available, and foes, US forces successfully executed their mission to capture the city in every case. American losses were certainly not light, civilian casualties were often extensive, as was damage to the city, and the tempo of operations was typically slow, but each battle ended with US forces victorious.

Urban warfare was of only episodic importance to the US military for the period of this study. Prior to World War II it was generally ignored, and after the war given only modest attention, mostly in doctrine. Outside of the World War II years, urban warfare had little impact on training, organization, force structure, or equipment decisions in either the US Army or Marine Corps. Absent evidence of any serious effort to prepare specifically for urban warfare, one can instead trace the successful results of all four battles back to two factors: transferable competence and battlefield adaptation.

Transferable Competence

In preparing for other aspects of warfare the Army and Marine Corps generated capabilities that proved effective in urban combat, despite that environment not having been a driver in the creation of those capabilities. For the latter two battles, it seems unlikely the Marine Corps thought combat in urban terrain would not occur again, but it is more likely they considered it a rarely occurring problem already well covered, in other words, a lesser included case. This transferable competence can be broken down into five elements that, while not equally related to each battle, were frequently evident across the four battles.

The first element was the quality of American small unit leaders. Hampered communications, short lines of sight, and short engagement ranges made all four battles small unit fights. The American advance depended more on squad-vs.-squad and platoon-vs.-platoon engagements than would have been the case in more open terrain. Key to those engagements was small unit leadership. These leaders could not see their superiors and often did not know the enemy disposition until they were in contact (sometimes inside the same building), so they had to be capable of solving problems on their own and pressing on despite heavy losses at times. And they were.

The emphasis on aggressiveness and initiative for small unit leaders was an early and prominent theme in Army doctrine, even back to the first overarching *Field Service Regulations* (1923) issued after World War I:

> Officers and men of all ranks and grades are given a certain independence in the execution of the tasks to which they are assigned and are expected to show initiative in meeting the different situations as they arise. Every individual, from the highest commander to the lowest private, must always remember that inaction and neglect of opportunities will warrant more severe censure than an error in the choice of the means.[1]

That theme was carried through to all subsequent versions of *FM 100-5* (a follow-on overarching Army doctrinal publication), along with other Army publications describing the broader principles of warfare. While the importance of initiative and flexibility was sometime discussed in the context of urban warfare, or some other form of close combat, it was treated as a much broader principle applicable to warfare in general.[2] This ethos was also present in the Marine Corps, as stated in the 1966 manual for rifle squads. "The outcome of the fighting depends largely upon initiative and aggressive leadership of unit leaders."[3] The philosophy and preparation to instill initiative, aggression, and flexibility in leaders paid dividends in decentralized urban combat, but without urban warfare as a central motivation for that effort.

A second element of transferable competence was the American emphasis on firepower, combined with the logistical support to make it employable. The American military was the first to equip its infantry with a standard-issue auto-loading rifle. While auto-loaders were common by the end of World War II in many armies, American infantry began the war with the M-1. Another important man-portable weapon, the bazooka, proved an important source of firepower in all four battles. Although the Army developed that weapon primarily for anti-tank use, it could go anywhere the infantry could go in a rubble-clogged urban landscape. It was used extensively to engage forces in heavy cover. World War II field reports repeatedly praised the bazooka's role in urban combat, and two decades later Marines in Hue were wearing out their larger "super" bazookas in a matter of days from heavy use.[4]

US infantry battalions possessed a robust suite of organic heavy weapons, but equally important was their ability to supply vast quantities of ammunition for those weapons. A combat observer report from Aachen, highlighting the key lessons, included a reference to "the employment of all available firepower."[5] At Manila one infantry battalion fired more than 4000 rounds of 81mm mortar ammunition in a single night onto buildings scheduled for assault the next morning.[6] Marine water-cooled heavy machine guns generated piles of expended shell casings as they cut down charging enemy infantry during the night-time NKPA counterattack in Seoul. In Hue Marine 106mm recoilless rifles were a key source of firepower, given the many limitations with artillery and air support. Observers with South Vietnamese units in Hue cited the Vietnamese unit's lack of organic infantry firepower as a key reason why those units were less effective than Marine Corps infantry in the city.[7]

In addition to their organic heavy weapons, the infantry battalions usually received large amounts of artillery and armor support, and to a lesser extent air support. Even in Hue, where the number of armored vehicles was modest, robust maintenance, repair, and logistical support kept most vehicles on the line each day. When the rules of engagement at Manila prohibited air support, American commanders made up the difference with the heavy use of artillery. Although a combination of rules of engagement and a compact battlefield limited artillery support in Hue, armor, mortars, and the infantry's recoilless rifles took up the slack. When a Marine battalion was under heavy pressure in Seoul during the night-time attack by the NKPA, and supporting Marine artillery had to cease fire due to overheated artillery tubes, a lowly US Army lieutenant succeeding in reassigning an entire Army artillery battalion to lend support. At times, the logistical system struggled to keep up with the demand for ammunition, such as the pauses in the advance in Hue, but these events were the exception and not the rule.[8] Whether it was Lieutenant Colonel Daniel in Aachen, stockpiling ammunition in dumps close to the front, or Marine helicopters flying into Hue stacked so heavily with ammunition that infantry were sometimes bumped from flights, American forces had both the weapons and ammunition to make firepower central to their tactics. One author, writing about American urban battles, put it well in describing Americans as often outnumbered but never outgunned.[9]

A third element contributing to American transferable competence in urban warfare was skill in the orchestration of combined arms. Infantry, armor, artillery, engineers, and air support all have their strengths and weaknesses. However, with careful coordination, each can cover the limitations of the others, creating a whole that is greater than the sum of the parts.

The concept of combined arms was slow to mature in the American military. Combined arms at the small unit level was rare before World War I, but during that war the Army had formed battalion level task forces. The 1923 *Field Service Regulations* emphasized this, although its focus was limited to the pairing of infantry and artillery. The Army's Infantry School did conduct some combined arms exercises in the 1920s, but these were constrained by the paucity of military resources in the interwar period. The independence of the various Army branches, combined with the lack of a forcing function from the Army's senior leaders, hindered the development of combined arms.[10]

Once World War II began, and the Germans demonstrated the efficacy of combined arms, thought in the US military began to change. Combined with the lessons learned in the Army's 1941 maneuvers, the Army began changing the organization of its forces. For example, by 1942 the Army had reconfigured its armored divisions by adding more infantry, self-propelled artillery that could keep up with the tanks, and command elements designed to control ad hoc and mixed collections of forces as needed on the battlefield.[11] This evolution was clearly evident within the Army's tank destroyer community, as it changed from an almost independent force to one where by war's end, small units of tank destroyers were routinely parceled out to support the infantry.[12]

In this area, Army doctrine was rapidly catching up with

changes in the field. The Army's overarching doctrinal manual had always included a section on the various combat arms, but the 1939 version was still focused on the infantry-artillery facet of combined arms while undervaluing the role of aircraft and armor. Not until the June 1944 version of *FM 100-5* did the "combat arms" section include a separate section on armor.[13]

These organizational and doctrinal changes, though not motivated by thoughts of urban warfare, were only the first step. The effective orchestration of supporting arms, which allowed the outnumbered American infantry in Aachen to capture the city, would require on-the-job training.

Experience gained in other combat environments was the fourth element of transferable competence. Before American forces began fighting major urban battles, in mid-1944, they learned valuable lessons and skills, which would later prove useful in those urban battles, from a range of other environments. The combined arms skills of the 1st Infantry Division improved steadily as it fought in the deserts and hills of North Africa and Sicily. The hedgerow fighting in Normandy further refined the skill set of the troops, forcing them to learn how to deal with short lines of sight and an abundance of cover.[14] For units assaulting Manila, the warm-up examination took place in the jungle. The 37th Infantry Division had spent several years clearing Japanese bunker complexes prior to Manila. A Sixth Army after-action report noted how similar the Japanese defensive tactics in Manila had been to their jungle tactics.[15] Recent battlefield experience was less of a factor for Seoul, but in Hue the Marines had ample experience dealing with short lines of sight from jungle combat.

The fifth and final element of transferable competence was the design of American armored vehicles. While the Sherman has been widely criticized for its weaknesses against German armor, the streets of Aachen and Manila proved an environment well suited to its design. Its faster rotating turret and large load of onboard ammunition served it well on the short-range firepower-heavy urban battlefield. Because the Infantry Branch had strongly influenced the Sherman's development, its design had more to do with supporting infantry and less to do with fighting other tanks.[16] In Aachen and Manila, that is exactly what it did. The vehicle the Army had designed to fight tanks, the M10 tank destroyer, also found a niche, where its high velocity gun was more effective at punching through thicker walls or bunkers. That ability, plus its mobility, compared to towed anti-tank guns, made the M10 a favorite of American troops clearing Brest.[17] In both Aachen and Manila, the large number of self-propelled artillery pieces proved useful in the close-range direct fire role. Because the engagement ranges were often short, dictated by short lines of sight, an exposed crew unlimbering a towed artillery piece was more vulnerable to small arms fire. A self-propelled piece could quickly move into place, fire, and depart. At Hue, the recoilless rifle-equipped Ontos, originally designed as a lightweight anti-tank system, provided crucial direct fire support when air support was mainly absent and artillery support limited. Its agility also made up for its lack of armor, usually allowing it to shoot and scoot before the NVA could bring to bear their RPGs. In sum, many of the vehicles used by American forces in urban combat proved adept in that role, despite their not having been designed for that purpose.

Adaptation

As useful as those transferable capabilities were, there was still a gap between existing capability and the demands of the urban battlefield. This led to the second major factor behind the success of American forces in the urban battles in this study: battlefield adaptation.

Despite the lack of any direct experience in urban warfare, the forces in Aachen and Manila adapted to the particulars of that environment. Senior commanders at Aachen saw to it that two scarce self-propelled 155mm guns, a weapon usually held at the corps level, were attached to the battalions clearing the city. As the American infantrymen advanced across the city, they adapted to German infiltration via the sewers by systematically blocking all manhole covers in areas they captured. To counter the problem of indistinguishable buildings, the 2nd Battalion commander assigned numbers to every building to better track sub-unit locations. In Manila the engineers, infantry, and tankers worked out a system for dismantling the mixed belts of Japanese minefields and barricades that allowed the engineers to work behind the cover of armor. Commanders in Manila also adapted to the denial of air support in MacArthur's rules of engagement by compensating with additional artillery.

That pattern of adaptation continued in Seoul and Hue. When an Army artillery liaison officer, on a hill outside of Seoul at night, had trouble seeing the fall of artillery spotting rounds among all the other explosions and burning buildings, he ordered the firing unit to switch to white phosphorous rounds, which were more visible among the other light sources. Elsewhere in Seoul, advancing Marine units worked out a coordinated system where tanks, aircraft, engineers, and infantry would methodically break down NKPA barricades. In Hue, Marines learned they could use the back-blast from a recoilless rifle as a smoke screen to cover infantry crossing open ground. When Lieutenant Colonel Ernie Cheatham learned that his battalion was to enter Hue, he quickly augmented his unit's firepower and ammunition supply. Inside the city Marines learned that for enemy firing from the windows of strongly built buildings, it was best to fire bazooka rounds at the window's edge rather than through the window. A young Marine officer came up with the idea of pairing one Ontos with one M48A3, to best support infantry assaults while maximizing the survivability of both vehicles. In its after-action report for Hue, one of the Marine battalions involved characterized the unit's transition from rice paddy and jungle fighting to urban fighting, as taking "a matter of hours."[18]

In general, across the four battles, senior commanders usually showed a willingness to adapt to the short lines of sight in the city, and the often-hampered radio signals, by allowing small unit leaders to conduct their own fight. To better cope with the command and control problems, the rate of advance was usually methodical, with phase line halts and requirements to link up with adjacent units. Communications by wire took on a greater role, as land lines were well suited for the slow rate of advance and signal interference problems presented by urban structures. Commanders adapted to the sharply increased ammunition expenditures by pushing ammunition dumps well forward and giving high priority to ammunition resupply. They formed combined arms task forces, at the company level and below, to adjust to the more confined battle space. In cases where the rules of engagement were initially restrictive, commanders usually relaxed them, once it was clear the enemy was present in strength and willing to fight (MacArthur's prohibition on air support in Manila being an exception).

This culture of adaptation was no accident; rather, it was pervasive, long standing, and emphasized in US doctrine. The 1923 version of the Army's *Field Service Regulations* expressed the expectation that men of all ranks "show initiative in meeting the different situations as they arise." That emphasis on initiative continued as a central theme in the subsequent 1939, 1941, and 1944 versions of *FM 100-5*.[19] During his tenure as assistant commandant of the Army's Infantry School in the 1920s, George C. Marshall worked to revamp the curriculum to instill a greater sense of flexibility and adaptation in the students.[20] One can find examples of American troops improvising to adapt to urban terrain dating back to the Mexican-American War of 1846, when troops breached interior walls to stay off the street, organized into small groups to better fit down narrow streets, and used small artillery projectiles as improvised grenades to clear rooms.[21] Even back in the 1770s a former captain in the British Army, after immigrating to America and working with American troops, stated "the privates are all generals" because of the way they thought for themselves.[22]

This is not the first study to identify battlefield adaptation as a key American strength.[23] In his excellent study of the US Army in Europe in World War II, Michael Doubler found that adaptation, and not just simple mass or raw firepower, was central to American success in meeting several challenges. However, he found that successful adaption was not a constant. While the GIs successfully discerned and implemented the needed tactical changes for the hedgerow country, urban terrain, close air support, and defensive warfare (e.g., the Battle of the Bulge), they were not successful in solving the problem of forest fighting. Doubler traces the roots of those successes back to a decentralized American society that encouraged problem solving.[24] This study reinforces those judgments about the important role of adaptation in World War II in Europe, and expands them to find adaptation a consistent factor in four successful US urban battles, involving two different services, across three wars, and over three decades.

Performance Across the Four Battles

Across all four battles command and control at the regiment and below level was effective, and communications were not a significant problem in any of the battles. Commanders at the regimental level and below adjusted well to the limitations in command and control caused by the urban terrain (e.g., short lines of sight). The differences emerge at the higher echelons of command. US forces cut off Aachen about midway through the battle, and the isolation of Manila was achieved even earlier with the convergence of three divisions from three different directions. At Seoul, however, the back door to the city to the northeast remained open throughout the battle. That back door served as an escape route for substantial NKPA forces, from within the city and further south. At Hue, the communists maintained an open corridor to the southwest of the Citadel throughout the battle. This corridor prolonged the battle and increased the cost to American and SVN forces.

Isolating Seoul and Hue certainly entailed serious challenges. The second two regiments to land at Inchon were not available until several days after the initial landings. At Hue, senior commanders had to contend with a nationwide communist offensive and a major communist effort to cut off the city from US and SVN reinforcements. The issue was not that effort was lacking to isolate Seoul or Hue, but rather the relative priority and the resources commanders allotted to the task. Almond had the first two regiments ashore attack the city itself, while the following two regiments were to isolate the city, and one of those (32nd Infantry) he later ordered to attack into the city from the south. At Hue, around the midpoint of the battle, commanders sent a newly arrived Marine battalion not to secure the still open enemy-held corridor from the southwest, but instead into the Citadel to assist the stalled SVN forces. Given the heavy demand for near continual ammunition resupply for US forces, one has to wonder how long the communist forces could have resisted in the Citadel had they been cut off. As it was, they fought on for approximately two weeks.

It is unclear if Army or Marine Corps doctrine was a contributing factor to this reduced emphasis on isolation. Although both Army and Marine urban doctrine described the isolation of an urban battlefield as "Phase I," the small unit focus of that doctrine may have left commanders unguided as to the role of isolation when larger units were involved.[25] Both the 1944 and 1952 versions of FM 31-50 describe its applicability as for units up to reinforced regiments, as does the Marine Corps urban manual (MCS

3-15).[26] For the 1964 version of FM 31-50, however, that statement of limited scope was deleted.[27]

Intelligence and reconnaissance were a challenge across all four battles. The specific location of enemy forces was often not known until contact was made. Aachen does stand out from the rest, as US forces were able to determine the southern orientation of the German defenses and launch their assault from another direction. The assault into Manila was similar in that the main American assault came from the north while the Japanese had built their strongest defenses to the south. This appears attributable more to luck than insight, however, as the orientation of Japanese defenses in the city does not appear to have been understood by American planners before the battle. At Seoul the initial Marine thrust into the city ran directly into the primary NKPA defensive position, the hills northwest of the city, and the fighting capability of NKPA units was initially underestimated. At Hue US forces were slow to realize the size of the occupying communist force, its determination to hold the city, and the degree to which the communists were feeding reinforcements and supplies into the city during the battle.

Firepower was a consistent strong suit of American forces in all four battles. The specific solutions varied, but American forces always had a large advantage over their enemies in this area and firepower was key for dealing with an enemy holding good defensive terrain. In Aachen US commanders found a highly successful role for the self-propelled 155mm guns, and commanders at Manila adjusted to the prohibition on air support with an increased use of artillery. In Seoul, on the first night the Marines were in the city, US firepower destroyed an attacking North Korean reinforced infantry battalion. In Hue the Marines made up for the paucity of air support and the limitations on artillery support by emphasizing tanks, Ontos, and 106mm recoilless rifles. Casualties were never light but they were sustainable for the duration of each battle.

Mobility was not a major problem in any of the battles. Infantrymen minimized their exposure by often moving from building to building through walls, and although vehicle movement was sometimes hampered by rubble or narrow streets, this did not significantly impact the contribution of those vehicles to the advance. When the NKPA emphasized barricades in Seoul, the Marines quickly devised a combined arms process for pushing through the barricades. At Hue, the major communist effort to cut the city off was countered by the Americans with a flexible mix of ground vehicles, boats crossing the Perfume River, and helicopters. The ability to counter the enemy's mobility in the city was roughly equal in the four battles. In each case, night-time halts preserved the integrity of the front line and nightly harassing artillery and mortar fires reduced enemy movement in enemy held portions of the city. In Aachen and Seoul, where air support played a greater role, US aircraft made daylight movement by enemy forces dangerous.

Logistical shortfalls significantly hampered operations only at Hue. Due to ammunition shortfalls, the 1st Battalion, 5th Marine Regiment had to halt operations on several occasions. As a general rule, US commanders accurately anticipated that ammunition use would be heavy and took steps that usually addressed the need.

US forces had their greatest difficulty in dealing with the civilian population in Manila. The huge population overwhelmed elements of the American plan to care for them. That large population also meant there were more people at risk from American firepower, and more people the Japanese could use as shields or attack directly.[28] In Aachen most of the population had left the city, and in both Seoul and Hue US allies were able to lend assistance in caring for the population and screening for enemy troops in civilian clothes.

In light of the aspects of tactical performance evaluated for each battle the most impressive overall performance was at Aachen, particularly given the 3-to-1 German advantage in manpower (See Table B). That performance was aided in part by the smaller population in Aachen as compared to the other battles. The second best performance was at Manila, impressive in part because of the large and fanatical defending force present. Greater problems emerged in Seoul and Hue, notably the failure to isolate each of those cities. The overall trend was thus one where US forces were gradually less effective over time. Relative to the other battles, the performance at Hue was the least impressive. However, it would be easy to overstate the American performance issues at Hue as the overall

Table B: Comparison of Tactical Performance (Symbols in each city column denote success (+) or difficulties (-) relative to the other battles)				
Aspects of Tactical Performance	Aachen	Manila	Seoul	Hue
Command, Control, and Communications	+	+	-	-
Intelligence and Reconnaissance	+	-	-	-
Firepower and Survivability	+	+	+	+
Mobility and Counter-mobility	+	+	+	+
Logistics	+	+	+	-
Dealing with the Population	+	-	+	+
Total Number of "+"	6	4	4	3

mission was still achieved. The city was captured and a large number of enemy forces were killed in the battle.

The failure to isolate Seoul and Hue may have been the byproduct of the rarity of major urban operations. When formulating their approaches for capturing Seoul and Hue, senior American commanders most likely simply lost touch with some of the fundamentals of urban warfare. This may have been because the challenge of fighting for a major urban area was rare in warfare, and not something extensively prepared for by the US Army or Marine Corps.

Myths

The overall performance of American forces in these four urban battles undermines two myths about urban warfare. The first is that the inherent advantages of defending in urban terrain require any attacking force to possess a large advantage in numbers, even well beyond the 3-to-1 sometimes referred to as the rule-of-thumb for offensive operations against prepared defenses.[29] Urban terrain does offer some advantages for the defender, most importantly because it can force a slower tempo of operations while requiring the attacker to choose between high casualties or extensive damage to the city (along with possibly high civilian casualties). However, in none of the four successful battles assessed in this study did US forces enjoy such numerical superiority.

The two reinforced infantry battalions that cleared Aachen were outnumbered 3-to-1 by the defending Germans. Counting the total strength of the two divisions that attacked into Manila itself, American forces captured that city with a modest advantage of approximately 1.5-to-1. The ratio of attacker to defender in Seoul itself is obscured by the number of units that fought near the city, but not inside it, and by the NKPA's retreat out of the city as the battle raged. If one tallies the total strength of each side's forces in or near the city, the result is approximately 1.3-to-1 in favor of US forces. At Hue as well, the flow of forces for both sides, in and out of the city, makes estimating force ratios difficult. However, the approximately 5000 communist forces killed inside the city would suggest that the combined US-SVN force in the city was modestly outnumbered.

The second myth is that urban warfare is a fight best left to the infantry.[30] Infantry certainly plays an essential role, but if left to function alone, its casualties would be much higher. As the cases examined here show, infantry is most effective when part of a combined arms team, which, if applied correctly, can largely trump the defensive advantages of urban terrain. This was the case in all four of the battles in this study. The tempo was slow and losses were not light, but the ability to methodically advance was demonstrated in all four battles via the careful coordination of armor, infantry, engineers, artillery (direct and indirect fire), and air support. The contribution of the latter two was episodic, but American forces consistently applied the first three.

Civilian Casualties

Across these four urban battles, American commanders solved many of the problems presented to them; however, they were not able to keep civilian casualties low when a large number of civilians were present. In the cases where the enemy decided to make the population a battlefield feature, Aachen being the exception with the German-ordered evacuations, American commanders had no answer that would spare those civilians. Avoiding a direct assault, by opting for an extended siege, would have killed many civilians from starvation, the breakdown of city services, or giving the enemy more time to kill them (e.g., Japanese in Manila, communists in Hue). Simultaneously, the larger war effort would have been hurt by delaying capture of the city and tying down forces needed for other operations, and that delay would have its own consequences for civilians under the control of the enemy elsewhere.

The best available option for American commanders was to rapidly clear the enemy from the city with a firepower-heavy approach. When possible, the Americans modified this approach when civilians appeared to be most directly threatened, but the overall heavy use of firepower was the general modus operandi. As American forces encountered civilians in Aachen they moved them out of the city. In Manila, when US troops discovered that the Japanese holding fortified positions inside the Philippine General Hospital held civilian hostages, US troops restricted their artillery fire to the first floor and foundation level. When it was learned the Japanese intended to destroy Manila's water system, the XIV Corps commander ordered the 1st Cavalry Division to swing wide outside the city to secure key nodes in the city's water system. In Seoul the invasion fleet that landed at Inchon carried with it rice for the population, and some Marine Corps medical units treated more civilian casualties than Marines. The plan for Seoul also included the rapid transport of South Koreans into the city to reconstitute local government and services. The Marines in Hue used tear gas to clear communist forces from a hospital complex and the Treasury Building, and almost five hundred civilians were rescued from within.

However, in the end, these American measures could only mitigate, not prevent, civilian casualties. The city's defenders could force the substantial loss of civilian life if they so chose. This unsolved aspect of urban warfare may, at least in part, explain the overall post-Vietnam American aversion to urban warfare.

Urban Warfare After Hue and Into the Future

Since the battle for Hue, the prominence of urban warfare has further increased, in large part because the continued global population migration into urban areas. After the disintegration of the Soviet Union, superpower versus superpower maneuvering was replaced with a proliferation of state versus non-state actor conflicts. These non-state actors often used the protection and concealment afforded by urban structures and populations to survive against conventional militaries.

While urban terrain was no guarantee of success for the military underdog, be they a state or non-state actor, the willingness to mass and fight there indicated that cities have become a popular venue. The Chechens made a stand in Grozny twice in the 1990s. The Israeli military has conducted sweeps to clear insurgents from Palestinian refugee camps and the Brazilian military has done the same against criminal gangs in Brazilian ghettos. Libyan mechanized forces sought shelter in urban areas from NATO aircraft. Aleppo and Damascus have become key battlegrounds in the Syrian civil war. Terrorists chose Mumbai (2008) and Nairobi (2013) for direct engagements against civilians.

The advantages afforded by urban terrain have been particularly important for opponents of the United States, as its military has become by far the world's most powerful. Somali militias challenged US forces in Mogadishu in 1993, providing a reminder that while helicopters are important for urban mobility they also have significant vulnerabilities in that environment. In 1991, even before US and other coalition forces began their air attacks, the Iraqi regime discussed plans to fall back into urban areas to force a close-range fight.[31] In 2003 Iraqi forces fought hard in Nasiriyah and Baghdad, and in both cases US forces learned the hazards of depending on supply lines that ran through unsecured urban areas. Post-Saddam insurgents also chose to mass and fight in Fallujah and Sadr City.

The slower tempo that can be forced upon US forces with an urban fight also has an appeal for combatants. US forces initially backed off from Fallujah in 2004, in part because of pressure from the Iraqi government, but also out of reluctance to get bogged down in an enduring fight, particularly while Washington's strategic narrative described nation building and a minimal enemy threat.[32] With the massive fiscal and political capital expenditures for the two nation-building wars in Iraq and Afghanistan, political will and resources will be scarce for future extended duration conflicts in urban terrain. Brief assaults into urban areas are more feasible, but sometimes the "you break it, you bought it" rule applies. Policing a large city with tens of thousands of troops for a year or more, while indigenous security organizations are created or rebuilt, could easily involve a billion-dollar price tag.

The "lesser included case" relationship between urban warfare and the general preparations for combat by the US military has been less true since Hue, and that trend will continue into the future. Central to this are changing performance standards. World War II was a war for national survival, and while Korea and Vietnam were not, they occurred under the shadow of a threat of national extinction from the Soviet Union. Post-Cold War conflicts have involved a lower tier of national interests, and as in all marketplaces, lower value warrants lower costs. Not only is the American public more sensitive to collateral damage and civilian casualties, but so are US allies, the coalition of the willing that really matters. Much of America's global military posture depends on access granted by allies. It is not difficult to imagine in today's world that a repeat of Manila's massive civilian death toll in some US urban operation would seriously damage US-ally relations.

Because of these changing performance standards, the US military will need to treat urban warfare as a special case, one not wholly addressed by general preparations for combat. The experiences in Mogadishu, Nasiriyah, Baghdad, and the Russian experience in Grozny rekindled an interest in urban warfare in the US military. Since the early-1990s, the US military has made some urban-specific training and equipment decisions. For example, the M1 Abrams tank can now be equipped with the Tank Urban Survival Kit, a collection of improvements to the tank's defensive and offensive capabilities. Also available for the M1 is a canister round for the 120mm main gun, a round optimized for engaging infantry at close range. The Army has built several urban warfare training complexes. After having issued no new urban warfare doctrinal manual in the 1980s or 1990s, the Army issued Field Manual 3-06 (*Urban Operations*) in 2003, and then revised and reissued it in 2006.[33]

Specific attention on urban warfare will need to continue, but many of the factors that favored US forces from 1944–1968 still apply today. The American cultural trait of adaptation still permeates the ranks. Despite the slow recognition by senior US leaders of the changing nature of the fight in Iraq in 2003, many US military personnel in Iraq recognized those changes and adapted. US forces were impressive in their operations in both Fallujah and Sadr City. US forces still possess an abundance of firepower, only now much of it is precise. The logistical capabilities necessary to support extended high tempo operations still exist as well. Small unit combined arms remains a core competency for US ground forces. Russian forces in Grozny in 1995 lacked that competency, and US forces in Mogadishu were prevented from employing a combined arms team; in both cases the results were costly. But in Fallujah and Sadr City effective combined arms played a key role in those successful operations.

Several technologies offer promise for the sensing challenges of future urban operations. Cyber warfare may allow existing urban sensors (e.g., traffic cameras, security cameras, personal cellphones) to be exploited. Small drones will make distributed short-range sensor grids possible, an effective work-around to the short lines of sight in urban areas. Small drones in the city, and even in buildings, and larger drones flying above a city, can act as communications relays. But today's cities also have more crowded signal environments, making communications for any military force more challenging. Light-weight night vision devices have proliferated to the extent that the US military now has to worry about non-state actors buying them on the open market. A variety of powered weapons sights are now available that facilitate more accurate snap-shots, the quick reaction shots taken at close range that are common in the close urban fight. Weapon-mounted high-performance flashlights have become common although they garner less attention, but they are a key capability when clearing the dark interior of a building. Small biometric data collection devices can make it somewhat harder for combatants to blend into the population, but those devices must be integrated into larger databases and the larger intelligence apparatus to be effective.

However, as technologies for surveillance, reconnaissance, communications, and precision strike have continued to advance, urban terrain has served to blunt some of those improvements. Most sensors employed on drones or satellites still require a line of sight, something in short supply in urban terrain. The flight trajectories for precision munitions are sometimes blocked in the urban canyons. Pervasive and instant media can produce images that trump subsequent investigation. Same-day images of a school struck by US munitions will often carry more weight than a report issued a week later stating that insurgents were based at that school. Perceptions of overall US power and precision strike capabilities have resulted in an increased sensitivity to civilian casualties, both with American and foreign publics. Those perceptions sometimes translate accidental civilian casualties into willful American acts.

The new capabilities for sensing can also be employed by enemy forces. The 2008 terrorist attack in Mumbai was notable for the degree to which broadcast and social media was used by the attackers. A command and control node in Pakistan was monitoring Twitter and other Internet sources to feed updates to the ten men shooting their way across the city, to warn them of the responses of Indian security forces and other key pieces of information, such as where a large number of civilians were hiding in one particular hotel.[34]

Both the US Army and Marine Corps are developing power management systems for their dismounted soldiers, to feed the increasing demand by man-portable electronics. The ability of those systems to harvest power from urban sources (e.g., wall plugs, car batteries), in addition to natural sources (e.g., solar), might actually make US forces more self-sustaining in urban environments in that respect.

Capabilities to protect US personnel in the urban environment have advanced greatly since 1968. Advances in materials have allowed body armor to play a role not seen in some 400 years, since firearms became dominant on the battlefield. Armor that could stop pistol rounds had been around since the 1970s but it was the plate inserts fielded extensively in the 2000s that could stop assault rifle rounds that were the game changer. In an environment that fosters many close-range engagements, getting the first hit in a gunfight no longer assures success. One could argue that that body armor worn by US forces in both Iraq and Afghanistan significantly reduced the effectiveness of insurgent attacks with small arms, and may have contributed to the insurgent reliance on improvised explosive devices (IEDs). Less prominent but also important have been the plethora of other protective equipment US personnel now consider essential for urban operations, such as improved helmets, ballistic eyewear, gloves, and knee and elbow pads. The urban environment is full of hard surfaces, jagged edges, and broken glass, all of which can cause injuries that put a warfighter out of action.

US offensive capabilities have advanced as well since Hue. Weapon magazines are larger, with standard issue pistols now holding fifteen rounds versus seven in 1968, and assault rifle magazines have grown from twenty to thirty rounds. A derivative of the M-16 is still the standard issue rifle, but now some have M203

40mm grenade launchers attached, unlike in Vietnam where a Marine had to choose between the M16 and the M79 40mm grenade launcher. This merge of rifle and grenade launcher has allowed the standard Marine rifle squad to increase its number of grenade launchers from one to three. The Marine Corps has also explored a six-shot 40mm grenade launcher (M32) which would further expand Marine infantry firepower if adopted.

A major leap forward may be possible with the experimental XM-25 assault rifle currently in development. The XM-25 is a magazine-fed 25mm grenade launcher that fires rounds with a programmable airburst capability. A sighting system measures the range to the target and then feeds that data to the round, which then airbursts just above and behind the target, bypassing the cover the target may be hiding behind. Technical challenges remain with this weapon, including its weight, durability, and cost, but it could alter the basic value of cover in urban terrain. Several dozen launchers were tested in combat operations in Afghanistan starting in 2010 with promising results. Development continues and low-rate initial production is possible in the near future.[35]

Not a weapon per se but rather a warhead design, thermobaric warheads have great potential in urban warfare. Thermobaric warheads are optimized for pressure generation, unlike the combined effects of pressure and fragmentation in conventional high explosive warheads. This reliance on pressure as the kill mechanism is key in urban environments, where the plethora of enclosed spaces used for cover, can then be used against the target, as thermobaric weapons are actually more effective in enclosed spaces. The pressure generated is contained and amplified, even allowing it to move to adjacent rooms within a structure. They were first widely used by Russian forces in Grozny, in the form of disposable rocket launchers (RPO-A) that resembled US Vietnam-era LAAWs. Since then a range of warheads have been developed by various militaries, including for the RPG, the Marine SMAW (Shoulder-launched

Multipurpose Assault Weapon), the US Hellfire missile (helicopter-launched) and even larger Russian artillery rockets (e.g., 220mm).

These advances in sensors, protective equipment, and offensive capabilities notwithstanding, urban warfare is and will continue to be a nasty, difficult business. The insurgent weapon of choice in recent conflicts, the improvised explosive device (IED), is a good fit for urban terrain. The clutter of people, structures, metal, and electromagnetic signals all make it harder to find and defeat IEDs.

As the world has grown more urbanized, cities have grown both larger and more complex. In many of the world's cities it is now possible to travel ten miles in a straight line and never leave the built-up area. Aside from all the people and structures, there are the complex interdependent infrastructure networks. Destroying a node in the power system could in turn shut down a city's water supply and healthcare facilities. This in turn increases the demands for intelligence on a city, not just where the enemy is, and where the people are, but what role a particular building plays in that city's infrastructure. With industrialization has come added threats, such a chemical plants. In 1984 a chemical leak in Bhopal, India, killed approximately 2,000, and during combat in a city chemical facilities could easily be damaged.

With all the complexities of urban warfare and the many variables at play, modeling and simulation can have a role in understanding that chaos. Their use can span doctrine development, weapons development, training, and even mission planning during a combat operation. A learning cycle combining simulations and field exercises could yield many lessons about tactics and new weapons, even before the weapons exist. The United States Navy learned a great deal in the 1920s and 1930s about carrier aviation, despite treaty limitations that kept the numbers of carriers low, and while the associated technologies were rapidly changing. That learning came from an integrated cycle of wargames at the Naval War College and fleet exercises. [36]

In Sum

By focusing on four case studies across a significant timespan, this study has been able to delve down to a detailed level of tactical assessment spanning two services, three wars, and three decades. That detailed tactical assessment reveals just how similar the formula for success was for American forces in each battle. Consideration of urban warfare had, to put it generously, only a modest effect on the US military's overall preparations for war. Nevertheless, the units tasked with capturing each of these cities proved up to the task, principally by way of their overall preparation for war and their ability to adapt under fire.

Notes

Introduction

1 Brunn, Stanley D., Jack F. Williams, and Donald J. Zeigler, eds., *Cities of the World: World Regional Urban Development*, 3rd ed. (Lanham, MD: Rowman and Littlefield Publishing Group, 2003), 6, 24.

2 This source estimates the world population in 1900 as 1.65 billion, and 2.52 billion by 1950. United Nations, Population Division, *The World At Six Billion*, (undated) <http://www.un.org/esa/population/publications/sixbillion/sixbilpart1.pdf> [accessed 8 May 2010] (p. 5)

3 United Nations, Population Division, *World Urbanization Prospects: the 2007 Revision*, (2007) <http://www.un.org/esa/population/publications/wup2007/2007wup.htm> [accessed 8 May 2010] (p. 1)

4 For two concise summaries of the advances in weaponry in the nineteenth century, and their impacts on military tactics, see John A. English, and Bruce I. Gudmundsson, *On Infantry*, rev. ed. (Westport, CT: Praeger, 1994), chapters 1–2; Bernard and Fawn M. Brodie, *From Crossbow to H-Bomb*, rev. ed. (Bloomington: Indiana University Press, 1973), chapter 6.

5 For an excellent examination of the struggle within the pre-World War I German military to adapt to the changes in technology, see Eric Dorn Brose, *The Kaiser's Army: The Politics of Military Technology in Germany During the Machine Age, 1870–1919* (Oxford: Oxford University Press, 2001).

6 "Targets are usually briefly exposed at ranges of 100 meters or less." Department of the Army, *An Infantryman's Guide to Combat in Built-Up Areas*, Field Manual 90-10-1 (1993). <http://www.globalsecurity.org/military/library/policy/army/fm/90-10-1/index.html> [accessed 1 July 2010] (p. 1-5)

7 Jonathan A. Beall, "The United States Army and Urban Combat in the Nineteenth Century," *War in History* 16 (2009): 157–188.

8 Martin Kitchen, *A Military History of Germany* (Bloomington: Indiana University Press, 1975), 75–85, 129–131, 164, 356–357; Anja Johansen, *Soldiers as Police: The French and Prussian Armies and the Policing of Popular Protest, 1889–1914* (Aldershot, UK: 2005), 65.

9 Johansen, *Soldiers as Police*, 2.

10 The quote is from a November 1945 conference. General Board, United States Forces, European Theater, *Organization, Equipment, and Tactical Employment of the Infantry Division*, Study No. 15, undated, Military History Institute, Carlisle, Pennsylvania (henceforth MHI), Minutes of Conference on the Infantry Division, p. 2.

11 Within the Department of Defense, C³ (command, control, communications), and ISR (intelligence, surveillance, reconnaissance) are commonly used acronyms when discussing organization, battlefield performance, capabilities, or acquisition. Sometimes these are combined into C⁴ISR, with the fourth C representing computers. The next three subtopics in this study's framework are common subjects within DoD as well, though not necessarily combined as some are in this framework. The last subcategory, "dealing with the population," primarily comes from the author's experience in assessing urban operations. While not all releasable to the general public, this author has written or co-written several reports for the Department of Defense on urban operations. *Military Operations in Urban Terrain: A Survey of Journal Articles* (Alexandria, VA: Institute for Defense Analyses, 2000); *Department of Defense Roadmap for Improving Capabilities for Joint Urban Operations*, two vols, restricted distribution (Alexandria, VA: Institute for Defense Analyses, 2002); *Exploring New Concepts for Joint Urban Operations* (Alexandria, VA: Institute for Defense Analyses, 2003); *Urban Resolve Phase I Final Report*, two vols, restricted distribution (Alexandria, VA: Institute for Defense Analyses, 2005).

12 Several Japanese freighters left the island of Luzon in the Philippines for Japan, just thirteen days before the Sixth Army landed there. Onboard were 1300 Allied POWs from Bilibid Prison in Manila, only 400 of whom would survive the journey. George Weller, *First Into Nagasaki* (New York: Crown, 2006), 177–239.

13 Friedrich Koechling, The Battle of the Aachen Sector (September to November 1944), Interviews with captured commander of German LXXXI Corps, MHI, Foreign Military Studies Collection, D739.F6713, Box 9, Folder A-989; Alfred Zerbel, The Battle for the Aachen Sector (Sep–Nov 1944), MS # A-997, NA, Microfiche Publication M1035, 6 July 1950; US Army, Headquarters 1st Infantry Division, Commanding Officer Battle Group Aachen, Annex No. 4 to G-2 Periodic Report No. 125, 22 October 1944, CMH, 228.01, HRC Geog. M Germany, 370.2 – Aachen; US Army, Headquarters 1st Infantry Division, Germans Compare Russian and U.S. Army, Annex No. 2 to G-2 Periodic Report No. 124, 21 October 1944, CMH, 228.01, HRC Geog. M Germany, 370.2 – Aachen.

14 Korea Institute of Military History, *The Korean War*, 3 vols (Lincoln: University of Nebraska Press, 2000).

15 *PLAF Directive on Tet 68 Offensive in Hue Area*, VVA, Item Number: 2131101005, Douglas Pike Collection; *Recapitulative Report: Phase of Attack on Hue from 31 Jan to 25 Feb 1968*, 30 March 1968, VVA, Item Number: 2131101002, Douglas Pike Collection; *Hue City Yearend (1968) Assessment Report*, 7 February 1969, VVA, Item Number: 2131107005, Douglas Pike Collection. *Fifth Columnist Activities in Thua Thien Prov, Tri-Thien-Hue MR*, 30 September 1970, VVA, Item Number: 2311312013, Douglas Pike Collection; *Scenes of the General Offensive and Uprising*, Foreign Languages Publishing House, Hanoi, 1968, VVA, Item Number: 2131012040, Douglas Pike Collection.

16 Pham Van Son, Chief, Military History Division, Joint General Staff, Republic of Vietnam Armed Forces, *The Viet Cong Tet Offensive (1968)*, translated from the original Vietnamese by the Joint General Staff Translation Board, undated, GRC, Vietnam Tet Offensive, Box 24, Folder 3; Australian Army Training Team in Vietnam, "Victory at Hue," *Army Journal*, 1 February 1969, pp. 3–20, VVA, Item Number: 2131109002, Douglas Pike Collection.

17 John Antal, and Bradley Gericke, eds., *City Fights: Selected Histories of Urban Combat from World War II to Vietnam* (New York: Ballantine Books, 2003); William G. Robertson, and Lawrence A. Yates, eds., *Block by Block: The Challenges of Urban Warfare* (Fort Leavenworth, KS: US Army Command and General Staff College Press, 2003); Louis A. DiMarco, *Concrete Hell: Urban Warfare from Stalingrad to Iraq* (Oxford, UK: Osprey, 2012).

18 Not all of *City Fights'* chapters were similar. For example, chapter seven (Aschaffenburg 1945) was almost exclusively based on primary sources.

Chapter 1

1 William O. Odom, *After the Trenches: The Transformation of U.S. Army Doctrine, 1918–1939* (College Station: Texas A&M University Press, 1999), chapters 1–3.

2 David E. Johnson, *Fast Tanks and Heavy Bombers: Innovation in the U.S. Army, 1917–1945* (Ithaca, NY: Cornell University Press, 1998), 103; Mark D. Sherry, "Armored Force Organization," in *A History of Innovation: U.S. Army Adaptation in War and Peace*, ed. Jon T. Hoffman (Washington, DC: Center for Military History, United States Army, 2009), 53.

3 The second amendment gives the right to citizens to keep and bear arms, while the third amendment bans the government from forcibly quartering troops in civilian homes.

4 Patrick O'Sullivan and Jesse W. Miller, *The Geography of Warfare* (New York: St. Martin's Press, 1983), 136.

5 Jonathan A. Beall, "The United States Army and Urban Combat in the Nineteenth Century," *War in History* 16 (2009), 157–188.

6 Lou DiMarco, "Attacking the Heart and Guts: Urban Operations Through the Ages," in *Block by Block: The Challenges of Urban Warfare*, ed. William G. Robertson and Lawrence A. Yates (Fort Leavenworth, KS: US Army Command and General Staff College Press, 2003), 13–14.

7 War Department, *Field Service Regulations United States Army 1923* (Washington, DC: Government Printing Office, 1924), 87, 114–120, MHI.

8 The Infantry School, US Army, *Infantry in Battle*, 2nd ed. (Richmond, VA: Garrett and Massie, 1939), 10–14, CARL.

9 War Department, *Tentative Field Service Regulations—Operations*, FM 100-5 (Washington, DC: Government Printing Office, October 1939), 218–222, MHI.

10 Odom, *After the Trenches*, 95.

11 Dewar describes World War I as having "surprisingly little urban combat" while referencing the Spanish Civil War as a conflict in which urban operations "became a regular phenomenon." Michael Dewar, *War in the Streets: The Story of Urban Combat from Calais to Khafji* (Devon, UK: David & Charles, 1992), 16.

12 This first article is the one that gave the most significant attention to urban combat. E. D. Cooke, "The Japanese Attacks at Shanghai and the Defense by the Chinese, 1931–1932," *Review of Military Literature* 17 (December 1937): 5–28; William H. Hobbs, "Needed—More Riot Training," *Infantry Journal* 43 (November–December 1936): 542; Wendell G. Johnson, "Spain: A Year and a Half of Modern War," *Infantry Journal* 45 (March–April 1938): 133–141.

13 Wendell G. Johnson, "The Spanish War: A Review of the Best Foreign Opinion," *Infantry Journal* 45 (July–August 1938): 351–356.

14 Odom, *After the Trenches*, 201.

15 H. H. Smith Hutton, "Lessons Learned at Shanghai in 1932," *U.S. Naval Institute Proceedings* 64 (August 1938): 1167–1174; Vincent Usera, "Some Lessons of the Spanish War," *U.S. Naval Institute Proceedings* 65 (July 1939): 969–972; Robert Blake, "War in Spain," *Marine Corps Gazette* 21 (February 1937): 5–10.

16 War Department, *List of Publications for Training*, FM 21-6 (Washington, DC: Government Printing Office, October 1940), 10–22, 28–48, MHI.

17 Christopher R. Gabel, *The U.S. Army GHQ Maneuvers of 1941* (Washington, DC: Center of Military History, US Army, 1991), 85–86, 139–140, 159, 164.

18 Dewar, *War in the Streets*, 24–25.

19 Bull stated the first US Army manual on urban warfare drew heavily from German doctrine, including lifting some sections without change. However, he did not clarify the degree to which this German doctrine was developed during or before the war. Bull also stated American doctrine and British doctrine were very similar. Stephen Bull, *World War II Street-Fighting Tactics* (Oxford: Osprey, 2008), 41, 54–55.

20 For a complete listing of all urban warfare-related journal articles see the periodicals section of this study's bibliography.

21 The quote is from the first article, page 22. Bert Levy, "Street Fighting," *Infantry Journal* 51 (September 1942): 22–29; Bert Levy, "Street Fighting," *The Cavalry Journal* 51 (September–October 1942): 46–51.

22 The quote is from page 58. V. L. Chuykov, "Tactics of Street Fighting: Military Lessons of Stalingrad," *The Cavalry Journal* 52 (September–October 1943): 58–62.

23 Operations Division, US War Department, *Combat Lessons No. 2*, 1942, pp. 6–13, CARL. See also, Operations Division, US War Department, *Combat Lessons No. 4*, 1944, p. 11, CARL; Operations Division, US War Department, *Combat Lessons No. 6*, 1945, pp. 11-21, CARL.

24 Military Intelligence Service, War Department, "German Combat Tactics in Towns and Cities," *Intelligence Bulletin* 2, no. 5 (Washington, DC: January

1944) <http://www.lonesentry.com/intelbulletin/index.html> [accessed 30 January 2010].

25 Military Intelligence Service, War Department, "How the Enemy Defended the Town of Ortona," *Intelligence Bulletin* 2, no. 11 (Washington, DC: July 1944) <http://www.lonesentry.com/intelbulletin/index.html> [accessed 30 January 2010]. Military Intelligence Service, War Department, "The British Discuss Combat in Towns," *Intelligence Bulletin* 2, no. 12 (Washington, DC: August 1944) <http://www.lonesentry.com/intelbulletin/index.html> [accessed 30 January 2010]. Military Intelligence Service, War Department, "Street Fighting by Panzer Grenadiers," *Intelligence Bulletin* 2, no. 2 (Washington, DC: October 1943) <http://www.lonesentry.com/intelbulletin/index.html> [accessed 30 January 2010].

26 See the April, May, June, and August issues. <http://www.lonesentry.com/intelbulletin/index.html> [accessed 30 January 2010].

27 Military Intelligence Division, War Department, *Tactical and Technical Trends No. 26* (Washington, DC: 3 June 1943) <http://www.lonesentry.com/intelbulletin/tt_trends.html> [accessed 30 January 2010] (pp. 53–59). Military Intelligence Division, War Department, *Tactical and Technical Trends No. 36* (Washington, DC: 21 October 1943) <http://www.lonesentry.com/intelbulletin/tt_trends.html> [accessed 30 January 2010] (pp. 22–27).

28 While Doubler states these reports supported the publication of the issues of "Information Bulletin" he likely misstated what was actually "Intelligence Bulletin." Michael D. Doubler, *Closing With the Enemy: How GIs Fought the War in Europe, 1944–1945* (Lawrence: University of Kansas Press, 1994), 270.

29 See this study's bibliography for the complete entries for Combat Observer's reports numbers: 18, 37, 39, 45, 68, 80, 85, 88, 93, and 94.

30 Headquarters VII Corps, US Army. *Combat Observer's Report No. 88*, 26 October 1944, NA, Record Group 498 (Records of the Headquarters, European Theater of Operations, US Army [World War II]), ETO, G-3 Division, Observers' Reports, 1944–1945, box 5.

31 War Department, *Field Service Regulations—Operations*, FM 100-5 (Washington, DC: Government Printing Office, May 1941), MHI, pp. 209–210; War Department, *Field Service Regulations—Operations*, FM 100-5 (Washington, DC: Government Printing Office, June 1944), MHI, pp. 246–249.

32 Bull also used the term "remarkable" to describe *FM 31-50*. Bull, *World War II Street-Fighting Tactics*, 31.

33 War Department, *Attack on a Fortified Position and Combat in Towns*, Field Manual FM 31-50, January 1944, MHI, pp. 60–61, 65, 73, 92–94, 112–114.

34 US Army, Headquarters Sixth Army, *Japanese Defense of Cities as Exemplified by the Battle for Manila—Report by XIV Corps*, 1 July 1945, MHI, D767.4J36, p. 21.

35 Robert R. Palmer, Bell I. Wiley, and William R. Keast, *The Procurement and Training of Ground Combat Troops* (Washington, DC: Center for Military History, U. S. Army, 2003), 59, 442–452.

36 The 37th Infantry Division had deployed overseas in June 1942 and the 1st Infantry Division deployed two months later, while the 1st Cavalry deployed in May 1943. Center for Military History, US Army, *World War II Divisional Combat Chronicles*, CMH.

37 Headquarters 16th Infantry Regiment, *Historical Report January 1944*, NA, Record Group 407, Entry 427, File 301-INF(16)-0.3, Report of Operations, Sept 43–Mar 44, Box 5232; Headquarters 16th Infantry Regiment, *Historical Report March 1944*, NA, Record Group 407, Entry 427, File 301-INF(16)-0.3, Report of Operations, Sept 43-Mar 44, Box 5232; Headquarters 18th Infantry Regiment, *Historical Report December 1943*, NA, Record Group 407, Entry 427, File 301-INF(18)-0.3, Report of Operations, Dec 43, Box 5254; Headquarters 18th Infantry Regiment, *Historical Report January 1944*, NA, Record Group 407, Entry 427, File 301-INF(18)-0.3, Report of Operations, Jan 44, Box 5254; Headquarters 18th Infantry Regiment, *Historical Report February 1944*, NA, Record Group 407, Entry 427, File 301-INF(18)-0.3, Report of Operations, Feb 44, Box 5254; Headquarters 1st Infantry Division, *G-3 Periodic Report*, 29 February 1944, NA, Record Group 407, Entry 427, File 301—3.1, G-3 Periodic Reports, Feb-Mar 44, Box 5112, pp. 1–3.

38 D. M. Daniel, *The Capture of Aachen (personal experience of a battalion commander)*, School of Combined Arms, Regular Course, 1946–1947 (Fort Leavenworth, KS: Command and Staff College), CARL.

39 Doubler, *Closing With the Enemy*, 90–98; Ken Casey, "Urban Combat in World War II: How Doctrine Changed as the War Progressed," *Armor* 108 (November-December 1999): 10-11. Unfortunately, Gawne gives no citation for his reference to the distribution of lessons learned from the 2nd Infantry Division. Jonathan Gawne, *1944 Americans in Brittany: The Battle for Brest* (Paris: Histoire & Collections, 2002), 138.

40 Doubler, *Closing With the Enemy*, 5–6, 28, 58, 106–107, 269, 282; Headquarters XX Corps, US Army, *Combat Observer's Report No. 37*, 8 November 1944, NA, Record Group 498 (Records of the Headquarters, European Theater of Operations, US Army [World War II]), ETO, G-3 Division, Observers' Reports, 1944–1945, box 11.

Chapter 2

1 The Allied Control Commission for Germany was "called upon to make itself ready to operate in Berlin by 1st November." Max Hastings, *Armageddon: The Battle for Germany, 1944–1945* (New York: Knopf, 2004), 15.

2 Harry Yeide, *The Longest Battle: September 1944 to February 1945 from Aachen to the Roer and Across* (St. Paul, MN: Zenith, 2005), 24.

3 Charles B. MacDonald, *United States Army in World War II: The European Theater of Operations: The Siegfried Line Campaign* (Washington, DC: Department of the Army, Office of the Chief of Military History, 1963), 20.

4 Ibid., 20, 37–38.

5 Ibid., 66–67, 72.

6 Ibid., 81–95.

7 Ibid., 109–115.

8 US Army, 1st Infantry Division, *1st Infantry Division: Report of Breaching the Siegfried Line and the Capture of Aachen,* November 1944, NA, 407/427/270//54/15/1/5664, p. 12 (henceforth *Report of Breaching the Siegfried Line*).

9 MacDonald, *United States Army,* 83; Lucian Heichler, *The Germans Opposite VII Corps in September 1944* (Washington, DC: Office of the Chief of Military History, Department of the Army, 1952) D 756 .H45 1952 c.2, MHI, pp. 87–88, 98. [The latter source was created by the Army to give the German perspective, as it drew entirely upon German sources.]

10 Milton Shulman, *Defeat in the West* (London: Cassell, 2003), 228; MacDonald, *United States Army,* 5, 16–18, 70–71, 87–88, 91; Heichler, *The Germans,* 83.

11 MacDonald, *United States Army,* 284.

12 Ibid., 91.

13 Aside from the 34th Machine Gun Battalion and the 433rd Replacement Battalion, this source also mentions the XIX Luftwaffe Battalion. US Army, Headquarters 1st Infantry Division, *The Battle of Aachen,* Annex No. 2 to G-2 Periodic Report No. 141, 7 November 1944, CMH, 228.01, HRC Geog. M Germany, 370.2—Aachen, p. 2. (henceforth Headquarters 1st Infantry Division, *The Battle of Aachen*)

14 Friedrich Koechling, *The Battle of the Aachen Sector (September to November 1944),* Interviews with captured commander of German LXXXI Corps, MHI, Foreign Military Studies Collection, D739.F6713, Box 9, Folder A-989, p. 3.

15 There is one mention of a PzKw VI (Tiger) in Aachen in the 26th Infantry Regiment's S-3 log on 14 October. However, this isolated reference was most likely a misidentification in the heat of battle. US Army, Headquarters 26th Infantry Regiment, 1st Infantry Division, *S-3 Unit Report for the Month of October,* NA, 407/427/x/x/x/x/5955. (henceforth *26th Infantry S-3 Unit Report for the Month of October*)

16 MacDonald, *United States Army,* 308.

17 US Army, Headquarters 1st Infantry Division, *The Battle of Aachen,* 3, 7.

18 *Report of Breaching the Siegfried Line,* 8.

19 US Army, Headquarters 1st Infantry Division, *Commanding Officer Battle Group Aachen,* Annex No. 4 to G-2 Periodic Report No. 125, 22 October 1944, CMH, 228.01, HRC Geog. M Germany, 370.2—Aachen. (henceforth *Commanding Officer Battle Group Aachen*)

20 *Report of Breaching the Siegfried Line,* 12.

21 Harry D. Condron, 2nd Information and History Service, 1st US Army, *The Fall of Aachen,* undated, NA, 407/427/270/65/24/7/24012, p. 4.

22 MacDonald, 281, 307, 308.

23 *Commanding Officer Battle Group Aachen,* p. 2. There is some disagreement between this source and the US Army's official history of the campaign cited earlier. That source states the entire 404th Regiment, along with a battalion

from the other two regiments, was detached from the 246th in the week before the assault—to fortify the line north of Aachen opposite the US XIX Corps. But the source in this footnote has the 404th with Wilck. It could be that the 404th returned to the city before the assault, or Wilck was making reference to the forces under his command at any point in the fight, not just those present when the assault began.

24 This source refers to the replacement battalion as the 453rd while the previous footnote source calls it the 433rd. Robert E. Price, III, *The Battle of Aachen*, Combat Studies Institute Battlebook 13-C (Fort Leavenworth, KS: Combat Studies Institute, US Army Command and General Staff College, 1984), 63.

25 MacDonald, *United States Army*, 312. Another source states that no substantial reinforcements were fed into the city during the assault. It could be that Battlegroup Rink was not considered substantial by this source, or this source was written too soon after the battle (only one month later) to benefit from later information on German actions. Headquarters 1st Infantry Division, *The Battle of Aachen*, 3.

26 Price, *The Battle of Aachen*, 63; Yeide, *The Longest Battle*, 79–80.

27 Koechling, *The Battle of the Aachen Sector*, 3–4.

28 Alex Buchner, *The German Infantry Handbook 1939–1945* (Atglen, PA: Schiffer Military History, 1991), 15, 142–144.

29 Heichler, *The Germans*, 35–36; *Report of Breaching the Siegfried Line*, 2–3, 11.

30 Heichler, *The Germans*, 18–20, 33–34, 55–56; MacDonald, *United States Army*, 71, 81.

31 H. R. Knickerbocker, *Danger Forward: The Story of the First Infantry Division in World War II* (Nashville, TN: The Battery Press, 1947), 260; Irving Werstein, *The Battle of Aachen* (New York: Thomas Y. Crowell Company, 1962), 31; *Report of Breaching the Siegfried Line*, 5.

32 *Report of Breaching the Siegfried Line*, 5–6; Colonel Jay P. Dawley (commander 238th), *The Capture of Aachen, Germany—October, 1944: Actions by the 238th Engineer Combat Battalion*, History, CMH, HRC 2, 254 Holocaust, Aachen, p. 2.

33 The reduced frontage was possible because the American Ninth Army had just arrived, after completing operations in France. MacDonald, *United States Army*, 251–252, 285.

34 Elbert E. Stickels, *The Operations of Company K, 18th Infantry Regiment (1st Infantry Division) In the Defense of the Ravelsberg, At Haaren, Northeast of Aachen, Germany, 15–19 October 1944*, monograph written for Advanced Infantry Officer's Course 1949–1950 by officer who participated in the action, The Infantry School, Fort Benning Georgia, DRL, pp. 7–9; Bobbie E. Brown, *The Operations of Company C, 18th Infantry (1st Infantry Division) in the Attack on Crucifix Hill, 8 October 1944 (Rhineland Campaign)(Aachen Offensive)(Personal Experience of a Company Commander)*, monograph written for the 1946–1947 Advanced Infantry Course, Infantry School, DRL, pp. 6–15; US Army, History, *Rhineland: The U.S. Army Campaigns of World*

War II, CMH publication 72-25, CMH; Koechling, *The Battle of the Aachen Sector*, 3–6.

35 Armand R. Levasseur, *The Operations of the 1st Battalion, 26th Infantry (1st Infantry Division) During the Initial Penetration of the Siegfried Line in the Vicinity of Nutheim, Germany, 13–20 September 1944 (Rhineland Campaign) (Aachen Offensive)(Personal Experience of a Battalion Operations Officer)*, monograph written for the 1947–1948 Advanced Infantry Course, Infantry School, DRL, pp. 27–28.

36 Headquarters 1st Infantry Division, *The Battle of Aachen*, 5; *Report of Breaching the Siegfried Line*, 8.

37 Interestingly, the ultimatum begins by saying the city is completely surrounded, which it was not at that time. A copy of the ultimatum can be found at: Combat Interviews: 1st Infantry Division, NA, 407/427/270/65/24/7/24012.

38 Derrill Daniel, *The Capture of Aachen*, Lecture given in 1950 at Quantico Virginia, 9 January 1950, CMH, Folder 228.01, HRC Geog. M Germany, 370.2—Aachen, p. 7. Headquarters 1st Infantry Division, *The Battle of Aachen*, 5, 12. *26th Infantry S-3 Unit Report for the Month of October*. 26th Infantry Regiment Association, *Account of the Battle of Aachen*, p. 10, <www.bluespader.org/uploads/aachen/02Contents.html> [accessed 17 December 2005] (p. 12). (henceforth *Account of the Battle of Aachen*)

39 Headquarters 1st Infantry Division, *The Battle of Aachen*, 6.

40 Daniel, *Capture*, 8.

41 Michael D. Runey, "Chaos, Cohesion, and Leadership: An American Infantry Battalion in Europe, October–December 1944" (master's thesis, Department of History, Pennsylvania State University, 2001), copy MHI, pp. 46–49, 52–53.

42 There is considerable confusion in the various accounts of Aachen regarding these terrain objectives. This reference to three objectives comes from Runey (pp. 53–54), but this author changed the terminology of the last two objectives to match with his own interpretation of Aachen's geography. This author cross-referenced a number of secondary sources and primary sources—including a map at the National Archives that appeared to have been marked by US troops involved in the battle. These references led this author to conclude that the Lousberg Heights refers to all three hills, the Lousberg refers to the tallest of the three, the middle height the Salvatorberg, and that Observatory Hill and Farwick Park are one and the same and the lowest of the three hills. Farwick Park also contains the spa complex and Quellenhof Hotel.

43 Runey, "Chaos...," 53–54.

44 MacDonald, *United States Army*, 290–293, 313; Koechling, *The Battle of the Aachen Sector*, 14; Stickels, *Operations*, 18–20.

45 Daniel, *Capture*, 13–14; MacDonald, *United States Army*, 303–306.

46 Headquarters 1st Infantry Division, *The Battle of Aachen*, 7; Runey, "Chaos...," 63–78; John D. Stromer and Paul W. Lunnie, compilers, *Journal for the 3rd Battalion, 26th Infantry, 1st Infantry Division*, October to December 1944

<http://www.historicaltextarchive.com/books.php?op=viewbook&bookid=2 2&cid=9> [accessed 4 December 2005].

47 Runey, "Chaos...," 78–84; Stromer, *Journal for the 3rd Battalion*, October to December 1944. *26th Infantry S-3 Unit Report for the Month of October. Report of Breaching the Siegfried Line.*

48 Armored infantry was mechanized infantry that had organic halftracks for transport. MacDonald, *United States Army*, 314; US Army, Headquarters VII Corps, *VII Corps Operations Memo 107, 18 October 1944*, MHI, Foreign Military Studies Collection, The Orlando C. Troxel, Jr. Papers.

49 *Report of Breaching the Siegfried Line.*

50 Daniel, *Capture*, 9–16. The 26th Infantry Regiment's 1st Battalion had recovered from its heavy losses in September around Stolberg, but it was tied down backing up the other 1st Infantry regiments maintaining the encirclement. See *Report of Breaching the Siegfried Line*, 11. This source states that one company from the 1st Battalion did make it into Aachen, starting on 18 October. Christopher R. Gabel, *Military Operations on Urbanized Terrain: The 2nd Battalion, 26th Infantry, at Aachen, October 1944*, (undated) <http://wwwglobalsecurity.org/military/library/report/1999/99-16/ chap1.htm> [accessed 4 December 2005]. U. S. Army, Headquarters 110th Infantry Regiment, 28th Infantry Division, *Journal*, 18 October 1944, NA, 407/427/270/56/5/2-4/8599, pp. 3–4.

51 Daniel, *Capture*, 16–17.

52 MacDonald, *United States Army*, 316; *26th Infantry S-3 Unit Report for the Month of October.* While the number of prisoners did spike at the end of the battle, the two infantry battalions had been processing a steady stream of German POWs throughout the battle. The 3rd Battalion averaged seventy-two captured Germans a day before 21 October. Stromer, *Journal for the 3rd Battalion*, October to December 1944; Runey, "Chaos...," 83–84; *Report of Breaching the Siegfried Line*, 11.

53 MacDonald, *United States Army*, 320.

54 Daniel, *Capture*, 5–6.

55 Ibid., 6.

56 Ibid., 18–19.

57 Stromer, *Journal for the 3rd Battalion*, October to December 1944; Runey, "Chaos...," 78–80.

58 Paul F. Gorman, *Aachen 1944: Implications for Command Post of the Future* (study conducted at the Institute for Defense Analyses, 2000) <http://cpof. ida.org/MOUT-Aachen-1944.pdf> [accessed 3 December 2005] (pp. 16, 29). Another source cites problems with wire often being cut by German artillery fire. Price, *The Battle of Aachen*, unnumbered page, Command Control and Communications subsection.

59 US Army, Headquarters 1106th Engineer Combat Group, *Lessons Learned by the 1106th Engineer Combat Group During the Aachen Operation*, 1 November 1944, NA, 407/427/270/62/13/6/19304, Folder: A/A Rpt Jun-Dec 44, p. 2. (henceforth *Lessons Learned by the 1106th*)

60 Steven J. Zaloga, *Sherman Medium Tank 1942–45* (Oxford: Osprey, 2001), 11.

61 Harry Yeide, *Steel Victory: The Heroic Story of America's Independent Tank Battalions at War in Europe* (New York: Presidio Press, 2003), 31–31, 77–79, 152–153; Yeide, *The Longest Battle*, 151.

62 *26th Infantry S-3 Unit Report for the Month of October.*

63 Daniel, *Capture*, 7.

64 War Department, *Field Service Regulations: Operations*, Field Manual 100-5, MHI, June 1944, p. 247.

65 The M12 was a scarce asset, only seventy-five having been shipped with US forces to Europe. It was also a corps-level asset, something a battalion commander seldom controlled. *M12 155mm U.S.A's Motor Gun Carriage*, (undated) <http://www.wwiivehicles.com/usa/self_propelled_guns/m12_gun_motor_carriage.html> [accessed 14 January 2007]. George Forty, *U.S. Army Handbook 1939–1945* (New York: Barnes and Noble, 1995), 67–86. War Department, *Field Artillery Tactical Employment*, Field Manual 6-20, MHI, February 1944, p. 65.

66 MacDonald, *United States Army*, 312; Richard W. Van Horne, "History of the 991st Field Artillery Battalion," 1955, <http://www.3ad.com/history/wwll/feature.pages/991st.pages/991st.history.htm> [accessed 30 July 2011]

67 Corley's main command post was further back and run by his staff. Runey, "Chaos...," 63–64; Charles Whiting, *Bloody Aachen* (London: Leo Cooper, 1976),137.

68 Knickerbocker, *Danger Forward*, 410–411; Runey, "Chaos...," 14–15, 21.

69 Runey, "Chaos...," 85-95; War Department, *Field Service Regulations United States Army 1923*, MHI, p. III.

70 Runey, "Chaos...," 50.

71 Daniel, *Capture*, 12.

72 Gabel, *Military Operations on Urbanized Terrain*; MacDonald, *United States Army*, 308; *Report of Breaching the Siegfried Line*, 8.

73 Koechling, *The Battle of the Aachen Sector*, 24.

74 Belton Y. Cooper, *Death Traps: The Survival of an American Armored Division in World War II* (Novato, CA: Presidio, 1998), 223.

75 MacDonald, *United States Army*, 26–27.

76 Cooper, *Death Traps*, 218–219.

77 Price, *The Battle of Aachen*, 93; *Account of the Battle of Aachen*, 10. "In anticipation of the attack on the city of Aachen the Division Engineer Section reproduced five hundred copies of a town plan of the city for Combat Team 26." Headquarters 1st Engineer Combat Battalion, *Report on October 1944 Operations.*

78 NA 407/427/270/65/24/7/24012, Combat Interviews: 1st Infantry Division folder.

79 While Whiting states US forces did know from "intelligence" that the hotel was Wilck's first headquarters, he provides no footnote. More convincingly, the journal for the 26th Infantry used the phrase "proved to be" when referencing the hotel and its status as a German headquarters, when the 3rd

Battalion captured the hotel. See Whiting, *Bloody Aachen*, 112–113; Stromer, *Journal for the 3rd Battalion*, October to December 1944.

80 Daniel, *Capture*, 10, 14–15.

81 Daniel, *Capture*, 15–16; MacDonald, *United States Army*, 311; Yeide, *The Longest Battle*, 113–114.

82 US Army, 1st Infantry Division, Military Police Platoon, *Journal October 1944*, NA, 407/427/270/54/21/5/5968, p. 3.

83 US Army, 1106th Engineer Combat Group, *Group History: 1106th Engineer Combat Group, October 1944*, NA 407/427/270/62/13/6/19304, Folder: Hist—1106th Engr C Gp Jun-Dec 44, p. 7 (henceforth *Group History: 1106th*).

84 *26th Infantry S-3 Unit Report for the Month of October.*

85 *Group History: 1106th*, 5.

86 Dawley, *Actions by the 238th*, 4–5.

87 26th Infantry Regiment commander, Colonel Seitz, attributed the success of his battalions in Aachen to "Common sense, normal tactical principles, and maximum firepower." *Account of the Battle of Aachen*, 17.

88 After the war Daniel described having a general sense of apprehension before Aachen, a feeling influenced by the difficult time Allied forces had taking Cassino. Daniel, *Capture*, 4–5.

89 Cooper, *Death Traps*, 40; Yeide, *Steel Victory*, 60, 83.

90 Yeide, *Steel Victory*, 88, 103.

91 War Department, *Armored Force Field Manual: Tactics and Technique*, Field Manual 17-10, March 1942, MHI, pp. 17, 142. War Department, *Field Service Regulations: Operations*, Field Manual 100-5, May 1941, p. 210. FM 100-5, June 1944, p. 248.

92 Yeide, *Steel Victory*, 80–82, 271–281.

93 US Army, Headquarters 1st Engineer Combat Battalion, *Report on October 1944 Operations*, 4 November 1944, NA, 407/427/270/54/19/6/5877. (henceforth Headquarters 1st Engineer Combat Battalion, *Report on October 1944 Operations*)

94 Daniel, *Capture of Aachen*, 7; Runey, "Chaos...," 40–43.

95 US Army, Headquarters 634th Tank Destroyer Battalion, *After Action Report for the Month of October 1944*, NA 407/427/270/50/31/3/23593. (henceforth Headquarters 634th Tank Destroyer Battalion, *After Action Report*) US Army, Headquarters 745th Tank Battalion, *S-3 Journal, October 1944*, November 1944, NA, 407/427/270/60/30/7/16710, Folder: A/A Rpt Jun-Dec 44. (henceforth 745th Tank Battalion, *S-3 Journal*)

96 *26th Infantry S-3 Unit Report for the Month of October.*

97 Christopher R. Gabel, "Knock'em All Down: The Reduction of Aachen, October 1944," in *Block by Block: The Challenges of Urban Operations*, ed. William G. Robertson and Lawrence A. Yates (Fort Leavenworth, KS: U.S. Army Command and General Staff College Press, 2003), 72; War Department, *Attack on a Fortified Position and Combat in Towns*, Field Manual FM 31-50, January 1944, MHI, pp. 65, 81–82.

98 Stephen Bull, *World War II Infantry Tactics: Company and Battalion* (Oxford: Osprey, 2005), 63; Ian V. Hogg, *The American Arsenal: The World War II Official Standard Ordnance Catalog of Small Arms, Tanks, Armored Cars, Artillery, Antiaircraft Guns, Ammunition, Grenades, Mines, etcetera* (London: Greenhill, 2001), 242–243, 327–329.

99 Alfred Zerbel, *The Battle for the Aachen Sector (Sep–Nov 1944)*, MS # A-997, NA, Microfiche Publication M1035, 6 July 1950, p. 33. US Army, Headquarters 1st Infantry Division, *Germans Compare Russian and U.S. Army*, Annex No. 2 to G-2 Periodic Report No. 124, 21 October 1944, CMH, 228.01, HRC Geog. M Germany, 370.2—Aachen, p. 2. (from here on called *Germans Compare Russian and U.S. Army*)

100 The German LXXXI Corps commander described the MP44 as "dominant" in urban fighting, along with the hand grenade and Panzerfaust. Koechling, *The Battle of the Aachen Sector*, 33.

101 Harold D. Howenstine, ed., *History of the 745th Tank Battalion: August 1942 to June 1945*, 302 -745TK 1945, MHI, p. 60.

102 The three rifle companies averaged 78 percent strength when they entered the city. Runey, "Chaos...," 26–27.

103 For 3rd Battalion the non-battle casualties were 112, including about thirty cases of combat fatigue. Ibid., 13, 22, 30, 41, 74, 85–95.

104 There is some disparity in the casualty figures given by various sources. While Runey's focus was on the 3rd Battalion's losses, which he chronicles in extreme detail, his figures (2nd Bn—206, 3rd Bn—292) also agree exactly with the 498 total of the official US Army history (MacDonald, 318). The 26th Regiment's history also gives the same 498 figure (Cantigny, 87). If one adds up the reported casualties in the 3rd Battalion's October–December journal, the total is 270 for 8 to 21 October. While that number is modestly less than Runey's, the unit journal is not as detailed as documents Runey used. See Stromer, *Journal for the 3rd Battalion*, October to December 1944. The key divergence from Runey's figures comes from a source that cannot easily be dismissed, the commander of the 2nd Battalion, Lieutenant Colonel Daniel. In a lecture given to an audience of Marines in 1950 he stated, "The total losses from all causes in the 2d Battalion and attached units throughout the entire Aachen operation were less than 100." (Daniel, p. 17) Two factors work against Daniel's total, one being his nonspecific number, and second, the five-year-old memories. It is not clearly stated in the written version of his remarks from 1950, but the round number suggests it was from memory, which could have lost some of its detail over the years.

105 Runey, "Chaos...," 67–78; Stromer, *Journal for the 3rd Battalion*, October to December 1944.

106 Yeide, *The Longest Battle*, 88.

107 Brown, *Operations of Company C*, 15.

108 Levasseur, *Operations of the 1st Battalion*, 27–28.

109 The HE round for the M10's 3 inch gun weighed ~12.7 lbs., while the Sherman's 75mm HE round weighed 14.7 lbs., and the 105mm weighed thirty-three lbs. Hogg, *The American Arsenal*, 182, 278, 281. The assault

gun Sherman should not be confused with the Jumbo Sherman, a 75mm-equipped Sherman with roughly double the armor on the frontal arc. Jumbo Shermans were not present at Aachen.

110 Zaloga, *Sherman Medium*, 9–10. It required nearly eighty seconds to rotate an M10's turret 180 degrees. Steven J. Zaloga, *M10 and M36 Tank Destroyers 1942–53* (Oxford: Osprey, 2002), 24; Yeide, *Steel Victory*, 26. Of the German PzKw IVs at Aachen it is unclear which model they were. They were most like the H or J models, the most common at that point in the war. The H model did have a powered traverse while the J did not. Both the H and J models carried eighty-seven rounds for their 75mm gun. Peter Chamberlain, and Hilary Doyle, *Encyclopedia of German Tanks of World War Two* (London: Arms and Armour, 1999), 98–99; Hogg, *The American Arsenal*, 98–99.

111 FM 18-5, *Tank Destroyer Field Manual, Organization and Tactics of Tank Destroyer Units*—officially published June 1942. Christopher R. Gabel, *Seek, Strike, and Destroy: U.S. Army Tank Destroyer Doctrine in World War II* (Fort Leavenworth, KS: Combat Studies Institute, 1985), 24–26, 49–50. To mount the larger and heavier 3-inch gun (2000 lbs. vs. 900 lbs. for the 75mm), and a larger diesel engine (3500 lbs. heavier than the early model Sherman gasoline engines), the M10 had to make do with less armor. Hogg, *The American Arsenal*, 29, 37, 51, 179–180. One advantage of the M10 was cost, about 25 percent less than a M4A2 Sherman. Zaloga, *M10*, 8.

112 Gerald Astor, *The Bloody Forest: Battle for the Huertgen: September 1944–January 1945*, (Novato, CA: Presidio, 2000), 218; Zaloga, *M10*, 16–21.

113 Chamberlain, *Encyclopedia of German Tanks*, 245. A Panzerfaust could penetrate the thickest armor on a King Tiger—the 8.5-inch front turret plate—which was twice the thickness of a Sherman's armor. Cooper, *Death Traps*, 257. The Panzerschreck could penetrate the frontal armor of a German Panther. Yeide, *Steel Victory*, 19.

114 Headquarters 634th Tank Destroyer Battalion, *After Action Report*.

115 745th Tank Battalion, *S-3 Journal*.

116 Headquarters 634th Tank Destroyer Battalion, *After Action Report*.

117 Yeide, *Steel Victory*, 146–150. The loss rate was a mix of total losses and vehicles that could be repaired and returned to service. Cooper, *Death Traps*, viii, 303.

118 David S. Wilson, "Evolution of Artillery Tactics in General J. Lawton Collins' U.S. VII Corps in WWII" (master's thesis, Command and General Staff College, US Army, Fort Leavenworth, KS. 1996) <http://stinet.dtic.mil/cgi-bin/GetTRDoc?AD=ADA312682&Location=U2&doc=GetTRDoc.pdf> [accessed 14 January 2007] (p. 21).

119 FM 100-5, May 1941, p. 210.

120 Daniel, *Capture*, 9–10.

121 Ibid., 7.

122 Ibid., 11, 18–19.

123 Hogg, *The American Arsenal*, 182, 302–303. In one instance, not in Aachen, a M12 155mm gun came around a bend in a road and met a German King

Tiger. The M12 fired off the first shot, blowing the turret completely off, killing all the crew. Cooper, *Death Traps*, 171.

124 Rounds from 155mm guns were found to penetrate only eighteen inches of concrete on bunkers but they would produce a severe concussion that often forced the Germans to surrender; bleeding out of their eyes, ears, nose and mouth. Levasseur, *Operations of the 1st Battalion*, 18–20.

125 *Account of the Battle of Aachen*, 17. The German commander was particularly impressed with the 155mm guns. *Commanding Officer Battle Group Aachen*, 2; Daniel, *Capture*, 13–15.

126 MacDonald, *United States Army*, 316.

127 Several sources misidentify this device as the V-3, but this first source contains a picture of one of the street cars with V-13 clearly painted on the side. The source of the confusion may be a humorous intelligence report written at the time, citing the wonders of the "V-3." Dawley, *Actions by the 238th*, 4 and Figure 6. *Group History: 1106th*, 3.

128 *Lessons Learned by the 1106th*, 3.

129 Price, *The Battle of Aachen*, 57.

130 Gorman, *Aachen 1944*, 1.

131 In their approach to the factory district on 10 October, 3rd Battalion suffered nine casualties while riding on tanks. Runey, "Chaos...," 49. This author could find no other references to infantry riding on tanks in Aachen after this.

132 Daniel, *Capture*, 11. *FM 31-50* contains a diagram showing building-to-building movement. FM 31-50, p. 93. German forces did much the same. In setting up their new headquarters on 19 Oct the SS men were digging from cellar to cellar. Whiting, *Bloody Aachen*, 132–133.

133 *Account of the Battle of Aachen*, 13.

134 Headquarters 1st Engineer Combat Battalion, *Report on October 1944 Operations*.

135 Yeide, *The Longest Battle*, 92.

136 Gorman, *Aachen 1944*, 16.

137 This problem was not unique to the urban environment. Replacement tires were in high demand in the 3rd Armored Division because of the frequent puncture from road debris, often from shell or mortar fragments. Cooper, *Death Traps*, 156, 263.

138 MacDonald, *United States Army*, 311.

139 Headquarters First Medical Battalion, First Infantry Division, *Operations Report for October 1944*, 31 October 1944, NA, 407/427/270/54/21/5/5966.

140 The M4 Sherman had the advantage of being narrower than the M10, 2.58m versus 3.00m, a plus when driving down narrow streets or those partially blocked off by rubble. Forty, *U.S. Army Handbook*, 139.

141 Price, *The Battle of Aachen*, 94.

142 Daniel, *Capture*, 9–12.

143 *Group History: 1106th*, 10–12.

144 Interviews with Colonel Wilck after his capture confirmed the German focus on the southern threat, and the difficulty he had in later shifting forces

during the day to counter the attack from the east. *Commanding Officer Battle Group Aachen*, 2.

145 A 12 October reference to extensive artillery fires, "We also have harassing fires all over town." *26th Infantry S-3 Unit Report for the Month of October.*

146 Koechling, *The Battle of the Aachen Sector*, 28; Daniel, *Capture*, 9–10.

147 *Account of the Battle of Aachen*, 12; *26th Infantry S-3 Unit Report for the Month of October.*

148 For the first two days of the assault (11–12 October) flying weather was good; but over 13 to 15 October the weather turned bad, allowing the Germans to "Reinforce the defenders of Aachen without the threat of interdiction." From 16 October until the surrender the flying weather was generally good. Price, *The Battle of Aachen*, 56–57.

149 "Only forty enemy aircraft were sighted during the entire battle." Price, *The Battle of Aachen*, 57.

150 *Germans Compare Russian and U.S. Army*, 3.

151 Hogg, *The American Arsenal*, 225–227, 245–246. A medium rate of fire of 125 rounds/minute could be sustained almost indefinitely. Bull, *World War Two Infantry Tactics: Company and Battalion*, 16.

152 MacDonald, *United States Army*, 311; Yeide, *The Longest Battle*, 93; Whiting, *Bloody Aachen*, 113–114.

153 US Army, *After Action Report, 1106th Engineer Combat Group*, NA, 407/427/270/62/13/6/19304.

154 Daniel, *Capture*, 11.

155 Ibid., 6.

156 Headquarters 634th Tank Destroyer Battalion, *After Action Report.*

157 Yeide, *The Longest Battle*, 90-91.

158 Gorman, *Aachen 1944*, 16.

159 *Group History: 1106th*, 4–5.

160 *26th Infantry S-3 Unit Report for the Month of October.*

161 Ian V. Hogg, *Mortars* (Ramsbury: Crowood Press, 2001), 67, 87.

162 *26th Infantry S-3 Unit Report for the Month of October.*

163 Astor, *The Bloody Forest*, 63.

164 Heichler, *The Germans*, 18–20, 33–34. Estimates range from 7–15,000 civilians for the number left in the city when the assault began. (7000—Gabel, 10,000—Price, 15,000—Parrish) Gabel, in *Block by Block*, 82; Price, *The Battle of Aachen*, 63; Monte M. Parrish, *The Battle of Aachen: An Analysis of City Fighting Tactics*, research paper written for the Infantry Officer Advanced Course 4-72, US Army Infantry School, Fort Benning, Georgia, 30 June 1972, DRL, p. 3.

165 Daniel, *Capture*, 5.

166 Price, *The Battle of Aachen*, 92–93.

167 Runey, "Chaos...," 83–84; Stromer, *Journal for the 3rd Battalion*, October to December 1944.

168 Daniel, *Capture*, 13–15.

169 *Account of the Battle of Aachen*, 22–23.

170 *Group History: 1106th*, 6.

171 *26th Infantry S-3 Unit Report for the Month of October.*

172 Yeide, *Steel Victory*, 157–158.

173 Gorman, *Aachen 1944*, 13.

174 *26th Infantry S-3 Unit Report for the Month of October.* The destruction of that particular church may not have been from the assault. According to one source the city's damage level from earlier bombing raids included the destruction of 43 percent of the buildings and twenty-five churches. Whiting, *Bloody Aachen*, 20–21.

175 *Account of the Battle of Aachen*, 21–22.

176 Gabel, in *Block by Block*, 77.

177 2nd Battalion (26th Infantry) commander Lieutenant Colonel Daniel realized that evacuating all civilians would slow his troops down somewhat, but he saw it as worthwhile to reduce the risk of sniping. Daniel, *Capture*, 6.

178 *Lessons Learned by the 1106th*, 3.

179 One source identifies the location of the camp but states it had a population of approximately forty-five hundred by the end of October. It is possible this source is referencing a peak population count that occurred at battle's end and not really the end of October. Gorman, *Aachen 1944*, 15. However, the following primary source gives a different population estimate. As of 14 October the Military Government Section in the 1st ID headquarters was reporting 1600 civilians evacuated from Aachen. On 15 October they reported 2750 civilians being cared for at the Brand Camp (former German barracks). By 31 October this number increased to 3301. US Army, Headquarters 1st Infantry Division, Military Government Section, *Monthly Report of Activities: October 1944*, November 1944, NA, 407/427/270/54/19/1/5841.

180 Gabel, *Block by Block*, 82; 1st Infantry Division, Military Police Platoon, *Journal October 1944*, 3.

181 Gabel, *Block by Block*, 76.

182 *Germans Compare Russian and U.S. Army*, 1.

183 War Department, *Field Service Regulations United States Army 1923*, MHI, p. III. War Department, *Tentative Field Service Regulations—Operations*, FM 100-5, October 1939, MHI, p. II. FM 100-5, May 1941, pp. II, 209. FM 100-5, June 1944, p. II.

184 Brown, *Operations of Company C*, 15; Stickels, *Operations*, 20.

185 Astor, *The Bloody Forest*, 356.

186 J. Lawton Collins, interviewed by Charles C. Sperow, *Senior Officers Oral History Program*, *Project 72-1*, Volume I, MHI, p. 222.

Chapter 3

1 Robert Ross Smith, *Triumph in the Philippines: The War in the Pacific* (Honolulu, HI: University Press of the Pacific, 2005), 6–17.

2 US Army, XIV Corps, *After Action Report—XIV Corps M1 Operation*, 29 July 1945, NA, 407/427/270/56/ 34/ 5/10033, p. 27.

3 Smith, *Triumph*, 22–26.
4 Walter Krueger, *From Down Under to Nippon: The Story of Sixth Army in World War II* (Washington, DC: Combat Forces Press, 1953), 226–227; Gordon L. Rottman, *Japanese Army in World War II: Conquest of the Pacific* (Oxford: Osprey, 2005), 61–73; Buddy Buck, *Battle of Manila*, Combat Studies Institute Battlebook 13-B (Fort Leavenworth, KS: Combat Studies Institute, US Army Command and General Staff College, 1984), CARL, p. IV-1.
5 XIV Corps, *After Action Report*, 53, 58.
6 Krueger, *From Down Under*, 227–228. XIV Corps commander Griswold was also less optimistic than MacArthur. Oscar W. Griswold, *Diary of Lieutenant General Oscar W. Griswold 1943–1945*, MHI, Oscar W. Griswold Papers, Box 1, entry for 14 January.
7 There are indications that Yamashita planned on counterattacking US forces, using the open terrain of the Central Plain for "skillful maneuver," once the Americans had taken Manila. However, counterattacks executed once American forces were in Manila were weak and ineffective. US Army, Headquarters XIV Corps, Allied Translator and Interpreter Section (ATIS) Advanced Echelon, *Prisoner of War Preliminary Interrogation Report*, 18 March 1945, 26-IR-63, microfiche, MHI, D 735 .W3713 1988, pp. 8, 13. US Army, Headquarters XIV Corps, Allied Translator and Interpreter Section (ATIS) Advanced Echelon, *Prisoner of War Preliminary Interrogation Report*, 7 April 1945, 26-IR-82, microfiche, MHI, D 735 .W3713 1988, p. 4. [All subsequent interrogation and translated document citations will be referred to with: ATIS, their document code (e.g., 26-IR-82), and a page number.]
8 Smith, *Triumph*, 88–92.
9 XIV Corps, *After Action Report*, 69.
10 Ibid., 75.
11 Giles H. Kidd, *The Operations of the 37th Infantry Division in the Crossing of the Pasig River and Closing to the Walls of Intramuros, Manila 7–9 February 1945 (Luzon Campaign)*, 1950, paper written for the Advanced Infantry Course, 1949–1950, The Infantry School, Fort Benning, Georgia, DRL, p. 10.
12 US Army, Headquarters 11th Airborne Division, *Report After Action with the Enemy, Operational Mike VI Luzon Campaign*, 24 January 1946, MHI, S.l., 1946, #05-11-1946/2, pp. 3–5; Krueger, *From Down Under*, 235–241.
13 Smith, *Triumph*, 217–220.
14 Krueger, *From Down Under*, 237.
15 XIV Corps, *After Action Report*, 80; Krueger, *From Down Under*, 239–242.
16 Kevin C. M. Benson, "Manila 1945: City Fight in the Pacific," in *City Fights: Selected Histories of Urban Combat from WWII to Vietnam*, ed. John Antal and Bradley Gericke (New York: Ballantine, 2003), 237; Smith, *Triumph*, 217–220.
17 Smith, *Triumph*, 224–231.
18 Headquarters 11th Airborne Division, 5.
19 Richard Connaughton, John Pimlott, and Duncan Anderson, *The Battle for Manila* (Novato, CA: Presidio Press, 1995), 46–47, 65–66.

20 Ibid., 65–71.
21 Smith, *Triumph*, 94–97.
22 This handover of command occurred on or after 13 January. Smith, *Triumph*, 241–243; XIV Corps, *After Action Report*, 86.
23 ATIS, 26-IR-63, pp. 8, 13; Smith, *Triumph*, 240–243.
24 US Army, Headquarters Sixth Army, *Japanese Defense of Cities as Exemplified by the Battle for Manila—Report by XIV Corps*, 1 July 1945, MHI, D767.4J36, p. 1. ATIS, 26-T-60, p. 2. A US congressional committee's report on the battle attributed the destruction plan to the High Command in Tokyo. US Congress, Senate, Committee on Military Affairs, *Sack of Manila*, 16 July 1945, MHI, pp. 2–3.
25 Headquarters Sixth Army, 2. One source suggests the Japanese were influenced in this by the naval facilities south of the city. Charles A. Henne, *Battle History of the 3rd Battalion, 148th Infantry*, vol. 6, "Manila, the Unwanted Battle (4 February through 7 March 1945)," MHI, D811H454, p. 34.
26 ATIS, 26-T-52, pp. 1–3.
27 US Army, 37th Infantry Division Headquarters, *Report After Action 37th Infantry Division—The Luzon Operation (M-1 Campaign)*, NA 407/427/270/56/34/5/10033, Part II, pp. 31–32.
28 Smith, *Triumph*, 246–248; Headquarters 640th Tank Destroyer Battalion, *Intelligence Report on Luzon Campaign, 9 Jan 45 to 19 Mar 45*, January to March 1945, NA 407/427/270/64/32/1/23633, p. 1.
29 "The enemy took excellent advantage of the specialized topography of the city." Headquarters Sixth Army, 14.
30 Headquarters Sixth Army, 15.
31 Yamashita's armor was largely lost in the first week of February in a failed Japanese attempt to stop I Corps' movement south. Smith, *Triumph*, 190–202; Rottman, *Japanese Army*, 7; 37th Infantry Division Headquarters, *Report After Action 37th Infantry Division—The Luzon Operation*, Part IV, pp. 8, 46; Headquarters Sixth Army, 15. Most of the Japanese anti-tank weapons were man-portable and hand-thrown. Buck, *Battle*, Appendix 19.
32 Buck, *Battle*, Appendix 19; Headquarters Sixth Army, 10–11.
33 Buck, *Battle*, p. III-15. ATIS, 26-IR-63, p. 10.
34 From the Lingayen landing until the capture of Manila, the 37th Infantry Division captured only six Japanese radios capable of both transmitting and receiving. 37th Infantry Division Headquarters, *Report After Action 37th Infantry Division—The Luzon Operation*, Part IV, 21. One captured Japanese document refers to getting information from other Japanese units via carrier pigeon while battling radio-equipped Filipino guerrillas. ATIS, 26-T-119, p. 11; XIV Corps, *After Action Report*, 86; Headquarters Sixth Army, 9.
35 Headquarters Sixth Army, 4–5, 9, 16. US Army, 37th Infantry Division Headquarters, *G-2 Journal, 4–6 February 1945*, NA, 407/427/270/57/2/1/10058, sheet 159.
36 Connaughton, *The Battle for Manila*, 73; Smith, *Triumph*, 246–248.
37 Headquarters Sixth Army, 2.
38 Connaughton, *The Battle for Manila*, 91–92; Smith, *Triumph*, 251–252.

39 Griswold, *Diary*, entry for 4 February 1945. US Army Military History Collection, Senior Officers Debriefing Program, *Conversations Between General Paul L. Freeman, USA (Ret.), and Colonel James N. Ellis—US Army War College*, compilation of three interviews, 1973-74, MHI, pp. 73-74.

40 37th Infantry Headquarters, *Report After Action 37th Infantry Division—The Luzon Operation*, 25.

41 Smith, *Triumph*, 220, 250–251.

42 Henne, *Battle History*, 43–47; Headquarters Sixth Army, 7–8; Smith, *Triumph*, 254–256.

43 Smith, *Triumph*, 258–260; Henne, *Battle History*, 56; 37th Infantry Headquarters, *Report After Action 37th Infantry Division—The Luzon Operation*, Part II, pp. 29–30.

44 Headquarters Sixth Army, 20; 37th Infantry Headquarters, *Report After Action 37th Infantry Division—The Luzon Operation*, Part II, 29; Smith, *Triumph*, 256–257.

45 Smith, *Triumph*, 266–268.

46 Ibid., 264–265.

47 Ibid., 271.

48 Thomas M. Huber, "The Battle of Manila," in *Block by Block: The Challenges of Urban Operations*, ed. William G. Robertson and Lawrence A. Yates (Fort Leavenworth, KS: US Army Command and General Staff College Press, 2003), 101–102; 37th Infantry Headquarters, *Report After Action 37th Infantry Division—The Luzon Operation*, Part II, p. 32.

49 37th Infantry Headquarters, *Report After Action 37th Infantry Division—G-3 Periodic Report, 5 February 1945*, NA, 407/427/270/57/2/1/10083, p. 2. Kevin T. McEnery, "The XIV Corps Battle for Manila: February 1945" (master's thesis, US Army Command and General Staff College, 1993), MHI, p. 82; Stanley A. Frankel and Frederick Kirker, eds., *The 37th Infantry Division in World War II* (Washington, DC: Infantry Journal Press, 1948), 240.

50 Smith, *Triumph*, 280–283.

51 Ibid., 272–273.

52 Headquarters 11th Airborne Division, 5–6, 17.

53 Smith, *Triumph*, 269–270, 277–279; 37th Infantry Headquarters, *Report After Action 37th Infantry Division—The Luzon Operation*, Part II, p. 35; Krueger, *From Down Under*, 248; Headquarters 11th Airborne Division, 6.

54 Smith, *Triumph*, 239–240, 275, 291–294; Griswold, *Diary*, entries for 11–17 February 1945; XIV Corps, *After Action Report*, 114–130.

55 XIV Corps, *After Action Report*, 130–134; Huber, in *Block by Block*, 108; Connaughton, *The Battle for Manila*, 171.

56 Krueger, *From Down Under*, 211–222. In the nineteen-page "planning" section of the Sixth Army G-4 report on Luzon no mention is made of Manila, though there is a page on civilian relief. US Army, Sixth Army, *G-4 Report Luzon Campaign*, MHI, #03-6.1945/6, pp. 2–21.

57 Krueger had received intelligence on 5 February that the Japanese were planning to destroy the nodes so he ordered the XIV Corps to take them. Krueger, *From Down Under*, 245.

58 Griswold, *Diary*, entries for 4, 7, 11–17 February 1945; Stephen L. Garay, *The Breach of Intramuros*, Armored School student paper, 1948, MHI, U423 .5 R32 1947–1948 G37, p. 9.

59 Henne, *Battle History*, 16 and VIII of the Appendix A Postscript . *Biographic information on MG Robert Sprague Beightler, commander, 37th Infantry Division*, NA, 407/427/270/56/34/5/10048, Biographical Sketches Folder, p. 1. Robert H. Berlin, *U.S. Army World War II Corps Commanders: A Composite Biography* (Fort Leavenworth, KS: US Army Command and General Staff College, 1989), CARL.

60 37th Infantry Headquarters, *Report After Action 37th Infantry Division—The Luzon Operation*, Part II, pp. 28, 31. Frankel, *The 37th*, 263, 284.

61 Griswold, *Diary*, entries for 6, 7, 28 February 1945.

62 37th Infantry Headquarters, *Report After Action 37th Infantry Division—The Luzon Operation*, Part II, p. 35; Headquarters 11th Airborne Division, 5–6, 17; Krueger, *From Down Under*, 248.

63 Krueger, *From Down Under*, 249.

64 37th Infantry Headquarters, *Report After Action 37th Infantry Division—The Luzon Operation*, Part II, p. 31.

65 War Department, *Field Service Regulations United States Army 1923*, MHI, p. III; War Department, *Tentative Field Service Regulations—Operations*, FM 100-5, MHI, p. II; War Department, *Field Service Regulations—Operations*, FM 100-5, MHI, p. 209; The Infantry School, US Army, *Infantry in Battle*, 2nd ed. (Richmond, VA: Garrett and Massie, 1939), CARL, Introduction; War Department, *Attack on a Fortified Position and Combat in Towns*, Field Manual FM 31-50, January 1944, MHI, p. 61.

66 Buck, *Battle*, pp. III-4 to III-6.

67 Headquarters 11th Airborne Division, 5–6, 17.

68 Henne, *Battle History*, 74–82.

69 Forty men were wounded. Henne, *Battle History*, 69–70.

70 US Army, 37th Infantry Division Artillery Headquarters, *Report After Action – Journal and Reports, From 1 November 1944 to 30 June 1945*, undated, NA, 407/427/270/57/2/1/10157, pp. 48, 50, 51, 77.

71 Smith, *Triumph*, 260–263.

72 Headquarters Sixth Army, 26. Henne, *Battle History*, 74.

73 Henne, *Battle History*, 75–76. Buck, *Battle*, p. III-5.

74 Headquarters Sixth Army, 21.

75 XIV Corps, *After Action Report*, 53. 37th Infantry Headquarters, *Report After Action 37th Infantry Division—The Luzon Operation*, Part VII, 54.

76 Headquarters 640th Tank Destroyer Battalion, *640th Tank Destroyer Battalion Operations Report (M-1 Operation), Island of Luzon, P.I., 9 January to 19 March 1945*, 5 August 1945, NA 407/427/270/64/32/1/23631, pp. 10–11.

77 Headquarters I Corps Artillery, US Army, "Jap Artillery in Northern Luzon," *Field Artillery Journal* 36 (Jan 1946): 21.

78 XIV Corps, *After Action Report*, 45; William S. McElhenny, et al., *Armor on Luzon: Comparison of Employment of Armored Units in the 1941–42 and 1944–45 Luzon Campaigns*, Armored School paper, 1950, MHI, D767.4A55, p. 68.

79 One 3 February 37th Infantry intelligence journal entry noted a large force defending Manila but estimated it at 12,000. 37th Infantry Headquarters, *G-2 Journal*, 3 February 1945; 37th Infantry Headquarters, *Report After Action 37th Infantry Division—The Luzon Operation*, Part II, pp. 2, 11, 29; XIV Corps, *After Action Report*, 86.

80 Griswold, *Diary*, entry for 7 February 1945. On 5 February Krueger stated it was clear the city would be defended. Krueger, *From Down Under*, 227–228, 245. Not until 12 February did MacArthur's headquarters change its estimate of Japanese defenses in Manila. McEnery, "The XIV Corps...," 90.

81 Headquarters Sixth Army, 14, 19. 37th Infantry Headquarters, *Report After Action 37th Infantry Division—The Luzon Operation*, Part VII, pp. 12–13, 16–17, Part IV, p. 7. Buck, *Battle*, pp. III-7 to III-8. XIV Corps, *After Action Report*, Part II, p. 50.

82 37th Infantry Headquarters, *Report After Action 37th Infantry Division—The Luzon Operation*, Part IV, p. 11.

83 Headquarters Sixth Army, 14, 19. 37th Infantry Headquarters, *Report After Action 37th Infantry Division—The Luzon Operation*, Part VII, 12–13, 16–17, Part IV, p. 7. XIV Corps, *After Action Report*, p. 50.

84 37th Infantry Headquarters, *Report After Action 37th Infantry Division—The Luzon Operation*, Part IV, p. 1, Part VII, p. 10. Krueger, *From Down Under*, 245; Smith, *Triumph*, 250–251.

85 Headquarters Sixth Army, 4–5, 9.

86 37th Infantry Headquarters, *Report After Action 37th Infantry Division—The Luzon Operation*, Part IV, pp. 8, 46. 37th Infantry Artillery Headquarters, *Report After Action*, p. 51.

87 Headquarters Sixth Army, p. 16. 37th Infantry Headquarters, *G-2 Journal*, 4–6 February 1945.

88 Henne, *Battle History*, 83.

89 XIV Corps, *After Action Report*, 54–55; Headquarters 640th Tank Destroyer Battalion, *Intelligence Report*, 2.

90 37th Infantry Headquarters, *Report After Action 37th Infantry Division—The Luzon Operation*, Part VII, pp. 8–9, 13.

91 Exact prisoner counts for Manila are difficult to derive from the various unit reports. The 37th Infantry reports 459 POWs for its operations from the Lingayen landing up through the surrender of Manila, but does not break out how many of those were taken inside the city. The Sixth Army reports cite 1579 POWs taken in all of its operations up through 10 March, but again, there is no breakout for Manila. The "fewer than 1000" figure is this author's rough estimate. 37th Infantry Headquarters, *Report After Action 37th Infantry Division—The Luzon Operation*, Part II, p. 54. Sixth Army, *G-4 Report Luzon Campaign*, p. 37.

92 37th Infantry Headquarters, *Report After Action 37th Infantry Division—The Luzon Operation*, Part VII, p. 14.

93 Smith, *Triumph*, 302–303.

94 For example, the 37th Infantry assaulted major bunker complexes at Munda (1943) and Bougainville (1943–1944). McEnery, "The XIV Corps...," 63; Headquarters Sixth Army, p. 22; Smith, *Triumph*, 275.

95 Headquarters Sixth Army, p. 21.

96 War Department, FM 31-50 (January 1944), pp. 28, 48, 50–75.

97 McEnery, "The XIV Corps...," 21–31. For an argument that the smaller unit tactics had to be improvised as well, see: Buck, *Battle*, pp. III-9 to III-10.

98 37th Infantry Headquarters, *Report After Action 37th Infantry Division—The Luzon Operation*, Section III, p. 1, Part VII, p. 40. Headquarters Sixth Army, 21–22.

99 US Army, Headquarters 754th Tank Battalion, *Battle of Luzon: 9 Jan–30 June '45*, undated, NA, 407/427/270/60/31/7/16760, unnumbered page.

100 Headquarters Sixth Army, 21–22.

101 Henne, *Battle History*, 42, 74–77.

102 37th Infantry Headquarters, *The Luzon Operation*, Part II, p. 30. 37th Infantry Headquarters, *Report After Action 37th Infantry Division—G-3*, p. 2.

103 37th Infantry Headquarters, *Report After Action 37th Infantry Division—The Luzon Operation*, Part II, p. 42.

104 Smith, *Triumph*, 285–290.

105 George Forty, *US Army Handbook 1939–1945* (New York: Barnes and Noble, 1995), 70–71; George Forty, *Japanese Army Handbook: 1939–1945* (Stroud, UK: Sutton, 2002), 60–61.

106 Headquarters 640th Tank Destroyer Battalion, *Intelligence Report*, 1.

107 Ibid., 1.

108 Henne, *Battle History*, 74, 78.

109 37th Infantry Headquarters, *Report After Action 37th Infantry Division—The Luzon Operation*, Part VII, p. 64.

110 XIV Corps, *After Action Report*, 64–65, 67.

111 Smith, *Triumph*, 285–290.

112 As in *FM 31-50*. Headquarters Sixth Army, p. 21.

113 Smith, *Triumph*, 275; Connaughton, *The Battle for Manila*, 156–157.

114 37th Infantry Headquarters, *Report After Action 37th Infantry Division—The Luzon Operation*, Part VII, p. 29. Headquarters Sixth Army, 22–24.

115 Henne, *Battle History*, 62–63.

116 One survived; both received the Medal of Honor. Frankel, *The 37th*, 274.

117 Ibid., 281–285.

118 The 240mm howitzer was a rare piece of equipment; only 315 were produced during World War II. Steven J. Zaloga, *US Field Artillery of World War II* (Oxford: Osprey, 2007), 9, 24–35. Starting in May 57mm and 75mm recoilless rifles would be used in clearing Japanese positions east of Manila, but they did not arrive in time to be used in Manila. Smith, *Triumph*, 421.

119 The shorter M3 series 105mm towed gun weighed about half the standard M2 series towed 105mm, but its range was 40 percent less. Ian Hogg, *The American Arsenal: The World War II Official Standard Ordnance Catalog of Small Arms, Tanks, Armored Cars, Artillery, Antiaircraft Guns, Ammunition, Grenades, Mines, etcetera* (London: Greenhill, 2001), 52–55.

120 The cannon companies attached to infantry regiments had been upgraded from towed short-barrel 105mm howitzers for the units at Manila. Zaloga, *US Field Artillery of World War II*, 14.

121 McEnery, "The XIV Corps...," 141–143; Krueger, *From Down Under*, 248.

122 Smith, *Triumph*, 339–357; Terrance C. McGovern and Mark A Berhow, *American Defenses of Corregidor and Manila Bay 1898-1945* (Oxford: Osprey, 2003), 37–41.

123 37th Infantry Headquarters, *Report After Action 37th Infantry Division—The Luzon Operation*, 45; Smith, *Triumph*, 303.

124 As I Corps cleared northern Luzon from January to August 1945 it reported only having to displace artillery three or four times due to Japanese counterbattery fire. Headquarters I Corps Artillery, "Jap Artillery in Northern Luzon," 23. The only mention of US artillery losses to Japanese counterbattery fire in the 37th Infantry after-action report is of two 155mm howitzers damaged by mortar fire on 25 February. 37th Infantry Headquarters, *Report After Action 37th Infantry Division—The Luzon Operation*, Part II, p. 51.

125 37th Infantry Headquarters, *Report After Action 37th Infantry Division—The Luzon Operation*, Section III, p. 7; Smith, *Triumph*, 303. The 37th Division artillery headquarters log for the dates of the battle of Manila notes six killed, sixty-three wounded in action, and two howitzers damaged. US Army, 37th Infantry Division Artillery Headquarters, *Daily Unit Logs: Jan-March 1945*, NA, 407/427/270/57/2/1/10157.

126 37th Infantry Artillery Headquarters, *Report After Action*, 42–43, 53.

127 Smith, *Triumph*, 263–264.

128 37th Infantry Headquarters, *Report After Action 37th Infantry Division—The Luzon Operation*, Part II, p. 32.

129 See, 37th Infantry Artillery Headquarters, *Report After Action*.

130 Headquarters Sixth Army, pp.22–25. 37th Infantry Headquarters, *Report After Action 37th Infantry Division—The Luzon Operation*, Section III, p. 7.

131 Headquarters Sixth Army, 22–24.

132 XIV Corps, *After Action Report*, 63, 67; Garay, *The Breach*, 11.

133 37th Infantry Headquarters, *Report After Action 37th Infantry Division—The Luzon Operation*, Part II, pp. 30, 43, 50.

134 McEnery, "The XIV Corps...," 141–143. The 754th Tank Battalion was equipped with early model M4 and M4A1 tanks. McElhenny, *Armor on Luzon*, 106.

135 640th Tank Destroyer Battalion, *S-3 Reports*, 10 January to 5 March 1945, NA 407/427/270/64/32/1/23633.

136 Steven J. Zaloga, *M26/M46 Pershing Tank 1943–53* (Oxford: Osprey, 2000), 16–19.

137 37th Infantry Headquarters, *Report After Action 37th Infantry Division—The Luzon Operation*, Part II, p. 36. Headquarters 754th Tank Battalion, unnumbered page.

138 Headquarters Sixth Army, 25.

139 McElhenny, *Armor on Luzon*, 107.

140 Frankel, *The 37th*, 266.

141 37th Infantry Headquarters, *Report After Action 37th Infantry Division—The Luzon Operation*, Part VII, p. 36. XIV Corps, *After Action Report*, 92.
142 Headquarters Sixth Army, 25.
143 Headquarters 754th Tank Battalion, unnumbered page. 37th Infantry Headquarters, *Report After Action 37th Infantry Division—The Luzon Operation*, Part VII, pp. 36, 44. XIV Corps, *After Action Report*, 64–65, 67.
144 A 37th Infantry source mentions eighteen sorties over 9 and 10 February. 37th Infantry Headquarters, *Report After Action 37th Infantry Division—G-3*. Smith lists ten to twelve sorties. Smith, *Triumph*, 291–294.
145 Headquarters 754th Tank Battalion, unnumbered page.
146 Smith, *Triumph*, 280–290.
147 37th Infantry Headquarters, *Report After Action 37th Infantry Division—G-3*. 37th Infantry Headquarters, *Report After Action 37th Infantry Division—The Luzon Operation*, Part II, pp. 28–52.
148 37th Infantry Headquarters, *Report After Action 37th Infantry Division—The Luzon Operation*, Part II, pp. 47–51. *Headquarters Sixth Army*, 24–25.
149 Glenn A. Steckel, *The Role of Field Artillery in the Siege on Intramuros, Manila, P.I.*, Student paper, Armored School, May 1948, MHI, U423.5R32, p. 13.
150 Griswold, *Diary*, entry for 23 February 1945.
151 37th Infantry Headquarters, *Report After Action 37th Infantry Division—The Luzon Operation*, Part II, pp. 47–51; Smith, *Triumph*, 300–301.
152 In mid-March C-47s would spray DDT repeatedly over the city ending the plague of flies. Also by mid-March, civilians work crews had buried most the dead. Henne, *Battle History*, 95.
153 XIV Corps, *After Action Report*, 135, 141.
154 37th Infantry Headquarters, *Report After Action 37th Infantry Division—The Luzon Operation*, Part VI, pp. 6, 14.
155 XIV Corps, *After Action Report*, Part II, p. 147.
156 Smith, *Triumph*, 652.
157 Henne, *Battle History*, 72.
158 Most secondary sources probably get the commonly used casualty figures from the US Army's official history of the campaign. Smith, *Triumph*, 306–307. Moreover, the 37th Infantry's after-action report cannot be taken at face value because it lumps the casualties suffered in Manila with all those suffered since the Lingayen landings. This inflates the losses by approximately 20 percent as those suffered clearing Clark Field are then included. This author found the division's daily G-3 reports a more accurate source. 37th Infantry Headquarters, *Report After Action 37th Infantry Division—G-3*. 37th Infantry Headquarters, *Report After Action 37th Infantry Division—The Luzon Operation*, Part II, p. 54, Part VI, p. 11.
159 In both of these sources the Japanese losses do not include estimates on those who were killed but whose bodies were not found. Krueger, *From Down Under*, 271; XIV Corps, *After Action Report*, 135.
160 Headquarters 640th Tank Destroyer Battalion, *Operations Report*, A Company Journal annex, pp. 1–5. 640th Tank Destroyer Battalion, *Casualty Reports*, January to March 1945, NA 407/427/270/64/32/1/23631. *History of the*

640th Tank Destroyer Battalion, NA 407/427/270/64/32/1/23631, Appendix C.

161 Headquarters 640th Tank Destroyer Battalion, *Intelligence Report*, 1.

162 US Army, Headquarters 672nd Amphibian Tractor Battalion, *Historical Record of the 672d Amphibian Tractor Battalion During Luzon Campaign*, NA, 407/427/270/60/29/6/16652, pp. 2–4. US Army, Headquarters 672nd Amphibian Tractor Battalion, *Historical Report of Luzon Campaign: 9 January 1945–30 June 1945*, NA, 407/427/270/60/29/6/16652.

163 Headquarters 754th Tank Battalion, chart preceding Lessons Learned During Luzon Campaign section, several unnumbered pages in the Phase IV section. Many other secondary sources and the unit reports of other units report several "lost" Shermans. This discrepancy likely stems from the 754th Tank Battalion headquarters knowing which vehicles were later put back into service, while the reports of other units had only the initial incident to report.

164 Headquarters 754th Tank Battalion, unnumbered pages in the Battle of Manila section.

165 Headquarters 754th Tank Battalion, unnumbered page.

166 Headquarters 640th Tank Destroyer Battalion, *Operations Report*, A Company Journal annex, 14.

167 Gordon L. Rottman, *World War II Infantry Anti-Tank Tactics* (Oxford: Osprey, 2005), 57.

168 37th Infantry Headquarters, *Report After Action 37th Infantry Division—G-3*, 5 *February 1945*, p. 2; McEnery, "The XIV Corps...," 82; Frankel, *The 37th*, 240.

169 Headquarters Sixth Army, 7–8; Henne, *Battle History*, 43–44.

170 The 37th Infantry suffered fourteen killed and 101 wounded on that day, most associated with the crossing of the Pasig. 37th Infantry Headquarters, *Report After Action 37th Infantry Division—The Luzon Operation*, Part II, p. 28.

171 US Army, 117th Engineer Combat Battalion, *117th Engineer Combat Battalion: Report After Action Against the Enemy in the Luzon Campaign, 1 November 1944 to 30 June 1945*, undated, NA, 407/427/270/57/3/4/10166, pp. 14–15. Henne, *Battle History*, 52–57; Kenneth J. Deacon, "Assault Crossings on the Pasig River," *The Military Engineer* 50 (Jan–Feb 1958): 8–9; Headquarters 672nd Amphibian Tractor Battalion, *Historical Record*, 2–4, Unit Report No. 25, p. 1. 37th Infantry Headquarters, *Report After Action 37th Infantry Division—The Luzon Operation*, Part II, p. 28.

172 37th Infantry Headquarters, *Report After Action 37th Infantry Division—The Luzon Operation*, Part V, p. 13.

173 Deacon, "Assault Crossings on the Pasig River," 8–9.

174 Headquarters 672nd Amphibian Tractor Battalion, *Historical Record*, 4–5, Unit Report No. 29, p. 1, Unit Report No. 31, p. 1. Buck, *Battle*, pp. IV-8 to IV-9. Deacon, "Assault Crossings on the Pasig River," 9.

175 117th Engineer Combat Battalion, 14–15; Deacon, "Assault Crossings on the Pasig River," 9–10.

176 Benson, in *City Fights*, 234; Buck, *Battle*, p. III-3. Kenneth J. Deacon, "Mine Warfare in Manila, 1945," *The Military Engineer* 57 (Sept–Oct 1965): 348.

177 FM 31-50 (January 1944), 96–97.

178 Headquarters Sixth Army, 6; Connaughton, *The Battle for Manila*, 189.

179 Deacon, "Mine Warfare in Manila, 1945," 348; 117th Engineer Combat Battalion, 21; Connaughton, *The Battle for Manila*, 197; 37th Infantry Headquarters, *Report After Action 37th Infantry Division—The Luzon Operation*, Part VII, p. 29.

180 McEnery, "The XIV Corps...," 51–52; Garay, *The Breach*, 13.

181 FM 31-50 (January 1944), 81; Smith, *Triumph*, 275; Henne, *Battle History*, 68.

182 37th Infantry Artillery Headquarters, *Report After Action*, 58, 74–75.

183 37th Infantry Headquarters, *Report After Action 37th Infantry Division—The Luzon Operation*, Part II, pp. 51–53.

184 Milton T. Hunt, *Use of Armor on Luzon*, Armored School paper, 1948, MHI, U423.5.R32.1947–1948.H86, p. 9.

185 Frankel, *The 37th*, 261, 284.

186 37th Infantry Artillery Headquarters, *Report After Action*, 70; US 37th Infantry Headquarters, *Report After Action 37th Infantry Division—The Luzon Operation*, Part II, p. 35. 37th Infantry Headquarters, *G-2 Journal*, 10 February 1945, sheet 132, 21 February 1945, sheet 179.

187 XIV Corps, *After Action Report*, p. 114. While many sources mention tunnels, this source is the only one that mentions them under the Pasig. 37th Infantry Headquarters, *G-2 Journal*, 10 February 1945, sheet 133.

188 XIV Corps, *After Action Report*, Part II, pp. 103–105.

189 By morning most of the paint had burned off the mortar tubes. Henne, *Battle History*, p. 78.

190 37th Infantry Headquarters, *Report After Action 37th Infantry Division—The Luzon Operation* Part II, p. 49.

191 37th Infantry Headquarters, *Report After Action 37th Infantry Division—The Luzon Operation*, Part V, p. 13.

192 XIV Corps, *After Action Report*, Part II, p. 103.

193 Sixth Army, *G-4 Report Luzon Campaign*, 38–39.

194 37th Infantry Headquarters, *Report After Action 37th Infantry Division—The Luzon Operation*, Part VII, p. 61. Sixth Army, *G-4 Report Luzon Campaign*, 17, 38–39.

195 Headquarters 640th Tank Destroyer Battalion, *Operations Report*, 11–12; *History of the 640th Tank Destroyer Battalion*, unnumbered page; Headquarters 754th Tank Battalion, unnumbered page.

196 Unit reports from the 672nd Amphibian Tractor Battalion make many references to the Alligators having already reached their life expectancy and imminent large-scale breakdowns. However, the Alligators always appeared in sufficient number when needed. Headquarters 672nd Amphibian Tractor Battalion, *Historical Report*, Unit Reports No. 20, 25, 26, 29, 32, 38, 1–26 February 1945. XIV Corps, *After Action Report*, Part II, p. 81.

197 XIV Corps, *After Action Report*, Part II, pp. 133–136.

198 MacArthur had issued general orders on Luzon that civilian movement was not to be impeded. Krueger, *From Down Under*, 244.

199 Smith, *Triumph*, 40.

200 24,000 tons of civilian supplies were scheduled to land on Luzon within the first sixty days. Sixth Army, *G-4 Report Luzon Campaign*, 17, 38–39. There was some confusion and delay within the Sixth Army headquarters about repairing and operating the civilian infrastructure of Manila. McEnery, "The XIV Corps...," 72, 79.

201 XIV Corps, *After Action Report*, 2–3.

202 See US Army, Headquarters XIV Corps, *Report of Investigation of Atrocities—Committed by Japanese Imperial Forces in Intramuros (Walled City) Manila, P.I.—During February 1945*, 6 April 1945, MHI, Russel B. Reynolds Papers, Box 1. US Army Forces Pacific—Headquarters, *Arraignment Proceedings of Tomoyuki Yamashita—United States of America vs. Tomoyuki Yamashita*, 8 October 1945, MHI, Russel B. Reynolds Papers, Box 1, pp. 42–58.

203 This figure was the estimate of the International Military Tribunal of the Far East, the Pacific equivalent of Nuremburg. Iris Chang, *The Rape of Nanking* (New York: Basic Books, 1997), 4.

204 37th Infantry Division Headquarters, *G-2 Journal*, 15 February 1945, sheet 159.

205 37th Infantry Headquarters, *G-2 Journal*, 15 February 1945, sheet 158. ATIS, 26-T-93, p. 7.

206 Headquarters Sixth Army, 16; 37th Infantry Headquarters, *G-2 Journal*, 5 and 11 February 1945.

207 Smith, *Triumph*, 307.

208 One tentative estimate attributed 60 percent to Japanese actions. Connaughton, *The Battle for Manila*, 122–123, 195.

209 For example, see Connaughton, *The Battle for Manila*, 200.

210 Unit reports during the battle are replete with references to Japanese atrocities in and around Manila. For example: 37th Infantry Artillery Headquarters, *Report After Action*, 40; US Army, 37th Infantry Division Headquarters, *G-2 Journal*, 1, 4, 11 February 1945.

211 The documentation on this was extensive in the proceedings of General Yamashita's war crimes trial after the war. Yamashita was found responsible for the atrocities in Manila and elsewhere on Luzon and executed by hanging in February 1946 outside of Manila. US Army Forces Pacific—Headquarters, *Trial of Tomoyuki Yamashita—Vol. 34, Findings*, 7 December 1945, MHI, Russel B. Reynolds Papers, Box 1, pp. 4057, 4062–4063. US Army Forces Pacific—Headquarters, *Arraignment Proceedings of Tomoyuki Yamashita*, 42–58. See also, Headquarters XIV Corps, *Report of Investigation of Atrocities*.

212 ATIS, 26-T-36, p. 4. ATIS, 26-IR-60, p. 1. ATIS, 26-T-84, p. 9. ATIS, 26-T-102, p. 5. ATIS, 26-T-119, p. 1.

213 Griswold wrestled with this moral issue in his diary, but he concluded his first duty was to protect the lives of his soldiers. Griswold, *Diary*, entries for 11–17 February 1945.

214 Several Japanese frcighters left Lingayen Gulf for Japan, just thirteen days before the Sixth Army landed. Onboard were 1300 Allied POWs from Bilibid Prison in Manila, only 400 of whom would survive the journey. George Weller, *First Into Nagasaki* (New York: Crown, 2006), 177–239.

215 McEnery, "The XIV Corps...," 63, 110; Headquarters Sixth Army, 13.

216 Headquarters Sixth Army, p. 26. Henne, *Battle History*, 74.

217 Michael D. Doubler, *Closing With the Enemy: How GIs Fought the War in Europe, 1944–1945* (Lawrence: University of Kansas Press, 1994), 282.

Chapter 4

1 Michael D. Doubler, *Closing With the Enemy: How GIs Fought the War in Europe, 1944–1945* (Lawrence: University of Kansas Press, 1994), 270.

2 General Board, United States Forces, European Theater, *Strategy of the Campaign in Western Europe 1944–1945*, Study No. 1, undated, MHI, pp. iv, 32, 50, 54–55, 59–60.

3 General Board, United States Forces, European Theater, *Organization, Equipment, and Tactical Employment of Separate Tank Battalions*, Study No. 50, undated, CARL; General Board, *Organization, Equipment, and Tactical Employment of the Infantry Division*, Study No. 15, undated, MHI, pp. 12–14.

4 General Board, United States Forces, European Theater, *Study of Organization, Equipment, and Tactical Employment of Tank Destroyer Units*, Study No. 60, undated, CARL, p. 18.

5 Gerald Astor, *The Bloody Forest: Battle for the Huertgen: September 1944– January 1945* (Novato, CA: Presidio, 2000), 356. In terms of destroyed ve-hicles, only one M10 was lost in Manila while eleven Shermans were lost in the first four days on Iwo Jima. See the Manila chapter for further details.

6 George S. Patton, *War As I Knew It* (New York: Houghton Mifflin Company, 1947), 343.

7 Robert A. Doughty, *The Evolution of US Army Tactical Doctrine, 1946–76* (Fort Leavenworth, KS: US Army Command and General Staff College, 1979), 14.

8 Thomas G. Mahnken, *Technology and the American Way of War* (New York: Columbia University Press, 2008), 27, 50.

9 Mahnken, *Technology and the American Way of War*, 52–54, 65; Oscar E. Gilbert, *Marine Corps Tank Battles in Vietnam* (Drexel Hill, PA: Casemate, 2007), 25.

10 Doughty, *The Evolution of US Army Tactical Doctrine*, 2–3, 46; Combat Studies Institute, *Sixty Years of Reorganizing for Combat: A Historical Trend Analysis*, CSI Report No. 14 (Ft. Leavenworth, KS: US Army Command and General Staff College, 1999), CARL, p. 45.

11 Lynn Montross, "Fleet Marine Force Korea," *U.S. Naval Institute Proceedings* 79 (August 1953): 829–841; Nicholas A. Canzona, "Dog Company's Charge," *U.S. Naval Institute Proceedings* 82 (November 1956): 1203–1211.

12 See the bibliography for the complete list of these articles.

13 M. E. Holt, "Street Fighting," *Marine Corps Gazette* 29 (September 1945): 27–33; R. C. Williams, Jr., "Defense in Towns," *Marine Corps Gazette* 32 (September 1948): 48–51.

14 Lynn Montross, "The Inchon Landing," *Marine Corps Gazette* 35 (July 1951): 26–35; Lynn Montross, "The Capture of Seoul: Battle of the Barricades," *Marine Corps Gazette* 35 (August 1951): 26–37; Hans W. Henzel, "The Stalingrad Offensive, Part I," *Marine Corps Gazette* 35 (August 1951): 46–53; Hans W. Henzel, "The Stalingrad Offensive, Part II," *Marine Corps Gazette* 35 (September 1951): 46–57; Ernest H. Giusti and Kenneth W. Condit, "Marine Air Over Inchon-Seoul," *Marine Corps Gazette* 36 (June 1952): 18–27.

15 Department of the Army, *Combat in Fortified Areas and Towns*, Field Manual 31-50, August 1952, MHI, pp. 55, 65, 78–80, 96–97.

16 Headquarters, Department of the Army, *Combat in Fortified and Built-Up Areas*, Field Manual 31-50, March 1964, MHI, p. 27.

17 FM 31-50, 1944, pp. 84–90, 109; FM 31-50, 1964, pp. 40–53.

18 War Department, *Attack on a Fortified Position and Combat in Towns*, Field Manual 31-50, January 1944, MHI, pp. 73–74, 101, 104.

19 Quote is from page 30. Headquarters, Department of the Army, *Combat in Fortified and Built-Up Areas*, Field Manual 31-50, March 1964, MHI, pp. 30, 36.

20 Marine Corps Schools, *The Marine Rifle Squad in Combat*, MCS 3-26, 2nd ed. (Quantico, VA: August 1945), GRC, pp. 96–102.

21 United State Marine Corps, *Marine Rifle Squad*, Fleet Marine Force Manual 6-5, 6 April 1966, GRC, pp. 430–450; United State Marine Corps, *Marine Rifle Company/Platoon*, Fleet Marine Force Manual 6-4, 10 August 1965, GRC, pp. 271–277, 345–347.

22 Marine Corps Schools, *Combat in Towns*, MCS 3-15, GRC, pp. 8, 27–38.

23 United State Marine Corps, *Marine Infantry Battalion*, Fleet Marine Force Manual 6-3, 16 April 1964, GRC, pp. 73–74.

24 United State Marine Corps, *Field Artillery Support*, Fleet Marine Force Manual 7-4, 6 March 1964, GRC, pp. 354–355, 370–371; United State Marine Corps, *Air Support*, Fleet Marine Force Manual 7-3, 10 February 1966, GRC, p. ix.

25 United State Marine Corps, *Tank Employment*, Fleet Marine Force Manual 9-1, 15 April 1965, GRC, pp. 224–227.

26 United State Marine Corps, *Marine Engineer Operations*, Fleet Marine Force Manual 4-4, 7 May 1963, GRC, p. 97.

27 Eric Hammel, *Marines in Hue City: A Portrait of Urban Combat, Tet 1968* (St. Paul, MN: Zenith Press, 2007), 60–61.

28 Hammel, *Marines in Hue City*, 14; Eric Hammel, *Fire in the Streets: The Battle for Hue, Tet 1968* (New York: Dell, 1991), 97. Gott makes the same overstatement. Kendall D. Gott, *Breaking the Mold: Tanks in the Cities* (Fort Leavenworth, KS: Combat Studies Institute Press, 2006), 113.

29 History and Museums Division, Headquarters, US Marine Corps, *Oral History Transcript: Major General Raymond L. Murray*, 1988, GRC, pp. 205–206.

30 W. Scott Payne and Jean G. Taylor, *Fighting in Cities* (Arlington, VA: Institute for Defense Analyses, 1970), 38–48.

31 Clay Blair, *The Forgotten War: America in Korea 1950–1953* (Annapolis, MD: US Naval Institute Press, 1987), 192, 282, caption in first picture section.

32 Charles Melson, *US Marine Rifleman in Vietnam 1965–73* (Oxford: Osprey, 1998), 17.

33 Health may have been a factor as upon his return to the US he entered a US Navy hospital where he remained until retirement in August of that same year. History and Museums Division, Headquarters, US Marine Corps, *Oral History Transcript: Major General Raymond L. Murray*, 1988, GRC, Introduction.

Chapter 5

1 MacArthur, accompanying his father, had spent time in Korea after his father's tour as a military observer in the Russo-Japanese War of 1905. Bascom N. Timmons, "MacArthur's Greatest Battle," *Collier's* 126 (16 December 1950): 64.

2 General Douglas MacArthur, Commander in Chief Far East, *Outgoing Message for Joint Chiefs of Staff*, C 62423, 8 September 1950, GRC, Korean War Project, Box 27, Incoming/Outgoing Messages Folder, p. 1. Headquarters X Corps, G-1 Section, *Operation Chromite*, For 15 August to 30 September 1950, NA, 407/429/270/66/34/1/1968, p. 5.

3 Operation Plan No. 100-B was dated 12 August. Headquarters X Corps Command, *Operation Chromite: 15 August to 30 September 1950*, NA, 407/429/270/66/34/1/1968, Preface.

4 Gordon L. Rottman, *Inchon 1950: The Last Great Amphibious Assault* (Oxford: Osprey, 2006), 44.

5 Headquarters X Corps Command, *Operation Chromite*, Preface.

6 Headquarters 1st Marine Division, *Special Action Report for the Inchon-Seoul Operation: 15 September–7 October 1950: Volume One*, 2 May 1951, GRC, Korean War Project, Box 8, Folder 2, pp. 22–23. (Subsequent references to this three-volume report will be in this form: SAR-V1, SAR-V2, or SAR-V3.) Roy E. Appleman, *United States Army in the Korean War: South to the Naktong, North to the Yalu (June–November 1950)* (Washington, DC: Center of Military History, 1961), 491.

7 Rottman, *Inchon*, 31, 44, 55–60.

8 Headquarters X Corps, G-1 Section, *Operation Chromite*, 11–12.

9 Rottman, *Inchon*, 73, 76.

10 Headquarters 1st Marine Division, *SAR-V1*, Folder 3, Annex Charlie, pp. 14–19. Robert Debs Heinl, Jr., *Victory at High Tide: The Inchon-Seoul*

Campaign (Baltimore, MD: Nautical & Aviation Publishing Company of America, 1979), 29.

11 Lynn Montross and Nicholas A. Canzona, *U.S. Marine Corps Operations in Korea 1950–1953, Volume II: The Inchon-Seoul Operation* (Washington, DC: Historical Branch, Headquarters US Marine Corps, 1955), 251–252.

12 Headquarters X Corps, *Inchon Seoul Invasion—Periodic Operations Report, No. 6*, 24 September 1950, MHI, DS 919.U53.

13 Headquarters 1st Marine Division, *SAR-V1*, Folder 3, Annex Baker, Appendix 2, pp. 12–13.

14 Joseph H. Alexander, *Battle of the Barricades: U.S. Marines in the Recapture of Seoul* (Washington, DC: US Marine Corps Historical Center, 2000), 20–21.

15 History and Museums Division, Headquarters, US Marine Corps, *Oral History Transcript: Major General Raymond L. Murray*, 1988, GRC, p. 207.

16 Headquarters X Corps, G-1 Section, *Operation Chromite*, 12; Montross, *U.S. Marine Corps Operations*, 212; Korea Institute of Military History, *The Korean War, Volume One*, 3 vols (Lincoln: University of Nebraska Press, 2000), 640–641.

17 Montross, *U.S. Marine Corps Operations*, 253–254.

18 James H. Dill, *Personal Adventures—Inchon-Seoul 1950*, unpublished memoir, undated, James H. Dill Papers, MHI, p. 39.

19 Montross, *U.S. Marine Corps Operations*, 26.

20 Headquarters 1st Marine Division, *SAR-V2*, Folder 6, Annex Oboe Oboe, p. 1.

21 Montross, *U.S. Marine Corps Operations*, 19–20.

22 Appleman, *United States Army*, 491–492. Headquarters 7th Infantry Division, *War Diary 7th Infantry Division, September 1950*, NA, 407/429/270/67/23/5/3171, pp. 1–2, Narrative section, p. 2.

23 Modest fortification efforts, prior to the Inchon landings, were noted in US intelligence reports. Headquarters X Corps, Special Planning Staff, G-2 Section, *Intelligence Bulletin #1*, 4 September 1950, NA, 407/429/270/66/34/1/1969, section I, p.10. An NKPA radio message warning Pyongyang the landings were likely, was intercepted (source does not say by whom) on 13 September. However, the degree of NKPA preparation would suggest the North Korean leadership did not fully accept the warning. Montross, *U.S. Marine Corps Operations*, 145.

24 Headquarters X Corps, *Estimate of the Enemy Situation: No. 7*, NA, 407/429/270/66/34/1/1969, Annex 2, pp. 1–2; John W. Riley, Jr. and Wilbur Schramm, *The Reds Take a City: The Communist Occupation of Seoul* (Westport, CT: Greenwood Press, 1973), 149–150.

25 Headquarters 1st Marine Division, *Periodic Intelligence Report No. 7*, 22 September 1950, GRC, Korean War Project, Box 3, Folder 13, Enclosure 1, p. 2.

26 Headquarters X Corps, *Estimate of the Enemy Situation: Inchon-Seoul Area*, 28 August 1950, NA, 407/429/270/66/34/1/1970, p. 2.

27 Headquarters 1st Marine Division, *SAR-V1*, Folder 3, Annex Baker, Appendix 2, p. 17; Appleman, *United States Army*, 590.

28 Headquarters 1st Marine Division, *SAR-V1*, Folder 2, Annex Baker, pp. 15–19; Headquarters X Corps, *Estimate of the Enemy Situation: Inchon-Seoul Area*, 2, 10; Headquarters X Corps, *War Diary Summary for Operation Chromite 15 August to 30 September 1950*, NA, 407/429/270/66/34/1/1968, p. 5; Headquarters X Corps, Special Planning Staff, G-2 Section, *Intelligence Bulletin #1*, 7–8; Alexander, *Battle of the Barricades*, 13, 26; Korea Institute of Military History, *The Korean War*, 627; Heinl, *Victory at High Tide*, 30.

29 Headquarters 1st Marine Division, *Periodic Intelligence Report No. 6*, 21 September 1950, GRC, Korean War Project, Box 3, Folder 13, Enclosure 1, p. 3.

30 Appleman, *United States Army*, 519.

31 Also information from a NKPA POW. Headquarters 1st Marine Division, *Periodic Intelligence Report No. 6*, Enclosure 1, p. 3.

32 Headquarters 1st Marine Division, *SAR-V1*, Folder 2, Annex Baker, pp. 8–9.

33 Headquarters 1st Marine Division, *SAR-V3*, Folder 7, Annex Queen Queen, p. 21.

34 Montross, *U.S. Marine Corps Operations*, 243.

35 Headquarters 1st Marine Division, *SAR-V1*, Folder 2, Annex Baker, p. 23; Headquarters 1st Marine Division, *SAR-V1*, Folder 2, Annex Baker, p. 25.

36 Headquarters US Marine Corps, *Tactical Lessons of Present Korean Fighting*, 29 September 1950, GRC, Korean War Project, Box 1, Folder 19, p. 4.

37 Headquarters 1st Marine Division, *SAR-V3*, Folder 7, Special Action Report 1st Battalion 5th Marines, pp. 14–15, and Annex Queen Queen, p. 18.

38 Headquarters 1st Marine Division, *SAR-V2*, Folder 6, Annex Oboe Oboe, p. 43.

39 Chris Bishop, ed., *The Encyclopedia of Weapons of World War Two* (New York: Metro Books, 1998), 187–188; Headquarters 1st Marine Division, *SAR-V1*, Folder 2, Annex Baker, p. 25.

40 Montross, *U.S. Marine Corps Operations*, 272.

41 Headquarters 1st Marine Division, *SAR-V2*, Folder 6, Annex Oboe Oboe, p. 43.

42 Headquarters 1st Marine Division, *SAR-V3*, Folder 7, Annex Queen Queen, p. 18; Steven J. Zaloga and Jim Kinnear, *T-34-85 Medium Tank 1944–1994* (Oxford: Osprey, 2000), 19; Steven J. Zaloga, *M26/M46 Pershing Tank 1943–1953* (Oxford: Osprey, 2000), plate D.

43 Headquarters 1st Marine Division, *SAR-V1*, Folder 2, Annex Baker, p. 18; Korea Institute of Military History, *The Korean War*, 627.

44 Headquarters 1st Marine Division, *SAR-V1*, Folder 2, Annex Baker, p. 12.

45 *Informal Statement of 1st Lieutenant James McGhee*, 15 February 1951, GRC, Korean War Project, Box 3, Folder 8, p. 6; Headquarters 1st Marine Division, *SAR-V3*, Folder 7, Annex Queen Queen, p. 18; Headquarters US Marine Corps, *Tactical Lessons of Present Korean Fighting*, 18 September 1950, GRC, Korean War Project, Box 1, Folder 19, p. 2; Headquarters 1st Marine Division, *SAR-V1*, Folder 3, Annex Baker, Appendix 5, pp. 2–3.

46 Headquarters X Corps, G-2 Section, *Periodic Intelligence Report No. 9*, For 27 September 1950, NA, 407/429/270/66/34/1/1969, p. 2.

47 Alexander, *Battle of the Barricades*, 37. Sergeant Kumagai (no identified first name), *Letter to Colonel Ralph Bing*, 12 March 1952, Sergeant Kumagai Papers, MHI, pp. 11–12. This source mentions 15 Soviet advisors in Seoul in July. Headquarters X Corps, Special Planning Staff, G-2 Section, *Intelligence Bulletin #1*, 7.

48 Headquarters 1st Marine Division, *SAR-V2*, Folder 6, Annex Peter Peter, p. 13.

49 General Headquarters Far East Command, Military Intelligence Section, *Chinese Communist Reference Manual for Field Fortifications—Translation*, 1 May 1951, NA, 554/-/290/48/9/3/54, pp. 6, 14, 21, 27, 76–77.

50 General Headquarters Far East Command, Military Intelligence Section, Military Intelligence Group Far East, *Enemy Documents—Korean Operations*, Issue No. 38, 21 December 1951, NA 554/-/290/48/9/3/54, pp. 170–176.

51 Headquarters 1st Marine Division, *SAR-V3*, Folder 7, Annex Queen Queen, p. 16.

52 Headquarters 1st Marine Division, *Periodic Intelligence Report No. 12*, 27 September 1950, GRC, Korean War Project, Box 3, Folder 16, p. 3.

53 Headquarters 1st Marine Division, *SAR-V2*, Folder 6, Annex Peter Peter, p. 13.

54 Headquarters 1st Marine Division, *SAR-V2*, Folder 6, Annex Peter Peter, p. 13, and Appendix 4, pp. 4–7.

55 Headquarters 1st Marine Division, *SAR-V1*, Folder 3, Annex Charlie, pp. 23–24.

56 Korea Institute of Military History, *The Korean War*, 643; Headquarters X Corps, *Inchon Seoul Invasion—Periodic Operations Report, No. 7*, 25 September 1950, MHI, DS 919.U53; Montross, *U.S. Marine Corps Operations*, 254–255; Rottman, *Inchon*, 69; Headquarters 7th Infantry Division, *War Diary*, 4; Appleman, *United States Army*, 519–520, 529–530.

57 Headquarters 1st Marine Division, *SAR-V1*, Folder 3, Annex Baker, Appendix 2, pp. 12–13; Headquarters 1st Marine Division, *SAR-V3*, Folder 7, Annex Queen Queen, pp. 11–14.

58 Headquarters X Corps, G-1 Section, *Operation Chromite*, 20.

59 Headquarters 1st Marine Division, *SAR-V1*, Folder 3, Annex Charlie, p. 26; Headquarters 1st Marine Division, *SAR-V2*, Folder 6, Annex Peter Peter, p. 9; Headquarters 1st Marine Division, *SAR-V3*, Folder 7, Annex Queen Queen, pp. 11–14; Appleman, *United States Army*, 529–530.

60 Headquarters 1st Marine Division, *SAR-V3*, Folder 7, Annex Queen Queen, p. 10; Montross, *U.S. Marine Corps Operations*, 238–239, 244–245, 255–257; Appleman, *United States Army*, 519–520.

61 Headquarters 1st Marine Division, *SAR-V2*, Folder 6, Annex Peter Peter, pp. 9–10; Thomas A. Kelly, "Seoul, 1950: City Fight After Inchon," in *City Fights: Selected Histories of Urban Combat from World War II to Vietnam*, ed. John Antal and Bradley Gericke (New York: Ballantine, 2003), 325–327.

62 Headquarters 1st Marine Division, *SAR-V1*, Folder 3, Annex Charlie, p. 27; Headquarters 1st Marine Division, *SAR-V3*, Folder 7, Special Action Report 3rd Battalion 5th Marines, Annex Peter, p. 12.

63 Headquarters 7th Infantry Division, *War Diary*, 5.

64 Headquarters 7th Infantry Division, *War Diary*, Narrative section, 26 September; Headquarters X Corps, G-2 Section, *Periodic Intelligence Report No. 9*, For 27 September 1950, p. 4.

65 Headquarters 1st Marine Division, *SAR-V3*, Folder 7, Special Action Report 3rd Battalion 5th Marines, Annex Peter, p. 12. Headquarters 1st Marine Division, *SAR-V1*, Folder 3, Annex Baker, Appendix 2, p. 15.

66 Headquarters 1st Marine Division, *Periodic Intelligence Report No. 12*, p. 3; Headquarters 1st Marine Division, *SAR-V1*, Folder 3, Annex Charlie, p. 29.

67 Headquarters 1st Marine Division, *Periodic Intelligence Report No. 13*, 28 September 1950, GRC, Korean War Project, Box 3, Folder 16, p. 1.

68 Headquarters X Corps Command, *Operation Chromite*, X Corps Chief of Staff log, entry for 28 September.

69 Headquarters X Corps Command, *Operation Chromite*, X Corps Chief of Staff log, entry for 28 September; Headquarters 1st Marine Division, *SAR-V2*, Folder 6, Annex Peter Peter, p. 10.

70 Headquarters X Corps, G-3 Section, *Operation Chromite: Operations 15 August to 30 September 1950*, NA, 407/429/270/66/34/1/1970, p. 8; Headquarters X Corps Command, *Operation Chromite*, Preface.

71 Headquarters 1st Marine Division, *SAR-V1*, Folder 2, p. 14.

72 Headquarters X Corps Command, *Operation Chromite*, X Corps Chief of Staff log, entry for 23 September. Montross, *U.S. Marine Corps Operations*, 244–245.

73 Almond had commanded a machine-gun battalion in World War I and been decorated for bravery. In World War II he had commanded the 92nd Infantry Division in Italy. Appleman, *United States Army*, 490–491.

74 Alexander, *Battle of the Barricades*, 8; Heinl, *Victory at High Tide*, 199.

75 Historical Division, Headquarters, US Marine Corps, *Oral History Transcript: General Oliver P. Smith*, 1973, GRC, pp. 199–203; Montross, *U.S. Marine Corps Operations*, 244.

76 Alexander, *Battle of the Barricades*, 36; Appleman, *United States Army*, 534.

77 The underlining of "now" comes from the original source. Headquarters 1st Marine Division, *SAR-V1*, Folder 3, Annex Charlie, p. 25.

78 Historical Division, Headquarters, US Marine Corps, *Oral History Transcript: General Oliver P. Smith*, 199–203.

79 Historical Division, Headquarters, US Marine Corps, *Oral History Transcript: General Oliver P. Smith*, 199–203; Headquarters X Corps Command, *Operation Chromite*.

80 Marine Corps Schools, *Combat in Towns*, MCS 3-15, December 1949, GRC, p. 5.

81 Alexander, *Battle of the Barricades*, 24.

82 Heinl, *Victory at High Tide*, 200.

83 Headquarters 1st Marine Division, *Periodic Intelligence Report No. 4*, 19 September 1950, GRC, Korean War Project, Box 3, Folder 13, Enclosure 2, p. 1. A US Army history called this area "susceptible to a quick organization for defense." Appleman, *United States Army*, 523. A Marine Corps history

of the campaign specifically mentions the northwest hill mass as part of this training area and pre-equipped with fighting positions. Alexander, *Battle of the Barricades*, 13.

84 Blair describes Almond as having an "obsession" with September 25, as the ninety-day anniversary of Seoul's fall to the NKPA. Clay Blair, *The Forgotten War: America in Korea 1950–1953* (Annapolis, MD: US Naval Institute Press, 1987), 274.

85 History and Museums Division, Headquarters, US Marine Corps, *Oral History Transcript: Major General Raymond L. Murray*, Introduction.

86 Blair, *The Forgotten War*, 273.

87 Historical Division, Headquarters, US Marine Corps, *Oral History Transcript: Lieutenant General Edward A. Craig*, 1968, GRC, pp. 166, 198.

88 History and Museums Division, Headquarters, US Marine Corps, *Oral History Transcript: Major General Raymond L. Murray*, 204–208.

89 Alexander, *Battle of the Barricades*, 41; History and Museums Division, Headquarters, US Marine Corps, *Oral History Transcript: Major General Raymond L. Murray*, 204–205.

90 Headquarters 1st Marine Division, *SAR-V1*, Folder 3, Annex Charlie, p. 26; Appleman, *United States Army*, 532.

91 Montross, *U.S. Marine Corps Operations*, 274; Headquarters X Corps, G-1 Section, *Operation Chromite*, 21.

92 Headquarters 96th Field Artillery Battalion, *War Diary 96th Field Artillery Battalion: 1 July to 30 September 1950*, 27 November 1950, NA, 407/429/270/68/19/2/4681, p. 2.

93 Dill, *Personal Adventures*, 54.

94 Montross, *U.S. Marine Corps Operations*, 335.

95 Headquarters 1st Marine Division, *SAR-V3*, Folder 7, Special Action Report 1st Battalion 5th Marines, p. 21; Headquarters 1st Marine Division, *SAR-V2*, Folder 5, Annex Charlie Charlie, p. 7; Commanding Officer, Marine Fighter Squadron 214, *Close Air Support from CVE in the Korean Theatre*, 10 October 1950, GRC, Korean War Project, Box 25, Folder 13, p. 1.

96 Dill, *Personal Adventures*, 102–110.

97 Matthew Fath, "How Armor Was Employed in the Urban Battle of Seoul," *Armor* 110 (September/October 2001): 28.

98 Headquarters 1st Marine Division, *SAR-V3*, Folder 7, Annex Queen Queen, pp. 11–14, and Special Action Report 1st Battalion 5th Marines, pp. 10–11.

99 Headquarters X Corps Command, *Operation Chromite*.

100 Headquarters X Corps, *Inchon Seoul Invasion—Operations Instruction No. 6*, Annex 2. Headquarters 96th Field Artillery Battalion, *War Diary*, Annex C, p. 6. Dill, *Personal Adventures*, 97. History and Museums Division, Headquarters, US Marine Corps, *Oral History Transcript: Major General Raymond L. Murray*, 207–208.

101 Montross, *U.S. Marine Corps Operations*, 215–216.

102 Headquarters 1st Marine Division, *SAR-V2*, Folder 6, Annex Peter Peter, Appendix 9, p. 9; Montross, *U.S. Marine Corps Operations*, 110–111, 271.

103 Headquarters 1st Marine Division, *SAR-V1*, Folder 4, Annex Victor, pp. 6–7.

104 Headquarters 1st Marine Division, *SAR-V2*, Folder 6, Annex Peter Peter, p. 17, and Appendix 7, p. 6. Headquarters 1st Marine Division, *SAR-V3*, Folder 7, Special Action Report 1st Battalion 5th Marines, pp. 22-26, Annex Queen Queen, Annex King, p. 3, and Folder 8, Annex SS, Appendix Two, p. 12; Headquarters 32nd Infantry Regiment, *War Diary, RCT 32 of the Seventh Infantry Division: Operations in Korea: Period of 16–30 September 1950*, NA, 407/429/270/67/23/5/3180, p. 2.

105 Headquarters 1st Marine Division, *SAR-V2*, Folder 6, Annex Peter Peter, Appendix 7, p. 4.

106 These first two Marine after-action report sources stated communications worked well, but the last source stated the Marines were having "a terrible time with their radios." This suggests wire communications made up the difference. Headquarters 1st Marine Division, *SAR-V2*, Folder 6, Annex Peter Peter, p. 9; Headquarters 1st Marine Division, *SAR-V3*, Folder 7, Annex Queen Queen, Annex Jig, p. 2; Dill, *Personal Adventures*, 93–94.

107 Headquarters 1st Marine Division, *SAR-V3*, Folder 7, Annex Queen Queen, Annex Mike, p. 3; Headquarters 1st Marine Division, *SAR-V2*, Folder 5, Annex Charlie Charlie, p. 7, and Appendix 2, pp. 5–6; Commanding Officer, Marine Fighter Squadron 214, *Close Air Support*, 4.

108 Dill, *Personal Adventures*, 93–94.

109 Headquarters X Corps, Provost Marshal Section, *History of Provost Marshal Operations*, 24 October 1950, NA, 407/429/270/66/34/1/1968, Section III; Headquarters 1st Marine Division, *SAR-V2*, Folder 5, Annex George George, p. 12.

110 Heinl, *Victory at High Tide*, 176–177, 283; Montross, *U.S. Marine Corps Operations*, 225–231.

111 Headquarters X Corps, G-1 Section, *Operation Chromite*, 14–15; Appleman, *United States Army*, 518–519; Montross, *U.S. Marine Corps Operations*, 225–231.

112 Marine Corps Schools, *Combat in Towns, MCS 3-15*, p. 3.

113 James O. Mortrude, *Korean War Veterans Survey*, October 1990, MHI, James O. Mortrude Papers, pp. 4–9.

114 Headquarters 1st Marine Division, *SAR-V1*, Folder 3, Annex Baker, Appendix 2, p. 17; Headquarters X Corps, *Estimate of the Enemy Situation: No. 7 Inchon-Seoul Area*, Annex 2, pp. 1–2; Headquarters X Corps, Special Planning Staff, G-2 Section, *Intelligence Bulletin #1*, section I, pp. 1–10.

115 Headquarters X Corps, *War Diary Summary*, 5; Headquarters X Corps, *Estimate of the Enemy Situation: Inchon-Seoul Area*, 1–2.

116 Headquarters X Corps, *Estimate of the Enemy Situation: Inchon-Seoul Area*, 2.

117 Headquarters 1st Marine Division, *SAR-V1*, Folder 2, Annex Baker, p. 15.

118 Headquarters 1st Marine Division, *SAR-V3*, Folder 7, Annex Queen Queen, Annex Baker, p. 3. For a good summary of the X Corps intelligence picture just before US forces entered the city, see Headquarters X Corps,

G-2 Section, *Periodic Intelligence Report No. 4*, For 22 September 1950, NA, 407/429/270/66/34/1/1969, pp. 1–2.

119 Headquarters X Corps, G-2 Section, *Periodic Intelligence Report No. 3*, For 21 September 1950, NA, 407/429/270/66/34/1/1969, p. 4; Headquarters 1st Marine Division, *SAR-V1*, Folder 3, Annex Baker, Appendix 2, p. 17.

120 Headquarters X Corps, *War Diary Summary*, 5.

121 Headquarters X Corps, G-2 Section, *Periodic Intelligence Report No. 6*, For 24 September 1950, p. 2.

122 Eliot A. Cohen and John Gooch, *Military Misfortunes: The Anatomy of Failure in War* (New York: Free Press, 2006), 175–178.

123 Headquarters X Corps, *History of the G-2 Section*, NA, 407/429/270/66/34/1/1969, pp. 4–5; Headquarters X Corps, *Map Distribution Table*, 29 August 1950, NA, 407/429/270/66/34/1/1969, pp. 1–3.

124 Headquarters 2nd Engineer Special Brigade, *Unit Activities Report (9 July 1950 to 1 October 1950)*, NA, 407/429/270/68/19/2/4665, pp. 2, 10.

125 Far East Command, Military Intelligence Section, *Terrain Handbook No. 65—Seoul and Vicinity*, 16 August 1950, MHI.

126 Headquarters 1st Marine Division, *SAR-V1*, Folder 2, Annex Baker, p. 26; Headquarters 1st Marine Division, *SAR-V2*, Folder 5, Annex Charlie Charlie, p. 7.

127 Montross, *U.S. Marine Corps Operations*, 155, 234–238; Headquarters 1st Marine Division, *SAR-V2*, Folder 6, Annex Oboe Oboe, p. 30. For a 1st lieutenant's recollection of good map support, see Dill, *Personal Adventures*, 70–86.

128 Headquarters 1st Marine Division, *Periodic Intelligence Report No. 4*, Enclosure 2, p. 1.

129 Headquarters 1st Marine Division, *Periodic Intelligence Report No. 6*, Enclosure 3, pp. 1, 4.

130 Headquarters X Corps, G-2 Section, *Periodic Intelligence Report No. 4*, For 22 September 1950, p. 3.

131 Headquarters 1st Marine Division, *Periodic Intelligence Report No. 9*, 24 September 1950, GRC, Korean War Project, Box 3, Folder 13, p. 3.

132 Headquarters X Corps Command, *Operation Chromite*, X Corps Chief of Staff log, entries for 25 and 26 September; Headquarters X Corps, G-2 Section, *Periodic Intelligence Report No. 7*, For 25 September 1950, NA, 407/429/270/66/34/1/1969, p. 3; Headquarters 1st Marine Division, *Periodic Intelligence Report No. 11*, 26 September 1950, GRC, Korean War Project, Box 3, Folder 16, p. 2.

133 Headquarters 1st Marine Division, *Periodic Intelligence Report No. 9*, Enclosure 2, p. 1.

134 Headquarters 1st Marine Division, *Periodic Intelligence Report No. 10*, 25 September 1950, GRC, Korean War Project, Box 3, Folder 16, pp. 2–3.

135 Headquarters X Corps, G-2 Section, *Periodic Intelligence Report No. 8*, for 26 September 1950, NA, 407/429/270/66/34/1/1969, pp. 1, 3.

136 Headquarters X Corps, *History of the G-2 Section*, 5.

137 Headquarters 1st Marine Division, *SAR-V1*, Folder 3, Annex Baker, Appendix 4, pp. 1–2.

138 Headquarters 1st Marine Division, *SAR-V1*, Folder 2, pp. 25–26; Headquarters 1st Marine Division, *SAR-V2*, Folder 6, Annex Peter Peter, pp. 16-17, and Appendix 4, p. 9.

139 Headquarters X Corps, *History of the G-2 Section*, 6.

140 Headquarters X Corps, G-2 Section, *Periodic Intelligence Report No. 9*, For 27 September 1950, p. 3; Headquarters 1st Marine Division, *SAR-V3*, Folder 8, Annex SS, p. 24, and Annex William William, p. 3; Headquarters 1st Marine Division, *SAR-V2*, Folder 5, Annex Charlie Charlie, pp. 5-6, and Appendix 2, pp. 5–6.

141 Headquarters 1st Marine Division, *SAR-V3*, Folder 7, Special Action Report 3rd Battalion 5th Marines, Annex Peter, pp. 15–16; Headquarters 1st Marine Division, *Periodic Intelligence Report No. 13*, p. 2.

142 Headquarters 1st Marine Division, *SAR-V1*, Folder 2, Annex Baker, p. 27.

143 Headquarters 1st Marine Division, *SAR-V3*, Folder 7, Annex Queen Queen, p. 22.

144 Appleman, *United States Army*, 515, 532–533.

145 Headquarters X Corps, Provost Marshal Section, *History of Provost Marshal Operations*, Annex 6. Headquarters 7th Infantry Division, *War Diary*, 3.

146 Headquarters 1st Marine Division, *SAR-V2*, Box 8, Folder 6, Annex Peter Peter, Appendix 4, pp. 4–5.

147 Headquarters 1st Marine Division, *SAR-V2*, Folder 6, Annex Peter Peter, p. 18.

148 *Informal Statement of 1st Lieutenant Robert E. Jochums*, 15 February 1951, GRC, Korean War Project, Box 3, Folder 8, p. 1.

149 As quoted in Matthew Fath, "How Armor Was Employed in the Urban Battle of Seoul," 28.

150 Rottman, *Inchon*, 33–34.

151 *Informal Statement of 1st Lieutenant Robert E. Jochums*, 1.

152 Donald W. Boose, Jr., *U.S. Army Forces in the Korean War 1950–53* (Oxford: Osprey, 2005), 12, 43.

153 *Informal Statement of 1st Lieutenant James McGhee*, 4–5.

154 History and Museums Division, Headquarters, US Marine Corps, *Oral History Transcript: Major General Raymond L. Murray*, 205–206; Headquarters 1st Marine Division, *SAR-V3*, Folder 7, Annex Queen Queen, pp. 4–6, and Special Action Report 1st Battalion 5th Marines, p. 2.

155 Headquarters 1st Marine Division, *SAR-V3*, Folder 7, Special Action Report 3rd Battalion 5th Marines, Annex Peter, pp. 20–21, and Special Action Report 1st Battalion 5th Marines, p. 21, and Annex Oboe, p. 11. Dill, *Personal Adventures*, 6–7.

156 Rottman, *Inchon*, 33–34; Alexander, *Battle of the Barricades*, 36; Boose, *U.S. Army Forces*, 12, 25–27.

157 Headquarters 1st Marine Division, *SAR-V2*, Folder 6, Annex Peter Peter, p. 18.

158 Headquarters 1st Marine Division, *SAR-V3*, Folder 7, Special Action Report 3rd Battalion 5th Marines, Annex Peter, pp. 20–21; Alexander, *Battle of the Barricades*, 8, 33; Headquarters 1st Marine Division, *SAR-V2*, Folder 6, Annex Peter Peter, Appendix 5, pp. 5–6.

159 Headquarters US Marine Corps, *Tactical Lessons of Present Korean Fighting*, 29 September 1950, p. 5.

160 Ibid., p. 5.

161 Headquarters X Corps, G-1 Section, *Operation Chromite*, 14–15; Appleman, *United States Army*, 518–519. Montross, *U.S. Marine Corps Operations*, 225–231.

162 Rottman, *Inchon*, 33–34, 92; Boose, *U.S. Army Forces*, 12, 25–27.

163 Headquarters 1st Marine Division, *SAR-V3*, Folder 7, Special Action Report 1st Battalion 5th Marines, p. 26, and Annex Queen Queen, Annex Dog, p. 2.

164 Headquarters 1st Marine Division, *SAR-V2*, Folder 6, Annex Peter Peter, Appendix 9, pp. 5–10.

165 Rottman, *Inchon*, 35, 92; Headquarters 7th Infantry Division, *War Diary 7th*, 2; Headquarters 1st Marine Division, *SAR-V1*, Folder 3, Annex Fox, p. 1; Headquarters 1st Marine Division, *SAR-V3*, Folder 7, Special Action Report 3rd Battalion 5th Marines, Annex Peter, pp. 20–21; Alexander, *Battle of the Barricades*, 29.

166 Jim Mesko, *Armor in Korea: A Pictorial History* (Carrollton, TX: Squadron/ Signal, 1984), 10–11.

167 Montross, *U.S. Marine Corps Operations*, 225–231.

168 Rottman, *Inchon*, 33-34, 92. Boose, *U.S. Army Forces*, 25–27, 51.

169 Headquarters 1st Marine Division, *SAR-V2*, Folder 6, Annex Peter Peter, Appendix 10, pp. 4–6. Headquarters US Marine Corps, *Tactical Lessons of Present Korean Fighting*, 1 September 1950, GRC, Korean War Project, Box 1, Folder 19, p. 7.

170 Headquarters 1st Marine Division, *SAR-V2*, Folder 6, Annex Oboe Oboe, p. 43.

171 Headquarters 1st Marine Division, *SAR-V2*, Folder 6, Annex Oboe Oboe, pp. 19–32, 42–43. Conversely, Heinl cites one case where an NKPA tank destroyed an American tank near Suwon, and the command tank commander was killed. Heinl, *Victory at High Tide*, 184.

172 Montross, *U.S. Marine Corps Operations*, 272; Alexander, *Battle of the Barricades*, 41.

173 Headquarters 1st Marine Division, *SAR-V2*, Folder 6, Annex Oboe Oboe, p. 43. While the preceding primary source is rather vague, this secondary source, a Marine Corps history, is more precise. "They lost 5 Pershings, one dozer Sherman, and one FT [flame thrower] Sherman while retaking Seoul." Alexander, *Battle of the Barricades*, 23.

174 Headquarters 1st Marine Division, *SAR-V2*, Folder 6, Annex Oboe Oboe, p. 24, and Annex Peter Peter, pp. 9–10.

175 Headquarters 1st Marine Division, *SAR-V2*, Folder 6, Annex Oboe Oboe, pp. 27, 43, 49–50; Rottman, *Inchon*, 34. Heinl, *Victory at High Tide*, 125.

176 Ian V. Hogg, *The American Arsenal: The World War II Official Standard Ordnance Catalog of Small Arms, Tanks, Armored Cars, Artillery, Antiaircraft Guns, Ammunition, Grenades, Mines, etcetera* (London: Greenhill, 2001), 29, 35, 179, 275–278, 292.

177 Headquarters 1st Marine Division, *SAR-V2*, Folder 6, Annex Oboe Oboe, pp. 3, 16–17, 50, and Appendix Two, pp. 3–4; Hogg, *The American Arsenal*, 182, 294–297; Mesko, *Armor in Korea*, 26.

178 Headquarters 1st Marine Division, *SAR-V2*, Folder 6, Annex Peter Peter, p. 18.

179 Headquarters X Corps, *Inchon Seoul Invasion—Periodic Operations Report, No. 6*; Montross, *U.S. Marine Corps Operations*, 178, 202; James O. Mortrude, *Korean War Veterans Survey*, 9.

180 Rottman, *Inchon*, 33–34; Boose, *U.S. Army Forces*, 12, 34; Headquarters 96th Field Artillery Battalion, *War Diary*, pp. 4–6; Dill, *Personal Adventures*, 51–53, 69–89; 1st Marine Division, *Operations Order 10-50*, 23 to 24 September 1950, GRC, Korean War Project, Box 3, Folder 10, p. 2.

181 Headquarters 96th Field Artillery Battalion, *War Diary*, 2, 11.

182 Dill, *Personal Adventures*, 101; Montross, *U.S. Marine Corps Operations*, 263; Headquarters 1st Marine Division, *SAR-V3*, Folder 8, Annex SS, Appendix Two, p. 7.

183 Dill, *Personal Adventures*, 45, 95–112.

184 Headquarters 1st Marine Division, *SAR-V3*, Folder 8, Annex SS, Appendix Two, p. 13.

185 Headquarters 1st Marine Division, *SAR-V3*, Folder 8, Annex SS, pp. 6, 10, and Folder 7, Annex Queen Queen, Annex King, p. 3; Headquarters 1st Marine Division, *SAR-V2*, Folder 6, Annex Peter Peter, Appendix 9, p. 7.

186 For examples of these shortfalls see, Headquarters 11th Marines, 1st Marine Division, *Report of Use and Effectiveness of 4.5" Rocket Launchers*, 3 November 1950, GRC, Korean War Project, Box 5, Folder 10, p. 2. See also Headquarters 1st Marine Division, *SAR-V2*, Folder 6, Annex Peter Peter, p. 17. See also the following portions of the *SAR-V3*: Folder 8, Annex SS, p. 6; Folder 7, Special Action Report 1st Battalion 5th Marines, p. 20; Folder 7, Special Action Report 1st Battalion 5th Marines, pp. 22-23; Folder 8, Annex SS, Appendix Two, p. 14.

187 Montross, *U.S. Marine Corps Operations*, 167–170; Commanding Officer, Marine Fighter Squadron 214, *Close Air Support*, 1–4; Warren Thompson, "Marine Corsairs in Korea," *International Airpower Review* 11 (Winter 2003/2004): 107–119.

188 Commanding Officer, Marine Fighter Squadron 214, *Close Air Support*, p. 1; Headquarters 1st Marine Division, *SAR-V2*, Folder 5, Annex Charlie Charlie, Appendix 2, pp. 5–6; Headquarters 1st Marine Division, *SAR-V1*, Folder 3, Annex Charlie, p. 29.

189 Headquarters 1st Marine Division, *SAR-V2*, Folder 5, Annex Charlie Charlie, Appendix 1, pp. 1–2; X Corps, Headquarters Tactical Air Command, *Operation Order 1-50*, 9 September 1950, NA, 407/429/270/66/34/1/1970, Annex How, p. 2.

190 Headquarters 1st Marine Division, *SAR-V3*, Folder 7, Special Action Report 1st Battalion 5th Marines, p. 21.

191 Headquarters 7th Infantry Division, *War Diary*, General comments section, pp. 1–2; Montross, *U.S. Marine Corps Operations*, 335.

192 Alexander, *Battle of the Barricades*, 26.

193 Headquarters 1st Marine Division, *SAR-V3*, Folder 8, Annex William William, p. 3; Headquarters 1st Marine Division, *SAR-V2*, Folder 5, Annex Charlie Charlie, Appendix 2, pp. 5–6.

194 Headquarters 1st Marine Division, *Medical Department Log—1st Marine Division*, 14 July to 26 October 1950, GRC, Korean War Project, Box 1, Folder 17, pp. 32–34, 40; Headquarters 1st Marine Division, *SAR-V2*, Folder 6, Annex Peter Peter, Appendix 8, p. 3.

195 Thompson, "Marine Corsairs in Korea," 250. Heinl notes that "virtually all" of the USMC aircraft shot down during CHROMITE were a result of hits on their oil coolers. Heinl, *Victory at High Tide*, 280.

196 Montross, *U.S. Marine Corps Operations*, 294–296; Thompson, "Marine Corsairs in Korea," 111–112.

197 Headquarters 1st Marine Division, *SAR-V3*, Folder 7, Annex Queen Queen, Annex Mike, pp. 4–5; Headquarters 1st Marine Division, *SAR-V3*, Folder 7, Special Action Report 1st Battalion 5th Marines, p. 21.

198 Headquarters X Corps, G-1 Section, *Personnel Daily Summary*, 16–30 September 1950, NA 407/429/270/66/34/1/1968.

199 1st Marine Division, *Personnel Periodic Report No. 1*, 24 September 1950, GRC, Korean War Project, Box 4, Folder 2, p. 1; Headquarters 1st Marine Division, *SAR-V2*, Folder 6, Annex Peter Peter, p. 11; Montross, *U.S. Marine Corps Operations*, 225.

200 Headquarters 1st Marine Division, *SAR-V3*, Folder 7, Annex Queen Queen, pp. 11–14, and Annex How, p. 3.

201 Montross, *U.S. Marine Corps Operations*, 244–245, 255–257, 264.

202 Headquarters 1st Marine Division, *SAR-V3*, Folder 7, Special Action Report 3rd Battalion 5th Marines, Annex Peter, p. 25, and Special Action Report 1st Battalion 5th Marines, pp. 10–11.

203 The chart on page 50 totals up to 711 casualties over the four days. Alexander, *Battle of the Barricades*, 46, 50.

204 Montross, *U.S. Marine Corps Operations*, 274.

205 Headquarters X Corps, G-1 Section, *Operation Chromite*, 25.

206 Headquarters 1st Marine Division, *SAR-V2*, Folder 6, Annex Peter Peter, Appendix 8, p. 3.

207 Alexander, *Battle of the Barricades*, 59; Headquarters 1st Marine Division, *SAR-V2*, Folder 6, Annex Peter Peter, Appendix 8, p. 3.

208 Montross, *U.S. Marine Corps Operations*, 129–130.

209 Headquarters 1st Marine Division, *SAR-V2*, Folder 5, Annex How How, Appendix Baker, pp. 4–5, and Appendix Charlie, pp. 3–5.

210 Headquarters 1st Marine Division, *SAR-V3*, Folder 7, Special Action Report 1st Battalion 5th Marines, p. 21. Headquarters 1st Marine Division, *SAR-V2*, Folder 6, Annex Peter Peter, Appendix 8, p. 3.

211 Headquarters 1st Marine Division, *Periodic Intelligence Report No. 12*, p. 3.
212 Headquarters 1st Marine Division, *SAR-V2*, Folder 6, Annex Oboe Oboe, pp. 21, 43; Headquarters 7th Infantry Division, *War Diary*, Narrative section, 20 September; Montross, *U.S. Marine Corps Operations*, 209–211; Headquarters 1st Marine Division, *SAR-V1*, Folder 2, Annex Baker, p. 11.
213 Headquarters 1st Marine Division, *SAR-V1*, Folder 3, Annex Charlie, p. 29; Headquarters 1st Marine Division, *SAR-V2*, Folder 6, Annex Peter Peter, Appendix 4, p. 7; Alexander, *Battle of the Barricades*, 37.
214 Far East Command, Military Intelligence Section, *Terrain Handbook No. 65*, pp. 31–32.
215 Headquarters 1st Marine Division, *SAR-V3*, Folder 8, Annex SS, Appendix One, p. 4.
216 Headquarters 1st Marine Division, *SAR-V2*, Folder 6, Annex Peter Peter, Appendix 5, pp. 5–6.
217 Appleman, *United States Army*, 535.
218 Headquarters 1st Marine Division, *SAR-V2*, Folder 6, Annex Oboe Oboe, p. 43.
219 Headquarters 1st Marine Division, *SAR-V2*, Folder 6, Annex Peter Peter, pp. 9–10.
220 Alexander, *Battle of the Barricades*, 37.
221 Marine Corps Schools, *The Marine Rifle Squad in Combat*, MCS 3-26, 2nd ed, August 1945, GRC, p. 103; Marine Corps Schools, *Combat in Towns*, 20.
222 *Informal Statement of 1st Lieutenant James McGhee*, 4–5; *Informal Statement of 1st Lieutenant Robert E. Jochums*, 1; Headquarters 1st Marine Division, *SAR-V1*, Folder 3, Annex Fox, p. 4, and Annex Charlie, pp. 23–24.
223 Headquarters 1st Marine Division, *SAR-V3*, Folder 8, Annex William William, p. 1; Headquarters 1st Marine Division, *SAR-V2*, Folder 6, Annex Peter Peter, Appendix 8, p. 3; Headquarters 1st Marine Division, *Medical Department Log*, 30–34; Heinl, *Victory at High Tide*, 142.
224 Korea Institute of Military History, *The Korean War*, 610–615; Appleman, *United States Army*, 497.
225 Montross, *U.S. Marine Corps Operations*, 102, 105.
226 Headquarters X Corps Command, *Operation Chromite*, X Corps Chief of Staff log, entry for 16 September.
227 Montross, *U.S. Marine Corps Operations*, 170.
228 Thompson, "Marine Corsairs in Korea," 116.
229 Headquarters 1st Marine Division, *SAR-V1*, Folder 3, Annex Charlie, p. 26; Appleman, *United States Army*, 532–533.
230 Headquarters 1st Marine Division, *SAR-V2*, Folder 6, Annex Peter Peter, Appendix 9, p. 4.
231 Headquarters 11th Marines, 1st Marine Division, *Report of Use and Effectiveness of 4.5" Rocket Launchers*, 1–2; Headquarters 1st Marine Division, *SAR-V3*, Folder 8, Annex SS, Appendix Two, p. 14; Montross, *U.S. Marine Corps Operations*, 215–216.

232 Headquarters 1st Marine Division, *SAR-V1*, Folder 2, p. 33; Headquarters, 1st Marine Division, *Daily Logistical Reports Nos. 12-14*, 26 to 29 September 1950, GRC, Korean War Project, Box 4, Folder 3.

233 Headquarters 1st Marine Division, *SAR-V2*, Folder 5, Annex Fox Fox, pp. 3–5.

234 Headquarters 1st Marine Division, *SAR-V2*, Folder 6, Annex Peter Peter, Appendix 5, pp. 5–6; Montross, *U.S. Marine Corps Operations*, 225–231.

235 Headquarters 1st Marine Division, *SAR-V2*, Folder 6, Annex Oboe Oboe, pp. 2, 24, and Appendix One, p. 21, and Appendix Two, pp. 3–4.

236 Headquarters 1st Marine Division, *SAR-V2*, Folder 6, Annex Peter Peter, pp. 9–10, 18.

237 Montross, *U.S. Marine Corps Operations*, 272.

238 Headquarters 1st Marine Division, *SAR-V1*, Folder 2, p. 28.

239 Headquarters 1st Marine Division, *SAR-V2*, Folder 6, Annex Oboe Oboe, p. 49, and Annex Peter Peter, pp. 9–10.

240 Headquarters 96th Field Artillery Battalion, *War Diary*, 4–5; Headquarters 2nd Engineer Special Brigade, *Unit Activities Report*, 12–13; Headquarters 7th Infantry Division, *War Diary*, Narrative section, September 22.

241 Montross, *U.S. Marine Corps Operations*, 199–200; Dill, *Personal Adventures*, 77–79.

242 Headquarters 2nd Engineer Special Brigade, *Unit Activities Report*, 11–13; Montross, *U.S. Marine Corps Operations*, 129; Headquarters X Corps, *Inchon Seoul Invasion—Periodic Operations Report, No. 7*; Headquarters X Corps, *Inchon Seoul Invasion—Periodic Operations Report, No. 8*, 26 September 1950, MHI, DS 919.U53; Headquarters X Corps, *Inchon Seoul Invasion—Periodic Operations Report, No. 9*, 27 September 1950, MHI, DS 919.U53; Headquarters 1st Marine Division, *SAR-V2*, Folder 6, Annex Love Love, p. 22; Headquarters 1st Marine Division, *Medical Department Log*, 29.

243 Far East Command, Military Intelligence Section, *Terrain Handbook No. 65*, p. 30; Headquarters X Corps, *Civil Affairs Historical Activities*, NA, 407/429/270/66/34/1/1968, p. 1; Headquarters X Corps, G-1 Section, *Report of Activities: For the Period of 17 August to 30 September 1950*, NA 407/429/270/66/34/1/1968, p. 2; Headquarters X Corps, Provost Marshal Section, *History of Provost Marshal Operations*, Section II.

244 Far East Command, Military Intelligence Section, *Terrain Handbook No. 65*, p. 33; Headquarters 1st Marine Division, *SAR-V1*, Folder 3, Annex Baker, Appendix 5, p. 1.

245 Headquarters 1st Marine Division, *Medical Department Log*, 40.

246 Headquarters X Corps, *Civil Affairs Historical Activities*, 2–3; Headquarters 1st Marine Division, *Medical Department Log*, 30, 38.

247 Headquarters 1st Marine Division, *Medical Department Log*, 42–46; Headquarters 1st Marine Division, *SAR-V1*, Folder 4, Annex Zebra, p. 2; Headquarters 1st Marine Division, *SAR-V2*, Folder 5, Annex How How, p. 9, and Folder 6, Annex Peter Peter, Appendix 8, p. 3.

248 Appleman, *United States Army*, 536–537; 1st Marine Division, *Personnel Periodic Report No. 1*, p. 3.

249 Headquarters 1st Marine Division, *SAR-V1*, Folder 4, Annex Zebra, p. 2.

250 Headquarters X Corps, Provost Marshal Section, *History of Provost Marshal Operations*, Section III, and Annex 6; Headquarters 7th Infantry Division, *War Diary*, General comments section, pp. 1–2; Headquarters 1st Marine Division, *SAR-V1*, Folder 3, Annex Charlie, p. 33.

251 Headquarters 1st Marine Division, *SAR-V1*, Folder 4, Annex Zebra, p. 2, and Folder 2, Annex Able, p. 10; Headquarters 1st Marine Division, *Compilation of Comments and Recommendations from the Special Action Report, Staff Sections 1st Marine Division Inchon-Seoul Operation*, 5 December 1950, GRC, Korean War Project, Box 8a, Folders 2, p. 31.

252 Headquarters X Corps Command, *Operation Chromite*; Alexander, *Battle of the Barricades*, 8; Headquarters 11th Marines, 1st Marine Division, *Report of Use and Effectiveness of 4.5" Rocket Launchers*, 2.

253 Headquarters 1st Marine Division, *SAR-V2*, Folder 6, Annex Peter Peter, Appendix 9, pp. 5–7; Headquarters 96th Field Artillery Battalion, *War Diary*, 14.

254 Headquarters X Corps, *Inchon Seoul Invasion—Operations Instruction No. 6*, Annex 2; Headquarters 96th Field Artillery Battalion, *War Diary*, Annex C, p. 6; Dill, *Personal Adventures*, 97; History and Museums Division, Headquarters, US Marine Corps, *Oral History Transcript: Major General Raymond L. Murray*, 204–208.

255 Richard K. Tucker, "Marine Artillery Takes Heavy Toll of Seoul As Well As Enemy Troops," *Baltimore Evening Sun*, 27 September 1950, pp. 1–2.

256 Headquarters 1st Marine Division, *SAR-V1*, Folder 3, Annex Baker, Appendix 5, p. 3.

257 Headquarters 1st Marine Division, *Periodic Intelligence Report No. 13*, p. 2; Riley, *The Reds Take a City*, 80–102.

258 General Headquarters Far East Command, Military Intelligence Section, Allied Translator and Interpreter Section, *Enemy Documents*, Issue No. 9, NA, 242/-/190/17/2/5/1, p. 102.

259 Far East Command, Military Intelligence Section, *Terrain Handbook No. 65*, p. 30.

260 Korea Institute of Military History, *The Korean War*, 645–656.

261 Blair estimates "Hundreds, perhaps thousands." Blair, *The Forgotten War*, 293.

262 Headquarters 1st Marine Division, *Periodic Intelligence Report No. 13*, p. 3.

263 The NKPA lost over three hundred tanks and self-propelled guns in the last two weeks of September. Heinl, *Victory at High Tide*, 248.

Chapter 6

1 Willard Pearson, *Vietnam Studies: The War in the Northern Provinces* (Washington, DC: Department of the Army, 1975), 5; James R. Arnold, *Tet Offensive 1968* (Oxford: Osprey, 1990), 68.

2 While the US efforts to seal off the enemy with US Army units outside the city were important to the overall course of the battle, they are not extensively covered in this chapter. The actions of these units did not involve urban terrain, and the effects in the city of those open communist supply routes are addressed.

3 While several well-researched secondary sources (Hammel, Nolan, Shulimson) list Hue's population as 140,000, this is likely a peacetime figure. Primary sources from around the time of the battle, from both the communist and US perspective, list the city's population as 200,000. This larger figure is likely the result of an influx of war refugees from the rural combat zones. Keith William Nolan, *Battle for Hue: Tet 1968* (New York: Dell, 1983), 22; Eric Hammel, *Fire in the Streets: The Battle for Hue, Tet 1968* (New York: Dell, 1991), 7–9; Jack Shulimson, and others, *U.S. Marines in Vietnam: The Defining Year, 1968* (Washington, DC: Headquarters US Marine Corps, 1997), 164; *PLAF Directive on Tet 68 Offensive in Hue Area*, VVA, Item Number: 2131101005, Douglas Pike Collection, p. 2; Ellsworth Bunker, *For the President from Bunker: Herewith My Forty-First Weekly Message*, 29 February 1968, VVA, Item Number: 0241013003, Larry Berman Collection, p. 6.

4 Oscar E. Gilbert, *Marine Corps Tank Battles in Vietnam* (Drexel Hill, PA: Casemate, 2007), vi, 137.

5 Hammel, *Fire in the Streets*, 12–15.

6 Nicolas Warr, *Phase Line Green* (Annapolis, MD: US Naval Institute Press, 1997), 18, 32; Nolan, *Battle for Hue*, 23.

7 Don Oberdorfer, *Tet: The Turning Point of the Vietnam War* (Baltimore, MD: Johns Hopkins University Press, 2001), 136.

8 Hammel, *Fire in the Streets*, 3–9.

9 Oberdorfer, *Tet*, 43–45, 52–54, 116; Hammel, *Fire in the Streets*, 3–5.

10 D. J. Robertson, *1st Marine Division Commanders After Action Report, Tet Offensive, 29 January–14 February 1968*, 25 May 1968, GRC, Vietnam Tet Offensive, Box 24, Folder 2, p. 50.

11 Arnold, *Tet Offensive*, 44; Oberdorfer, *Tet*, 136.

12 David Ewing Ott, *Vietnam Studies: Field Artillery, 1954–1973* (Washington, DC: Department of the Army, 1975), 138; Ron Christmas, *Hue City*, undated paper, GRC, Vietnam Tet Offensive, Box 24, Folder 5, pp. 2–3; Oberdorfer, *Tet*, xi, 121.

13 Fleet Marine Force, Pacific, *Operations of U.S. Marine Forces Vietnam, February 1968*, undated, GRC, p. 8; Nolan, *Battle for Hue*, 55–56; Pearson, *Vietnam Studies*, 39.

14 This document is an exact translation of a captured North Vietnamese document. *Recapitulative Report: Phase of Attack on Hue from 31 Jan to 25 Feb 1968*, 30 March 1968, VVA, Item Number: 2131101002, Douglas Pike Collection, p. 16.

15 Pham Van Son, Chief, Military History Division, Joint General Staff, Republic of Vietnam Armed Forces, *The Viet Cong Tet Offensive (1968)*, trans-

lated from the original Vietnamese by the Joint General Staff Translation Board, undated, GRC, Vietnam Tet Offensive, Box 24, Folder 3, p. 291.

16 Fleet Marine Force, *Operations*, 18, 46–47.

17 As of October 1967 the US Central Intelligence Agency estimated there were 54,000 NVA and 64,000 VC in South Vietnam. Director of Central Intelligence, "Capabilities of the Vietnamese Communists for Fighting in South Vietnam," Special National Intelligence Estimate, Number 14.3-67, 13 November 1967, in *Estimate Products on Vietnam 1948–1975* (Pittsburgh, PA: National Intelligence Council, 2005), 11.

18 Fleet Marine Force, *Operations*, 8.

19 *Hue City Yearend (1968) Assessment Report*, 7 February 1969, VVA, Item Number: 2131107005, Douglas Pike Collection, p. 17.

20 D. J. Robertson, p. 50.

21 *Recapitulative Report*, 9–10, 13.

22 Captured and translated North Vietnamese documents. *Fifth Columnist Activities in Thua Thien Prov, Tri-Thien-Hue MR*, 30 September 1970, VVA, Item Number: 2311312013, Douglas Pike Collection; Oberdorfer, *Tet*, 206–208, 213.

23 Hammel, *Fire in the Streets*, 28–30.

24 *Recapitulative Report*, 9.

25 Oberdorfer, *Tet*, 57.

26 *Recapitulative Report*, 11.

27 *PLAF Directive on Tet 68 Offensive in Hue Area*, 5.

28 Headquarters 2nd Battalion, 5th Marines, *Command Chronology for the Period 1 February 1968 to 29 February 1968*, GRC, pp. 4–7.

29 Director of Central Intelligence, Estimate Products, p. 19; Bunker, *For the President from Bunker*, 10.

30 Headquarters 1st Battalion, 5th Marines, 1st Marine Division, *Command Chronology for the Period 1–31 March 1968*, 1 April 1968, GRC, Part IV, pp. 12, 47; *Recapitulative Report*, 14, 20–21, 35; Headquarters 1st Battalion, 5th Marines, *Command Chronology for the Period 1 February 1968 to 29 February 1968*, 1 March 1968, GRC, Part II, p. 8; Gordon L. Rottman, *The Rocket Propelled Grenade* (Oxford: Osprey, 2010), 19, 40.

31 J2, Joint General Staff, Army of the Republic of Vietnam, *VC/NVA Offensive Techniques in Cities and Towns*, 29 August 1968, VVA, Item Number: 2131007010a, Douglas Pike Collection, p. 14.

32 Headquarters 2nd Battalion, 5th Marines, 1st Marine Division, *Command Chronology for the Period 1 February 1968 to 29 February 1968*, 4 March 1968, GRC, pp. 26–27; *Recapitulative Report*, 13, 25; Ian V. Hogg, *The American Arsenal: The World War II Official Standard Ordnance Catalog of Small Arms, Tanks, Armored Cars, Artillery, Antiaircraft Guns, Ammunition, Grenades, Mines, etcetera* (London: Greenhill, 2001), 730–731; Gilbert, *Marine Corps Tank Battles*, 48, 80; Headquarters 1st Battalion, 5th Marines, *Command Chronology for the Period 1–31 March 1968*, Part IV, p. 47; Talman C. Budd, Office of the Senior Marine Advisor, *Combat Operations After Action Report (RCS MACJ 3-32)*, 25 July 1968, GRC, pp. 9–10.

33 Hammel, *Fire in the Streets*, 268.

34 Australian Army Training Team in Vietnam, "Victory at Hue," *Army Journal*, 1 February 1969, pp. 3–20, VVA, Item Number: 2131109002, Douglas Pike Collection, p. 16.

35 *Recapitulative Report*, 15, 25-26, 35, 41–42, 47; *PLAF Directive on Tet 68 Offensive in Hue Area*, 8; Pham Van Son, p. 267; Oberdorfer, *Tet*, 211–212; Hammel, *Fire in the Streets*, 132.

36 These two battalions report recapturing a total of forty-three CS grenades. Headquarters 1st Battalion, 5th Marines, *Command Chronology for the Period 1–31 March 1968*, Part IV, pp. 41–42; Headquarters 2nd Battalion, 5th Marines, *Command Chronology for the Period 1 February 1968 to 29 February 1968*, pp. 4–7.

37 Australian Army Training Team in Vietnam, "Victory at Hue," 16.

38 Budd, *Combat Operations*, 8; *Recapitulative Report*, 44; Eric Hammel, *Marines in Hue City: A Portrait of Urban Combat, Tet 1968* (St. Paul, MN: Zenith Press, 2007), 146; J2, Joint General Staff, Army of the Republic of Vietnam, pp. 9, 31–32.

39 Nolan, *Battle for Hue*, 176–178; Hammel, *Fire in the Streets*, 10; Shulimson, *U.S. Marines in Vietnam*, 164.

40 Christmas, *Hue City*, 2–3; Pham Van Son, pp. 248–249.

41 Ott, *Vietnam Studies*, 140.

42 Hammel, *Marines in Hue City*, 36; Arnold, *Tet Offensive*, 73; Nolan, *Battle for Hue*, 27–29, 57.

43 D. J. Robertson, pp. 52–54; Hammel, *Marines in Hue City*, 35, 41, 115–119; Fleet Marine Force, *Operations*, 10.

44 D. J. Robertson, pp. 51–52; Nolan, *Battle for Hue*, 45–49, 81; Christmas, *Hue City*, 7.

45 Fleet Marine Force, *Operations*, 14.

46 To simplify reference the various United States Marine Corps (USMC) units involved at Hue, a scheme will be used, where F/2/5 will equate to F Company, 2nd Battalion, 5th Marine Regiment, and 1/5 refers to the 1st Battalion, 5th Marine Regiment (or 5th Marines for short).

47 Nolan, *Battle for Hue*, 176–178.

48 D. J. Robertson, pp. 46, 49.

49 Budd, *Combat Operations*, 5.

50 *Recapitulative Report*, 11.

51 Christmas, *Hue City*, 18–21; Fleet Marine Force, *Operations*, 10, 16–17.

52 Fleet Marine Force, *Operations*, 16.

53 Headquarters 1st Battalion, 5th Marines, *Command Chronology for the Period 1–31 March 1968*, Part IV, pp. 12–24, 43–48.

54 Headquarters 1st Battalion, 5th Marines, *Command Chronology for the Period 1 February 1968 to 29 February 1968*, Part II, p. 7.

55 Budd, *Combat Operations*, 9.

56 Pham Van Son, pp. 269–271; Oberdorfer, *Tet*, 224.

57 Ott, *Vietnam Studies*, 138–139; Pearson, *Vietnam Studies*, 45–47.

58 Hammel, *Fire in the Streets*, 12–15.

59 Nolan, *Battle for Hue*, 30–32.

60 George S. Eckhardt, *Vietnam Studies: Command and Control, 1950–1969* (Washington, DC: Department of the Army, 1991), 74.

61 Interestingly, the Deputy Commander of III MAF had been Major General Raymond Murray, up until February 1968, when he returned to the United States and retired later that year. Murray was a veteran of Seoul as commander of the 5th Marines, but there is no evidence his experience had any direct influence on the USMC approach at Hue. History and Museums Division, Headquarters, US Marine Corps, *Oral History Transcript: Major General Raymond L. Murray*, 1988, GRC, Introduction.

62 D. J. Robertson, pp. 51–52; Nolan, *Battle for Hue*, 45–54; Hammel, *Fire in the Streets*, 82; Shulimson, *U.S. Marines in Vietnam*, 173. A US Fleet Marine Force, Pacific, summary of operations for February sheds no light on this subject as it misidentifies the company crossing the bridge as A/1/1 (actually was G/2/5), states tanks supported the push into the Citadel (tanks did not cross the bridge), and states that ARVN units relieved the Marines at the bridge when they came back into south Hue (no organized ARVN units were in south Hue at this time). Fleet Marine Force, *Operations*, 10. Neither the Fleet Marine Force nor the 1st Marine Division report states where the order for Gravel to go into the Citadel came from.

63 Hammel, *Fire in the Streets*, 112–113; Nolan, *Battle for Hue*, 61; D. J. Robertson, p. 52.

64 Headquarters 1st Battalion, 1st Marines, 1st Marine Division, *Command Chronology for the Period 1 February 1968 to 29 February 1968*, 5 March 1968, GRC, p. 1-2-5; Christmas, *Hue City*, 5; Headquarters 2nd Battalion, 5th Marines, *Command Chronology for the Period 1 February 1968 to 29 February 1968*, pp. 8–9.

65 Headquarters 1st Battalion, 5th Marines, *Command Chronology for the Period 1-31 March 1968*, Part IV, pp. 3, 17–18.

66 Budd, *Combat Operations*, 12–13. Apparently the Vietnamese Joint General Staff had issued orders that the SVN Marines were not to be sent to Hue piecemeal. Shulimson, *U.S. Marines in Vietnam*, 197.

67 D. J. Robertson, p. 52; Nolan, *Battle for Hue*, 74–75; Hammel, *Fire in the Streets*, 137.

68 D. J. Robertson, pp. 69–71. One exception to this lack of urban warfare experience was the battalion sergeant major for 2/5, who was a veteran of the battle for Seoul in 1950. Nolan, *Battle for Hue*, 152.

69 Hammel, *Fire in the Streets*, 91.

70 Hammel, *Marines in Hue City*, 60–61; Hammel, *Fire in the Streets*, 141. While Hammel does not specify which manuals Cheatham read, the titles he mentions, and the key lessons drawn, make it likely the US Army's FM 31-50, *Combat in Fortified and Built-Up Areas*, was part of the set. The 1964 version of FM 31-50 mentions the utility of nonlethal chemical agents twice. Headquarters, Department of the Army, *Combat in Fortified and Built-Up Areas*, Field Manual 31-50, March 1964, MHI, pp. 30, 36.

71 Nolan, *Battle for Hue*, 76, 126, 270–276.

72 Ibid., 179–180.

73 Hammel, *Fire in the Streets*, 257–258.

74 Hammel, *Marines in Hue City*, 129–133; Nolan, *Battle for Hue*, 223, 230–233.

75 Cushman would announce Thompson's relief to reporters, but Thompson would not hear of this pseudo-relief until weeks later, in a letter from his wife. Hammel, *Fire in the Streets*, 303.

76 Christmas, *Hue City*, 13; D. J. Robertson, p. 71; Hammel, *Marines in Hue City*, 70–72.

77 United State Marine Corps, *Marine Rifle Squad*, Fleet Marine Force Manual 6-5, GRC, p. 432.

78 R. Scot Hopkins, *Interview of Colonel Ron Christmas, USMC, on the Battle of Hue City During Tet Offensive, January-March 1968*, 21 April 1987, GRC, Vietnam Tet Offensive, Box 24, Folder 4, p. 5; Hammel, *Fire in the Streets*, 68–74.

79 Nolan, *Battle for Hue*, 206–207.

80 Fleet Marine Force, *Operations*, 17–18; Nolan, *Battle for Hue*, 223, 230–233.

81 Hammel, *Marines in Hue City*, 99; Nolan, *Battle for Hue*, 32–38, 104–106.

82 Christmas, *Hue City*, 22.

83 Headquarters 2nd Battalion, 5th Marines, *Command Chronology for the Period 1 February 1968 to 29 February 1968*, pp. 2–3.

84 Nolan, *Battle for Hue*, 270–276.

85 Fleet Marine Force, *Operations*, 10.

86 Nolan, *Battle for Hue*, 179–180, 184; Hammel, *Marines in Hue City*, 125–127; Fleet Marine Force, *Operations*, 16–17.

87 Budd, *Combat Operations*, 2–4, 12.

88 Australian Army Training Team in Vietnam, "Victory at Hue," 16; Ott, *Vietnam Studies*, 142–143.

89 Ott, *Vietnam Studies*, 142–143. US Joint Chiefs of Staff, *Combat Air Activities Files (CACTA)*, created October 1965–December 1970, original data from the Electronic and Special Media Records Services Division, NA, Record Group 218, Records of the US Joint Chiefs of Staff. Data was processed by US Air Force personnel into a more user friendly format, with access granted to this author by Lt. Col. Jenns Robertson and Mr. Ryan Burr in March 2009.

90 Headquarters 1st Battalion, 5th Marines, *Command Chronology for the Period 1–31 March 1968*, Part IV, pp. 7–8, 47–48; Fleet Marine Force, *Operations*, 20; D. J. Robertson, p. 71.

91 Nolan, *Battle for Hue*, 113–114.

92 Headquarters 1st Battalion, 5th Marines, *Command Chronology for the Period 1–31 March 1968*, Part IV, pp. 8–9, 48; Ed Gilbert, *U.S. Marine Corps Tank Crewman 1965–70* (Oxford: Osprey, 2004), 47–48; Peter Bush, "The Ontos Was One of the More Interesting Developments to Come Down the Road...," *Vietnam* 15 (October 2002): 12–14.

93 Gilbert, *Marine Corps Tank Battles*, x, 103.

94 Hammel, *Marines in Hue City*, 51–52.

95 Headquarters 1st Battalion, 5th Marines, *Command Chronology for the Period 1–31 March 1968*, Part IV, p. 9.

96 Headquarters 1st Battalion, 5th Marines, *Command Chronology for the Period 1–31 March 1968*, Part IV, pp. 20–21, 27–32; Headquarters 1st Battalion, 1st Marines, *Command Chronology for the Period 1 February 1968 to 29 February 1968*, Part IV, Journal for 11 February 1968; Headquarters 2nd Battalion, 5th Marines, *Command Chronology for the Period 1 February 1968 to 29 February 1968*, p. 18, journal entries for 18, 19, and 24 February.

97 Headquarters 2nd Battalion, 5th Marines, *Command Chronology for the Period 1 February 1968 to 29 February 1968*, pp. 29–30.

98 Nolan, *Battle for Hue*, 104–106.

99 Hammel, *Fire in the Streets*, 348–349.

100 Budd, *Combat Operations*, 8; Headquarters 2nd Battalion, 5th Marines, *Command Chronology for the Period 1 February 1968 to 29 February 1968*, Journal for 24 February; Headquarters 1st Battalion, 1st Marines, *Command Chronology for the Period 1 February 1968 to 29 February 1968*, Part IV, Journal for 22 February 1968.

101 Headquarters 1st Battalion, 5th Marines, *Command Chronology for the Period 1–31 March 1968*, Part IV, p. 45.

102 Ibid., 45.

103 Headquarters 2nd Battalion, 5th Marines, *Command Chronology for the Period 1 February 1968 to 29 February 1968*, pp. 34–35; Headquarters 1st Battalion, 1st Marines, *Command Chronology for the Period 1 February 1968 to 29 February 1968*, p. 1-2-8.

104 Warr, *Phase Line Green*, 157.

105 Warr, *Phase Line Green*, 12, 102; Hammel, *Marines in Hue City*, 134; Raymond A. Stewart, "Marine Tanks in the Battle for Hue City: Tet 1968," *Leatherneck* 91 (February 2008): 12; Gilbert, *Marine Corps Tank Battles*, 100.

106 Fleet Marine Force, *Operations*, 9–10.

107 Australian Army Training Team in Vietnam, "Victory at Hue," 17–18; D. J. Robertson, p. 50; Fleet Marine Force, *Operations*, 8.

108 Australian Army Training Team in Vietnam, "Victory at Hue," 17–18.

109 Oberdorfer, *Tet*, 119–120, 131–134, 209-210; Hammel, *Fire in the Streets*, 2–6, 23–24.

110 D. J. Robertson, pp. 51–52.

111 Headquarters, US Military Assistance Command Vietnam, *Monthly Summary: February 1968*, 29 April 1968, VVA, Item Numbers: 7390103001a and 7390103001b, John M. Shaw Collection, p. 29.

112 Earle Wheeler, Chairman Joint Chiefs of Staff, *Memorandum for the President: Telephone Conversation with General Westmoreland*, 11 February 1968, VVA, Item Number: 0010244008, Veteran Members of the 109th Quartermaster Company Collection, p. 1. Earle Wheeler, Chairman Joint Chiefs of Staff, *Memorandum for the President: Telephone Conversation with General Westmoreland*, 16 February 1968, VVA, Item Number: 0010245001, Veteran Members of the 109th Quartermaster Company Collection, p. 1.

113 Nolan, *Battle for Hue*, 30–32, 45–53, 61; Oberdorfer, *Tet*, 216–218.

114 Christmas, *Hue City*, 9.
115 Headquarters 1st Battalion, 5th Marines, *Command Chronology for the Period 1–31 March 1968*, Part IV, pp. 9–10.
116 Budd, *Combat Operations*, 4–5.
117 Earle Wheeler, Chairman Joint Chiefs of Staff, *Memorandum for the President: Situation in Vietnam*, 11 February 1968, VVA, Item Number: 0010244008, Veteran Members of the 109th Quartermaster Company Collection, p. 1.
118 Headquarters 1st Battalion, 5th Marines, *Command Chronology for the Period 1–31 March 1968*, Part IV, pp. 9–10.
119 D. J. Robertson, p. 50.
120 Christmas, *Hue City*, 9–10.
121 Australian Army Training Team in Vietnam, "Victory at Hue," 9.
122 Headquarters 1st Battalion, 5th Marines, *Command Chronology for the Period 1–31 March 1968*, Part IV, pp. 21–22.
123 Headquarters, US Military Assistance Command Vietnam, pp. 28–60.
124 Nolan, *Battle for Hue*, 54.
125 Wheeler, *Memorandum for the President: Telephone Conversation with General Westmoreland*, p. 1; Nolan, *Battle for Hue*, 183; Hammel, *Marines in Hue City*, 142–143; Hammel, *Fire in the Streets*, 190–204, 278.
126 Nolan, *Battle for Hue*, 125, 160–161, 204–205; Hammel, *Fire in the Streets*, 60–65, 185, 291; Warr, *Phase Line Green*, 159–161.
127 Hammel, *Marines in Hue City*, 110; Nolan, *Battle for Hue*, 129–130.
128 Ron Christmas, "A Company Commander Remembers the Battle for Hue," *Marine Corps Gazette* 61 (February 1977): 23.
129 J2, Joint General Staff, Army of the Republic of Vietnam, p. 14; Hammel, *Marines in Hue City*, 142.
130 Nolan, *Battle for Hue*, 179–180; Russell W. Glenn, et al., *Ready for Armageddon* (Santa Monica, CA: Rand, 2002), 64–65.
131 Ray Smith, 2nd Lieutenant (USMC), *Letter to Captain Batcheller Regarding Hue City Fighting*, 25 March 1968, GRC, Vietnam Tet Offensive, Box 24, Folder 1, pp. 2–3; Headquarters 1st Battalion, 5th Marines, *Command Chronology for the Period 1–31 March 1968*, Part IV, p. 13.
132 Fleet Marine Force, *Operations*, 46–47; Headquarters 1st Battalion, 1st Marines, *Command Chronology for the Period 1 February 1968 to 29 February 1968*, Part IV, Journal for 12 February 1968.
133 Australian Army Training Team in Vietnam, "Victory at Hue," 16; Headquarters 2nd Battalion, 5th Marines, *Command Chronology for the Period 1 February 1968 to 29 February 1968*, p. 4, Journal for 6 February.
134 Headquarters 1st Battalion, 5th Marines, *Command Chronology for the Period 1–31 March 1968*, Part IV, pp. 9–10. While counter-mortar radar is mentioned several times in this source, it is not clear it made much of a contribution in finding enemy mortars. Headquarters 1st Battalion, 5th Marines, *Command Chronology for the Period 1 February 1968 to 29 February 1968*, Part III, pp. 1, 11.
135 Shulimson, *U.S. Marines in Vietnam*, 204.

136 Fleet Marine Force, *Operations*, 13. In a US military database of sorties for USAF/USMC/SVN aircraft over or close to Hue (within a kilometer), only one of 195 sorties is listed as being dedicated to reconnaissance. But this database did not include the sort of light aircraft supporting 2/5. US Joint Chiefs of Staff, *Combat Air Activities Files (CACTA)*; Marine Medium Helicopter Squadron 364, Marine Aircraft Group 36, 1st Marine Aircraft Wing, *Command Chronology for 1 February Through 29 February 1968*, 5 March 1968, GRC, p. 10; Headquarters 2nd Battalion, 5th Marines, *Command Chronology for the Period 1 February 1968 to 29 February 1968*, p. 32.

137 Hammel, *Fire in the Streets*, 255–258.

138 R. Scot Hopkins, *Interview of Colonel Ron Christmas*, 5; Nolan, *Battle for Hue*, 77–78; Shulimson, *U.S. Marines in Vietnam*, 185.

139 Hammel, *Fire in the Streets*, 147–149; Hammel, *Marines in Hue City*, 93; Warr, *Phase Line Green*, 4, 47, 55.

140 Fleet Marine Force, *Operations*, 12–13; Nolan, *Battle for Hue*, 57, 81; Shulimson, *U.S. Marines in Vietnam*, 176.

141 Christmas, *Hue City*, 11.

142 Hammel, *Fire in the Streets*, 82–91.

143 Nolan, *Battle for Hue*, 86; US Joint Chiefs of Staff, *Combat Air Activities Files (CACTA)*.

144 This personal account was from a platoon commander in C/1/5. Warr calls the command chronology incorrect. He states on one page that the strict rules of engagement were in place until 16 Feb, but on another page describes F-4s dropping bombs on a tower in the Citadel on 15 February (see pages 124 and 139–144). Warr, *Phase Line Green*, x, 91–95, 104–125, 137–144.

145 Headquarters 1st Battalion, 5th Marines, Command Chronology for the Period 1–31 March 1968, Part IV, pp. 17–18, 47–48.

146 Nolan, *Battle for Hue*, 185, 193–194, 205; Hammel, *Marines in Hue City*, 127–133; Hammel, *Fire in the Streets*, 270–271; Pham Van Son, p. 266.

147 Fleet Marine Force, *Operations*, 18; Michael Herr, *Dispatches* (New York: Vintage International, 1991), 84.

148 This report from Australian advisors to the ARVN called the weather seasonal. Australian Army Training Team in Vietnam, "Victory at Hue," 16.

149 Marine Aircraft Group 36, *Command Chronology for 1 February–29 February 1968*, pp. 6–18; D. J. Robertson, p. 51.

150 Headquarters 1st Battalion, 1st Marines, *Command Chronology for the Period 1 February 1968 to 29 February 1968*, p. 1-2-5.

151 Headquarters 1st Battalion, 5th Marines, *Command Chronology for the Period 1–31 March 1968*, Part IV, p. 48.

152 Headquarters 2nd Battalion, 5th Marines, *Command Chronology for the Period 1 February 1968 to 29 February 1968*, p. 32.

153 US Joint Chiefs of Staff, *Combat Air Activities Files*; Headquarters 2nd Battalion, 5th Marines, *Command Chronology for the Period 1 February 1968 to 29 February 1968*, p. 32; Headquarters 1st Battalion, 5th Marines, *Command*

Chronology for the Period 1–31 March 1968, Part IV, p. 48; Hammel, *Fire in the Streets*, 275.

154 Headquarters 1st Battalion, 5th Marines, *Command Chronology for the Period 1–31 March 1968*, Part IV, pp. 7, 47–48; Headquarters 2nd Battalion, 5th Marines, *Command Chronology for the Period 1 February 1968 to 29 February 1968*, p. 2.

155 Fleet Marine Force, *Operations*, 20; Budd, *Combat Operations*, 3; Hammel, *Marines in Hue City*, 51–52. Thompson viewed the naval gunfire support his battalion received as not very useful, as the height of the Citadel wall kept many of the low-flying rounds from landing in his area. Shulimson, *U.S. Marines in Vietnam*, 200.

156 Headquarters 2nd Battalion, 5th Marines, *Command Chronology for the Period 1 February 1968 to 29 February 1968*, pp. 31–32; Nolan, *Battle for Hue*, 136–138. While most of the artillery was outside the city, one battery of USMC 105mm howitzers did operate within south Hue during the last half of the battle. Shulimson, *U.S. Marines in Vietnam*, 194.

157 Hammel, *Fire in the Streets*, 231–232.

158 Gilbert, *Marine Corps Tank Battles*, 146–147; Jim Mesko, *M48 Patton in Action* (Carrollton, TX, 1984), 27. Stewart, "Marine Tanks...," 11–12.

159 Note, Hammel states there were five M48s in south Hue. Hammel, *Marines in Hue City*, 51, 63; Hammel, *Fire in the Streets*, 77–78; Nolan, *Battle for Hue*, 78; Shelby L. Stanton, *Vietnam Order of Battle* (Mechanicsburg, PA: Stackpole, 2003), 278.

160 Headquarters, 1st Tank Battalion, 1st Marine Division, *Command Chronology, 1 February 1968 to 29 February 1968*, undated, VVA, Item Number: 1201012113, US Marine Corps History Division, Vietnam War Documents Collection, pp. 118, 126 of an electronic document that is a collection of 1st Tank Battalion documents. Headquarters 1st Battalion, 5th Marines, *Command Chronology for the Period 1–31 March 1968*, Part IV, pp. 8–9; Gilbert, *US Marine Corps Tank Crewman*, 47–48; Gilbert, *Marine Corps Tank Battles*, 159; Stewart, "Marine Tanks...," 13.

161 D. J. Robertson, p. 69; Headquarters 1st Battalion, 5th Marines, *Command Chronology for the Period 1–31 March 1968*, Part IV, pp. 9, 48; Fleet Marine Force, *Operations*, 18; Gilbert, *Marine Corps Tank Battles*, 62, 158–159.

162 Mesko, *M48 Patton*, 27; Gilbert, *Marine Corps Tank Battles*, 27–28, 52, 155.

163 Headquarters 2nd Battalion, 5th Marines, *Command Chronology for the Period 1 February 1968 to 29 February 1968*, p. 24; Fleet Marine Force, *Operations*, 17.

164 United State Marine Corps, *Marine Infantry Battalion*, 73–74.

165 Headquarters 2nd Battalion, 5th Marines, *Command Chronology for the Period 1 February 1968 to 29 February 1968*, Journal for 4 February; Nolan, *Battle for Hue*, 87.

166 Headquarters 2nd Battalion, 5th Marines, *Command Chronology for the Period 1 February 1968 to 29 February 1968*, pp. 13–14; Christmas, *Hue City*, 11–13.

167 Headquarters 2nd Battalion, 5th Marines, *Command Chronology for the Period 1 February 1968 to 29 February 1968*, p. 2.

168 Nolan, *Battle for Hue*, 208–209.
169 Budd, *Combat Operations*, 13; Australian Army Training Team in Vietnam, "Victory at Hue," 11, 15.
170 Hammel, *Fire in the Streets*, 304, 339.
171 *Hue City Yearend (1968) Assessment Report*, 7.
172 D. J. Robertson, p. 51.
173 Hammel, *Marines in Hue City*, 60–61, 121; D. J. Robertson, p. 71; Headquarters 2nd Battalion, 5th Marines, *Command Chronology for the Period 1 February 1968 to 29 February 1968*, pp. 2, 9–10; Headquarters 1st Battalion, 5th Marines, *Command Chronology for the Period 1–31 March 1968*, Part IV, pp. 17–18.
174 Hammel, *Marines in Hue City*, 68; Hammel, *Fire in the Streets*, 116–122, 166–172.
175 Nolan, *Battle for Hue*, 80, 85–91, 152; Hammel, *Marines in Hue City*, 70–72.
176 Headquarters 2nd Battalion, 5th Marines, *Command Chronology for the Period 1 February 1968 to 29 February 1968*, pp. 12–13; Fleet Marine Force, *Operations*, 13.
177 R. Scot Hopkins, *Interview of Colonel Ron Christmas*, 6.
178 Stanton, *Vietnam Order of Battle*, 276.
179 Ibid., 276.
180 Gary's US Infantry Weapons Reference Guide <http://www.inetres.com/gp/military/infantry/index.html#rifle> [accessed 28 June 2009].
181 Hammel, *Marines in Hue City*, 70–72.
182 Warr, *Phase Line Green*, 102, 123–124.
183 Charles Melson, *U.S. Marine Rifleman in Vietnam 1965–73* (Oxford: Osprey, 1998), 16–17.
184 Hammel, *Marines in Hue City*, 51, 74, 134, 144.
185 Fleet Marine Force, *Operations*, 17, 20; Headquarters 1st Battalion, 5th Marines, *Command Chronology for the Period 1–31 March 1968*, Part IV, pp. 19, 26-27; Headquarters 2nd Battalion, 5th Marines, *Command Chronology for the Period 1 February 1968 to 29 February 1968*, pp. 18–19.
186 Erik Villard, Erik, *The 1968 Tet Offensive Battles of Quang Tri City and Hue* (Washington, DC: Center for Military History, 2008), CMH, p. 61.
187 Matthew S. Meselson, "Chemical and Biological Weapons," *Scientific American* 222 (May 1970): 15, 21–22, 24; E. E. Westbrook and L. W. Williams, *A Brief Survey of Nonlethal Weapons* (Columbus, OH: Columbus Laboratories, 1971), pp. A-1 to A-2; Robert J. Bunker, ed., *Nonlethal Weapons: Terms and References*, Occasional Paper 15 (Colorado Springs, CO: United States Air Force Institute for National Security Studies, US Air Force Academy, 1997), 25–27; Department of the Army, *The Law of Land Warfare*, Field Manual 27-10, July 1956, MHI, pp. 18–19.
188 The date this guidance was issued is unclear. Ott, *Vietnam Studies*, 173–174.
189 Headquarters 1st Battalion, 1st Marines, *Command Chronology for the Period 1 February 1968 to 29 February 1968*, Part IV, Journal for 10 February 1968; Headquarters 1st Battalion, 5th Marines, *Command Chronology for the Period 1–31 March 1968*, Part IV, pp. 17–18, 46; Headquarters 2nd Battalion, 5th

Marines, *Command Chronology for the Period 1 February 1968 to 29 February 1968*, pp. 10–13, 31–32; Nolan, *Battle for Hue*, 236; Melson, *U.S. Marine Rifleman*, 16–17; Shulimson, *U.S. Marines in Vietnam*, 183.

190 D. J. Robertson, p. 69; Westbrook, *A Brief Survey*, 14; Headquarters 2nd Battalion, 5th Marines, *Command Chronology for the Period 1 February 1968 to 29 February 1968*, p. 9; Headquarters 1st Battalion, 5th Marines, *Command Chronology for the Period 1–31 March 1968*, Part IV, p. 46.

191 Fleet Marine Force, *Operations*, 20; Budd, *Combat Operations*, 8; *Recapitulative Report*, 44; *Scenes of the General Offensive and Uprising*, Foreign Languages Publishing House, Hanoi, 1968, VVA, Item Number: 2131012040, Douglas Pike Collection, p. 40; J2, Joint General Staff, Army of the Republic of Vietnam, pp. 9, 31–32.

192 Marine All Weather Fighter Squadron 235, Marine Aircraft Group 11, 1st Marine Aircraft Wing, *Command Chronology for 1 February–29 February 1968*, 7 March 1968, GRC, Enclosure 1, p. 4.

193 Of the 196 sorties over or near the city (within one kilometer) twenty-nine involved damage to the aircraft, an abort, or a diversion. US Joint Chiefs of Staff, *Combat Air Activities Files (CACTA)*. Hammel describes in detail one strike by two USMC A-4s where one of the aircraft suffered serious damage. This may indicate some gaps in the Joint Chiefs of Staff database as it does not report any damaged A-4s. Hammel, *Fire in the Streets*, 341–346.

194 Marine Aircraft Group 36, *Command Chronology for 1 February–29 February 1968*, p. 19.

195 Marine Medium Helicopter Squadron 364, pp. 4, 8; Wilfred A. Jackson, "Stay Clear of Hue," *United States Army Aviation Digest* 16 (April 1970): 12–14.

196 Christopher F. Foss, *Jane's Main Battle Tanks* (London: Jane's, 1986), 146–152; Steven J. Zaloga, *M26/M46 Pershing Tank 1943–1953* (Oxford: Osprey, 2000), picture plate D.

197 Gilbert, *Marine Corps Tank Battles*, 80, 158–159, 263; Foss, *Jane's Main Battle Tanks*, 146–152; Headquarters 1st Battalion, 5th Marines, *Command Chronology for the Period 1–31 March 1968*, Part IV, pp. 8–9, 48; Headquarters, 1st Tank Battalion, pp. 5, 131–179 of an electronic document that is a collection of 1st Tank Battalion documents.

198 Gilbert, *Marine Corps Tank Battles*, 46; Mesko, *M48 Patton*, 36.

199 Headquarters 1st Battalion, 1st Marines, *Command Chronology for the Period 1 February 1968 to 29 February 1968*, Part IV, Journal for 9 February 1968; Gilbert, *Marine Corps Tank Battles*, 151; Gilbert, *US Marine Corps Tank Crewman*, 47; Hammel, *Marines in Hue City*, 106–107.

200 Gilbert, *Marine Corps Tank Battles*, 25–26, 148, 162, picture section caption; Mesko, *M48 Patton*, 14.

201 Headquarters 1st Battalion, 5th Marines, *Command Chronology for the Period 1–31 March 1968*, Part IV, p. 48; Bush, "The Ontos...," p. 14; D. J. Robertson, p. 57; Fleet Marine Force, *Operations*, 20; Headquarters 2nd Battalion, 5th Marines, *Command Chronology for the Period 1 February 1968 to 29 February 1968*, Journal for 6 February.

202 Headquarters 2nd Battalion, 5th Marines, *Command Chronology for the Period 1 February 1968 to 29 February 1968*, p. 34; Christmas, *Hue City*, 7–9, 11–13; Headquarters 2nd Battalion, 5th Marines, *Command Chronology for the Period 1 February 1968 to 29 February 1968*, pp. 27–29; Nolan, *Battle for Hue*, 45–53; Hammel, *Marines in Hue City*, 107–109; Hammel, *Fire in the Streets*, 85, 248.

203 Fleet Marine Force, *Operations*, 19.

204 Nolan, *Battle for Hue*, 268; Michael Dewar, *War in the Streets: The Story of Urban Combat from Calais to Khafji* (Devon, UK: David and Charles, 1992), 68; Arnold, *Tet Offensive*, 84.

205 Headquarters 1st Battalion, 1st Marines, *Command Chronology for the Period 1 February 1968 to 29 February 1968*, pp. 1-2-1 to 1-2-5; Headquarters 2nd Battalion, 5th Marines, *Command Chronology for the Period 1 February 1968 to 29 February 1968*, pp. 19–20; Headquarters 1st Battalion, 5th Marines, *Command Chronology for the Period 1-31 March 1968*, Part IV, pp. 15–33.

206 The commander of the armor in the Citadel would estimate his tank crewmen suffered approximately four killed and at least forty wounded. Gilbert, *Marine Corps Tank Battles*, 158–159.

207 Christopher G. Blood and Marlisa E. Anderson, *The Battle for Hue: Casualty and Disease Rates During Urban Warfare*, Report No. 93-16 (San Diego, CA: Naval Health Research Center, 1993), 2, 5.

208 Fleet Marine Force, *Operations*, 19; Budd, *Combat Operations*, 9.

209 Headquarters 2nd Battalion, 5th Marines, *Command Chronology for the Period 1 February 1968 to 29 February 1968*, pp. 1–2; Headquarters 2nd Battalion, 5th Marines, *Command Chronology for the Period 1 March 1968 to 31 March 1968*, 4 April 1968, GRC, p. 2.

210 Nolan, *Battle for Hue*, 245; Melson, *US Marine Rifleman*, 16–17; Hammel, *Fire in the Streets*, 297.

211 Nolan, *Battle for Hue*, 154.

212 R. Scot Hopkins, *Interview of Colonel Ron Christmas*, 6.

213 Gilbert, *US Marine Corps Tank Crewman*, 20–21.

214 Headquarters 1st Battalion, 5th Marines, *Command Chronology for the Period 1-31 March 1968*, Part IV, pp. 43–44; Headquarters 2nd Battalion, 5th Marines, *Command Chronology for the Period 1 February 1968 to 29 February 1968*, pp. 35–36.

215 Hammel, *Fire in the Streets*, 9–10.

216 Hammel, *Fire in the Streets*, 251, 258–259; Headquarters 1st Battalion, 5th Marines, *Command Chronology for the Period 1-31 March 1968*, Part IV, p. 3; Christmas, "A Company Commander Remembers the Battle for Hue," 150–151.

217 Hammel, *Marines in Hue City*, 136–137, 284.

218 Australian Army Training Team in Vietnam, "Victory at Hue," 16.

219 Fleet Marine Force, *Operations*, 12; Headquarters 1st Battalion, 5th Marines, *Command Chronology for the Period 1-31 March 1968*, Part IV, pp. 3, 15.

220 This unit was based offshore on a US Navy amphibious assault ship. Marine Medium Helicopter Squadron 165, Marine Aircraft Group 15, 9th Marine

Amphibious Brigade, *Command Chronology for 1 February Through 3 March 1968*, 6 March 1968, GRC, pp. 1–6.

221 Nolan, *Battle for Hue*, 62–63, 136–138.

222 *Recapitulative Report*, 6–7.

223 Budd, *Combat Operations*, 4.

224 D. J. Robertson, pp. 58–59.

225 Headquarters 1st Battalion, 5th Marines, *Command Chronology for the Period 1–31 March 1968*, Part IV, p. 45.

226 Headquarters 1st Battalion, 5th Marines, *Command Chronology for the Period 1–31 March 1968*, Part IV, pp. 44, 49; Marine Aircraft Group 36, *Command Chronology for 1 February–29 February 1968*, Enclosure 1, pp. 6–18.

227 US Army Transportation Command Museum website <http://www.tran-school.eustis.army.mil/museum/MECHANICALMULE.htm> [accessed 15 November 2008]. Headquarters 1st Battalion, 5th Marines, *Command Chronology for the Period 1–31 March 1968*, Part IV, pp. 44–45, 49.

228 Nolan, *Battle for Hue*, 45–53; Gilbert, *Marine Corps Tank Battles*, 146–147; Australian Army Training Team in Vietnam, "Victory at Hue," 9; *PLAF Directive on Tet 68 Offensive in Hue Area*, 8; Headquarters 2nd Battalion, 5th Marines, *Command Chronology for the Period 1 February 1968 to 29 February 1968*, Journal for 7 February.

229 Fleet Marine Force, *Operations*, 16–17; Headquarters 1st Battalion, 5th Marines, *Command Chronology for the Period 1-31 March 1968*, Part IV, pp. 44–45.

230 D. J. Robertson, pp. 58–61; Hammel, *Fire in the Streets*, 276–277, 337–340.

231 Hammel, *Marines in Hue City*, 131–132, 136–137; Nolan, *Battle for Hue*, 181–182, 186–192.

232 Fleet Marine Force, *Operations*, 83.

233 Headquarters 1st Battalion, 5th Marines, *Command Chronology for the Period 1–31 March 1968*, Part IV, p. 48.

234 Stewart, "Marine Tanks...," 14.

235 Nolan, *Battle for Hue*, 45–53.

236 Headquarters 1st Battalion, 5th Marines, *Command Chronology for the Period 1–31 March 1968*, Part IV, p. 13. Fleet Marine Force, *Operations*, 12.

237 Headquarters 1st Battalion, 5th Marines, *Command Chronology for the Period 1–31 March 1968*, Part IV, p. 47; Blood, *The Battle for Hue*, 3.

238 Headquarters 2nd Battalion, 5th Marines, *Command Chronology for the Period 1 February 1968 to 29 February 1968*, pp. 13–14; R. Scot Hopkins, *Interview of Colonel Ron Christmas*, 8.

239 Headquarters 1st Battalion, 5th Marines, *Command Chronology for the Period 1–31 March 1968*, Part IV, p. 46.

240 Nolan, *Battle for Hue*, 62–63, 87.

241 D. J. Robertson, p. 50.

242 Fleet Marine Force, *Operations*, 15, 18.

243 Nolan, *Battle for Hue*, 55–56; Hammel, *Marines in Hue City*, 133, 142–143; Fleet Marine Force, *Operations*, 8; Pearson, *Vietnam Studies*, 39.

244 Pham Van Son, p. 267.

245 Headquarters 2nd Battalion, 5th Marines, *Command Chronology for the Period 1 February 1968 to 29 February 1968*, pp. 15–18; Hammel, *Marines in Hue City*, 103–104, 109–110, 244.

246 Gilbert, *Marine Corps Tank Battles*, 156.

247 Headquarters 1st Battalion, 5th Marines, *Command Chronology for the Period 1–31 March 1968*, Part IV, pp. 7–8.

248 Pham Van Son, pp. 288–290; *Recapitulative Report*, 18.

249 J2, Joint General Staff, Army of the Republic of Vietnam, pp. 16, 22.

250 Marine Heavy Helicopter Squadron 463, Marine Aircraft Group 16, 1st Marine Aircraft Wing, *Command Chronology for February 1968*, 7 March 1968, GRC, pp. 5, 10, 32–35.

251 Nolan, *Battle for Hue*, 115.

252 Fleet Marine Force, *Operations*, 13, 88; D. J. Robertson, pp. 56–57.

253 Commander US Naval Forces, Vietnam, *U.S. Naval Forces, Vietnam Monthly Historical Supplement, February 1968*, 29 June 1968, VVA, Item Number: 13120202001, United States Naval Forces, Vietnam Monthly historical summaries, 1966–1972, 1973 Collection, pp. 89–93, 97.

254 Australian Army Training Team in Vietnam, "Victory at Hue," 15, 19; Budd, *Combat Operations*, 11.

255 Fleet Marine Force, *Operations*, 88.

256 Four Wheel Drive Online website <http://www.4wdonline.com/Mil/M422/MightyMite.html> [accessed 15 November 2008].

257 Headquarters 2nd Battalion, 5th Marines, *Command Chronology for the Period 1 February 1968 to 29 February 1968*, p. 34; Headquarters 1st Battalion, 5th Marines, *Command Chronology for the Period 1–31 March 1968*, Part IV, p. 49; US Army Transportation Command Museum website.

258 Hammel, *Marines in Hue City*, 51–52, 116–122.

259 Nolan, *Battle for Hue*, 145, 208–209; Hammel, *Marines in Hue City*, 51–52.

260 Headquarters 1st Battalion, 5th Marines, *Command Chronology for the Period 1–31 March 1968*, Part IV, pp. 43–44, 48.

261 Nolan, *Battle for Hue*, 205, 214, 218; Hammel, *Marines in Hue City*, 139–143, 297.

262 D. J. Robertson, p. 66.

263 Headquarters 1st Battalion, 5th Marines, *Command Chronology for the Period 1–31 March 1968*, Part IV, pp. 44, 48.

264 Gilbert, *US Marine Corps Tank Crewman*, 47–48.

265 D. J. Robertson, pp. 52–54, 57–58; Fleet Marine Force, *Operations*, 3; Pham Van Son, p. 257.

266 Hammel, *Fire in the Streets*, 130–131, 240.

267 Fleet Marine Force, *Operations*, 45.

268 Australian Army Training Team in Vietnam, "Victory at Hue," 20; Bunker, *For the President from Bunker*, 6; Fleet Marine Force, *Operations*, 3, 46–47.

269 Fleet Marine Force, *Operations*, 46–47.

270 Headquarters 1st Battalion, 5th Marines, *Command Chronology for the Period 1–31 March 1968*, Part IV, p. 13; Hammel, *Marines in Hue City*, 78–81, 85, 142.

271 Headquarters 1st Battalion, 5th Marines, *Command Chronology for the Period 1–31 March 1968*, Part IV, pp. 32–33; Nolan, *Battle for Hue*, 133–134, 252.

272 Headquarters 1st Battalion, 5th Marines, *Command Chronology for the Period 1–31 March 1968*, Part IV, pp. 16–17; Bunker, *For the President from Bunker*, 7.

273 Pham Van Son, pp. 281, 291–293.

274 Oberdorfer, *Tet*, 224.

275 Headquarters 2nd Battalion, 5th Marines, *Command Chronology for the Period 1 February 1968 to 29 February 1968*, pp. 10–13; Fleet Marine Force, *Operations*, 13.

276 Fleet Marine Force, *Operations*, 20.

277 D. J. Robertson, p. 50; *Hue City Yearend (1968) Assessment Report*, 7, 12.

278 Pham Van Son, p. 281.

279 *PLAF Directive on Tet 68 Offensive in Hue Area*, 2, 9. For details of their intelligence preparation see this captured document. *Fifth Columnist Activities*. This captured document also lists a large number of killed local administrative personnel. *Recapitulative Report*, 47.

280 Oberdorfer, *Tet*, 201, 214–215, 231–232.

281 Oberdorfer, *Tet*, 201; Nolan, *Battle for Hue*, 267; Fleet Marine Force, *Operations*, 43; Pham Van Son, pp. 273–278, 284.

282 Some civilians in Hue were critical of the heavy American use of firepower. Bunker, *For the President from Bunker*, 7.

283 *Hue City Yearend (1968) Assessment Report*, 17.

284 Hammel, *Fire in the Streets*, 132.

285 Ibid., 91.

286 Nolan, *Battle for Hue*, 45–53.

287 Fleet Marine Force, *Operations*, 18, 46–47.

288 Headquarters 2nd Battalion, 5th Marines, *Command Chronology for the Period 1 February 1968 to 29 February 1968*, p. 9.

289 Nolan, *Battle for Hue*, 96.

Conclusion

1 War Department, *Field Service Regulations United States Army 1923*, 1924, MHI, p. III.

2 War Department, *Tentative Field Service Regulations—Operations*, FM 100-5, October 1939, MHI, p. II; War Department, *Field Service Regulations—Operations*, FM 100-5, May 1941, MHI, p. 209; The Infantry School, US Army, *Infantry in Battle*, 2nd ed. (Richmond, VA: Garrett and Massie, 1939), CARL, Introduction; War Department, *Attack on a Fortified Position and Combat in Towns*, Field Manual 31-50, January 1944, MHI, p. 61.

3 United State Marine Corps, *Marine Rifle Squad*, Fleet Marine Force Manual 6-5, 6 April 1966, GRC, p. 432.

4   For just two examples of World War Two reports, see, Headquarters VI
    Corps, US Army, *Combat Observer's Report No. 39*, 27 December 1944, NA,
    RG 498, ETO, G-3 Division, Observers' Reports, 1944–1945, box 3, p.
    1. Headquarters XII Corps, US Army, *Combat Observer's Report No. 18*, 7
    December 1944, NA, RG 498, ETO, G-3 Division, Observers' Reports,
    1944-1945, box 6.

5   Headquarters VII Corps, US Army, *Combat Observer's Report No. 88*, 26
    October 1944, NA, RG 498, ETO, G-3 Division, Observers' Reports, 1944–
    1945, box 5.

6   Charles A. Henne, *Battle History of the 3rd Battalion, 148th Infantry*, vol. 6,
    "Manila, the Unwanted Battle (4 February through 7 March 1945)," MHI,
    D811H454, p. 78.

7   Talman C. Budd, Office of the Senior Marine Advisor, *Combat Operations
    After Action Report (RCS MACJ 3-32)*, 25 July 1968, GRC, p. 13; Australian
    Army Training Team in Vietnam, "Victory at Hue," *Army Journal*, 1 February
    1969, pp. 3–20, VVA, Item Number: 2131109002, Douglas Pike Collection,
    pp. 11, 15.

8   Jonathan Gawne, *1944 Americans in Brittany: The Battle for Brest* (Paris:
    Histoire & Collections, 2002), 80, 82, 157.

9   Mark J. Reardon, "Evolution of Urban Combat Doctrine," in *City Fights:
    Selected Histories of Urban Combat from World War II to Vietnam*, ed. John
    Antal and Bradley Gericke (New York: Ballantine Books, 2003), 393.

10 William O. Odom, *After the Trenches: The Transformation of U.S. Army
    Doctrine, 1918–1939* (College Station: Texas A&M University Press, 1999),
    48–50, 70, chapter 12; War Department, *Field Service Regulations United
    States Army 1923*, p. 11.

11 Christopher R. Gabel, *The U.S. Army GHQ Maneuvers of 1941* (Washington,
    DC: Center of Military History, US Army, 1991), 178–180, 188.

12 Christopher R. Gabel, *Seek, Strike, and Destroy: U.S. Army Tank Destroyer
    Doctrine in World War II* (Fort Leavenworth, KS: Combat Studies Institute,
    1985).

13 War Department, *Tentative Field Service Regulations—Operations*, FM 100-
    5, 1939, Chapter 2; War Department, *Field Service Regulations—Operations*,
    FM 100-5, June 1944, Chapter 2; Odom, *After the Trenches*, 134–137; War
    Department, *Field Service Regulations United States Army 1923*, p. 11.

14 Michael D. Doubler, *Closing With the Enemy: How GIs Fought the War in
    Europe, 1944–1945* (Lawrence: University of Kansas Press, 1994), 17, 41.

15 Kevin T. McEnery, "The XIV Corps Battle for Manila: February 1945" (the-
    sis, US Army Command and General Staff College, Fort Leavenworth, KS,
    1993), p. 63; US Army, Headquarters Sixth Army, *Japanese Defense of Cities as
    Exemplified by the Battle for Manila—Report by XIV Corps*, 1 July 1945, MHI,
    D767.4J36, p. 13.

16 David E. Johnson, *Fast Tanks and Heavy Bombers: Innovation in the U.S. Army,
    1917–1945* (Ithaca, NY: Cornell University Press, 1998), 59, 72–80, 120.

17 Gawne, *1944 Americans in Brittany*, 48, 62, 84–85.

18 Headquarters 2nd Battalion, 5th Marines, 1st Marine Division, *Command Chronology for the Period 1 February 1968 to 29 February 1968*, 4 March 1968, GRC, pp. 1–2.

19 War Department, *Field Service Regulations United States Army 1923*, p. III; War Department, *Tentative Field Service Regulations—Operations*, FM 100-5, October 1939, p. II; War Department, *Field Service Regulations—Operations*, FM 100-5, May 1941, pp. II, 209; War Department, *Field Service Regulations—Operations*, FM 100-5, June 1944, p. II.

20 John R. Mass, "The Benning Revolution," in *A History of Innovation: U.S. Army Adaptation in War and Peace*, ed. Jon T. Hoffman (Washington, DC: Center for Military History, United States Army, 2009), 27–32.

21 Jonathan A. Beall, "The United States Army and Urban Combat in the Nineteenth Century," *War in History* 16 (2009): 168–169.

22 Don Higgenbotham, *The War of American Independence: Military Attitudes, Policies, and Practices, 1763–1789* (New York: Macmillan, 1971), 111.

23 See James Jay Carafano, *GI Ingenuity: Improvisation, Technology, and Winning WWII* (Mechanicsburg, PA: Stackpole Books, 2006), xiii, 216; Brian M. Linn, "The American Way of War Revisited," *The Journal of Military History* 66 (2002): 506.

24 Doubler, *Closing With the Enemy*, 282.

25 Department of the Army, *Combat in Fortified Areas and Towns*, Field Manual 31-50, August 1952, pp. 76–77; United State Marine Corps, *Marine Rifle Company/Platoon*, Fleet Marine Force Manual 6-4, 10 August 1965, pp. 273–274.

26 War Department, *Attack on a Fortified Position and Combat in Towns*, Field Manual FM 31-50, January 1944, p. 60; Department of the Army, *Combat in Fortified Areas and Towns*, Field Manual 31-50, August 1952, p. 51. In a section on planning, this manual begins with discussing regiments, and then works own down to smaller units. Marine Corps Schools. *Combat in Towns*, MCS 3-15, December 1949, p. 7.

27 Headquarters, Department of the Army, *Combat in Fortified and Built-Up Areas*, Field Manual 31-50, March 1964, p. 33.

28 The discussion in Chapter 3 about the relative culpability of American and Japanese forces for the large loss of civilian life in Manila will not be repeated here.

29 Ashworth cites a Soviet rule of thumb, learned from World War II, of 10-to-1 needed for urban operations. G. J. Ashworth, *War and the City* (London: Routledge, 1991), 120.

30 For example, Ashworth, *War and the City*, 116–122; Barry R. Posen, "Urban Operations: Tactical Realities and Strategic Ambiguities," in *Soldiers in Cities: Military Operations in Urban Terrain*, ed. Michael C. Desch (Carlisle, PA: Strategic Studies Institute, US Army War College, October 2001), 153–154; S. L. A. Marshall, *Notes on Urban Warfare* (Aberdeen Proving Ground, MD: Army Materiel Systems Analysis Agency, 1973), 40.

31 The utility of urban terrain was an ongoing theme for the Iraqis. An Iraqi intelligence report created before the raid on Khafji described its urban terrain

as a possible safe haven for raids further into Saudi Arabia. Several months before the American-led counterattack, Saddam emphasized the importance of making the Americans fight in urban terrain. But despite those comments Iraqi commanders made few preparations to defend inside Kuwait City. As the Iraqi front was collapsing from the allied ground offensive, Saddam issued orders to one corps commander to withdraw back toward Basra as part of a redistribution of Iraq forces into various Iraqi cities. Kevin M. Woods, *The Mother of All Battles: Saddam Hussein's Strategic Plan for the Gulf War*, Official U.S. Joint Forces Command Report (Annapolis, MD: Naval Institute Press), 16, 23, 27, 137, 227, 237, 285.

32 The initial step back took place in April 2004, and the subsequent successful assault occurred in November of that same year.

33 The preceding urban warfare manual was Field Manual 90-10, issued in 1979.

34 See chapter two. David Kilcullen, *Out of the Mountains: The Coming Age of the Urban Guerrilla* (New York: Oxford University Press, 2013).

35 Project Manager Soldier Weapons, United States Army, "XM25 Individual Semi-Automatic Airburst System," briefing, 26 May 2011, accessed 9 January 2014, http://www.dtic.mil/ndia/2011smallarms/Thursday12439Stucki.pdf C. Todd Lopez, "XM25 Counter Defilade Target Engagement System May Lose 'X' by Next August," 9 August 2013, accessed 19 January 2014, http://www.army.mil/article/109049/

36 See, Thomas C. Hone, Norman Friedman, and Mark D. Mandeles, *American and British Aircraft Carrier Development 1919–1941* (Annapolis, MD: Naval Institute Press, 1999).

Glossary

4.2-inch Mortar: US heavy mortar sometimes referred to as a chemical mortar because of its role in firing smoke-generating rounds.

AK-47: Soviet 7.62mm caliber rifle used by some Communist forces in Vietnam, used a 30-round magazine, fired a larger but slower bullet than the American M-16.

Alligator: US amphibious tractor that combined light armor protection, water crossing capability, and full tracked propulsion, used for both river crossings and assaults on ocean beaches.

Anti-Tank Rifle: Man-portable Soviet 14.5mm weapon from WWII used by North Korean forces during the Korean War, but with little effect against heavier armored vehicles.

Bazooka: US reusable rocket launcher for use by the infantry, came in 2.36-inch and 3.5-inch versions (the latter called the Super Bazooka), used from WWII to Vietnam.

CH-46 Sea Knight: US medium helicopter cargo and troop transport with two rotors used in Vietnam.

Citadel: 19th Century French fort which constituted the bulk of Hue's built-up area north of the Perfume River.

Demilitarized Zone: Zone that separated North and South Vietnam, just north of Hue.

E-8 CS Gas Launcher: Backpack-size launcher containing 64 CS gas grenades.

F4U-4B Corsair: US aircraft used in WWII and the Korean War, capable of flying from aircraft carriers or land bases, armed with four 20mm cannons plus a wide assortment of other ordnance.

HO3S-1: First generation US helicopter used in the Korean War, could only evacuate one casualty at a time, also gave commanders who were not located close to landing strips the ability to quickly visit units across the battlefield.

Intramuros: 16th Century Spanish fort in the heart of Manila.

Luftwaffe: Germany's air force.

Luzon: Largest and northernmost of islands in the Philippines, also the location of the largest city in the Philippines, Manila.

M1 Garand: US semi-automatic .30 caliber rifle, used in WWII and Korea.

M4 Sherman: US tank that served in both WWII and Korea, depending on the model, equipped with a 75mm, 76mm, or 105mm gun.

M10: US tank destroyer that served in the US Army in WWII, armed with a 76mm gun, distinguishing feature from the Sherman was the open-top turret.

M12: US self-propelled 155mm gun.

M-16: US 5.56mm caliber rifle used by US forces in Vietnam, at that time with 20-round magazines.

M26 Pershing: US tank that served during the last few months of WWII and the first year of the Korean War. Armed with a 90mm gun the Pershing was the replacement for the M4 Sherman.

M48A3 Patton: US tank that served in Vietnam, armed with a 90mm gun.

M1917: US heavy .30 caliber water-cooled machine gun.

M1919: US light .30 caliber air-cooled machine gun.

M274 Mechanical Mule: Small US 4-wheel general purpose cargo vehicle.

Ontos: Small US tracked vehicle armed with six 106mm recoilless rifles, lightly armored.

Panzerfaust: German single-shot disposable anti-tank weapon for use by the infantry.

Panzerschreck: German 88mm reusable anti-tank rocket launcher for use by the infantry.

Recoilless Rifles: Used by US forces in both Korea and Vietnam (75mm and 106mm versions) these eliminated the need for heavy recoil mechanisms by allowing the blast from firing the weapon to eject out the back, allowing for a far lighter weapon that could be carried by infantry short distances.

Siegfried Line: Belt of German WWII fortifications extending largely along the German-French border.

SU-76: Soviet self-propelled 76mm gun with light armor. First used in WWII it was also used by North Korean forces during the Korean War.

T34/85: Soviet tank that was first fielded in 1944 during WWII. It served with North Korean forces in the Korean War, armed with an 85mm gun.

UH-1 Huey: Small US troop transport helicopter used in Vietnam.

Viet Cong: Communist guerrillas in Vietnam, distinct from the North Vietnamese Regulars who were often encountered by US forces, particularly in Hue.

Wehrmacht: Germany's main army, a separate organization from the notorious "SS."

Bibliography

National Archives, College Park, Maryland
(Abbreviated "NA" in endnotes)

Some National Archive citations will use x/x/x/x/x/x/x with each x corresponding to (in order): record group, entry, stack area, row, compartment, shelf, and box, followed by folder and page notations as needed, with an x remaining for any missing information.

Overall body of sources drawn from the National Archives was a broad range of unit reports and other sources largely residing in record groups:

- 407 (entries 427 and 429, stack area 270)

- 338 (entry 37042, stack area 290)

- 554 (stack arca 290)

- 242 (stack area 190)

- 498

See footnotes for specific source information.

Military History Institute, Carlisle, Pennsylvania
(Abbreviated "MHI" in endnotes)

The sources below were accessed at the Military History Institute or through its website. (http://www.ahco.army.mil/site/index.jsp).

Collins, General J. Lawton, interviewed by Charles C. Sperow, *Senior Officers Oral History Program*, *Project 72-1*, Volume I.

Denkert, Walter, *3rd Panzer-Grenadier Division in the Battle of Aachen (October 1944)*, Headquarters US Army, Europe, Historical Division—Foreign Military Studies Branch, Box 8, D739 .F6713 no.A-979.

Department of the Army, *Combat in Fortified Areas and Towns*, Field Manual 31-50, August 1952.

Department of the Army, *The Law of Land Warfare*, Field Manual 27-10, July 1956.

Dill, James H., *Personal Adventures—Inchon-Seoul 1950*, unpublished memoir, undated, James H. Dill Papers.

Far East Command, Military Intelligence Section, *Terrain Handbook No. 65—Seoul and Vicinity*, 16 August 1950.

Garay, Stephen L., *The Breach of Intramuros*, Armored School student paper, 1948, U423 .5 R32 1947–1948 G37.

General Board, United States Forces, European Theater, *Organization, Equipment, and Tactical Employment of the Infantry Division*, Study No. 15, undated.

General Board, United States Forces, European Theater, *Strategy of the Campaign in Western Europe 1944–1945*, Study No. 1, undated.

Griswold, Oscar W., *Diary of Lieutenant General Oscar W. Griswold 1943–1945*, Oscar W. Griswold Papers, Box 1.

Headquarters 11th Airborne Division, US Army, *Report After Action with the Enemy, Operational Mike VI Luzon Campaign*, 24 January 1946, S.1., 1946, #05-11-1946/2.

Headquarters X Corps, *Inchon Seoul Invasion—Operations Instructions, No. 1-10*, 14 September to 4 October 1950, DS 919.U535 no. 1–10.

Headquarters X Corps, *Inchon Seoul Invasion—Periodic Operations Reports, No. 1-16*, 19 September to 4 October 1950, DS 919.U53 no. 1–16.

Headquarters, Department of the Army, *Combat in Fortified and Built-Up Areas*, Field Manual 31-50, March 1964.

Headquarters, Department of the Army, *Counterguerrilla Operations*, Field Manual 31-16, March 1967.

Heichler, Lucian, *The Germans Opposite VII Corps in September 1944* (Washington, DC: Office of the Chief of Military History, Department of the Army, 1952) D 756 .H45 1952 c.2.

Henne, Charles A., *Battle History of the 3rd Battalion, 148th Infantry*, vol. 6, "Manila, the Unwanted Battle (4 February through 7 March 1945)," D811H454.

Howenstine, Harold D., ed., *History of the 745th Tank Battalion: August 1942 to June 1945*, 302-745TK 1945.

Hunt, Milton T., *Use of Armor on Luzon*, Armored School paper, 1948, U423.5.R32.1947-1948.H86.

Koechling, Friedrich, *The Battle of the Aachen Sector (September to November 1944)*, Interviews with captured commander of German LXXXI Corps, Foreign Military Studies Collection, D739.F6713, Box 9, Folder A-989.

McElhenny, William S., and others, *Armor on Luzon: Comparison of Employment of Armored Units in the 1941–42 and 1944–45 Luzon Campaigns*, Armored School paper, 1950, D767.4A55.

McEnery, Kevin T., "The XIV Corps Battle for Manila: February 1945" (masters thesis, US Army Command and General Staff College, 1993).

Mortrude, James O., *Korean War Veterans Survey*, October 1990, James O. Mortrude Papers.

Rakestraw, Charles C. *Korean War Veterans Survey*, 2 November 1990, Charles C. Rakestraw Papers.

Regimental Staff 129th Infantry, *The 129th Infantry in World War II*, 1947, 603-129 1947 C.5.

Runey, Michael D., "Chaos, Cohesion, and Leadership: An American Infantry Battalion in Europe, October-December 1944" (masters thesis, Pennsylvania State University, 2001).

Sergeant Kumagai (no identified first name), *Letter to Colonel Ralph Bing*, 12 March 1952, Sergeant Kumagai Papers.

Steckel, Glenn A., *The Role of Field Artillery in the Siege on Intramuros, Manila, P.I.*, Armored School student paper, May 1948, U423.5R32.

US Army Forces Pacific, Headquarters, *Arraignment Proceedings of Tomoyuki Yamashita—United States of America vs. Tomoyuki Yamashita*, 8 October 1945, Russel B. Reynolds Papers, Box 1.

US Army Forces Pacific, Headquarters, *Trial of Tomoyuki Yamashita— Vol. 3, Closing Arguments*, 1 to 5 December 1945, Russel B. Reynolds Papers, Box 1.

US Army Forces Pacific, Headquarters, *Trial of Tomoyuki Yamashita—Vol. 34, Findings*, 7 December 1945, Box 1, Russel B. Reynolds Papers.

US Army Military History Collection, Senior Officers Debriefing Program, *Conversations Between General Paul L. Freeman, USA (Ret.), and Colonel James N. Ellis—US Army War College*, compilation of three interviews, 1973-74.

US Army Military History Institute, *Varlan D. Vancil papers*, Building 950, Bay 5, Row 159, Face G, Shelf 7, Box 8, Folder 26.

US Army, Headquarters Sixth Army, *Japanese Defense of Cities as Exemplified by the Battle for Manila—Report by XIV Corps*, 1 July 1945, D767.4J36.

US Army, Headquarters VII Corps, *VII Corps Operations Memo 100, 28 September 1944*, Foreign Military Studies Collection, The Orlando C. Troxel, Jr. Papers.

US Army, Headquarters VII Corps, *VII Corps Operations Memo 102, 5 October 1944*, Foreign Military Studies Collection, The Orlando C. Troxel, Jr. Papers.

US Army, Headquarters VII Corps, *VII Corps Operations Memo 106, 15 October 1944*, Foreign Military Studies Collection, The Orlando C. Troxel, Jr. Papers.

US Army, Headquarters VII Corps, *VII Corps Operations Memo 107, 18 October 1944*, Foreign Military Studies Collection, The Orlando C. Troxel, Jr. Papers.

US Army, Headquarters XIV Corps, Allied Translator and Interpreter Section (ATIS) Advanced Echelon, *Prisoner of War Preliminary Interrogation Report...*

- 11 February 1945, 26-IR-20, microfiche, D 735 .W3713 1988.
- 14 February 1945, 26-IR-28, microfiche, D 735 .W3713 1988.

- 16 February 1945, 26-IR-30, 26-IR-31, microfiche, D 735 .W3713 1988.

- 5 March 1945, 26-IR-53, microfiche, D 735 .W3713 1988.

- 13 March 1945, 26-IR-60, microfiche, D 735 .W3713 1988.

- 18 March 1945, 26-IR-61, 26-IR-63, microfiche, D 735 .W3713 1988.

- 19 March 1945, 26-IR-64, microfiche, D 735 .W3713 1988.

- 7 April 1945, 26-IR-82, microfiche, D 735 .W3713 1988.

US Army, Headquarters XIV Corps, Allied Translator and Interpreter Section (ATIS) Advanced Echelon, *Wartime Translation of Seized Japanese Document...*

- 1 February 1945, 26-T-36, microfiche, D 735 .W3713 1988.

- 9 February 1945, 26-T-52, microfiche, D 735 .W3713 1988.

- 11 February 1945, 26-T-56, microfiche, D 735 .W3713 1988.

- 13 February 1945, 26-T-60, microfiche, D 735 .W3713 1988.

- 14 February 1945, 26-T-61, microfiche, D 735 .W3713 1988.

- 23 February 1945, 26-T-74, 26-T-75, microfiche, D 735 .W3713 1988.

- 2 March 1945, 26-T-82, microfiche, D 735 .W3713 1988.

- 4 March 1945, 26-T-84, microfiche, D 735 .W3713 1988.

- 10 March 1945, 26-T-93, microfiche, D 735 .W3713 1988.

- 16 March 1945, 26-T-95, microfiche, D 735 .W3713 1988.

- 29 March 1945, 26-T-102, microfiche, D 735 .W3713 1988.

- 25 April 1945, 26-T-116, microfiche, D 735 .W3713 1988.

- 28 April 1945, 26-T-119, microfiche, D 735 .W3713 1988.

US Army, Headquarters XIV Corps, *Report of Investigation of Atrocities— Committed by Japanese Imperial Forces in Intramuros (Walled City) Manila, P.I.—During February 1945*, 6 April 1945, Russel B. Reynolds Papers, Box 1.

US Army, Sixth Army, *G-4 Report Luzon Campaign*, #03-6.1945/6.

US Congress, Senate, Committee on Military Affairs, *Sack of Manila*, 16 July 1945.

War Department, *Armored Force Field Manual: The Armored Battalion, Light and Medium*, Field Manual 17-33, September 1942.

War Department, *Attack on a Fortified Position and Combat in Towns*, Field Manual 31-50, January 1944.

War Department, *Field Artillery Tactical Employment*, Field Manual 6-20, February 1944.

War Department, *Field Service Regulations – Operations*, Field Manual 100-5, May 1941.

War Department, *Field Service Regulations – Operations*, Field Manual 100-5, June 1944.

War Department, *Field Service Regulations United States Army 1923*, 1924.

War Department, *Infantry Battalion*, Field Manual, 7-20,October 1944.

War Department, *List of Publications for Training*, Field Manual 21-6, October 1940.

War Department, *Tank Battalion*, Field Manual 17-33, December 1944.

War Department, *Tentative Field Service Regulations—Operations*, Field Manual 100-5, October 1939.

Gray Research Center, Marine Corps University, Quantico, Virginia (Abbreviated "GRC" in endnotes)

Many of these sources reside in the Archives and Special Collections section of the Gray Research Center.

1st Marine Division, *Administrative Order 7-50*, 25 September 1950, Korean War Project, Box 3, Folder 17.

1st Marine Division, *Operation Plan 3-50*, 16 September 1950, Korean War Project, Box 3, Folder 11.

1st Marine Division, *Operations Order 10-50*, 23 September 1950, Korean War Project, Box 3, Folder 10.

1st Marine Division, *Operations Order 11-50*, 24 September 1950, Korean War Project, Box 3, Folder 10.

1st Marine Division, *Personnel Periodic Report No. 1*, 24 September 1950, Korean War Project, Box 4, Folder 2.

1st Motor Transport Battalion, 1st Marine Division, *Command Chronology for Period 1-29 February 1968*, 9 March 1968.

Budd, Talman C., Office of the Senior Marine Advisor, *Combat Operations After Action Report (RCS MACJ 3-32)*, 25 July 1968.

Christmas, Ron, *Hue City*, undated paper, Vietnam Tet Offensive, Box 24, Folder 5.

Commanding Officer, Marine Fighter Squadron 214, *Close Air Support from CVE in the Korean Theatre*, 10 October 1950, Korean War Project, Box 25, Folder 13.

Fleet Marine Force, Pacific, *Operations of U.S. Marine Forces Vietnam, February 1968*, undated.

General Douglas MacArthur, Commander in Chief Far East, *Outgoing Message for Joint Chiefs of Staff*, C 62423, 8 September 1950, Korean War Project, Box 27, Incoming/Outgoing Messages Folder.

General Headquarters Far East Command, Military Intelligence Section, *Uniform, Insignia, Equipment North Korean Army*, August 1950, Korean War Project, Box 27.

Headquarters 11th Marines, 1st Marine Division, *Report of Use and Effectiveness of 4.5" Rocket Launchers*, 3 November 1950, Korean War Project, Box 5, Folder 10.

Headquarters 1st Battalion, 1st Marines, 1st Marine Division, *Command Chronology for the Period 1 February 1968 to 29 February 1968*, 5 March 1968.

Headquarters 1st Battalion, 5th Marines, 1st Marine Division, *Command Chronology for the Period 1 February 1968 to 29 February 1968*, 1 March 1968.

Headquarters 1st Battalion, 5th Marines, 1st Marine Division, *Command Chronology for the Period 1-31 March 1968*, 1 April 1968.

Headquarters 1st Marine Air Wing, *Summary of Missions Flown by the 1st Marine Air Wing While Operating in Korea*, 12 January 1951, Korean War Project, Box 1, Folder 25.

Headquarters 1st Marine Division, *Compilation of Comments and Recommendations from the Special Action Report, Staff Sections 1st Marine Division Inchon-Seoul Operation*, 5 December 1950, Korean War Project, Box 8a, Folder 2.

Headquarters 1st Marine Division, *Medical Department Log—1st Marine Division*, 14 July to 26 October 1950, Korean War Project, Box 1, Folder 17.

Headquarters 1st Marine Division, *Periodic Intelligence Report (No. 4-15)*, 19–30 September 1950, Korean War Project, Box 3, Folder 13 and 16.

Headquarters 1st Marine Division, *Special Action Report for the Inchon-Seoul Operation: 15 September–7 October 1950: Volumes 1–3*, 2 May 1951, Korean War Project, Box 8, Folders 2-8.

Headquarters 2nd Battalion, 5th Marines, 1st Marine Division, *Command Chronology for the Period 1 February 1968 to 29 February 1968*, 4 March 1968.

Headquarters 2nd Battalion, 5th Marines, 1st Marine Division, *Command Chronology for the Period 1 March 1968 to 31 March 1968*, 4 April 1968.

Headquarters US Marine Corps, *Tactical Lessons of Present Korean Fighting*, 28 July 1950, Korean War Project, Box 1, Folder 19.

Headquarters US Marine Corps, *Tactical Lessons of Present Korean Fighting*, 1 September 1950, Korean War Project, Box 1, Folder 19.

Headquarters US Marine Corps, *Tactical Lessons of Present Korean Fighting*, 18 September 1950, Korean War Project, Box 1, Folder 19.

Headquarters US Marine Corps, *Tactical Lessons of Present Korean Fighting*, 29 September 1950, Korean War Project, Box 1, Folder 19.

Headquarters, 1st Marine Division, *Daily Logistical Reports Nos. 12-14*, 26 to 29 September 1950, Korean War Project, Box 4, Folder 3.

Historical Division, Headquarters, US Marine Corps, *Oral History Transcript: Lieutenant General Edward A. Craig*, 1968.

Historical Division, Headquarters, US Marine Corps, *Oral History Transcript: General Oliver P. Smith*, 1973.

History and Museums Division, Headquarters, US Marine Corps, *Oral History Transcript: Major General Raymond L. Murray*, 1988.

Hopkins, R. Scot, *Interview of Colonel Ron Christmas, USMC, on the Battle of Hue City During Tet Offensive, January-March 1968*, 21 April 1987, Vietnam Tet Offensive, Box 24, Folder 4.

Informal Statement of 1st Lieutenant James McGhee, 15 February 1951, Korean War Project, Box 3, Folder 8.

Informal Statement of 1st Lieutenant Robert E. Jochums, 15 February 1951, Korean War Project, Box 3, Folder 8.

Joint Chiefs of Staff, *Outgoing Message for General MacArthur*, JCS 90958, 9 September 1950, Korean War Project, Box 27, Incoming/Outgoing Messages Folder.

Marine Aircraft Group 36, 1st Marine Aircraft Wing, *Command Chronology for 1 February–29 February 1968*, 18 March 1968.

Marine All Weather Fighter Squadron 235, Marine Aircraft Group 11, 1st Marine Aircraft Wing, *Command Chronology for 1 February–29 February 1968*, 7 March 1968.

Marine Corps Schools, *Combat in Towns*, MCS 3-15, December 1949.

Marine Corps Schools, *The Marine Rifle Squad in Combat*, MCS 3-26, 2nd ed., August 1945.

Marine Heavy Helicopter Squadron 463, Marine Aircraft Group 16, 1st Marine Aircraft Wing, *Command Chronology for February 1968*, 7 March 1968.

Marine Medium Helicopter Squadron 164, Marine Aircraft Group 36, 1st Marine Aircraft Wing, *Command Chronology for 1 February Through 3 March 1968*, 7 March 1968.

Marine Medium Helicopter Squadron 165, Marine Aircraft Group 15, 9th Marine Amphibious Brigade, *Command Chronology for 1 February Through 3 March 1968*, 6 March 1968.

Marine Medium Helicopter Squadron 364, Marine Aircraft Group 36, 1st Marine Aircraft Wing, *Command Chronology for 1 February Through 29 February 1968*, 5 March 1968.

Marine Medium Helicopter Squadron 364, Marine Aircraft Group 36, 1st Marine Aircraft Wing, *Command Chronology for 1 March Through 31 March 1968*, 5 March 1968.

Marine Observation Squadron-3, Marine Aircraft Group 36, 1st Marine Aircraft Wing, *Command Chronology for the Month of February 1968*, 3 March 1968.

Pham Van Son, Chief, Military History Division, Joint General Staff, Republic of Vietnam Armed Forces, *The Viet Cong Tet Offensive (1968)*, translated from the original Vietnamese by the Joint General Staff Translation Board, undated, Vietnam Tet Offensive, Box 24, Folder 3.

Robertson, D. J., *1st Marine Division Commanders After Action Report, Tet Offensive, 29 January–14 February 1968*, 25 May 1968, Vietnam Tet Offensive, Box 24, Folder 2.

Smith, Ray, *Letter to Captain Batcheller Regarding Hue City Fighting*, 25 March 1968, Vietnam Tet Offensive, Box 24, Folder 1.

Surgeon Generals' Office, Department of the Army, *Wound Ballistics Survey Korea: 15 November 1950–5 May 1951*(Washington, DC: undated).

United State Marine Corps, *Air Support*, Fleet Marine Force Manual 7-3, 10 February 1966.

United State Marine Corps, *Counterinsurgency Operations*, Fleet Marine Force Manual 8-2, 22 December 1967.

United State Marine Corps, *Employment of Chemical Agents*, Fleet Marine Force Manual 11-3, 1966.

United State Marine Corps, *Field Artillery Support*, Fleet Marine Force Manual 7-4, 6 March 1964.

United State Marine Corps, *Fire Support Coordination*, Fleet Marine Force Manual 7-1, 11 August 1967.

United State Marine Corps, *Helicopterborne Operations*, Fleet Marine Force Manual 3-3, 12 June 1963.

United State Marine Corps, *Marine Division*, Fleet Marine Force Manual 6-1, 28 March 1964.

United State Marine Corps, *Marine Engineer Operations*, Fleet Marine Force Manual 4-4, 7 May 1963.

United State Marine Corps, *Marine Infantry Battalion*, Fleet Marine Force Manual 6-3, 16 April 1964.

United State Marine Corps, *Marine Infantry Regiment*, Fleet Marine Force Manual 6-2, 6 April 1966.

United State Marine Corps, *Marine Rifle Company/Platoon*, Fleet Marine Force Manual 6-4, 10 August 1965.

United State Marine Corps, *Marine Rifle Squad*, Fleet Marine Force Manual 6-5, 6 April 1966.

United State Marine Corps, *Tank Employment*, Fleet Marine Force Manual 9-1, 15 April 1965.

Combined Arms Research Library, Command and General Staff College, Fort Leavenworth, Kansas (Abbreviated "CARL" in endnotes)
These sources were accessed through the library's website. (http://www.cgsc.edu/carl/).

Allied Force Headquarters, *Lessons from the Sicilian Campaign*, Training Memorandum No. 50, 20 November 1943.

Berlin, Robert H., *U.S. Army World War II Corps Commanders: A Composite Biography* (Fort Leavenworth, KS: US Army Command and General Staff College, 1989).

Buck, Buddy, *Battle of Manila*, Combat Studies Institute Battlebook 13-B (Fort Leavenworth, KS: Combat Studies Institute, US Army Command and General Staff College, 1984).

Combat Studies Institute, *Sixty Years of Reorganizing for Combat: A Historical Trend Analysis*, CSI Report No. 14 (Fort Leavenworth, KS: US Army Command and General Staff College, 1999).

Cooling, Norman Lee, "Shaping the Battlespace to Win the Street Fight" (masters degree thesis, Marine Corps University, 2000).

Daniel, D. M., *The Capture of Aachen (personal experience of a battalion commander)*, School of Combined Arms, Regular Course, 1946–1947 (Fort Leavenworth, KS: Command and Staff College).

Doughty, Robert A., *The Evolution o f U.S. Army Tactical Doctrine, 1946–76*, study No. 1 of the Leavenworth papers (Fort Leavenworth, KS: Combat Studies Institute, US Army Command and General Staff College, 1976).

General Board, United States Forces, European Theater, *Organization, Equipment, and Tactical Employment of Separate Tank Battalions*, Study No. 50, undated.

General Board, United States Forces, European Theater, *Study of Organization, Equipment, and Tactical Employment of Tank Destroyer Units*, Study No. 60, undated.

The Infantry School, US Army, *Infantry in Battle*, 2nd ed. (Richmond, VA: Garrett and Massie, 1939).

James, William T. Jr., "From Siege to Surgical: The Evolution of Urban Combat Doctrine from World War II to the Present and its Effect on Current Doctrine" (master's thesis, US Army Command and General Staff College, 1998).

Marshall, S. L. A., *Notes on Urban Warfare* (Aberdeen Proving Ground, MD: Army Materiel Systems Analysis Agency, 1973).

Operations Division, US War Department, *Combat Lessons No. 2*, 1942.

Operations Division, US War Department, *Combat Lessons No. 4*, 1944.

Operations Division, US War Department, *Combat Lessons No. 6*, 1945.

Center for Military History, Fort Mcnair, Washington, District of Columbia (Abbreviated "CMH" in endnotes)

The sources below were accessed at the Center for Military History or through its website. (http://www.history.army.mil/).

Center for Military History, US Army, *Rhineland: The U.S. Army Campaigns of World War II*, CMH publication 72-25.

Center for Military History, US Army, *World War II Divisional Combat Chronicles*.

Daniel, Derrill, *The Capture of Aachen*. Lecture given in 1950 at Quantico, 9 January 1950, Folder 228.01, HRC Geog. M Germany, 370.2—Aachen.

Dawley, Jay P., *The Capture of Aachen, German—October, 1944: Actions by the 238th Engineer Combat Battalion*, HRC 2, 254 Holocaust, Aachen.

Hoffman, Jon T., ed, *A History of Innovation: U.S. Army Adaptation in War and Peace* (Washington, DC: Center for Military History, United States Army, 2009).

US Army, Headquarters 1st Infantry Division, *Commanding Officer Battle Group Aachen*, Annex No. 4 to G-2 Periodic Report No. 125, 22 October 1944, 228.01, HRC Geog. M Germany, 370.2—Aachen.

US Army, Headquarters 1st Infantry Division, *Germans Compare Russian and US Army*, Annex No. 2 to G-2 Periodic Report No. 124, 21 October 1944, 228.01, HRC Geog. M Germany, 370.2—Aachen.

US Army, Headquarters 1st Infantry Division, *The Battle of Aachen*, Annex No. 2 to G-2 Periodic Report No. 141, 7 November 1944, 228.01, HRC Geog. M Germany, 370.2—Aachen.

Villard, Erik, *The 1968 Tet Offensive Battles of Quang Tri City and Hue* (Washington, DC: Center for Military History, 2008).

Donovan Research Library, Fort Benning, Georgia
(Abbreviated "DRL" in endnotes)
The sources below were accessed through the Donovan Library's website. (http://www.benning.army.mil/library/)

Beachler, William C., *The Operations of Company C, 63rd Infantry (6th Infantry Division) In the Attack on the Shimbu Line (Mount Mataba) East of Manila, Luzon, Philippine Islands 10–17 April 1945 (Luzon Campaign), Personal experience of a Rifle Company Commander*, monograph written for the 1949–1950 Advanced Infantry Officers Course, The Infantry School, Fort Benning, Georgia.

Brown, Bobbie E., *The Operations of Company C, 18th Infantry (1st Infantry Division) in the Attack on Crucifix Hill, 8 October 1944 (Rhineland Campaign)(Aachen Offensive)(Personal Experience of a Company Commander)*, monograph written for the 1946–1947 Advanced Infantry Course, The Infantry School, Fort Benning, Georgia.

Kidd, Giles H., *The Operations of the 37th Infantry Division in the Crossing of the Pasig River and Closing to the Walls of Intramuros, Manila 7–9 February 1945 (Luzon Campaign)*, 1950, paper written for the Advanced Infantry Course, 1949–1950, The Infantry School, Fort Benning, Georgia.

Levasseur, Armand R., *The Operations of the 1st Battalion, 26th Infantry (1st Infantry Division) During the Initial Penetration of the Siegfried Line in the Vicinity of Nutheim, Germany, 13–20 September 1944 (Rhineland Campaign)(Aachen Offensive)(Personal Experience of a Battalion Operations Officer)*, monograph written for the 1947–1948 Advanced Infantry Course, The Infantry School, Fort Benning, Georgia.

Parrish, Monte M., *The Battle of Aachen: An Analysis of City Fighting Tactics*, research paper written for the Infantry Officer Advanced Course 4-72, 30 June 1972, US Army Infantry School, Fort Benning, Georgia.

Stickels, Elbert E., *The Operations of Company K, 18th Infantry Regiment (1st Infantry Division) In the Defense of the Ravelsberg, At Haaren, Northeast of Aachen, Germany, 15–19 October 1944*, monograph written for Advanced Infantry Officer's Course 1949–1950, The Infantry School, Fort Benning, Georgia.

Virtual Vietnam Archive, Texas Tech University (Abbreviated "VVA" in endnotes)

These sources were accessed through the Archive's website: http://www.vietnam.ttu.edu/virtualarchive/

Australian Army Training Team in Vietnam, "Victory at Hue," *Army Journal*, 1 February 1969, Item Number: 2131109002, Douglas Pike Collection, 3-20.

Bunker, Ellsworth, *For the President from Bunker: Herewith My Forty-First Weekly Message*, 29 February 1968, Item Number: 0241013003, Larry Berman Collection.

Commander US Naval Forces, Vietnam, *U.S. Naval Forces, Vietnam Monthly Historical Summary, February 1968*, 5 March 1968, Item Number: 13120202001, United States Naval Forces, Vietnam Monthly historical summaries, 1966–1972, 1973 Collection.

Commander US Naval Forces, Vietnam, *U.S. Naval Forces, Vietnam Monthly Historical Supplement, February 1968*, 29 June 1968, Item Number: 13120202001, United States Naval Forces, Vietnam Monthly historical summaries, 1966–1972, 1973 Collection.

Fifth Columnist Activities in Thua Thien Prov, Tri-Thien-Hue MR, 30 September 1970, Item Number: 2311312013, Douglas Pike Collection.

Headquarters, 1st Tank Battalion, 1st Marine Division, *Command Chronology, 1 February 1968 to 29 February 1968*, undated, Item Number: 1201012113, US Marine Corps History Division, Vietnam War Documents Collection.

Headquarters, US Military Assistance Command Vietnam, *Monthly Summary: February 1968*, 29 April 1968, Item Numbers: 7390103001a and 7390103001b, John M. Shaw Collection.

Hue City Yearend (1968) Assessment Report, 7 February 1969, Item Number: 2131107005, Douglas Pike Collection.

J2, Joint General Staff, Army of the Republic of Vietnam, *VC/NVA Offensive Techniques in Cities and Towns*, 29 August 1968, Item Number: 2131007010a, Douglas Pike Collection.

Le Van Hao, Chairman, Alliance of National, Democratic, and Peaceful Forces in Hue, *The Alliance Addresses Appeal to World Leaders*, 23 February 1968, Item Number: 2311009016, Douglas Pike Collection.

NLF Policies in Urban Areas, 10 February 1968, Item Number: 2121007011, Douglas Pike Collection.

PLAF Directive on Tet 68 Offensive in Hue Area, Item Number: 2131101005, Douglas Pike Collection.

Recapitulative Report: Phase of Attack on Hue from 31 Jan to 25 Feb 1968, 30 March 1968, Item Number: 2131101002, Douglas Pike Collection.

Scenes of the General Offensive and Uprising, Foreign Languages Publishing House, Hanoi, 1968, Item Number: 2131012040, Douglas Pike Collection.

Wheeler, Earle, Chairman Joint Chiefs of Staff, *Memorandum for the President: Military Situation and Requirements in South Vietnam*, 27 February 1968, Item Number: 0241011010, Larry Berman Collection.

Wheeler, Earle, Chairman Joint Chiefs of Staff, *Memorandum for the President: Situation in Vietnam*, 11 February 1968, Item Number: 0010244008, Veteran Members of the 109th Quartermaster Company Collection.

Wheeler, Earle, Chairman Joint Chiefs of Staff, *Memorandum for the President: Telephone Conversation with General Westmoreland*, 16 February 1968, Item Number: 0010245001, Veteran Members of the 109th Quartermaster Company Collection.

Other Internet Sources

"Burning City," *Time*, 19 February 1945 <http://www.time.com/time/magazine/article/0,9171,778352,00.html> [accessed 18 November 2007].

26th Infantry Regiment Association, *Account of the Battle of Aachen*, (undated) <www.bluespader.org/uploads/aachen/02Contents.html> [accessed 17 December 2005].

Connolly, James, "Street Fighting—Summary." *Worker's Republic*, 24 July 1915 <http://www.marxists.org/archive/connolly/1915/rw/stfight. htm> [accessed 10 January 2010].

Department of the Army, *An Infantryman's Guide to Combat in Built-Up Areas*, Field Manual 90-10-1 (1993) <http://www.globalsecurity.org/ military/library/policy/army/fm/90-10-1/index.html> [accessed 1 July 2010].

Four Wheel Drive Online website <http://www.4wdonline.com/Mil/ M422/MightyMite.html> [accessed 15 November 2008].

Gabel, Christopher R., Military *Operations on Urbanized Terrain: The 2nd Battalion, 26th Infantry, at Aachen, October 1944*, (undated) <http:// www.globalsecurity.org/military/library/report/1999/99-16/chap1. htm> [accessed 4 December 2009].

Gary's US Infantry Weapons Reference Guide <http://www.inetres.com/ gp/military/infantry/index.html#rifle> [accessed 28 June 2009].

Gorman, Paul F., *Aachen 1944: Implications for Command Post of the Future*, (study conducted by the Institute for Defense Analyses, 2000) <http:// cpof.ida.org/MOUT-Aachen-1944.pdf> [accessed 3 December 2005].

James Boyd Coates, Jr., ed., *Wound Ballistics* (Washington, DC: Officer of the Surgeon General—US Army, 1962) <http://history.amedd.army. mil/booksdocs/wwii/woundblstcs/default.htm> [accessed 22 January 2007].

Leitch, R. A., H. R. Champion, and J. F. Navein, *Analysis of Casualty Rates and Patterns Likely to Result from Military Operations in Urban Environments* <http://www.smallwarsjournal.com/documents/urban-casstudy.pdf> [accessed 6 February 2006].

Lone Sentry Website, *Index of Intelligence Bulletin Series* <http://www. lonesentry.com/intelbulletin/index.html> [accessed 30 January 2010].

Lopez, C. Todd. "XM25 Counter Defilade Target Engagement System May Lose 'X' by Next August." 9 August 2013. <http://www.army.mil/ article/109049/> [accessed 19 January 2014].

M12 155mm U.S.A.'s Motor Gun Carriage,(undated) <http://www.wwiive-hicles.com/usa/self_propelled_guns/m12_gun_motor_carriage.html> [accessed 14 January 2007].

Military Intelligence Division, War Department, *Tactical and Technical Trends No. 26* (Washington, DC: 3 June 1943) <http://www.lonesentry.com/intelbulletin/tt_trends.html> [accessed 30 January 2010].

Military Intelligence Division, War Department, *Tactical and Technical Trends No. 36* (Washington, DC: 21 October 1943) <http://www.lonesentry.com/intelbulletin/tt_trends.html> [accessed 30 January 2010].

Military Intelligence Service, War Department, "City and Town Defense," *Intelligence Bulletin* 3, no.12 (Washington, DC: August 1945) <http://www.lonesentry.com/intelbulletin/index.html> [accessed 30 January 2010].

Military Intelligence Service, War Department, "German Combat Tactics in Towns and Cities," *Intelligence Bulletin* 2, no. 5 (Washington, DC: January 1944) <http://www.lonesentry.com/intelbulletin/index.html> [accessed 30 January 2010].

Military Intelligence Service, War Department, "How the Enemy Defended the Town of Ortona," *Intelligence Bulletin* 2, no. 11 (Washington, DC: July 1944) <http://www.lonesentry.com/intelbulletin/index.html> [accessed 30 January 2010].

Military Intelligence Service, War Department, "Jap Defense of a Town: Tanks Join the Banzai Charge," *Intelligence Bulletin* 3, no. 10 (Washington, DC: June 1945) <http://www.lonesentry.com/intelbulletin/index.html> [accessed 30 January 2010].

Military Intelligence Service, War Department, "Soviet Tanks in City Fighting," *Intelligence Bulletin* 4, no. 10 (Washington, DC: June 1946) <http://www.lonesentry.com/intelbulletin/index.html> [accessed 30 January 2010].

Military Intelligence Service, War Department, "Street Fighting by Panzer Grenadiers," *Intelligence Bulletin* 2, no. 2 (Washington, DC: October 1943) <http://www.lonesentry.com/intelbulletin/index.html> [accessed 30 January 2010].

Military Intelligence Service, War Department, "The British Discuss Combat in Towns," *Intelligence Bulletin* 2, no. 12 (Washington, DC: August 1944) <http://www.lonesentry.com/intelbulletin/index.html> [accessed 30 January 2010].

Military Intelligence Service, War Department, "TNT: A Preliminary Report on Jap Demolitions in Manila," *Intelligence Bulletin* 3, no. 9 (Washington, DC: May 1945) <http://www.lonesentry.com/intelbulletin/index.html> [accessed 30 January 2010].

Military Intelligence Service, War Department, "What the Germans Learned at Warsaw," *Intelligence Bulletin* 3, no. 8 (Washington, DC: April 1945) <http://www.lonesentry.com/intelbulletin/index.html> [accessed 30 January 2010].

Project Manager Soldier Weapons, United States Army. "XM25 Individual Semi-Automatic Airburst System." Briefing. 26 May 2011. <http://www.dtic.mil/ndia/2011smallarms/Thursday12439Stucki.pdf> [accessed 9 January 2014].

Stromer, John D., and Paul W. Lunnie, compilers, *Journal for the 3rd Battalion, 26th Infantry, 1st Infantry Division*, July to September 1944, <http://www.historicaltextarchive.com/books.php?op=viewbook&bookid=22&cid=8> [accessed 4 December 2005].

Stromer, John D., and Paul W. Lunnie, compilers, *Journal for the 3rd Battalion, 26th Infantry, 1st Infantry Division*, October to December 1944 <http://www.historicaltextarchive.com/books.php?op=viewbook&bookid=22&cid=9> [accessed 4 December 2005].

United Nations, Population Division, *The World At Six Billion*, (undated) <http://www.un.org/esa/population/publications/sixbillion/sixbilpart1.pdf> [accessed 8 May 2010].

United Nations, Population Division, *World Urbanization Prospects: The 2007 Revision*, (2007) <http://www.un.org/esa/population/publications/wup2007/2007wup.htm> [accessed 8 May 2010].

US Army Transportation Command Museum website <http://www.transchool.eustis.army.mil/museum> [accessed 15 November 2008].

Wilson, David S., "Evolution of Artillery Tactics in General J. Lawton Collins' U.S. VII Corps in WWII" (masters thesis, Command and General Staff College, US Army, Fort Leavenworth, KS. 1996) <http://stinet.dtic.mil/cgi-bin/GetTRDoc?AD=ADA312682&Location=U2&doc=GetTRDoc.pdf> [accessed 14 January 2007].

Van Horne, Richard W., "History of the 991st Field Artillery Battalion." 1955, <http://www.3ad.com/history/wwll/feature.pages/991st.pages/991st.history.htm> [accessed 30 July 2011].

McCormick Research Center, First Division Museum, Wheaton, Illinois

1st Infantry Division, *WWII Outstanding Combat Achievements by All Rifle Companies Report: 16 Inf – 18 Inf – 26 Inf,* undated.

Databases

US Joint Chiefs of Staff, *Combat Air Activities Files (CACTA),* created October 1965–December 1970, original data from the Electronic and Special Media Records Services Division, National Archives and Records Administration, College Park, MD, Record Group 218, Records of the US Joint Chiefs of Staff. Data was processed by US Air Force personnel into a more user friendly format, with access granted to this author by Lieutenant Colonel Jenns Robertson and Mr. Ryan Burr in March 2009.

Books and Reports

Alexander, Joseph H. *Battle of the Barricades: U.S. Marines in the Recapture of Seoul.* Washington, DC: US Marine Corps Historical Center, 2000.

Antal, John, and Bradley Gericke, eds. *City Fights: Selected Histories of Urban Combat from World War II to Vietnam.* New York: Ballantine, 2003.

———. *Forests of Steel: Modern City Combat from the War in Vietnam to the Battle for Iraq.* NP: Historical Explorations, 2007.

Appleman, Roy E. *United States Army in the Korean War: South to the Naktong, North to the Yalu (June–November 1950).* Washington, DC: Center of Military History, 1961.

Arnold, James R. *Tet Offensive 1968*. Oxford: Osprey, 1990.

Ashworth, G. J. *War and the City*. London: Routledge, 1991.

Astor, Gerald. *The Bloody Forest: Battle for the Huertgen: September 1944–January 1945*. Novato, CA: Presidio, 2000.

Badsey, Stephen. *The Franco-Prussian War 1870–1871*. Oxford: Osprey, 2003.

Berlin, Robert H. *U.S. Army World War II Corps Commanders: A Composite Biography*. Leavenworth, KS: US Army Combat Studies Institute, 1989.

Bishop, Chris, ed. *The Encyclopedia of Weapons of World War Two*. New York: Metro Books, 1998.

Blair, Clay. *The Forgotten War: America in Korea 1950–1953*. Annapolis, MD: US Naval Institute Press, 1987.

Blood, Christopher G., and Marlisa E. Anderson. *The Battle for Hue: Casualty and Disease Rates During Urban Warfare*, Report No. 93-16. San Diego, CA: Naval Health Research Center, 1993.

Boose, Donald W., Jr. *U.S. Army Forces in the Korean War 1950–53*. Oxford: Osprey, 2005.

Brodie, Bernard, and Fawn M. Brodie. *From Crossbow to H-Bomb*. rev. and enlarged ed. Bloomington: Indiana University Press, 1973.

Brose, Eric Dorn. *The Kaiser's Army: The Politics of Military Technology in Germany During the Machine Age, 1870–1919*. Oxford: Oxford University Press, 2001.

Brunn, Stanley D., Jack F. Williams, and Donald J. Zeigler, eds. *Cities of the World: World Regional Urban Development*. 3rd ed. Lanham, MD: Rowman and Littlefield Publishing Group, 2003.

Buchner, Alex. *The German Infantry Handbook 1939–1945*. Atglen, PA: Schiffer Military History, 1991.

Bull, Stephen. *World War II Infantry Tactics: Company and Battalion*. Oxford: Osprey Publishing, 2005.

———. *World War II Infantry Tactics: Squad and Platoon*. Oxford: Osprey Publishing, 2004.

———. *World War II Street-Fighting Tactics.* Oxford: Osprey, 2008.

Bunker, Robert J., ed. *Nonlethal Weapons: Terms and References.* Occasional Paper 15. Colorado Springs, CO: United States Air Force Institute for National Security Studies, US Air Force Academy, 1997.

Cantigny First Division Foundation. *Blue Spaders: The 26th Infantry Regiment, 1917–1967.* Steven Weingartner, ed. Wheaton, IL: Cantigny First Division Foundation, 1996.

Carafano, James Jay. *GI Ingenuity: Improvisation, Technology, and Winning WWII* Mechanicsburg, PA: Stackpole Books, 2006.

Chamberlain, Peter, and Hilary Doyle. *Encyclopedia of German Tanks of World War Two* London: Arms and Armour, 1999.

Chang, Iris. *The Rape of Nanking.* New York: Basic Books, 1997.

Cline, Ray S. *Washington Command Post: The Operations Division.* Washington, DC: Government Printing Office, 1990.

Close, Jacob. *Memoirs of a Groundpounder.* Sylvania, OH: by author, 1999.

Cohen, Eliot A., and John Gooch. *Military Misfortunes: The Anatomy of Failure in War.* New York: Free Press, 2006.

Conboy, Ken, and Ken Bowra. *The NVA and Viet Cong.* Oxford: Osprey, 1991.

Connaughton, Richard, John Pimlott, and Duncan Anderson. *The Battle for Manila.* Novato, CA: Presidio Press, 1995.

Cooper, Belton Y. *Death Traps: The Survival of an American Armored Division in World War II.* Novato, CA: Presidio, 1998.

Desch, Michael C., ed. *Soldiers in Cities: Military Operations in Urban Terrain.* Carlisle, PA: Strategic Studies Institute, US Army War College, October 2001.

Dewar, Michael. *War in the Streets: The Story of Urban Combat from Calais to Khafji.* Devon, UK: David & Charles, 1992.

Director of Central Intelligence. "Capabilities of the Vietnamese Communists for Fighting in South Vietnam." Special National Intelligence Estimate, Number 14.3-67, 13 November 1967, in *Estimate Products on Vietnam 1948–1975*. Pittsburgh, PA: National Intelligence Council, 2005.

Doubler, Michael D. *Closing With the Enemy: How GIs Fought the War in Europe, 1944–1945*. Lawrence: University of Kansas Press, 1994.

Doughty, Robert A. *The Evolution of US Army Tactical Doctrine, 1946–76*. Fort Leavenworth, KS: US Army Command and General Staff College, 1979.

Eckhardt, George S. *Vietnam Studies: Command and Control, 1950–1969*. Washington, DC: Department of the Army, 1991.

English, John A., and Bruce I. Gudmundsson. *On Infantry*. rev. ed. Westport, CT: Praeger, 1994.

Fleischer, Wolfgang. *Russian Tanks and Armored Vehicles 1917–1945*. Atglen, PA: Schiffer, 1999.

Forty, George. *Japanese Army Handbook: 1939–1945*. Stroud, UK: Sutton, 2002.

———. *US Army Handbook 1939–1945*. New York: Barnes and Noble, 1995.

Foss, Christopher F., ed. *Jane's Armour and Artillery 1979–1980*. New York: Jane's, 1979.

———. *Jane's Main Battle Tanks*. London: Jane's, 1986.

Frankel, Stanley A., and Frederick Kirker, eds. *The 37th Infantry Division in World War II*. Washington, DC: Infantry Journal Press, 1948.

Gabel, Christopher R. *Seek, Strike, and Destroy: U.S. Army Tank Destroyer Doctrine in World War II*. Fort Leavenworth, KS: Combat Studies Institute, 1985.

———. *The U.S. Army GHQ Maneuvers of 1941*. Washington, DC: Center of Military History, US Army, 1991.

Gawne, Jonathan. *1944 Americans in Brittany: The Battle for Brest*. Paris: Histoire & Collections, 2002.

Gilbert, Ed. *US Marine Corps Tank Crewman 1965–70*. Oxford: Osprey, 2004.

Gilbert, Oscar E. *Marine Corps Tank Battles in Vietnam*. Drexel Hill, PA: Casemate, 2007.

Glenn, Russell W., et al. *Ready for Armageddon*. Santa Monica, CA: Rand, 2002.

Gott, Kendall D. *Breaking the Mold: Tanks in the Cities*. Fort Leavenworth, KS: Combat Studies Institute Press, 2006.

Hammel, Eric. *Fire in the Streets: The Battle for Hue, Tet 1968*. New York: Dell, 1991.

———. *Marines in Hue City: A Portrait of Urban Combat, Tet 1968*. St. Paul, MN: Zenith Press, 2007.

Hastings, Max. *Armageddon: The Battle for Germany, 1944–1945*. New York: Knopf, 2004.

Hay, John H., Jr. *Vietnam Studies: Tactical and Materiel Innovations*. Washington, DC: Department of the Army, 1989.

Heinl, Robert Debs, Jr. *Victory at High Tide: The Inchon-Seoul Campaign*. Baltimore, MD: Nautical & Aviation Publishing Company of America, 1979.

Henke, Klaus-Dietmar. *Die amerikanische Besetzung Deutschlands*. Munich, Germany: Oldenbourg, 1996.

Herr, Michael. *Dispatches*. New York: Vintage International, 1991.

Higgenbotham, Don. *The War of American Independence: Military Attitudes, Policies, and Practices, 1763–1789*. New York: Macmillan, 1971.

Higgins, Marguerite. *War in Korea: The Report of a Woman Combat Correspondent*. Garden City, NY: Doubleday, 1951.

Hogg, Ian V. *The American Arsenal: The World War II Official Standard Ordnance Catalog of Small Arms, Tanks, Armored Cars, Artillery, Antiaircraft Guns, Ammunition, Grenades, Mines, etcetera*. London: Greenhill, 2001.

———, ed. *Jane's Infantry Weapons 1984–85*. London: Jane's, 1984.

———. *Mortars*. Ramsbury: Crowood Press, 2001.

Hone, Thomas C., Norman Friedman, and Mark D. Mandeles. *American and British Aircraft Carrier Development 1919–1941*. Annapolis, MD: Naval Institute Press, 1999.

Johansen, Anja. *Soldiers as Police: The French and Prussian Armies and the Policing of Popular Protest, 1889–1914*. Aldershot, UK: Ashgate Pub. Ltd., 2005.

Johnson, David E. *Fast Tanks and Heavy Bombers: Innovation in the U.S. Army, 1917–1945* Ithaca, NY: Cornell University Press, 1998.

Kilcullen, David. *Out of the Mountains: The Coming Age of the Urban Guerrilla*. New York: Oxford University Press, 2013.

Kitchen, Martin. *A Military History of Germany*. Bloomington: Indiana University Press, 1975.

Knickerbocker, H. R. *Danger Forward: The Story of the First Infantry Division in World War II*. Nashville, TN: The Battery Press, 1947.

Korea Institute of Military History. *The Korean War, Volume One*. 3 vols. Lincoln: University of Nebraska Press, 2000.

Krueger, Walter. *From Down Under to Nippon: The Story of Sixth Army in World War II*. Washington, DC: Combat Forces Press, 1953.

Lathrop, Richard, and John McDonald. *M60 Main Battle Tank 1960–91*. Oxford: Osprey, 2003.

Lucas, James. *German Army Handbook 1939–1945*. Gloucestershire, UK: Sutton Publishing, 2002.

MacDonald, Charles B. *United States Army in World War II: The European Theater of Operations: The Siegfried Line Campaign*. Washington, DC: Department of the Army, Office of the Chief of Military History, 1963.

Mahnken, Thomas G. *Technology and the American Way of War*. New York: Columbia University Press, 2008.

Manchester, William. *American Caesar: Douglas MacArthur 1880–1964*. Boston, MA: Little and Brown, 1978.

Marshall, Malcolm. *Proud Americans: Men of the 32nd Field Artillery Battalion in Action, World War II, as Part of the 18th Regimental Combat Team, 1st U.S. Infantry Division*. New London, NH: by author, 1994.

Mayo, Lida. *The Ordnance Department: On the Beachhead and Battlefront.* Washington, DC: Center of Military History, US Army, 1991.

McGovern, Terrance C., and Mark A. Berhow. *American Defenses of Corregidor and Manila Bay 1898–1945.* Oxford: Osprey, 2003.

Melson, Charles. *US Marine Rifleman in Vietnam 1965–73.* Oxford: Osprey, 1998.

Mesko, Jim. *Armour in Korea: A Pictorial History.* Carrollton, TX: Squadron/Signal, 1984.

———. *M48 Patton in Action.* Carrollton, TX: Squadron/Signal, 1984.

Montross, Lynn and Nicholas A. Canzona. *U.S. Marine Corps Operations in Korea 1950–1953, Volume II: The Inchon-Seoul Operation.* Washington, DC: Historical Branch, Headquarters US Marine Corps, 1955.

Murray, Williamson. *War and Urban Terrain in the Twenty-First Century.* Alexandria, VA: Institute for Defense Analyses, 2000.

Nolan, Keith William. *Battle for Hue: Tet 1968.* New York: Dell, 1983.

O'Sullivan, Patrick, and Jesse W. Miller. *The Geography of Warfare.* New York: St. Martin's Press, 1983.

Oberdorfer, Don. *Tet: The Turning Point of the Vietnam War.* Baltimore, MD: Johns Hopkins University Press, 2001.

Odom, William O. *After the Trenches: The Transformation of U.S. Army Doctrine, 1918–1939.* College Station: Texas A&M University Press, 1999.

Ott, David Ewing. *Vietnam Studies: Field Artillery, 1954–1973.* Washington, DC: Department of the Army, 1975.

Palmer, Robert R., Bell I. Wiley, and William R. Keast. *The Procurement and Training of Ground Combat Troops.* Washington, DC: Center for Military History, U S Army, 2003.

Patton, George S. *War as I Knew It.* New York: Houghton Mifflin Company, 1947.

Payne, W. Scott, and Jean G. Taylor. *Fighting in Cities.* Arlington, VA: Institute for Defense Analyses, 1970.

Pearson, Willard. *Vietnam Studies: The War in the Northern Provinces.* Washington, DC: Department of the Army, 1975.

Price, Robert E. III. *The Battle of Aachen.* Combat Studies Institute Battlebook 13-C. Fort Leavenworth, KS: Combat Studies Institute, US Army Command and General Staff College, 1984.

Rienzi, Thomas Matthew. *Vietnam Studies: Communications-Electronics, 1962–1970.* Washington, DC: Department of the Army, 1972.

Riley, John W., Jr., and Wilbur Schramm. *The Reds Take a City: The Communist Occupation of Seoul.* Westport, CT: Greenwood Press, 1973.

Robertson, William G., and Lawrence A. Yates, eds. *Block by Block: The Challenges of Urban Operations.* Fort Leavenworth, KS: US Army Command and General Staff College Press, 2003.

Rottman, Gordon L. *Inchon 1950: The Last Great Amphibious Assault.* Oxford: Osprey, 2006.

———. *Japanese Army in World War II: Conquest of the Pacific.* Oxford: Osprey, 2005.

———. *The Rocket Propelled Grenade.* Oxford: Osprey, 2010.

———. *World War II Infantry Anti-Tank Tactics.* Oxford: Osprey, 2010.

Short, Neil. *Germany's West Wall: The Siegfried Line.* Oxford: Osprey Publishing, 2004.

Shulimson, Jack, et al., *U.S. Marines in Vietnam: The Defining Year, 1968.* Washington, DC: Headquarters United States Marine Corps, 1997.

Shulman, Milton. *Defeat in the West.* London: Cassell, 2003.

Smith, R. Elberton. *The Army and Economic Mobilization.* Washington, DC: Department of the Army, 1959.

Smith, Robert Ross. *Triumph in the Philippines: The War in the Pacific.* Honolulu, HI: University Press of the Pacific, 2005.

Stanton, Shelby L. *Vietnam Order of Battle.* Mechanicsburg, PA: Stackpole, 2003.

Starry, Donn A. *Vietnam Studies: Mounted Combat in Vietnam.* Washington, DC: Department of the Army, 1989.

United Nations, Department of Economic and Social Affairs, Population Division. *World Urbanization Prospects: The 2005 Revision.* Working Paper No. ESA/P/WP/200.

Van Creveld, Martin. *Fighting Power: German and U.S. Army Performance, 1939–1945.* Westport, CT: Greenwood Press, 1982.

———. *Supplying War: Logistics from Wallerstein to Patton.* New York: Cambridge University Press, 1980.

———. *Technology and War: From 2000 B.C. to the Present.* New York: The Free Press, 1989.

Warr, Nicolas. *Phase Line Green.* Annapolis, MD: US Naval Institute Press, 1997.

Webster, Sir Charles, and Noble Frankland. *The Strategic Air Offensive against Germany 1939–1945.* 3 vols. London: Her Majesty's Stationery Office, 1961.

Weigley, Russell F. *The American Way of War: A History of United States Military Strategy and Policy.* Bloomington: Indiana University Press, 1977.

Weller, George. *First Into Nagasaki.* New York: Crown, 2006.

Werstein, Irving. *The Battle of Aachen.* New York: Thomas Y. Crowell Company, 1962.

Westbrook, E. E., and L. W. Williams. *A Brief Survey of Nonlethal Weapons.* Columbus, OH: Columbus Laboratories, 1971.

Whiting, Charles. *Bloody Aachen.* London: Leo Cooper, 1976.

Woods, Kevin M. *The Mother of All Battles: Saddam Hussein's Strategic Plan for the Gulf War.* Official U.S. Joint Forces Command Report. Annapolis, MD: Naval Institute Press, 2008.

Yeide, Harry. *The Longest Battle: September 1944 to February 1945 from Aachen to the Roer and Across.* St. Paul, MN: Zenith, 2005.

———. *Steel Victory: The Heroic Story of America's Independent Tank Battalions at War in Europe.* New York: Presidio Press, 2003.

Zaloga, Steven J. *M4 (76mm) Sherman Medium Tank 1943–65.* Oxford: Osprey, 2003.

———. *M10 and M36 Tank Destroyers 1942–53.* Oxford: Osprey, 2002.

———. *M26/M46 Pershing Tank 1943–53.* Oxford: Osprey, 2000.

———. *Sherman Medium Tank 1942–45.* Oxford: Osprey, 2001.

———. *US Field Artillery of World War II.* Oxford: Osprey, 2007.

Zaloga, Steven, J., and Jim Kinnear. *T-34-85 Medium Tank 1944–1994.* Oxford: Osprey, 2000.

Periodicals

"Aachen." *Infantry Journal* 55 (December 1944):16–19.

Ames, Glenn C. "Employment of Scout Cars in Civil Disturbances." *The Cavalry Journal* 50 (July–August 1941): 82–83.

"The Arnhem Victory—A German Account." *Military Review* 24 (February 1945): 111–112.

"Artillery in Combat on the Streets of Stalingrad." *Military Review* 23 (May 1943): 69.

"Attack on Inhabited Places." *Military Review* 23 (October 1943): 67–69.

"Attacking and Defending Populated Places." *Military Review* 24 (October 1944): 94–96.

Beall, Jonathan. "The United States Army and Urban Combat in the Nineteenth Century." *War in History* 16 (2009): 157–188.

Blake, Robert. "War in Spain." *Marine Corps Gazette* 21 (February 1937): 5–10.

Boucher, Francis H. "Artillery in Attacks on Stone Villages." *Field Artillery Journal* 34 (October 1944): 708–709.

Bush, Peter. "The Ontos Was One of the More Interesting Developments to Come Down the Road...." *Vietnam* 15 (October 2002): 10–14.

Canzona, Nicholas A. "Dog Company's Charge." *U.S. Naval Institute Proceedings* 82 (November 1956): 1203–1211.

"Capture of a Village at Night." *Military Review* 23 (July 1943): 71–73.

Casey, Ken. "Urban Combat in World War II: How Doctrine Changed as the War Progressed." *Armor* 108 (November–December 1999): 8–13.

Christmas, Ron. "A Company Commander Remembers the Battle for Hue." *Marine Corps Gazette* 61 (February 1977): 18–26.

Chuykov, V. I. "Street Fighting Tactics." *Infantry Journal* 53 (December 1943): 60–63.

———. "Tactics of Street Fighting: Military Lessons of Stalingrad." *The Cavalry Journal* 52 (September–October 1943): 58–62.

"Civil Affairs and Military Occupation." *Military Review* 23 (March 1944): 83–84.

Close, D. E. "The Siege of Nam-Tha." *Marine Corps Gazette* 49 (February 1965): 32–36.

Cohan, Leon, Jr. "Vulnerable." *Marine Corps Gazette* 51 (April 1967): 33–35.

"Combat in Inhabited Places." *Military Review* 24 (November 1944): 118–120.

"The Conditions of Fighting in the Leningrad Sector." *Military Review* 21 (January 1942): 69–70.

Cooke, E. D. "The Japanese Attacks at Shanghai and the Defense by the Chinese, 1931–1932." *Review of Military Literature* 17 (December 1937): 5–28.

Deacon, Kenneth J. "Assault Crossings on the Pasig River." *The Military Engineer* 50 (Jan–Feb 1958): 8–10.

———. "Mine Warfare in Manila, 1945." *The Military Engineer* 57 (Sept–Oct 1965): 348.

"The Defense of Aachen, City of the Emperors." *Military Review* 24 (March 1945): 88–90.

"The Defense of Hondeghem." *Field Artillery Journal* 31 (January 1941): 2–5.

"Defense of a Command Post in Street Combat." *Military Review* 23 (April 1943): 65.

"Defense of Inhabited Places." *Military Review* 23 (November 1943): 76–77.

Fath, Matthew. "How Armor Was Employed in the Urban Battle of Seoul." *Armor* 110 (September/October 2001): 25–29, 35.

"Fighting for Cities in Offensive and Defensive Action." *Military Review* 23 (January 1944): 92–93.

"German Engineers in the Attack on Stalingrad." *Military Review* 23 (November 1943): 82–83.

Giusti, Ernest, and Kenneth W. Condit. "Marine Air Over Inchon-Seoul." *Marine Corps Gazette* 36 (June 1952): 18–27.

Greene, W. M., Jr. "Shanghai 1937." *Marine Corps Gazette* 49 (November 1965): 62–63.

Greene, Wallace M. "The Employment of the Marine Rifle Company in Street Riot Operations." *Marine Corps Gazette* 24 (March 1940): 49–53.

"Guerrilla Attacks on Populated Places." *Military Review* 24 (August 1944): 96–98.

Headquarters I Corps Artillery, US Army. "Jap Artillery in Northern Luzon." *Field Artillery Journal* 36 (Jan 1946): 17–23.

Hemingway, Al. "Storming the Citadel." *Vietnam* 20 (February 2008): 42–49.

Henzel, Hans W. "The Stalingrad Offensive, Part I." *Marine Corps Gazette* 35 (August 1951): 46–53.

———. "The Stalingrad Offensive, Part II." *Marine Corps Gazette* 35 (September 1951): 46–57.

Hobbs, William H. "Needed—More Riot Training." *Infantry Journal* 43 (November–December 1936): 542.

Holt, M. E. "Street Fighting." *Marine Corps Gazette* 29 (September 1945): 27–33.

"How the City of Yukhnov Was Captured." *Military Review* 22 (January 1943): 72–73.

"How the Germans Defend Buildings." *Military Review* 24 (December 1944): 117–118.

Hutchison, William E. "Riots and Marines." *Marine Corps Gazette* 46 (March 1962): 45–49.

Hutton, H. H. Smith. "Lessons Learned at Shanghai in 1932." *U.S. Naval Institute Proceedings* 64 (August 1938): 1167–1174.

Jackson, Wilfred A. "Stay Clear of Hue." *United States Army Aviation Digest* 16 (April 1970): 12–14.

Johnson, Wendell G. "Spain: A Year and a Half of Modern War." *Infantry Journal* 45 (March–April 1938): 133–141.

———. "The Spanish War: A Review of the Best Foreign Opinion." *Infantry Journal* 45 (July–August 1938): 351–356.

Kononenko, A. "Attack on a Fortified Inhabited Point." *Infantry Journal* 51 (September 1942): 62–63.

"Lessons of One Battle." *Military Review* 23 (July 1943): 76–77.

Levy, Bert. "Street Fighting." *Infantry Journal* 51 (September 1942): 22–29.

———. "Street Fighting." *The Cavalry Journal* 51 (September–October 1942): 46–51.

Linklater, Eric. "The Defense of Calais." *Infantry Journal* 50 (June 1942): 12–25.

Linn, Brian M. "The American Way of War Revisited." *The Journal of Military History* 66 (2002): 501–533.

"Maneuver in Battles for Populated Places." *Military Review* 24 (January 1945): 117–120.

McGraw, Ralph C. "We Were First Into Manila." *The Cavalry Journal* 54 (July–August 1945): 2–5.

Meselson, Matthew S. "Chemical and Biological Weapons." *Scientific American* 222 (May 1970): 15–25.

Meyers, Lewis. "Japanese Civilians in Combat Zones." *Marine Corps Gazette* 29 (February 1945): 11–16.

Miller, Walter L., Jr. "Riot Control With Chemical Agents." *Marine Corps Gazette* 45 (March 1961): 28–31.

Montross, Lynn. "Fleet Marine Force Korea." *U.S. Naval Institute Proceedings* 79 (August 1953): 829–841.

———. "The Capture of Seoul: Battle of the Barricades." *Marine Corps Gazette* 35 (August 1951): 26–37.

———. "The Inchon Landing." *Marine Corps Gazette* 35 (July 1951): 26–35.

"Mortars in an Inhabited Place." *Military Review* 23 (February 1944): 66–68.

"Motorized Infantry Company Attacks Calais." *Military Review* 21 (October 1941): 79–81.

"Night Battle for a Populated Point." *Military Review* 22 (October 1942): 89–90.

"Planning an Attack Against a Village." *Military Review* 22 (January 1943): 94.

Q, Major. "When the Red Army Attacks a City." *Infantry Journal* 56 (March 1945): 52–57.

Randall, Nelson H. "The Battle of Manila." *Field Artillery Journal* 35 (August 1945): 451–456.

Samoilov, Boris. "How Artillery Captured a Town." *Field Artillery Journal* 35 (June 1945): 366–367.

Samuelsen, Lewis N. "Handling Enemy Civilians." *Marine Corps Gazette* 29 (April 1945): 14–16.

Scales, Robert H., Jr. "The Indirect Approach: How US Military Forces Can Avoid the Pitfalls of Future Urban Warfare." *Armed Forces Journal International* 136 (October 1998): 68+.

Shadel, W. F. "Street Fighting in Cassino." *Infantry Journal* 54 (June 1944): 24+.

Simonov, Konstantin. "Stalingrad Under Siege." *The Cavalry Journal* 51 (September–October 1942): 51.

"Snipers in Stalingrad." *Military Review* 23 (October 1943): 71–72.

"Street Fighting—The Lessons of Stalingrad." *Military Review* 24 (July 1944): 95–99.

"Street Fighting—Tips from a Platoon Commander in Italy." *Military Review* 24 (November 1944): 116–118.

"Street Fighting in Stalingrad." *Military Review* 23 (August 1943): 78–79.

"Street Fighting." *Military Review* 23 (February 1944): 75–76.

Stewart, Raymond A. "Marine Tanks in the Battle for Hue City: Tet 1968." *Leatherneck* 91 (February 2008): 10–14.

"Tactics of Combat for Inhabited Places." *Military Review* 23 (June 1943): 74–75.

"Tank Attacks on Occupied Villages." *Military Review* 22 (January 1943): 74.

"Tanks Against Warsaw." *Military Review* 21 (June 1941): 60–62.

"Tanks in Combat for Populated Areas." *Military Review* 21 (March 1941): 48.

Thompson, Paul W. "Capture of a Town." *Infantry Journal* 51 (September 1942): 46–48.

Thompson, Warren. "Marine Corsairs in Korea." *International Airpower Review* 11 (Winter 2003/2004): 104–119.

Timmons, Bascom N. "MacArthur's Greatest Battle." *Collier's* 126 (16 December 1950): 13–15, 64.

"Total Defense of a City." *Infantry Journal* 55 (December 1944): 53–54.

Tucker, Richard K. "Marine Artillery Takes Heavy Toll of Seoul As Well As Enemy Troops." *Baltimore Evening Sun*, 27 September 1950, pp. 1–2.

"The Use of Trench Mortars in Defending Inhabited Places." *Marine Corps Gazette* 27 (July 1943): 20.

Usera, Vincent. "Some Lessons of the Spanish War." *U.S. Naval Institute Proceedings* 65 (July 1939): 969–972.

Vagts, Alfred. "Stalingrad: City into Fortress." *Infantry Journal* 52 (January 1943): 44–45.

Williams, R. C., Jr. "Defense in Towns." *Marine Corps Gazette* 32 (September 1948): 48–51.

Wyatt, Richard B. "Marines vs Mobs." *Marine Corps Gazette* 49 (January 1965): 38–40.

Yarborough, William P. "House Party in Jerryland." *Infantry Journal* 55 (July 1944): 8–13.

Index